JEWISH THEMES IN SPINOZA'S PHILOSOPHY

SUNY series in Jewish Philosophy
Kenneth Seeskin, editor

Jewish Themes
in Spinoza's Philosophy

EDITED BY
Heidi M. Ravven
AND
Lenn E. Goodman

STATE UNIVERSITY OF NEW YORK PRESS

Published by
State University of New York Press, Albany

© 2002 State University of New York

For information, address State University of New York Press,
90 State Street, Suite 700, Albany, NY 12207

Production by Cathleen Collins
Marketing by Michael Campochiaro

Library of Congress Cataloging in Publication Data

Jewish themes in Spinoza's philosophy / edited by Heidi M. Ravven and Lenn E.
    Goodman.
        p. cm. — (SUNY series in Jewish philosophy)
    Includes bibliographical references and index.
    ISBN 0-7914-5309-X (alk. paper) — ISBN 0-7914-5310-3 (pbk. : alk. paper)
        1. Spinoza, Benedictus de, 1632–1677. 2. Philosophy, Jewish. I. Ravven,
Heidi M., 1952– II. Goodman, Lenn Evan, 1944– III. Series.

B3999.J8 J48 2002
199'.492—dc21

                                                                2001034412

10 9 8 7 6 5 4 3 2 1

Dedicated to lovers of Spinoza everywhere.

We understand what our salvation or blessedness or freedom consists in, namely, in the constant and eternal love
towards God, that is, in God's love toward humanity. This
love or blessedness is called glory in the Holy Scriptures,
and rightly so. . . . For it can properly be called spiritual
contentment.

—*Ethics*, VP36S, (as translated by
Samuel Shirley, emended slightly)

Contents

PART IV
The Historical Setting

Abbreviations

G I - IV *Spinoza Opera*, ed. C Gebhardt, 4 vols.
(Heidelberg: Carl Winter, 1925 (reprinted 1972 vols. I to IV, with a supplement, vol. V, 1987). References are given as G I to G IV, with page and line. G II 22/10 refers to volume II, page 22, line 10.

Van Vloten and Land

Benedicti de Spinoza opera quotquot reperta sunt. 3rd ed. 4 vols. (The Hague: M. Nijhoff, 1913 and 1914) References are by volume and page number: e.g., Van Vloten and Land, vol. 1: 268.

E References to the *Ethics* are in the format: e.g., EIIP13S1 means *Ethics* Part II, Proposition 13, first Scholium. A = Axiom, D = definition, dem = demonstration, C = corollary, Pref = Preface

TTP Spinoza's *Tractatus Theologico-Politicus*
References are by chapter: for example, *TTP* iv.

TdIE Spinoza's *Treatise on the Emendation of the Intellect*
References are by section: for example. *TdIE* 97

KV Spinoza's *Short Treatise on God, Man and His Well-Being* (*Korte verhandeling van God, de Mensch, en deszelfs Welstand*)
References are by part, chapter, and section: e.g., *KV* I, ii, 5

Guide Maimonides' *Guide to the Perplexed*
References are by part and chapter as follows: e.g., *Guide* II 33.

English translations used are specified by each author in the chapter Notes.

PART I

Laying the Groundwork

CHAPTER 1

Introduction

HEIDI M. RAVVEN AND LENN E. GOODMAN

The attitudes of Jewish thinkers toward Spinoza have defined a fault line between traditionalist and liberal ideas about Judaism and Jewish identity ever since the time of Moses Mendelssohn. Perhaps as a result, by the twentieth century many text-based historical studies of the impact of Jewish philosophy on Spinoza's ideas were available. Yet there have been remarkably few philosophical treatments of what is or is not Jewish in Spinoza's *philosophy*. The present volume speaks to that question. The authors address the question, directly in some cases and indirectly in others: Is Spinoza's a Jewish philosophy? What is its significance for Jewish philosophy as a living enterprise? What is its impact on the trajectory of such philosophy now and on the prospects of Jewish philosophy as we look to the future?

Among the works available in English that trace the impact on Spinoza's philosophy of his many Jewish predecessors, Wolfson's magisterial study still towers above the rest; Shlomo Pines's contribution is of lasting importance too, as is the work of many other scholars.[1] Yet that historical question is not ours. Nor do we aim to investigate the history of Jewish attitudes toward Spinoza and the varied appropriations of his thought that have been so much a part of the emergence of modern Jewish identities. These questions are fascinating in their own right but beyond our present concern. Mendelssohn, in his *Jerusalem*, to name just one important example, relied on the *Tractatus* as the model for a modern approach to Jewish philosophy. Such responses are of profound interest and are eminently worthy of further investigation than they have as yet received. So are the hagiographic attitudes of the Reformers toward Spinoza and those of some early Zionists and Yiddishists. Equally worthy of study is the contrasting approach of Hermann Cohen, for whom Spinoza's was the anti-Judaic philosophy par excellence, against which all subsequent Jewish philosophies must be tested. Cohen saw a stark dichotomy between Judaism and Spinozism, and many living philosophers and theologians still echo his views. Emil Fackenheim, for one, posed the fundamental choice of modern Judaism as a fateful decision to be made between Rosenzweig and Spinoza. Emmanuel Levinas made Spinoza the foil for his own Judaic philosophy. And David Novak's recent *Election of Israel* suggests that all modern Jewish thought must take its start from a successful response to Spinoza's challenge to the divine chosenness of Israel.

Sometimes Spinoza becomes a stalking horse, and less than dispassionate treatments yield troublesome results rather than philosophical clarity. Nor are the troubled waters always made clearer by Leo Strauss's further challenge, the claim that Spinoza's words bear an esoteric meaning conditioned by the hostile environment in which the philosopher lived and quite different from their seemingly candid, even outspoken lines of argument. We can learn much from Strauss about Spinoza, but in many of the writings of Strauss's less trenchant followers we learn more about Strauss than about Spinoza. Strauss did not distort Spinoza in the effort to surmount him. But with Cohen and Levinas that is less clear. The effort to set up Spinoza as the anti-figure of all that is Jewish may have helped these thinkers to clarify their own religious stance, but the resulting portrait of Spinoza grows twisted and distorted in the process, as areas of disagreement or disturbance are enlarged, and areas of profound affinity overlooked.

Many readers may be familiar with Julius Guttmann's claim that Spinoza's philosophy belongs more to European than to Jewish thought. But we think this claim rests on a false dichotomy. For Jewish philosophy and Jewish thought in general, in every period, have been actively engaged with the ideas of the surrounding environment, and have critically and creatively engaged those ideas. Nor can we concur with Guttmann's assumption that the primary goal of classical Jewish philosophy was apologetic. For to defend a tradition one must not only interpret it but also render it defensible, in one's own eyes as well as in those of others. For that reason, from its most ancient beginnings, Jewish thought in general and Jewish philosophy in particular have been engaged in tasks of critical reappropriation that have made Judaism and the Jewish tradition capable of impressive longevity and vitality. Guttmann's Spinoza is a cognitivist and a logicist, a deductivist philosopher who actively rejected "all considerations of value," the bearer of a philosophy that caricatures the depth and nuance, the subtle syntheses of Spinoza's philosophical theses and arguments. Guttmann's portrayal of Judaism is similarly pallid and cartoonish. It lacks in the depth and color, diversity and fluidity of the reality that he seeks to portray and contrast with Spinoza's views.

For our part, we do not undertake to predefine a Judaic philosophic stance against which Spinoza is to be judged (and found wanting). Rather, we have gathered together essays that explore Spinoza's philosophic ideas and raise the question of the resonance or dissonance of these ideas with the full array of Jewish sources, traditions, and themes. Are some of Spinoza's ideas secularizations of traditional Jewish values and concepts, in the way that, say, the capitalist work ethic is often said to be a secularization of Protestant religious values? What of the Kabbalah, the tradition of Jewish mysticism that grows out of ancient Neoplatonic thinking and explains all being as a declension form the divine Infinite (the *Ensof*) by way of hypostatic numbers (the *Sefirot*) that are given the names of God's attributes? To what extent, despite his disparagement of its extravagances, does Spinoza transform Kabbalistic ideas into authentic and viable Jewish philosophy?

And what of the political ideas of the *Tractatus Theologico-Politicus* and the unfinished *Tractatus Politicus*? Do they represent a Jewish politics, as Spinoza himself implied? Do Spinoza's reflections on language in his projected Hebrew grammar cast a light on his philosophy? Does his earliest encounter with the nexus between language and thought arise in the study of a non-European language that has formed a common pedagogic awakening for so many Jewish youngsters across the generations? Again, is there a deep structure to Spinoza's philosophic and political thought that expresses Jewish ideas or values, perhaps in a heterodox way, as Hegel, say, claimed that his central philosophical conception was a rational articulation of the ideas of Trinity and Incarnation? Our aim is to take the most empirical and wide-ranging view of what can and should be deemed Judaic and to seek the resonances and the enduring insights that re-echo from those resonances in the philosophy of Spinoza.

The contributors to this volume represent the rich diversity of Spinoza scholarship today: Jewish philosophical, Jewish historical, Cartesian-analytic, Continental-Marxist, political scientific, and intellectual historical. The essays can be divided by their major themes: Lenn Goodman argues that Spinoza grafts together and brings to fruition the parallel shoots of Jewish monotheism and Western philosophical monism. Lee Rice and Warren Montag suggest that some of Spinoza's ideas about divine immanence are philosophical elaborations of ancient Jewish religious insights. Warren Zev Harvey proposes that Spinoza found in the Hebrew language seeds or stimuli for the distinctive categories of his metaphysics and ethics. Kenneth Seeskin sounds a note of caution, reminding us that in denying the creation of the world and asserting its eternity Spinoza rejected a fundamental tenet of Jewish monotheism, a thesis that lay at the heart of Maimonides' adjudication of the issues between Judaism and rationalism. Edwin Curley assesses

Spinoza's response to Maimonides' theodicy, exposing both continuities and departures from Maimonides and the biblical tradition. Michael Rosenthal and Heidi Ravven assess Spinoza's conception of Judaism as a product of the imagination. Rosenthal finds in the Judaism of the *Tractatus Theologico-Politicus* a paradigm case of exemplars or normative ethical models that Spinoza proposes in the *Ethics*. And Ravven finds in Spinoza's critique of tradition a starting point for his philosophical journey. Both Ravven and Rosenthal conclude, however, that Spinoza made the Ancient Jewish Commonwealth the model for his ideal of a modern and tolerant democratic state. Richard Popkin in the concluding essay presented here, sets Spinoza's excommunication in its historical context, filling in our picture of the actual Jewish community with which Spinoza came into conflict. The impact of his paper is to debunk the tendentious image fostered by later writers, of Spinoza as a martyr to the dark forces of religious intolerance.

What follows is a brief overview of the chapters in this book:

LENN GOODMAN, "WHAT DOES SPINOZA'S *ETHICS* CONTRIBUTE TO JEWISH PHILOSOPHY?"

Lenn Goodman undertakes a complete review of Spinoza's philosophy. At every point along the way he finds Spinoza addressing classic problems that Jewish philosophy shares with the larger philosophical tradition and addressing them with creative and constructive solutions that draw upon Jewish themes. Goodman reconstructs Spinoza's philosophy and finds in its principal theses and arguments distinctive reconciliations of the classical oppositions of philosophy: the one and the many, freedom and determinism, mind and body, is and ought, power and justice, reason and emotion, creation and eternity, knowledge and skepticism, correspondence and coherence, matter as active and matter as inert, transcendence and immanence, finitude or infinitude in nature's scope or duration, and teleology and mechanism. The common thread in Spinoza's approach is a rigorous reconceptualization of the core concepts of philosophy. That radical conceptual reworking is what allows a synthesis, and it often leads Spinoza to a reappropriation of notions that seem at first blush to have been rejected. Behind Spinoza's approach, and making it possible, Goodman finds not only the dialectical skills of a conceptual genius but an uncompromising commitment to philosophical monotheism, a commitment that, in its tenacity and rigor, makes Spinoza's metaphysics the most coherent yet to be developed in the checkered history of philosophical speculation. On the basis of this analysis, Goodman finds Spinoza's philosophy to be Judaic to the core, Jewish not merely in ethos and outlook but also in its central philosophical values and conceptual commitments. In the course of his exposition, Goodman describes Spinoza's many points of engagement with his Jewish (and non-Jewish) philosophical predecessors, including the great Jewish rationalists Maimonides and Saadiah. But the thrust of these comparisons is not to discover sources or points of departure but to trace the course of an enduring thematic development.

The Jewish questions raised by Spinoza's philosophy prove, in Goodman's analysis, to be identical with the big questions of philosophy, and the understanding of Spinoza's theses and arguments that emerges from this perspective gives us new insight into the coherence and contemporary relevance of his philosophy. A sustained engagement with Spinoza's own dialogue with the tradition in which he was raised gives us a sense of the power of Spinoza's philosophic mind and character, of what Goodman calls the moral strength of Spinoza's independence of mind. We appreciate anew Spinoza's unflinching honesty as a model of philosophic praxis. Goodman shows us that at the roots of Spinoza's insights, and of the purity, force, and clarity of his thought, lies a Judaic monotheistic, and ethical motive. But beyond that, Spinoza's philosophic achievement casts Judaic monotheism itself in a new key. Thus, Goodman's synoptic account of Spinoza's thinking ends by pointing to Spinozist avenues yet to be taken, even continents to be explored.

LEE RICE, "LOVE OF GOD IN SPINOZA"

Lee Rice in his essay points to a particular Judaic theme that lies at the heart of Spinoza's project, the immanence of the divine. Rice shows how Spinoza's account of divine love articulates and specifies the Judaic notion. He argues that Spinoza identifies three kinds of love of God. Each is the affective expression or correlate of one of the three kinds of knowledge: imaginative, rational, and intuitive. Love at the level of imagination is characterized by its passivity to external events and phenomena. The imaginative knowledge of God "provides at best only a metaphorical knowledge," frequently miscasting God "as judge, a governor of nature capable of directing natural events to human ends." This kind of love for God presupposes a supernaturalist dualism. Yet it can be of considerable social utility when put to work as a motive for kindness and tolerance.

Rational love, unlike imaginational love, is "self-determined." It originates in *generositas* or "strength of mind." When its object is God, this love does not demand reciprocation, for that would entail a misunderstanding of the divine nature. Instead, it seeks union with God.

Spinoza's famous conception of the intellectual love of God is the correlate of the intuitive form of knowledge. Recognition of that fact returns us to Spinoza's thesis that intuitive knowing/loving allows God's act of loving and the human act of loving God to converge: Human knowing/loving is divine activity, the active expression of the immanence of the divine. This daring thesis, as Rice points out, is identified by Spinoza as an ancient Jewish insight.

Warren Montag, in his chapter on Spinoza and the Kabbalist idea of the Shekhinah, comes to a similar conclusion, as does Lenn Goodman in his discussion of immanence in the thinking of Saadiah and in the ancient Hebrew liturgy.

Taking these arguments together, one might justly argue that Spinoza regarded his own account of God, and of the human love and knowledge of God that perfect human existence, as a philosophically elevated and clarified Judaism.

WARREN ZEV HARVEY, "SPINOZA'S METAPHYSICAL HEBRAISM"

Warren Zev Harvey reminds us that Spinoza was an outstanding scholar of the Hebrew language and viewed himself "as a consummate authority on Hebrew." Harvey finds evidence that Spinoza's knowledge was not only theoretical. Spinoza was also an accomplished speaker, writer, and stylist in Hebrew. He apparently saw himself as the first true Hebrew grammarian and devoted much time toward the end of his life to an unfinished Hebrew grammar.

In his *Compendium of the Grammar of the Hebrew Language*, Spinoza set forth a novel theory of the significance of Hebrew nouns, undergirded with a metaphysical analysis of the parts of speech in terms of substance, attribute, and mode. He also sought to explain the distinctive aspects of the Hebrew language in terms of the cultural peculiarities of its speakers. In this way Spinoza linked language with cultural outlook—a natural connection for him to make, since he saw both language and tradition as products of the imagination.

Despite Spinoza's vociferous denial of any philosophic content in Scripture, Harvey shows that Spinoza regarded Hebrew as harboring a perfect conception of substance in its articulation of the idea of an absolute God in the Tetragrammaton. Further, Spinoza said that the Hebrew term *kabod* (glory) points to the (true) human *summum bonum*, the intellectual love of God. Thus Spinoza found elements of the true philosophy, his own, embedded in the Hebrew language, albeit naively and in pre-philosophical hints and gestures.

KENNETH SEESKIN, "MAIMONIDES, SPINOZA, AND THE PROBLEM OF CREATION"

Kenneth Seeskin argues that Spinoza opts for a non-Judaic position on divine Creation, where Maimonides chose the Judaic one. Seeskin explores the powerful arguments that Maimonides and Spinoza use to defend their opposed positions on the creation (versus the eternity) of the universe. They both take reasonable positions. Not only from the perspective of the science of their times but even from a contemporary point of view, both Spinoza's account of God as the infinite, immanent cause of the world and Maimonides' opposing claim that God is the transcendent creator seem plausible. Seeskin turns to contemporary cosmology to suggest that the matter remains unsettled: The historic conflict between Maimonides and Spinoza is still with us, albeit in a somewhat revised form.

Maimonides' preference for the creation of the world, Seeskin argues, expresses his belief that creation "is the primary way to account for separation" between God and the cosmos, a separation not just of degree but of kind. Maimonides, Seeskin notes, even "denies any sort of relation between God and other things." Thus from the knowledge of the world we can infer nothing about its origin. Spinoza's response, Seeskin argues, is that the Maimonidean model lacks explanatory power. Seeskin suggests that Maimonides would not deny the charge but would reply that his approach is to make us confront the limits of our knowledge even of our capacity to resolve the issue.

It remains a question today whether the explanatory categories of physics still apply when we are talking about a time zero "prior" to the Big Bang. Seeskin finds Maimonides' best resolution of the dilemma in rational restraint. But the dispute remains open between that Kantian position and Spinoza's pressing for fuller rational explanation and branding the Maimonidean restraint as mere mystification.

The traditional theist will probably view creation in the Maimonidean-Kantian way, Seeskin argues. "In the end," he says, "the reason people are so desperate to hold on to creation is that without it, we may have a necessary being, a being with infinite attributes, even a being who inspires love; but in the eyes of traditional theists, we do not have God." Yet these were not considerations that moved Spinoza nor would they move a contemporary Spinozist, Seeskin concludes.

Seeskin's position contrasts with that of Goodman, Rice, and Montag on the Jewishness of Spinoza's doctrines of divine immanence and monism. Goodman argues that Spinoza does not simply choose immanence over transcendence but seeks to synthesize the two, and he notes that Maimonides did not deny every kind of relation between God and the world: He did not deny the relation of Creator to creature, for example, and he did not think that his wide-ranging negative theology compromised theism. For Goodman, Spinoza's *Deus sive natura* is the descendant and counterpart of Maimonides' perfect and necessary Being. Seeskin, by contrast, argues, that Jewish theism stands or falls with the claim of divine transcendence expressed in a doctrine of temporal creation. What is perhaps most distinctive about this lively philosophical debate over Spinoza's relation to the Jewish tradition is that its focus is not on the terms and phrases that may mark the lines of historical filiation but on the question of which concepts are appropriable today by thinkers who take seriously the values and the problems of Jewish philosophical theology.

WARREN MONTAG, "'THAT HEBREW WORD': SPINOZA AND THE CONCEPT OF THE SHEKHINAH"

Warren Montag contributes to the same debate. He teases out a convincing answer to questions about the exact nature of the threat to Christian orthodoxy that Spinoza and Spinozism were feared to pose by the Amsterdam Reformed Church elders and the municipal council. Both groups strove to root out Spinozism in their investigations into the purportedly Spinozist belief in the Shekhinah, the indwelling divine presence as conceived in Jewish mystical sources. While he eschewed attaching any esoteric Kabbalistic meanings to the content of the Bible, Montag argues, Spinoza did draw on Kabbalistic themes for his own conception of God's immanence.

Spinoza's philosophical reworking of the idea of the Shekhinah, Montag argues, illustrates Spinoza's way of "systematically appropriating and then turning against the enemy his own weapons." Spinoza turned the Kabbalists' concept of Shekhinah against them in two ways, Montag suggests: First, he closed the gap between creator and creation. Second, he substituted the unity of the spiritual and material for the Kabbalists' hierarchically organized universe emergent from divine emanation. In the process Spinoza did away with the notion that materiality was a distancing from God.

It was not Kabbalism per se but what we might call Spinoza's Kabbalistic anti-Kabbalism that the would-be defenders of Christian orthodoxy held against him. As Montag suggests, the investigators had a pretty good idea what they were looking for. Spinoza's doctrine of divine immanence did pose a challenge not only to Christian theology but to widespread notions of Christian morality and to the associated assumptions of hierarchical thinking and oppressive praxis. Judaism and Jewish philosophy have also struggled with the challenge posed by Spinoza and by the immanentism he spoke for, but these challenging ideas were typically confronted as variations on core Jewish themes. Only occasionally did the more radical versions call forth any concerted response. Spinoza's philosophy, Montag concludes, serves Judaism as a test of its tolerance of internal diversity and as a reminder of some of the authentic and abiding streams of understanding within Judaism itself.

EDWIN CURLEY, "MAIMONIDES, SPINOZA AND THE BOOK OF JOB"

Edwin Curley carefully analyzes three texts in this essay: first, the biblical Book of Job; second, the chapters on Job in Maimonides' *Guide to the Perplexed*; and finally, Spinoza's references to Job in the *Tractatus Theologico-Politicus*. He finds a biblical precedent for Spinoza's denial of traditional theodicies. These ideas are developed by the medievals, particularly Maimonides but also Ibn Ezra. The Book of Job is the key text in this regard. It serves both Maimonides and Spinoza as the occasion for the reduction of moral virtue to (what is deemed to be) a more fundamental and encompassing intellectual virtue. That theme is carried further by Maimonides in his interpretation of the biblical narrative of the Garden of Eden, an interpretation adopted almost globally by Spinoza.

Although such rationalist exegeses may seem to torture the text in the interest of an alien Greek philosophical tradition (and in a way that Spinoza sometimes forcefully condemns), Curley shows how the seemingly heterodox themes have their biblical sources not only for the issues dealt with in the Book of Job but also for the apotheosis of wisdom and intellect in Koheleth. If these traditions seem to resonate with outside influence, it is clearly an influence adopted and transformed by the biblical writers and put into a Hebraic idiom. That idiom re-echoes, as Curley shows, from the Bible to modernity.

Further investigation of the *Guide* would uncover Maimonides' reconciliation of the strains Curley exposes—Aristotelian intellectualism, divergent understandings of Providence within the biblical and rabbinic traditions, and mainstream Jewish theodicy.

HEIDI RAVVEN, "SPINOZA'S RUPTURE WITH TRADITION—HIS HINTS OF A JEWISH MODERNITY"

Heidi Ravven argues that Spinoza regards the imagination, not only in the *Tractatus Theologico-Politicus* but also in the *Ethics*, as a vehicle of socialization and a medium for the transmission of tradition. She challenges the widespread assumption that the imagination in Spinoza only receives the images conveyed to it by sense perception. To understand the role of imagination in Spinoza's psychology we need to recognize its associative operations in connecting images and memories to make a meaningful scene and picture of the world. The world constructed by the imagination is, according to Spinoza, represented symbolically in language. The resultant vistas are transmitted by authoritative tradition, and the norms constructed as a result are enforced politically by rewards and punishments.

Spinoza identifies language and religion as the two great forces of the imagination that bring the individual into conformity with the group and under the authority of group traditions. The imagination thus becomes the basis of a primitive form of morals. Ravven argues that in both the *Ethics* and the *TTP* Spinoza lays out a path of intellectual and moral development and education that leads from religious authority, internalized but backed by external political coercion, to rational self-determination and ethical autonomy.

In the *TTP*, Spinoza finds the ideal use of the imagination in religion. Religion can legitimate and reinforce a democratic distribution of power and a just judicial system. It need not support only authoritarian powers. Religion and its imaginative suasions, used with proper restraint, can evoke enthusiastic obedience to a system of government that fosters self-determination and independence of mind. The imagination can thus be called into the service of a form of government that reason itself commends as the best support of human fulfillment. To illustrate the proper social function of the imagination, Spinoza chooses the example of the ancient Israelite commonwealth, as described in the Hebrew Bible. As Michael Rosenthal also argues in the present volume, Spinoza envisioned the reshaping of Holland—and of all modern polities—along the general lines of the democratic political constitution that he finds typified in the original Jewish commonwealth.

Spinoza's *Ethics* sets out a path of education that aims at transcending the hold of the traditional religious community over the individual. But his political theory embraces, reinvigorates, and hopes to universalize the Jewish political tradition as a means to that very end.

MICHAEL ROSENTHAL, "WHY SPINOZA CHOSE THE HEBREWS: THE EXEMPLARY FUNCTION OF PROPHECY IN THE *THEOLOGICAL-POLITICAL TREATISE*"

Michael Rosenthal explores Spinoza's use of the ancient Hebrew commonwealth as a historical exemplar that sets a universal standard. He raises both logical and historical issues: What is the status of a model of this kind for Spinoza? What did the polity of the Ancient Israelites connote for a Dutch audience who were asked to view it is a model? Rosenthal argues that Spinoza intended the original Mosaic state in the *Tractatus* as an imaginative universal, that is, a provisional exemplar of political behavior analogous to the exemplar of human nature that Spinoza proposes in the Fourth Part of the *Ethics*. Both models are provisional—indeed false if taken strictly literally. Yet, even as fictions, these models have moral and political utility.

An exemplar is an imaginative constuction, not a true idea. Its appeal is established not by philosophical arguments but by narratives and rhetoric. The aim of such suasions is not understanding but allegiance. Such is the strategy of the biblical prophets. As Rosenthal points out, Spinoza himself uses persuasion rather than strictly rational argumentation in the *TTP* when setting out his version of the biblical account of the ancient Israelite commonwealth. He writes with his eye on his Dutch audience, who identify with the Israelites and the circumstances of the Exodus. Spinoza's naturalized retelling of the founding of Mosaic society aims toward a systematic revision of our reading of the Bible. But it also aims to persuade his Dutch audience of the efficacy and value of the strategy that Spinoza imputes to the ancient Israelite commonwealth. Spinoza uses the ancient Israelites to argue the value of tolerance and to warn of the dangers of unchecked ecclesiastical power. "In the interpretation of this particular exemplar," Rosenthal concludes, Spinoza "is himself trying to govern its meaning and use in political life."

Spinoza, then, might legitimately be said to have revised the meaning of Ancient Judaism for his contemporaries—in this case for non-Jews. But his revision took on a new life within Judaism when Mendelssohn, the thinkers of the Haskalah, and later the Reformers, developed new models of Judaism inspired by Spinoza's proposals.

RICHARD POPKIN, "SPINOZA'S EXCOMMUNICATION"

Richard Popkin takes a hard look at what we really know about Spinoza's excommunication and what has passed into print by way of embellishment, much of it, ideologically motivated. Spinoza did not attend his excommunication, was already living apart from the Jewish community when it took place, and rarely referred to it later. The elaborate descriptions in some of the early accounts of Spinoza's life and work are not based on any data regarding Spinoza's case but are fabrications and fanciful dramatizations, extrapolated from general rabbinic accounts of how excommunications ought to be carried out.

Any analogy with the public condemnation of Galileo is utterly misleading, Popkin argues. Spinoza's excommunication did not occur in public in the synagogue but in a private chamber. It was hardly a momentous event within the Jewish community of Amsterdam, which was at the time much occupied with an influx of impoverished refugees from Poland. And it was not carried out by the rabbis of the Amsterdam synagogue (who were in any case not advocates of a rigid orthodoxy but enlightened and worldly figures). In fact, the excommunication was an act of the congregational lay leaders, the *parnassim*. Nor was Spinoza completely cut off from all Jewish contacts. Popkin cites evidence that Spinoza even served as a character witness for a Dutch Jewish army officer.

Popkin concludes that the excommunication "was not one of the traumatic events of the seventeenth century or a decisive turning point in the struggle between orthodoxy and modernity. It seems to have been a minor local event in the Amsterdam community, one that was never discussed later on." Moreover, Spinoza clearly benefited by his excommunication in many ways. It freed him to publish without fear of rabbinic censorship. All things considered, Spinoza may not have regretted paying the price of excommunication for the freedom to publish. He did, after all, later refuse the chair in philosophy at Heidelberg whose acceptance no doubt would have entailed embracing or at least mouthing Christian orthodoxies. Nor did Spinoza ever fully embrace another faith or religious community, not even of the most liberal or radical kind.

Popkin's essay is a sobering reminder of the difference between myth and reality and how much of what we think we know about Spinoza's life has been driven by those, on all sides, with axes to grind. It also reminds us that whatever Jewish currents we find in Spinoza's philosophy, his distancing from the Jewish community was at least to some extent mutual. If Spinoza's philosophy proves to be in important respects a Jewish philosophy, it is so obliquely and not because Spinoza intended to work from within to develop a new Judaism.

CONCLUDING REMARKS

Spinoza's philosophy is decisively Jewish in one respect we have not yet mentioned: Spinoza's philosophical anthropology reflects the biblical and Jewish understanding of the human person as fallible, poised between constructive and destructive tendencies and between perfection and imperfection. Spinoza's ethical project is to channel, not suppress, the unruly passions into constructive avenues. Desire, not a disembodied reason but a desire embracing mind and body as one, is the human essence. It is to be reformed and thereby most adequately satisfied, not subdued or denied. If one side of

Spinoza's ethical theory is the loosening of the bonds of tradition, freeing the human person and allowing individual movement toward increased independence of mind and action, the other side is learning to understand oneself in the fullest natural causal context. Spinoza's insistence that we— not only our bodies but our minds—are part of nature and must be understood in terms of physics, biology, psychology, and even sociology and anthropology, owes a debt to what one could call the Hebrew Bible's honest gaze, its refusal to take a falsely rosy view of human motives and its equal refusal of the notion (read into the text of Genesis by Christian salvation theory) of the utter corruption or natural depravity of our moral natures. In refusing to bemoan, ridicule, or lament our human nature, Spinoza is characteristically Jewish.

In rejecting Descartes' solution to the moral (and the epistemic) problem in a turn to inner psychic control by acts of will, Spinoza embraces the reality of our human limitations and resists the fantasy of our willful omnipotence, even in the inner citadel of individual subjectivity. Our minds are not of our own invention or subject to our direct and all-encompassing control, as our tendency toward magical thinking might suggest. Spinoza insists instead that our beliefs are more often than not socially constructed and uncritically held, and that our emotions follow naturally from those beliefs. Our minds, no less than our bodies, are subject to external influences of all kinds, social and natural. Our hope comes not from any ability to will ourselves free of external and internal determination and still less from casting ourselves on some mythic eschaton in a surrender of reason and intelligence to the sheer sense of our creatureliness. It comes from understanding ourselves and pursuing our interests within the largest causal and social nexus, one that recognizes and furthers our human connectedness rather than denies it.

That we are part of nature and cannot escape it is profoundly humbling. Honest ethics begins when we come to understand the contexts of our desires, beliefs, and actions, and thereby recognize that the same laws, the same desires and struggles, apply to us as to everyone and everything else. We realize our interdependence with all things, and most especially with the beings most fittingly allied with ourselves, that is, our fellow human beings. Ethics is not the assertion of a superhuman control over our thoughts and feelings, nor is its project the dream that Spinoza (using that word) defines as utopian, the project of a human nature remade. Such notions only open up a route to self-deception and can lead us into doing evil in the name of the good. Ethics involves our recognition both of our finitude and of our stake in the whole. It involves a recognition of the reality but the finitude of our powers. It is only through the understanding of ourselves and our passions and of the natural and social contexts in which they arise that we can reliably enhance those powers. The joy that results is the natural concomitant of our growth in understanding and as a result in power. This is the conceptually tough and philosophically enduring sense behind the ancient rabbinic idea that real power lies in self-governance, and in the still older, scriptural idea that wisdom opens the route to self-mastery.

Spinoza's ethics, in its own way, does express the Torah's insistence on the infinite distance between the human and the divine. But at the same time it discovers a spark of the divine in each human being, giving a new yet profoundly ancient meaning to the biblical trope that tells us, almost paradoxically, that God is near to those who call upon him. In this respect, regardless of his troubles with the synagogue and his disappointments with earlier attempts at a synthesis of the Mosaic and the philosophical ideals, Spinoza made a Jewish choice.

Spinoza had not the standing to create a new Judaism, and his ideas could not command the allegiance of his contemporaries, whether Jewish or non-Jewish. Yet Spinoza's philosophical ideas have long been a springboard to moral and intellectual independence for many, as much if not more for lovers of philosophical thinking as for professional philosophers. In an age like our own, when all thinking persons must construct their own thinking and reconstruct, if they can or will, the links that bind them to the cultures and traditions from which we all spring, Spinoza's radical reconstruction of Jewish ideas can provide an opening toward moral and intellectual rediscovery. For what is radical is what goes to the root, not merely for purposes of destruction or deracination but also, potentially, for creativity and growth.

NOTE

1. See, for example, Pines's essay, "Spinoza's *Tractatus Theologico-Politicus* and the Jewish Philosophical Tradition," in *Jewish Thought in the Seventeenth Century*, ed. Isadore Twersky and Bernard Septimus (Cambridge: Harvard University Press, 1987); "Spinoza's *Tractatus Theologico-politicus*, Maimonides, and Kant," in *Further Studies in Philosophy*, ed. Ora Segal, *Scripta Hierosolymitana*, vol. XX, Jerusalem (1968); "The Limitations of Human Knowledge According to Al-Farabi, ibn Bajja, and Maimonides," in *Studies in Medieval Jewish History*, ed. I. Twersky (Cambridge: Harvard University Press, 1979). Notable also in the first mentioned volume is Septimus's "Biblical Religion and Political Rationality in Simone Luzzato, Maimonides and Spinoza." Unfortunately, we do not have the space here to offer a comprehensive account of the scholarship on the influence upon Spinoza of his Jewish philosophical predecessors or even to name the full range of scholars who have addressed that issue.

CHAPTER 2

What Does Spinoza's *Ethics* Contribute to Jewish Philosophy?

LENN E. GOODMAN

1. The One and the Many
2. Freedom and Determinism
3. Mind and Body
4. Is and Ought
5. Power and Justice
6. Reason and Emotion
7. Creation and Eternity
8. Knowledge and Skepticism
9. Correspondence and Coherence
10. Matter as Active and Matter as Inert
11. Transcendence and Immanence
12. Finitude or Infinitude in Nature's Scope or Duration
13. Teleology and Mechanism

The list could be expanded, but these may suffice for now. Here we see some of the core issues that have dogged the heels, or paid the wages, of philosophers in the Western tradition from the beginning. They involve oppositions that arise in every area of philosophy, from metaphysics and cosmology to epistemology, philosophical anthropology, ethics, and politics. The oppositions have grown so hoary and canonical that the list acquires the look of the ancient Pythagorean table of opposites. But the terms subtend opposing theses, not just themes or tendencies. Philosophers are typically categorized by their stances on such issues as these, and those who cannot be neatly pigeon-holed are rarely said to have taught Yin to dance with Yang. More commonly they are called incoherent, or confused—a charge that A. E. Taylor, for one, was not displeased to bring against Spinoza.[1]

But Spinoza was not content to leave traditional oppositions where they lay and then line up on one side or the other of some conventional divide. More than an analytic thinker, he was a synthetic and constructive philosopher.[2] He saw it as part of his task to replow the great watersheds of philosophy. We can see the pattern in his earliest essays at philosophical writing, when he warns against hasty surrender to apparent paradoxes and urges that a sound account of nature must be set out in its proper order, with hard work and careful distinctions (*TdIE* 44–45; G II 17). We need not simply reject troublesome ideas. But we do need to purify and clarify our thinking, to free it from the misleading effects of common usage.[3] Hence Spinoza's bid for an emending of our thinking.[4] His call to order and clarity is an antidote and a rebuff to skeptical exercises. Thus the open rebuke of skepticism that immediately follows it (*TdIE* 46). The spirit, in fact, is Maimonidean.[5]

The intellectual elbow-room that allowed Spinoza to think his way clear of so many conventional oppositions was hard won. The moral strength that preserved his freedom was vividly demonstrated in his life—perhaps never more so than when he declined a university post, with all the strings and emoluments pertaining thereto. He had paid too dearly for intellectual liberty and honesty to sell his birthright for a mess of academic pottage.[6] That, in fact, is part of what I want to show: that, excommunicate or not, Spinoza never did give up his birthright. As a result, Jewish philosophy, as a living tradition, like the broader philosophical tradition of which it is a part, has much to glean from Spinoza's philosophical work—from his concrete ideas, and from the model of his synthetic vision.

Some historians of ideas lay claim to Spinoza as a kind of culture hero (or antihero), the Rambam of secularity or deracination, a Marrano of the mind. The appraisal grows from a response to Spinoza's understandable pain vis-à-vis his Jewish roots. It circles warily around a handful of prophetic, and prophetically bitter, remarks he made about circumcision, Zionism, and manliness—and responds with ethnically charged sensitivity to his uncharitable but irreversibly liberating reading of the Bible.[7] The tendency (as in endless discussions of Shakespeare's intent with Shylock) is focused more on the sharp edges and less on the broad surfaces and inner depths. It ignores the rabbinic caution against blaming words uttered in the heat of pain, and the rabbinic advice to look at the contents, not the container.

There is often a jolting bluntness to Spinoza's words, in the *Ethics* and elsewhere. Richard Mason rightly describes those words as sometimes brutal. Spinoza rarely writes with academic tact—although such tact is evident, curiously matched with solecism and reductionism, when he tries to accommodate his Christian friends' beliefs and attitudes.[8] More often his efforts at candor thwart moderation. But, beyond making allowance for the sense of hurt and isolation that both strengthens Spinoza's philosophical incisiveness and makes it ruthless, unfeeling, even unseeing, I will not try to deal with his attitudinal posture here. My present task is that of a miner, not a pardoner, and a miner needs to distinguish acid from ore.

A well-known alternative to ethnic apologues and ripostes has proved more fruitful: to examine Spinoza's philosophical work against the backdrop of intellectual history. We are shown—magisterially, in Wolfson's case— how Spinoza drew on and addressed the philosophical tradition in which his mind grew to maturity.[9] My goal here is quite different. It is not to probe Spinoza's mixed feelings about Jews and Judaism. But neither is it to reduce his philosophy to slips of paper emblematic of the sources that informed his thinking and his problematic.[10] Rather, I wish to show, all too schematically, how Spinoza was able, with each of our baker's dozen of oppositions, to sidestep the familiar dichotomies and frame a synthesis that avoided many of the worst repugnancies of the opposing theses.

Spinoza's means to this goal were philosophical—not dogmatic, dismissive, fideistic, or romantic. He exposed the doctrines commonly ranged on both sides of the table not as horns of a dilemma but as outgrowths of slipshod thinking—as he put it, of inadequate ideas. He articulated more adequate ideas by thinking more rigorously, and more freely, about the key notions that oriented each of these bones of contention and made it stick in the craw of philosophers, and nonphilosophers. A Hume might deem causal thinking irrational but indispensable. A Moore might use grammar as a club, to bully his way to perceptual knowledge. A Wittgenstein might dismiss solipsism by insisting that our patterns of life and language presuppose a social world. Even a Kant can tell us that if science does not countenance self-caused actions, law and morals cannot move without them—so, free volitions must be preserved, albeit in the sealed train of disciplines which they both justify and define.

But that was not Spinoza's way. Like any profound ideas, his syntheses rest on a background of prior analysis. But the distinctions he made were devised to reconcile oppositions long thought insuperable: By taking more seriously than others had the ideas of substance, freedom, knowledge, matter, truth, or mind, Spinoza finds ways to disarm the familiar dichotomies. The perennial disputes were the reflex of inadequate conceptual spadework. They persist, we might add, in part through the unwillingness or inability of later thinkers to pursue or even consider and develop Spinoza's conceptual achievements.

Not that Spinoza solved all philosophical problems—no one has done that. Nor does Spinoza gives us a cookbook method for solving the problems he did not resolve fully and to everyone's satisfaction. In philosophy, as in other fields, no method is a substitute for thinking. As Spinoza remarked,

> Method is nothing but a reflexive knowledge, or an idea of an idea; and because there is no idea of an idea, unless there is first an idea, there will be no method unless there is first an idea. (*TdIE* 38, cf. 23; G II 15–16, 12/7)

But what has all this to do, as the old joke has it, with the Jewish Problem? Nothing, if we confine Jewish Philosophy to the limited (if fascinating) issues of the philosophy of Judaism. Yet if we weigh the engagement of Jewish thought with the great issues of God and humanity, freedom, purpose, justice, knowledge, body and soul, might and right—an engagement that emerges with the dawn of Hebrew culture and gains philosophical articulacy pari passu with the growth of Western thought at large—why then everything.

Let us consider the issues themselves and not just how Spinoza's problematic responds to prior Jewish thinking, but, critically, how his analyses can contribute to future Jewish philosophical insight and exploration. Spinoza is claimed for many a fold: Jewish and Christian, pantheist and atheist, rationalist and mystic, realist and nominalist, analyst and continental, historicist and ahistorical metaphysician, ecologist, and, yes, Buddhist.[11] The tenor of my argument is less celebratory and possessive. My aim is not to claim Spinoza as a Jew but to reclaim his insights for Jewish philosophy. I will state boldly that if Jewish philosophers, speaking as such, hope once again to face the great questions of cosmology and metaphysics, ethical, social and political philosophy, epistemology and philosophy of mind, they will find no more powerful ally—and no more penetrating and demanding interlocutor—than Spinoza. He was the first great philosopher in the modern age to confront these problems from a background of learning in the Jewish canon and a deep commitment to the core ideas of the biblical and rabbinic traditions that he so profoundly scrutinized.

In *On Justice*, noting how alien to a Jewish ethos is preoccupation with death and afterlife,[12] I called Spinoza a true child of the Torah when he writes: "The free man thinks of nothing less than death; his wisdom is a contemplation not of death but of life" (E IV P67). Similarly with his distaste for remorse and regret. Not that death is absent from life, or that sin and redemption are irrelevant to religion, or to Judaism. But Spinoza faithfully reflects the Mosaic ethos in refusing to make death the cynosure of his philosophy, or sin the core of religion. Even when he castigates what he calls the unmanning of the Jews by the Judaism he knew, he is falling back to a robust humanism rooted in the Torah and vital in predecessors like Akiba, Halevi, and Maimonides.[13] He turns the focus from sin and death to the human potential for perfection and the love of God.

But my concern here is not with the ethos Spinoza commends but with his philosophical articulation of Judaic values and insights. He arrays the ideas that he can appropriate from his Judaic heritage in philosophical, indeed geometrical order, not as an apologist but as an inquirer who will trim his engagements to the demands of reason. That was Aristotle's posture when he asked himself what philosophy could make of received religious ideas (*Metaph.* Lambda, 1074b 1–14). It was Maimonides' too, when he argued that one can believe only what one understands—and that even creation would be allegorized, as anthropomorphism is, should reason prove it untenable (*Guide* I 50, II 25).

Let me tag at the outset some of the insights taken up by Spinoza, received not as theses but as themes that philosophical argument itself, in open encounter with experience, will cast into propositional form: the absoluteness of God and unity of nature; the bounty and intelligibility of the cosmos, as expressions of God's perfection; the centrality of charity to justice; and, within a comprehensive determinism, the human power and responsibility to shape our own destiny and take charge of our own character, individually and communally, so as to live by an ethic of love and understanding, in good fortune and adversity.

To specifics now. What I aim to show is that the core theses of Spinoza's *Ethics* address the central conundrums of Western philosophy with a rigor whose yield is a system of ideas deeply consonant with the core themes of Mosaic thinking and highly fruitful for future philosophical work that weighs the strengths of that tradition.

1. THE ONE AND THE MANY

Here, surely, is the oldest problem of philosophy—so old that it is not easy to state it as a problem. The Presocratics searched for a source of unity and stability underlying nature's variety and change. They wanted an account of diversity and variability, an intellectual assurance that the world will not fall away or come to pieces—and an explanation of its not having done so as yet. The biblical authors found answers to such questions in the idea of absolute creation and in the poetry of a divine promise: "While the earth remaineth, seedtime and harvest, cold and heat, summer and winter, day and night shall not cease" (Gen. 8:22). The rainbow, read with the eyes of hope, was the emblem of that promise (Gen. 9:10–17). Nature's stability is underwritten by God's grace and justice; and these in turn, by God's unity: No conflict of natural principles undermines the world, because God's mind is one. No passionate violence will pursue wrongdoers to the grave and beyond: Human failings are accountable to human justice (Gen. 9:6). God's justice works inwardly, through the dynamic of human actions. It gives room to human and natural freedom and will not rain constant judgments from the heavens. Rather, human weaknesses will be tolerated by nature and by nature's God (Gen. 8:21).

The *physikoi* sought the basis of unity and stability in some material substance, although they were not averse to assigning it some of the attributes of the divine. What material, they wondered, manifests so much variety as we encounter, and how does the flashing of change resolve itself into oneness without collapsing into nullity, as nature courses through the rhythms and cycles of life? Sublimated into metaphysics, such questions become Parmenides' quest for an absolute Unity that gives the lie to all mere appearances. At its heart the quest was religious, a search for ultimate explanations, "first principles," as Aristotle put it. As an intellectual quest this search for unity bespeaks the highest and most disinterested piety. But it is also a quest for perfect peace and stability, perfect reality, and deathlessness.

The same quest takes moral as well as cosmological form in the Mosaic Torah, with the dismissal of the pagan pantheon.[14] The beauty and bounty of nature—heaven and earth themselves—are not the fallout of some dreadful theomachy but the creative work of a single God, whose unity is reflected in the unity of all goods and virtues. The unity of the cosmos and the coherence of God's law can be seen in the purgation from the idea of divinity of the disparate and conflicting values of the pagan horrendum—terror, fever, blood, wanton sexuality, and violence, no longer confused with holiness, as in pagan cult and culture.[15]

Plato found Parmenides' arguments for ontic unity telling, and not unsound—only too rigorous for mere nature to live up to: This world of change and seeming, the world of becoming, was equivocal in its every move and claim (*Sophist* 241–61). But beyond it, in the ideal patterns of thoughts and things, lay reality itself. Moral unity too could be found, if not in the conflicting interests and opinions of this world of *parti pris*, then beyond it, in an intellectual realm where all values unite in their source.

Aristotle could not make much use of the unity Plato found in the Forms. Morals needs guidance in the here and now, and the Form of the Good is too general to give us adequate specificity (*NE* I 6–7, 1096b 15–1097a 24). Again, in the study of nature, we can learn why things must be as they are, but not by recourse to pure forms—as if deduction from definitions might yield discoveries (*An. Pr.* I 31)—but only from study of the specific natures of things in their natural settings. The forms we need are not There, but here.

Aristotle rejected Plato's concessions to Sophists and Eleatics. He denied that worldly facts are equivocal. But he respected Parmenides still and held to the idea that being must be, and in some sense must be one. So matter, species, God, the spheres—the cosmos itself—do not change: God is unmoved, nature eternal, species do not evolve; there is no void or absolute coming to be, or perishing. All these are Parmenidean thoughts, purchased at great cost, betraying Plato's Cratylean idea of becoming and nature's utter mutability.

But Aristotle could not give up his deep commitment to pluralism. So he could not mount a single-minded account of substance. His epistemic realism made no clear choice between species and particulars as candidates for the title of substance. For the epistemic criteria cut both ways: Both species and particulars have a kind of epistemic primacy—species conceptually and nomically; particulars, empirically and heuristically. Both, in different ways, are prime bearers of attributes and subjects of predication.

Applying the distinctive criterion of self-sufficiency that Aristotle deploys in so many realms—judging states and stories, plays, and sentences—the ambiguity about substance becomes even more pronounced. For an organism is self-sufficient, in a sense. But so, in a way, are its organs. Only God is self-sufficient fully. For God's pure activity of thought requires no external support. But Aristotle's commitment to the here-and-now conspires with his pagan religiosity to make him balk at any exclusivist conclusion. There are substances and substances, it seems.

Yet surely one of the marks of the category of substance, by Aristotle's own account, is that it brooks no relativity. A thing either is or is not real, either is or is not a member of its kind. Not so with qualities (*Cat.* 7). One can always ask the Johnny Carson question, "How hot is it?" But there is no corresponding question, "How dog is it?"or "How Socrates is he?"[16] So how is it that substances, critically identified by their self-sufficiency, are—like city-states, sentences, or stories—self-sufficient only in certain respects and to varying degrees, but never perfectly or absolutely so, except in the case of God?

The same question arises insistently from the Torah, becoming explicit in the philosophical and theosophical traditions that flow from the confluence of biblical with Neoplatonic thinking. If God is absolute, as is powerfully suggested in the Mosaic epiphany, I AM THAT I AM—if God, indeed, is infinite, as the Kabbalists affirm when they call God *Ensof,* the Boundless, if God is the Ground of being, as the rabbinic epithet *ha-Maqom*[17] entails—then how can there be anything besides God? The question was confronted in the philosophy of the Stoics and presaged in their Megarian, ultimately Eleatic heritage.[18]

The Sufi-inspired theologian al-Ghazālī finds the core of monotheism (*al-tawḥīd*), the "kernel of the kernel," in a monism that sees nothing in existence but God.[19] Ghazālī's spiritual cousin, the Jewish pietist philosopher Bahya Ibn Paquda, like Ghazālī, gives cognitive and ethical significance to this idea, laying out a way of life as its practical and spiritual interpretation.[20]

Writing of prophets as ecstatic visionaries in whom all human powers are fulfilled, Maimonides too assigns a practical significance to the unitive vision:

> a person of this description will undoubtedly have as perfect an imaginative faculty as can be. So, when that faculty functions [turning pure ideas into images, words, and institutions], it will receive from the [Active] Intellect an emanation commensurate with his intellectual development. As a result, he will apprehend only divine things, and those the most remarkable. He will see nought but God and His angels; he will sense and apprehend only true beliefs and universal principles of governance for the reform of human relations. (*Guide* II 36)

The blueprint matches Spinoza's: Monism on the upper storeys opens out onto (and rests upon) a naturalistic scientific enterprise and an integrated ethical program. The style may differ. For Maimonides, like Bahya, fills the space with the ethos and ritual of Halakha. Spinoza sets out the sparer furnishings of a more generic life plan. Its cosmopolitan humanism only faintly suggests the biblical heritage that frames it. But, despite this clearing, with all its benefits and costs, the monistic clerestory remains and preserves its articulation to the main body of theory and practice. For both are Mosaic.

The affinities here are generic and structural, not specific and lineal. Spinoza rejects the search for philosophy in scripture.[21] Where Maimonides and his Muslim predecessor al-Farabi saw philosophy as a prerequisite of genuine prophecy, the source of its claims to truth, Spinoza more closely tracks Isaac Pulgar (fourteenth century), who saw philosophy and prophecy as competing (if ideally complementary) avenues. Imagination, the classic fount of prophetic language and legislative concreteness, was not for Spinoza a vehicle but a rival of the pure intellect that yields philosophical understanding.[22] Yet, we must allow for Spinoza's political intent in the *Tractatus*.[23] As Michael Rosenthal shows, Spinoza writes, in part to defang the "priests." For appeals to scripture hamstring philosophy with the notion that revelation somehow obviates argument. When we make allowance for Spinoza's agenda and set his thoughts on prophecy alongside those of Maimonides, we can see the two great philosophers addressing distinctive solutions to the same problem.[24]

Behind Spinoza lies a heritage studded with monistic readings of experience. I have cited only a few. The compelling intuition of God's all-encompassing reality is unfolded with scholastic thoroughness and zeal in every branch of medieval philosophy, pietism, and mysticism. As Mason asks, citing Wolfson, "how could God *not* be said to be infinite by anyone in the monotheistic tradition?"[25] But the monistic nisus is fraught with dangers. And monism is only one reading of monotheism, powerfully attractive to philosophically inclined mystics and mystically inclined philosophers, but radical. It solves several problems but raises the ante on others—not least, the tension between timeless unity and the manifest diversity and change of nature and experience. Some mystics sidestep that challenge, deeming the Absolute unanswerable to the canons of ordinary experience, and making paradox the ultimate expression of ineffable unity.[26] But a truth that finds its voice only in paradox is an oxymoronic truth. It is not what Spinoza seeks.

He condemns appeals to ignorance and brands as such any attempt to leapfrog beyond nature to God's ultimate causality. Appeals to providence when ordinary causal accounts run dry under the pressure of repeated demands for (ultimately teleological) explanations, he insists, make God the refuge of ignorance, a substitute for causal explanations rather than their sponsor and unifier.[27] Yet Spinoza's naturalism is not materialism. His is not the monism of the *Physikoi*. But neither does he offer a Neoplatonic solution. He does not reject emanation so much as generalize it, bringing matter in from the Neoplatonic cold, making it constitutive·rather than remote, not alien to the divine, not a pole apart from intellect but one of the infinite ways in which the Infinite expresses its reality. Spinoza here does not abandon the tradition but offers new and radical answers to its ancient problems. He does not need the polarity of matter and form to see intellect as an expression of perfection; he need not denigrate matter to valorize mind: Extension too expresses divine creativity. But in reconfiguring the bearing walls of monotheistic ontology, Spinoza hews from the same quarry as his predecessors. If his house stands stronger it is because he has cut more sharply, set his angles more solidly, rejected flawed stones more resolutely.

Asked how God's omnipresence did not somehow overwhelm the world, the Talmudic rabbis replied in smiling, iridescent midrashim. Their childlike allegories cast vivid pinpricks of light but carefully, coyly deflect broader theological inferences—as if to say, *aggadah* sets no precedent. The Kabbalists, recoiling in voluntaristic reaction at the insistent surge of emanation, pronounce that God, by a special grace, contracts His godhead and withdraws His power and presence, to give space and specificity to the world and to His Laws, scope to natural actions and human choices.[28] But in the repertoire of midrashic tropes that contrast God's boundlessness with the works and deeds of, say, mortal kings,[29] Spinoza could find only a wish list. The voluntarism broached by Jewish philosophers like Ibn Gabirol, Halevi, and Maimonides had long grown stale and dogmatic. And, like Parmenides, Aristotle, Proclus, and Averroes, Spinoza found it arbitrary to expect God to alter vis-à-vis the world (EIP33S2). The real question was not whether God's act is free or determined (a false dichotomy, as Spinoza clearly saw) but whether God's absoluteness precludes the reality of anything else. Spinoza's characteristic answer was yes and no.

The question was misleading; it would find no coherent answer until formulated more adequately.

Combining Aristotle's working definition of substance, as what exists in itself, with Descartes' more epistemic definition, as what is conceived through itself—the definition that made thought and extension the two substances of Cartesian nature, since the two were independently conceived—Spinoza could reply that anything delimited will inevitably depend in part on other things, for its conception and its existence. It will inevitably be equivocal, then, to ascribe substantiality to finite things. When pressed, such claims will self-destruct. Yet finite things—bodies and minds—are not unreal. They are all expressions of God, specifying and differentiating His unity in a panoply of ways. They are as real as God is, but not self-sufficient. Their existence is dependent. They are attributes and adverbs—modifications, as Spinoza puts it. Yet attributes are of the essence. They are the reality of a thing. Spinoza's realism fits well within the Mosaic orbit: It too is innocent of the idealist thrust that philosophers have long used to discipline recalcitrant nature and secure divine hegemony. The monism too suits the Mosaic tradition, its drive to treat all creation as one within God. Spinoza acknowledges the affinity, with due allowance for the differences that sunder his work from the idiom of his predecessors:

> I maintain that God is the immanent cause, as the phrase is, of all things, not the transitive cause. All things, I say, are in God and move in God. This I affirm along with Paul ["For in Him do we live and move and have our being, Acts 17:28] and perhaps with all the ancient philosophers, though expressed in a different way; I would even venture to say, along with all the ancient Hebrews, as far as may be conjectured from certain traditions, though these have suffered much corruption. But those who think that the *Tractatus Theologico-Politicus* rests on identifying God with nature, meaning by that some sort of mass or corporeal matter, have missed the point completely (*totā errant viā*). (Ep. 73; G IV 307/5–14)

Like Bahya and Maimonides, Spinoza reaps a practical harvest from his monism:

> It remains to point out how helpful knowledge of this doctrine is to our lives. . . . i) in teaching that we act only at God's pleasure, share in God's nature, and do so the more, the more perfect our actions are and the more we understand God. Besides giving us complete peace of mind, then, this doctrine teaches us in what our greatest happiness, or blessedness consists: knowledge of God

alone, by which we are led to do only those things that love and morality advise. . . . ii) in teaching us how to handle ourselves in matters of fortune, things beyond our control. . . . to expect and bear calmly good fortune and ill, since all things follow from God's eternal decree. . . . (EII App.; G II 135–36; cf. Eps. 43, 75)

The fullest elaboration of the monotheistic idea will take normative rather than narrative form. But Spinoza touches on the normative only at its highest generality. He was not a legislator, nor a Talmudist. Metaphysics and philosophical anthropology undergird the ethical part of the *Ethics*, just as cosmology and ontology undergird what Maimonides archly calls the legal portions of the Mosaic law—and psychology and physiology underlie Maimonidean ethics. Clearly Spinoza had not the sympathy with the rabbinic or even the scriptural tradition fully to explore their normative potentials.[30] Nor would he anchor his metaphysics or cosmology in scriptural authority. "High speculative thought, in my view," he wrote, "has nothing to do with Scripture. For my part, I have never learned, nor could I have learned, any of God's eternal attributes from Holy Scripture" (Ep. 21; G IV 133/4–7). But what of the attributes he did learn of from the tradition and bent to the contour of his monism? What, specifically, of extension as an attribute of God?

Maimonides had long before tied matter and form to God by treating both as expressions of the divine. His rejection of the Neoplatonic exclusion of matter from the power and ken of God led directly to Spinoza's inclusion of extension, along with thought, among God's attributes. Strictly speaking, Maimonides argues, God's unity and uniqueness preclude all real attributes (*Guide* I 60). But in seeing nature as God's work and sphere of governance, we naturally project anthropomorphic traits: We see order and credit divine wisdom; events that seem incomprehensible, we ascribe to chance, or, in biblical parlance, to God's will. The diversity of these aspects of the Godhead, wisdom and will, is as subjective as the names are projective. All is ultimately resolved in God's absolute simplicity.[31]

That real attributes would compromise God's unity had long been urged in the Mu'tazilite polemics against the Trinity.[32] Divine unity, as Maimonides clearly saw, was no mere postulate of monotheism but an entailment of God's absolute and necessary being.[33] Mu'tazilite polemics, however, were now nearly a thousand years old. Spinoza could disengage from the Maimonidean constraints by treating not the attributes but their self-sufficiency as subjective. Thought and extension (to use the new, Cartesian names) had been shown by Descartes not to depend on one another for their conception. Having nothing in common, neither could they depend on one another for their existence (EIP3). Rather, both, as determinate natures, must depend on God.

The world, Maimonides argues, shows us not just order and wisdom but also what we see as disordered and tychistic. Piety ascribes all to God's will (*Guide* II 48). Philosophy may speak of the play of chance and the vagaries of matter. But both "design" and "chance" manifest God's rule. The differences we see reflect the limitations of our understanding. Even the 'good' and 'evil' of common parlance are names for what meets or resists our desires. That, for the Rambam, is the sense of the biblical story of the fall: that in the human condition as we know it value judgments do not directly reflect the true, divine imperatives but project our own wants and needs, passions and conventions (*Guide* I 2). Spinoza generalizes the point: Order and disorder, simplicity and complexity are among the notions that we humans shape to our finite perspectives (EIP33S2). Objectively, all is order when adequately understood—since all events are causal implications of God's decree/nature. Troublesome as some may seem, all are intelligible *in se*. As Heidi Ravven puts it:

> All of nature is self-ordering energy or a process of ordering and integration. There is no force of disintegration or entropy in Spinoza's conception. Disorder is a reordering, i.e., a transition to another ordered state.[34]

Spinoza washes away conventional distinctions between order and disorder much as Aristotle (also taking a God's eye view) dismissed Empedocles' demand for separate powers of Strife and Love to explain the buildup and breakdown of things (*Metaph.* III 4, 1000a 26–1000b 13). For in nature's eternal cycles, the buildup of one thing is the breakdown of another.

Maimonides links Aristotle to Spinoza here, in his expectation that the differences between divine will and wisdom dissolve, reducing what we know as chance ultimately to divine wisdom. Spinoza takes up the strategy as his rightful legacy. For to him, as Santayana put it, "the flux of things is the life of God."[35] Like Maimonides, Spinoza relied on the unity of God's attributes to overcome (that is, subjectivize) the notions of chance and disorder. But instead of rejecting real attributes Spinoza rejects the notion that God somehow, anthropomorphically, stands behind the attributes. Rather, He is constituted in them. The attributes are real; and, for Cartesian reasons, they remain distinct. It is the ultimacy—the substantiality—of their differences that is subjective.

Irrealism about nature, a price that Parmenides paid willingly for the metaphysical pleasure and religious repose of monism, was too high a price for Spinoza—although Berkeley, Leibniz, even Kant in time (by relativizing time and space, substances, causal relations, and modalities) would pay it. Maimonides had boldly called matter and form "attributes" of God— expressions through which human intelligence can appreciate God's reality and grace (*Guide* I 54). Spinoza adopted the language and extended the boldness, by defining thought and extension, with striking realism, as what intellect apprehends as constituting the essence of a substance. For, insofar as it is intellect that grasps a thing, it apprehends it as it is.[36] Spinoza preserves the unity and absoluteness of God by revisiting and revising, indeed intensifying, Maimonides' approach: Thought and extension are real, but not in their own right. Strict insistence on ontic and epistemic self-sufficiency reveals God as the only substance.[37] Other beings, while fully real, are not fully other. They are eddies in the timeless current of the life of God.

Spinoza's affirmation that thought and extension are real constituents in God's essence, does not lead to the pluralization of God that the Mu'tazilites had feared, since God/nature is united by the causal interconnectedness of the modes within each attribute and by the radial symmetry of the attributes themselves, as expressions of the divine unity. That unity is not set at a remove. Nor is nature set adrift from God's act and presence—leaving God to fish for it like a deus ex machina in a bad play.[38]

Here, at a stroke, core problems of biblical monotheism and metaphysical speculation are resolved: It becomes evident why divine existence cannot be problematized, and thus how the ontological argument can be sound as well as valid—since God, as the infinite totality, is the one reality that cannot fail to exist (EIP11; *TdIE* 54). It becomes clearer what is meant in the epiphany articulated in the words I AM THAT I AM. Maimonides took these words to express God's absolute and necessary existence and to voice an argument for God's reality that would be accessible to the wise of Israel.[39] The core intuition underlying both Parmenides' monism and the Mosaic I AM THAT I AM, the intuition that absolute perfection must be real (and that what necessarily exists can only be absolute perfection), is unfolded, by Spinoza, into the proposition that divine reality is the all (EIP15).[40]

Matter is no longer set at odds with God by a dualism that holds it suspect and then tries to insert some mysterious quasi-physical spirit or quintessence to mediate between the two. Spinoza does not disown the hard won medieval doctrine of God's incorporeality. Characteristically, he sets his own approach in a middle ground between the crude corporealism of the anthropomorphists and the reckless antimaterialism of the Neoplatonists, disparaging "those who fashion a God in the image of man, comprised of a body and a mind, vulnerable to the passions":

> But how far these have strayed from true apprehension of God is well enough established by what has already been proved. These I leave out of account. For everyone who has in any way considered the divine nature denies that God is a body. They prove this best from the fact that by body we understand any quantity,

with length, breadth, and depth, limited by some certain figure. Nothing more absurd can be said of God, a being absolutely infinite. (EIP15S)

The trouble with corporealism is that it treats the Infinite as finite. Nor will it do simply to stipulate that God's matter is infinite. For matter is infinite only in one respect, but God must be infinite absolutely. If matter is to be an attribute, then, it must be one of an infinite variety of attributes, each infinite in its own way.

The thesis that God's attributes express infinite reality in infinite ways preserves the transcendence that was critical in the idea of creation. Infinity becomes the guardian and repository of transcendence and the retort to those who imagine a reductive pantheism in Spinoza.[41] God is manifest in matter, as in thought, but neither of these determinate expressions fully compasses God's absoluteness or creative activity. Saadiah finds the same idea vividly presaged in the Book of Job. Where Elihu says, "God is great beyond knowing, and there is no tally to His years" (Job 36:26), Saadiah's Arabic translation renders: "The Almighty hath many attributes above what we know. And he hath not years that might be counted or spent."[42] Saadiah here places God beyond time, seeing not the suggestion of some large number but a denial of temporality in God. And he takes the reference to God's unknown greatness as an allusion to unknown attributes.

By understanding God in a way that precludes finitude, Spinoza becomes free to enclose matter in the Godhead, obviating the problem of God's relation to a nature with which He has nothing in common (EIP15S). Further, if God is all of nature, matter need no longer be the scapegoat, the feminine locus of insufficiency, potency without act, the shroud, receptacle, or shrine of deficiency and otherness. It could now become what the new physics called for—not a Cartesian substance, but an attribute, God's expression not in but *as* extension (EIIP2). And it could be active, conative, expressive in its own way,[43] like that other attribute, thought, which so long before and so much more readily, under the name of mind or logos, was assimilated to the action and expression, even the immanence of God.

God's immutability is intact. For the changes that modes undergo produce no change whatever in nature's overall pattern, the *totius facies universi*.[44] The medieval worry as to how God could know or govern changeable nature without Himself undergoing change is solved at a stroke, and much in keeping with the medieval project. Both Maimonides and Ghazali had long argued that God's nature does not change.[45] They meant God's plan, design, and will. But now Spinoza could say that God's objective nature does not change—"the face of the universe at large"—even though God is the locus and matrix of change.

The core doctrine then: that there is but one substance. Finite particulars are real, but their reality is derivative and dependent. In Avicenna's terms, they are contingent in themselves, necessary with reference to their causes.[46] But they are never found by themselves. Only by a wrenching act of abstraction are they wrested from their contexts. For reality need not serve our mental convenience: the givenness of things requires their thick embeddedness in their causal milieu. Their adequate conception, then, is achieved only in the measure that this milieu is conceptually preserved.

Spinoza's holism is rooted in monotheism and monism. It fuses themes broached in the Presocratic *physis* and the Noahian exegesis of the rainbow. Stuart Hampshire shows how far Spinoza traveled and how faithful he remained to these parallel traditions when he asks and answers the Spinozistic question: "What content is there to the thesis that the attributes are possessed by a single substance?" Hampshire's answer:

> The single "order and connection of things" . . . runs across, through and under all the attributes, giving the one substance its integrity, its unity, its wholeness. There is not the slightest threat that nature, just because its attributes are so disconnected from one another, will conceptually fall apart.[47]

Spinoza's God does not perform miracles, answer prayers by intervening from above, or single us out for arbitrary blessings. So it will be natural to identify that God with the God of the philosophers and not what is often called the God of faith. But faith, despite the burdens placed on it, is not a way of knowing but an attitude of hope, expectation, trust, accommodation. It cannot vindicate the reality of a personal God. Confronted with the reasonings of a Maimonides showing that the Infinite and Absolute transcends the virtues and deficiencies of human character and emotion (cf. EVP17), it only compromises the monotheistic idea—or takes refuge in the notion that the ultimate profundity is quirky and paradoxical. That, I think, is not just faith but bad faith. Spinoza holds true to the biblical idea that God is absolute. Perhaps one who takes literally the biblical stories of miracles and interventions has not reckoned fully with the power of those stories. A cow, as Nahmanides tells us, would not recognize a miracle; that demands some concept of a natural order. Similarly, one does not begin to reckon with the biblical claims about God in history until one calls to mind the biblical idea of God, not as some troll or spirit but as the All-inclusive, who yet had it in the plan of the universe that Israel would be chosen, the Torah inspired, the laws lived by. These are matters of faith, not in the expectation of nature's interruption by a creaky deus ex machina but in the recognition of God's pervasion of the cosmos.

2. FREEDOM AND DETERMINISM

Kant is a better foil than Aristotle in exposing what Spinoza did with the
classic aporia—the antinomy, as Kant conceived it—of free will and determinism. Here we see two modes of discourse, one scientific, explanatory,
even exculpatory; the other, judgmental, offering praise and blame, promis-
ing punishment and reward. The first, we are told, rests on the presumption
that comprehensive causal explanations are possible in principle. It assumes
that there is no event without a prior cause and makes no exception of
human acts of choice. These too, as a condition of their being understood,
are entered into the ranks of facts with explanations. They thus become
events determined by their causes, events that could not be otherwise. The
second mode of discourse, the one we use in admiring altruism or condemn-
ing selfishness, is incompatible with the first. It assumes, so we are told, that
outcomes might have been other than they were, and that we ourselves might
have made that difference. It sets aside all that we know of causal determinations and regards the self as a self-mover, operating causally, but in a different kind of world, where not every cause requires some prior cause, so
that ultimately all is determined externally from the start.[48]

Spinoza loathes the idea of free will, partly because it seems incoherent
to him. Free will is an otiose hypostasis, an inexplicable cause (even God
cannot be that!), an occult principle, a supposed faculty that is in fact only a
renaming of its putative effects. It is also a sinkhole of moralism, regret,
recriminations, paralyzing anxiety, and self-deception.[49] Spinoza likes determinism. It places acts and decisions in their causal contexts and teaches us
to understand rather than praise or blame. But it permits punishment or
reward. For strict liability needs no moralism. We may sanction desired or
undesired actions without recriminations or celebratory congratulations.[50]

Yet, despite Spinoza's preferences, he does not deny human freedom
but affirms it alongside the determinism he derives from the very determi-
nacy (and causal embeddedness) of all things. He even finds a meaning for
Rabbi Akiva's celebrated words (*Avot* 3.19): "Everything is foreseen, but
sway is given." As Ravven puts it:

> Spinoza is able to claim both the naturalistic determination of
> all choices and also a series of gradations within self-causation
> itself that makes improvement and development possible.[51]

Once again it is by clarity of reasoning that Spinoza untangles the classic
antinomy. Freedom is not a matter of indeterminism but of self-determination.
"We are," as he puts it, "a part of the whole of nature" (EIV App., 32)—no
more, but also no less:

> Man, insofar as he is part of Nature, constitutes a part of the power of Nature. Thus, whatever follows from the necessity of man's nature—that is, from Nature as we conceive her to be determinately expressed in man's nature—follows from human power, even though it does so necessarily. (*TTP* translated by Samuel Shirley (Leiden: Brill, 1989), 101)

Here, as with the reality of the modes (which is, after all, their expression), relativity is at issue. The real question is, to what extent can a thing be the determinant of its own actions? Classical determinists like Hobbes tend to make all determinations external. But that ignores the contribution of the individual. Pursued systematically, the familiar, externalist approach would empty the universe of agency. But God/nature is constituted in the being of things. There is, as Arne Naess insists, nothing more.[52] And things manifest themselves in their activity; they express themselves conatively, in pursuit of their own welfare.[53] Things act and are not just acted upon. So events can be understood in terms of each being's contributions—in concert with the actions of other beings alongside, or against, or upon its own effect. Does this mean that things can happen other than as they do? The question is misconceived: Given their causes, events must turn out as they do. But in a dynamic world those causes are given fully only at the very moment when an event takes place.

We humans, like all other beings, are both active and passive. Our passivity is plain in events beyond our control (EIV App., art. 32). But we do act, and by our actions can win more active control of our situations and our destinies.[54] The point is an old one. The Stoics, the Rabbis, the Mu'tazilites all argue that our actions may enhance or diminish our degrees of freedom. We can invent and use medicines and drugs, helpful or harmful to our project—as Maimonides stresses.[55] To deny that is to deny the causal nexus that underwrites Spinoza's determinism. What matters for ethics is the dynamic by which our choices enhance or curtail our freedom.[56] The thought is deeply embedded in Spinoza's psychology. For joy and sorrow (*laetitia* and *tristitia*) are transitions of the mind to greater or lesser perfection—greater or lesser degrees of power, adequacy, effectiveness. Indeed, ethics is the realm in which our choices can affect our further latitude for choice.[57] It is the growth or constraint of our thinking that gives us freedom or binds us in servitude to externals: The more adequate our ideas, the more adequate our self-governance.

For Spinoza our choices reflect, or rather *are* ideas, in some measure adequate or inadequate. We determine our own actions to the extent that those actions arise in adequate ideas (EVP20). We are passive victims of external agencies, chaff in the wind, to the extent that our actions express inadequate ideas. Since we are intellectual as well as physical beings, changing and dynamic, active as well as passive, we can, in some measure acquire more adequate ideas and in that measure make ourselves more free (EVP10, P14). It is here, where freedom is most clearly relevant, that we are free: As Mason puts it: "among the causes that will bring about the future are decisions I make now, based partly on what I have been able to discover about how I arrived where I am." For indeed, "my capacity to predict and affect the future may be improved by the exercise of my understanding."[58]

The old Platonic and Aristotelian project of placing education at the head and not the foot of the social agenda here gains a new dimension of meaning, as Spinoza considers the communal and public responsibility for human access to adequate ideas. The agenda is biblical as well. How, if not by education, can the Mosaic law achieve its goal of making the Israelites "a kingdom of priests and holy nation" (Ex. 19:6)? Thus, with all Spinoza's words in the *TTP* about the purely political aims and methods of the Mosaic Law, Heidi Ravven finds a current there expressive of Spinoza's educational understanding of politics:

> In the *TTP*, Spinoza argues that the ideal use of the imagination is in Religion. For Religion can serve to legitimate and reinforce a democratic distribution of power and a just judicial system as well as to support more authoritarian forms of government. . . . It is the irony of the public arena that the authority of religion and its mechanisms of suasion can be invoked, albeit with considerable restraint, to incur enthusiastic obedience to a system of government that fosters self-determination and independence of mind. The imagination can thus be called into the service of a form of government that Reason independently recommends as the one that best supports human fulfillment. The historical model that Spinoza chooses to illustrate the proper social function of the imagination, i.e., of religion, in the democratic and just society is the ancient Jewish commonwealth, as described in the Hebrew Bible.[59]

3. MIND AND BODY

Scripture ascribes to God the creation of the earth as well as the heavens. In setting matter apart, as the scapegoat of natural and human deficiency and excess, the Platonic tradition creates a tension within its own program. For it sought to show that whatever is real in the realm of becoming results from the saturation of matter by form. But at the same time it held matter alien and resistant to form. The Neoplatonists tried to ease the tension by insisting that matter is not just the sump at the base of the ontic cataract but also the most immediate manifestation of the One.[60] But this required treating matter not as a mere physical thing but as otherness itself—(recalcitrant) receptivity—a relative rather than categorical reality. Evil and deficiency remained, to be laid at matter's door.

Maimonides mitigates the charges against God's most elemental creation, by making matter neutral, not evil. It is the married harlot of Proverbs 7, with ever-changing forms as its "lovers," and no internal stability (*Guide* I, Introduction, Munk, 1.8a).[61] But it is also the good woman of Proverbs 31—a source of strength and potency, not just weakness and vulnerability. The body is not evil. It can be turned (by the soul, if the soul makes it a good husband!) either in the service of perfection, or toward servitude to the appetites and senses, made ends in themselves rather than lovely means to a higher end (*Guide* III 8).

I say lovely means because Maimonides defends beauty, delight and recreation, if they are sought in pursuit of our highest goal, knowledge of God:

> When a man makes this way of living his goal, he will find very many of his former sayings and doings futile; he will not trouble to decorate his walls with gold or to have gold embroidery on his clothes, unless to raise his spirits, so that his soul may be healthy and well removed from morbidity, to be clear and ready to learn. Thus the Sages said, "A pleasant house, a comely wife, and a comfortable bed for the scholar" (Shabbat 25b).[62]

But matter is still otherness, not one of the realia to be reckoned in the cosmic accounting—not one of the "sons of the Divine" (*Guide* III 22). And it is still the scapegoat. Indeed, Maimonides takes the Neoplatonists to task for not following through in exploiting the weaknesses of matter in their account of evil (*Guide* III 16).

If the Neoplatonic ambivalence toward matter created tensions, Descartes compounded the problem when his epistemic turn made matter and form separate substances. How could a nonphysical God have any causal or creative impact on materiality? Mind and body seemed forever to be seated at separate tables, with no chance of commerce between them for volition or perception. Princess Elisabeth was not alone in seeing that Cartesian dualism left no room for interaction.[63] As Spinoza notes with gentle irony, Descartes' appeal to the pineal gland proved only his ingenuity: "This is the opinion of this most celebrated man, so far as I can judge from his own words. I would scarcely have believed it was put forward by such a man, were it not so ingenious."[64]

Spinoza is not content with discontent. His disappointment with the dualism that Descartes presses to an endgame is the atrium to his own alternative, which Stuart Hampshire called "nearer to the truth at certain points than any other philosopher ever has been."[65] It is not just Spinoza's monism that gives him his opening, as if it sufficed to say that we are persons first and minds or bodies only by analysis. Descartes himself had said as much, when pressed to the wall by the Princess.[66] What matters is that Spinoza accepts the Cartesian problematic: Thought and extension are, inevitably, described in different terms and understood in different ways. Given that sort of independence, interaction is a non-starter for Spinoza, as he thinks it should have been for Descartes. For the epistemic turn means that each given must be taken to be what it presents itself to be conceptually. Spinoza declines Descartes' Copernican turn.[67] Yet for him things really are what the intellect conceives them to be. One might try to reduce mind to matter or matter to mind, or assign causal primacy to the one realm or the other. But Spinoza is untempted. He took seriously the phenomenological foundations of Descartes' dualism. And that makes his response especially valuable to us, even if we do not share all his premises and caveats. For his solution will not rest on the triumphalist reductions of materialists or idealists.[68] He will seek a more faithful description of the intimacy of mind and body than is afforded by the mysterious pervasion of matter by a nonphysical substance, or the pseudomechanism of a causal linkage between physical and nonphysical things. As he writes plainly: "The body cannot determine the mind to thinking, nor can the mind determine the body to motion, to rest, or to anything else (if there is anything else)" (EIIIP2).

Parity is maintained, emblematically in the dictum that the order and connection of ideas is the same as the order and connection of things: There will be a correspondence, a structural symmetry. But ideas are not *caused* by bodily movements or bodily movements by ideas. The relevant causes and explanations are of wholly different orders. Spinoza maintains the integrity of both realms and does not quail from the consequences of his characteristically outspoken rejection of interaction.

I can hardly endorse that rejection. It leaves unanswered far too many questions that we (like Princess Elisabeth) want to answer about our embodiment and about what Descartes himself, in remarks prophetic of phenomenology, came to call the unity of mind and body.[69] But Spinoza makes a major, much neglected, departure here: Construing the mind in terms of ideas allows him to ask what it is the idea of. His answer, framing an original and heuristic approach in the philosophy of mind, is that the mind is the idea of the body—not, in the first instance, the idea of its putative objects. For to put the matter that way would still leave unanswered the question that Descartes left unanswered: how consciousness can touch physical things, what fork it is to use.

Mind is the body made conscious. It is the consciousness of the body. For, in an important sense, it is not true (as Descartes and all philosophers of the Platonic tradition had supposed) that bodies cannot think. In one important case, bodies can think. Human bodies can think—and the human mind is their thinking. It makes the body conscious. But its consciousness, although of the body, is not chiefly about the body. Mind objectifies the affections of the body and thus knows other bodies (as Descartes suggested) through their impact on our own, and in particular on those parts of our body that are adapted to interact with other bodies in pragmatically informative ways.

Spinoza's calling the mind the idea of the body is perhaps the most original thing to be said on the subject since Aristotle labeled soul the first entelechy of a natural body potentially alive (*De An.* II 2). Indeed, Spinoza's description specifies and refines on Aristotle's but proves far more useful and perspicuous. It does not ignore or sidestep the brain as the organ of thought, or the senses as thought's messengers. But it allows thought its own dynamic, including the power to initiate, rather than remain a mere reflex of brain states. Spinoza's account thus addresses the ancient and abiding concern with the status of the person, without turning to any pseudospiritual ectoplasm that is called nonphysical but in the same breath or puff of smoke assigned many qualities of a body—as though reality or efficacy were assured only by corporeality. Spinoza's overture here needs to be explored and elaborated. Doing so, I believe, will advance our understanding of the nature of the mind or soul in its delicate relation with the body, a topic I hope to discuss elsewhere.

But to think of the mind as the consciousness of the body is not just to address the mind-body problem. It is also to reappropriate and reinvigorate the Aristotelian notion that the mind is its thoughts, that consciousness, to put it in a Cartesian way, is what I am. Spinoza here, addressing the phenomenology of consciousness as a philosopher and not as a mere philosophical diplomatist or catalog shopper, makes enduring contributions to our understanding of consciousness and cognition. Most telling is his all too telegraphic remark that our thinking is not like a picture painted on a pad (EIIP43S). This means a number of things. First, rejection of the spectator model of consciousness. The argument is clear: If thought, or experience, were something we watched as it goes by, the subject of consciousness would remain to be found, and the nature of consciousness would remain opaque—for how could these objective images or words ever become *ours*? The spectator in the back of the theater would need to have another spectator inside—and so, ad infinitum.

But taking seriously Aristotle's insight that when thought is actual, the subject, object, and act of thinking are the same,[70] Spinoza sees that thoughts are active and reflexive—self-conscious and dynamic. I am, as the cogito suggests, identical with my thoughts; and they are not mere symbols, signs, or images, but lively and interactive ideas. Subjecthood and subjectivity, attitude and emotion are already within them. Here we see answers to Hume's quandary about how thoughts can motivate. For thoughts are not just representations or impressions (see EIIIPref). And we see answers to many other questions about commitment and belief, since belief is not just willful attachment of an assertoric to a propositional content. It is a response (as Maimonides suggested, *Guide* I 50) to what I understand.

The Mosaic Torah does not make a topos, let alone a problem, of a disembodied soul. It does speak of souls and spirits. But, more importantly, its expectations address a dimension of humanity that is not reducible to the empiric—teaching the Israelites, in its own concrete idiom, the lesson of their trials: "that it is not by bread alone that a man liveth, but by all that cometh from the mouth of God" (Dt. 8:3). Strange foodstuffs in the desert, clothing that did not wear out, feet that did not swell—the message is spiritual, but the medium is material; and the response called for is spiritual in intent but worldly in expression. The Torah addresses a unified person as the subject of its commands and admonitions. That premise becomes explicit in rabbinic midrashim on the organicity of body and soul, and especially on moral agency.[71] Spinoza's even-handed rejection of both dualism and reductionism respects the biblical agenda, even as it articulates the values of that agenda by way of concepts and a syntax of relations never articulated in the tradition.

4. IS AND OUGHT

The idea of the conatus is among Spinoza's most fruitful—far more so than the modes and attributes, a legislative ontology that calls to mind Strawson's division of descriptive from revisionary metaphysics.[72] Few philosophers rush to accept the revisionary label. Even Berkeley calls his story common sense. And Spinoza's radical claims draw only half their power from their enhanced coherence vis-à-vis prior accounts of being. The rest comes from their ability to accommodate our ordinary usages and expectations—areas where, say, radical Eleatics notoriously stumbled. But metaphysical systems typically can save the phenomena, so they do not compete much with one another in point of verification (or falsification). That is what rankled the positivists about metaphysics, and still rankles their heirs, from Popper to Quine. Such systems should perhaps be compared as songs, poems, or artworks are, or comprehensive theories in the sciences, for elegance, scope, and beauty—responsiveness to the givens and to questions raised from rival standpoints, but also for fruitfulness in ethics, politics, the sciences and arts, in theological understanding and the general integration of experience. It is here that I find the conatus far richer in potential than the attributes and modes—even allowing for the secondary, but separable, yield of those ideas in addressing the mind-body problem, and for their primary impact, in satisfying (and putting to rest) the ancient and perennial quest for ultimate unity.

Spinoza's conatus is a rethinking of the idea of essence. It strips away the ancient association of essence with universals, allowing each individual to stand (not alone but on its own), not merely as an exemplar of a kind but as a unique particular, answering to various general descriptions, but bound, in the end, by no nature but its own, as that nature expresses itself and interacts with the natures of other things. Leibniz loved the idea, although he hated the monism in which it was embedded. It gave each being its own dynamic.[73] So essences were no longer static. Evolution would not somehow violate the logic of being or the law of self-identity. Even natural kinds could change, since they were now no more than populations of particulars with specific traits in common.

But the crucial impact of the idea of the conatus was on ethics; and, through ethics, on politics: The essence of each being is its project, the sum of its claims, projecting an identity beyond the empiric given and making demands on the environment in a way that both defines an emergent character and demands its recognition. Here, in the immediacy of the positive given, in the dynamic of any being's self-affirmation, Spinoza found an anchor for the idea of the good.

The good is not a property, natural or nonnatural. Rather, it is located in being itself.[74] Our notorious perspectivalism about the good reflects the diversity of claims, just as Maimonides suggested in his gloss of the biblical story of the fall (*Guide* I 2). The Aristotelian telos is discovered exactly where Aristotle sought it, in the demands projected by all beings. The social good lies in the complementarity of claims. That is why humans do not have the sort of obligations toward, say, animals as toward one another (I soften Spinoza's irritated tone here just a bit). For animals and humans do not have the same nature. So they cannot fully share in the same good—least of all in those intellectual and moral goods that are gained and grow only in the sharing (EIVP36&S1).[75]

In Spinoza's analysis we have an identity of being, good and power. But we must always note the direction of a reduction: Spinoza admires strength. Even more than weakness and servility, he loathes the confusion of weakness and servility with virtue. But his is not a celebration of brute power. Thus, in his cautious praise for Machiavelli, what he looks for in the dicta of "that shrewd observer" is a moral rootedness that modern readers find, say, in Machiavelli's thoughts about civic virtue.[76] Spinoza despises pity and the tyranny of words but loves honor, nobility, and principle. His argument is not that where principle and pragmatism part company one should pursue expedience. Rather, it is Plato's ancient insight that expedience is not adequately understood when presumed to part company with principle. For Plato reversed the ancient Sophists' reduction of goodness to power, arguing against Thrasymachus and all half-hearted defenders of principle (represented by Plato's brothers Glaucon and Adeimantus). Plato claimed not only that justice cannot be reduced to the interest of the stronger but also that the interest of the stronger, adequately understood is justice—meaning no blind pursuit of self-aggrandizement but the integration of the virtues—and, through that integration, the further integration of seemingly disparate interests.

Like Plato, Spinoza finds warrant for reversing the Sophists' arrow in his conception of our inner strength and genuine interest. And, like Plato, he does not rest his case on appeals to the cosmic supremacy of justice but on his appraisal of the human situation. Just as Plato set aside all talk of an afterlife when urging the inherent worth of justice, Spinoza finds no place for extrinsic sanctions in the ultimate evaluation of our choices. We know our strengths when they enhance our being. Reason gives adequacy to our thinking, and that lends power to our acts: "Blessedness is not the reward of virtue but is virtue itself; nor do we enjoy it because we restrain our lusts, but it is because we enjoy it that we are able to restrain them. . . . From this it is clear how effective the wise man is and how much more powerful than the ignorant, who is actuated only by his cravings" (EVP42&S).

The Mosaic faith that being is a good, and the highest being, the most perfect good, is alive and articulate in the elements of Spinoza's account: (1) the ontic anchoring of norms in the identity in each being; (2) the revalorization of the telic, by its immanentization;[77] (3) the demand for editing individual claims in the light of our need for cooperation, without which the human project is a dead letter; (4) the purgation of passive emotions like pity and fear from the idea of virtue. Classic ideals—as often Hebraic as Roman—here displace their medieval counterparts, through a restored faith in nature. Humility, abjectness, repentance, and regret are false virtues. Joy is a good; sorrow, an evil.

As always in ethics, some of the choices made are matters of style, reactions to prior conventions and present extremes—rejecting the pietist idea, for example, that one can never be too humble or forebearing. But many of Spinoza's ethical benchmarks express not just personal predilections but keen analyses. Thus arrogance, *superbia*, is a weakness not because it is a kind of pride but because it is a form of self-deception, an inadequate idea of one's strengths and weaknesses. It has much in common, then, with false modesty—and may cohabit with it, or with partiality (*existimatio*). Kindliness and benevolence are strengths. So are gratitude, courage, generosity, fortitude, spirit (*animositas*), and good cheer (*hilaritas*). Scorn, dolefulness, censoriousness, ambivalence (*fluctuatio*), ire, and spite are weaknesses. Many of Spinoza's judgments reflect those of the tradition. Thus the negative appraisal of anger, as in Maimonides. Defining *antipathia* as groundless hatred echoes the rabbinic term *sin'at ḥinam*. Clemency or mercy (unlike pity) is not a passivity but an active restraint of anger and vindictiveness (Defs. of the Emotions 38). Since it aims at the good of another, it is a kind of generosity (EIIIP59S).

One hallmark of a pietist heritage in Spinoza is the crucial import of subtle differences of intention. Thus *ambitio* is a desire to act so as to please others, "especially the vulgar." *Humanitas*, humaneness, differs only in intent: Its goal is others' good rather than their approbation (EIIIP29, 31; Defs. 43, 44; EVP4S). Spinoza equates *humanitas* with *pietas*, in keeping with the Hebraic tradition, where saintliness (*tzedek*) is called truth, and charity is called justice (*tzedakkah*)—but piety is called lovingkindness (*ḥesed*).

A virtue is what strengthens us in our project. But strength here is neither egotistical nor subjective. The idea of joy[78] distinctively colors Spinoza's conception of the good and orients the perspective of a subject, but one whose real interests are intimately bound up with those of his fellows and inadequately conceived in isolation.

5. POWER AND JUSTICE

We can see clearly the roots of Spinoza's political synthesis,[79] and how he can say, "A man guided by reason is more free in a state, where he lives according to a common decision, than in solitude, where he obeys only himself" (EIVP73). The point will be echoed by Locke:

> Freedom, then is not what Sir Robert Filmer tells us, "liberty for every one to do what he lists, to live as he pleases, and not to be tied by any laws," but freedom of men under government is to have a standing rule to live by, common to every one of that society. (*Second Treatise* IV 22)

Locke reasons that the enjoyment of liberty outside civil society is so uncertain as to be largely theoretical—indeed mythic! (*Second Treatise* IX 123). Spinoza, in the same vein, contends that our freedom (our power of action) is enhanced by our engagement in civil society. As Michael Rosenthal shows, Spinoza models the Hobbesian state of nature on the experience of ancient Israel as an exiled nation, in Sinaitic limbo between bondage in Egypt and the covenanted commonwealth in its new land. But Spinoza does not rely on the mythic notion of a wild and unfettered state of nature. He uses the Hobbesian idea of anarchy only to motivate the Mosaic use of religious suasions to govern an unruly populace unaccustomed to rule under their own law and untrained in civic virtues. Heidi Ravven's chapter shows how Spinoza thinks the Mosaic strategy worked. The key is the precedence over Hobbes that Spinoza gives to Plato's and Aristotle's account of human sodality: acceptance of Plato's idea that cooperation is prior in nature to enmity. Despite the prominence of the passions, human interdependence, not sheer aggression, is the prime fact of our political nature.

So Spinoza needs no narratives about the state of nature to prove civil society advantageous (EIVP73D). Those guided by reason will maintain the common life and pursue the common advantage. The ethical scholium makes clear why. For, as Spinoza says, it seems hardly to need argument that a man of genuine strength (*vir fortis*) is the least arrogant of men, hates and envies no one, is enraged at no one, holds no one in scorn or beneath notice (*indignetur*). The wise man knows that "hate is overcome by the return of love"; he wants for others the same good that he wants for himself and sees the weaknesses of others as natural facts, not personal affronts (G II 265).

The wise man, then, is not some titan rebel or anchorite in retreat from human society but a realist who knows how precious (and how deadly) human beings can be to each other and has found a way of living suited to that understanding. Spinoza's thinking here resonates with the Stoicism of Marcus Aurelius, but also with Maimonides and his biblically and rabbinically mediated response to Aristotle's idea of the *zoon politikon*:

> It has been made as clear as can be that man is a social being by nature, that his nature is civil, unlike other animals that do not need to congregate in groups. Because of the immense complexity in the make up of this organism, which, as you know, represents the final stage in the compounding of living species, individual differences abound—so much so that you are hardly more likely to find two individuals who match at all in any moral trait than to find two who look alike. The reason is the diverse make up of individuals: The matter is different, so the accidents attendant on its form will differ too. . . . Such immense individual diversity is not found in any other animal species. . . . with humans you might find two individuals who are as different in every character trait as if they belonged to different species: One might be so hard that he would slaughter his smallest child in the heat of anger, while the other might quail at killing a bedbug or some such insect, because his spirit is too soft to do it. And so with most accidents.

But since the nature of our species dictates that there must be so much diversity among its members, and yet requires that we live together socially, we need someone, necessarily, to regulate our actions. For without this, our social existence could not be achieved at all—someone to moderate our excesses and remediate our deficiencies, to model actions and characters for us all, instituting more constant and consistent patterns of behavior, to cover over the disparities of our natures with an abundance of conventional concord, so that society can function in an organized fashion. That is why I say that although the Law is not natural, it makes an entry into the natural order, and part of the wisdom of the Deity, in behalf of the survival of this species, which He was pleased to give existence, was to give it a nature such that its members have the ability to govern. (*Guide* II 40)

Compare Spinoza's model:

We can never make ourselves capable of needing nothing outside ourselves to preserve our being, or of living without dealings with external things. Besides, if we look at the mind, clearly it would be more imperfect if it were alone and knew only itself. So there are many things outside ourselves that are useful to us. And of these none better could be devised than those that are a perfect fit to our own nature. For if, say, two individuals of just the same nature are joined together, they form a new individual twice as capable as either alone. Nothing, then, is more useful to man than man; nothing, I say, can be wished for by men that would be more effective in preserving their own being than for all their minds and bodies so to come together in every way as to form, as it were, one body and one mind, and, all together, insofar as possible, strive to preserve their own being and seek for themselves the common benefit of all. (EIVP18S; G II 222–23)

Both the Torah and the philosophers of the great tradition—Socrates, Plato, Aristotle—argue that an enlightened self-interest counsels socially responsible and generous actions. It is by following the biblical injunction to love one's fellow as oneself that a follower of the Torah will optimize his individual interests, along with those of his community and the family who are his closest link to that community, its history, welfare, and destiny. It is by pursuing the life of justice, Plato and Aristotle find, that we humans fulfill and integrate ourselves, not only socially but as persons.

There is a warning as well as a promise here. In vivid historical vignettes, the Torah drives home the point later made so forcefully by Hobbes, that anarchy and desperation are the yield of lawlessness and statelessness. Thus the Book of Judges frames a ghastly narrative with mention of the days "when there was no king in Israel" and "every man did what was right in his own eyes" (Judg. 19:1, 21:25). Spinoza echoes the biblical caution in the passage already cited, where we found him anticipating Locke: "A man guided by reason is more free in a state, where he lives according to a common decision, than in solitude, where he obeys only himself" (EIVP73). One who is guided by reason can collaborate with others in building a common life. One who lives alone lives in fear, isolated from the sources of aid and cooperation.

The same reasoning that leads Spinoza to his affirmation of community allows him to build a bridge from egoism to altruism: "When each man most seeks his own advantage men are most useful to each other" (EIVP35C). Thus "One who lives according to the guidance of reason strives, so far as he is able, to repay another's hatred, anger and scorn with love and generosity" (EIVP46). The power of love to dissolve hatred was a Christian message, but also central to the Torah's ethics. A paradigm case, the biblical commandment to aid one's enemy in righting his fallen load (Ex. 23:4–5).[80] Spinoza understands the misery of living for hatred and revenge, a point long argued by Saadiah (*ED* X 13). Virtue is both an intrinsic and an instrumental good, its two sides, complementary and mutually reinforcing.

Spinoza's bridge from egoism to altruism[81] rests on the discovery of the true nature of the good, announced as early as the *TdIE* (1–13), the recognition of understanding as our highest goal. For it is in the quest for understanding that we find the surest grounds for human unity: "Only insofar as men live according to the guidance of reason must they always agree in nature" (EIIIP35). Reason teaches us that our highest and most fulfilling goal is that of our intellectual quest, the quest for a life guided by reason and aiming for the intellectual love of God. Such goods can be shared. They are optimally pursued, in fact, through shared efforts. And they foster our social nature, since what unites us optimally is not sheer physical sameness. That might make us competitors! Rather, it is reason's recognition that its highest aim is also what is most readily and equably shared (EIIIP36).

Maimonides may seem naive in finding more individual diversity among humans than among other animals. But he does attach this claim to moral differences, where freedom accentuates our underlying diversity of bent, and where patterns of behavior are entrenched in habit, custom and policy. Nor is his appraisal overly sanguine. While stressing our need for one another's aid, he offers a caveat as well: The wise leader will regard all people,

> as individuals—that is, inevitably, either as members of the flock or beasts of prey. If the perfectly developed man who holds himself aloof (*al-mutawaḥḥid*) thinks of them at all, it will be only

with a view to avoiding the harm the noxious ones may do him, should he chance to associate with them, or benefiting from the helpful ones, as his needs may require. (*Guide* II 36, Munk, 2.79b)

Spinoza may seem sunnier about complementarities. But he heeds the caveat: "Only insofar as men live by the guidance of reason will they necessarily agree in nature" (EIVP35). In tones that echo Maimonides and his admired Andalusian predecessor, Ibn Bājja, who gave special weight to the idea of the loner (*al-mutawaḥḥid*), Spinoza warns those who would be free, to beware the blandishments of the ignorant: "A free man who lives among the ignorant strives, as far as he can, to avoid their favors" (EIVP70).[82] Spinoza leaves the institutional task of reconciling diversities for his political writings.

Refracting the iridescence of Machiavelli's studied ambiguity into its diverse components, Spinoza offers alternative explanations of the shrewd Florentine's intent: Was he casting a jaundiced eye on foolish rebellions that would only entrench a hateful tyranny? Or was he warning "how chary a free people should be of entrusting its welfare entirely to one man"?[83] The latter reading may seem somewhat wishful,[84] but the bivalence he finds in Machiavelli does reflect Spinoza's own thoughts: Sovereignty of any kind reflects our human need for common rules and so is not lightly to be attacked—even if rebellion were not so dangerous. But usurpation also is all too human: One can hardly blame a sovereign for trying to defend its rule. But by the same token one cannot blame citizens who seek to defend their rights and interests, as they see them. Hence, a Hobbesian riposte aimed pointedly at Hobbes' own Elizabethan sounding appeal to good faith and loyalty:

> The pledging of faith to any man, where one has but verbally promised to do this or that, which one might rightfully leave undone or *vice versa* remains so long valid as the will of him that gave his word remains unchanged. For whoever has the power to break his word has given up his rights not at all in reality but only nominally. Thus, if he who is by the Law of nature his own judge determines—rightly or wrongly (for to err is human)—that from some pledging of faith more loss than benefit follows, then he determines by his own judgment that that pledge ought to be dissolved, and by natural Law he does dissolve it.[85]

Spinoza plainly takes delight in reminding those who follow Hobbes in his acid reading of the social contract, that part of the acidity derives from nominalism and its dissolution of word magic, which must include the magic of nominal promises, made in behalf of interests whose fulfillment is unseen.

The moral strand that survives in Machiavelli is the recognition that power in the state, as in the individual, depends on virtue. Machiavelli does have his own ideas of what counts as a virtue. Cunning and ruthlessness may eclipse clemency and truth. But the ancient claim survives, that power rests on moral qualities. Plato makes a case for social integration, paralleling his claims about personal integration: That society is most enduring that is most just: the society where reason rules, integrating diverse interests and coordinating complementary capabilities. Aristotle argues more concretely to the same effect: One cannot exclude whole classes from public deliberations without risking the stability of the state (*Pol.* I 2, 4, 6, 7, 12, 13, III 1, IV 4, 6, 7).

Barbarians, Aristotle argues (making a foil of the alien other and an object lesson of the ethos of historic enemies) equate women with slaves, not recognizing the partnership of couples and their need for cooperation rather than domination (*Pol.* I 2). The wise man knows that even a slave needs virtues, even if not those of the free. A fortiori will he want his wife and children to share in virtue, since the children will be adults, and women are half the population. So rule cannot be equated with despotism. Nor is government the same as "household management" (*Pol.* I 1)—or running a business. Our survival depends on communal engagement, and the human quality of our lives depends on the quality of that engagement. The integration of the individual in the social fabric, then, is the critical issue of politics, and the nature and tenor of that integration are the critical questions that set apart one polity from another. Those who confuse rule with domination or government with household management fail to see beyond the ends of economics—or self-aggrandizement. In effect, they make slaves, rather than citizens, of all. For they instrumentalize and dehumanize the populace by barring them from the deliberative process, in which we exercise the critical human function of choosing our own ends. Participation is pivotal in any polity, since it articulates our social integration. But rightly regulated modes of participation are the foundation of constitutional rule, which is, at bottom, the structuring of a polity on the basis of some system of mutuality in participation (*Pol.* III 1).

Spinoza follows in the biblical and Aristotelian tradition here, as synthesized by Maimonides. He recognizes that the rule of law humanizes human relations. For that is the heart of his argument that our best allies in attaining our human ends are our fellow human beings. Complementarily, he accepts the need for penal laws. Maimonides writes:

> if criminals are not punished, crime will not be diminished at all, and those who contemplate wrongdoing will not be deterred.

There is no more fatuous fool than those who claim that the abrogation of all penalties would be a kindness to mankind. That would be the most barbarous cruelty to men as well as the ruin of civil order. The compassionate thing, in fact, is to do as He commanded: "Establish judges and magistrates in all your precincts" (Dt. 16:18). (*Guide* III 35, cf. I 46)

Spinoza echoes the argument:

By this law, then, society can be sustained (*firmari*), if it retain for itself the right of reprisal that everyone has, and that of judging good and ill for itself. Indeed, that is how it has the power to institute a shared way of life, to make laws and enforce them—not by reason, which lacks the power to subdue the emotions (by P17S) but by threats. (EIVP37S2, G II 238)

Early on, defending his determinism, Spinoza wrote:

Again, you may ask, "Why then are the wicked punished, since they act by their own nature and according to the divine decree." But I answer: 'It is equally at the divine decree that they are punished. And if only those were to be punished whom we deem to have offended by their own free will, then why do men strive to exterminate poisonous snakes? For they too offend only by their own nature and cannot do otherwise.' (CM 2.8, G I 265)

He uses the same reasoning in the *Ethics*. After naming indignation an evil, he adds:

But be it noted that when the supreme power, out of a desire to keep the peace, punishes a citizen who has wronged another, I do not call that indignation. For it punishes him not because it is aroused by hatred to destroy him but because it is moved by duty. (EIVP51S)

Spinoza's word for duty here is *pietas*, synonymous for him, as we have seen, with *humanitas*, a linkage made by way of the Hebrew equation of piety with *ḥesed*, lovingkindness, the same motive that Maimonides urged in behalf of retributive punishment.

Again, in keeping with the rabbinic and Mosaic tradition, Spinoza mandates public responsibility for the needs of the poor. For, as he remarks, the need exceeds private sympathy and resource (EIV ad cap. 17). Further, as Rosenthal's and Ravven's chapters show, Spinoza adapts and adopts Maimonides' Farabian thought that prophecy mediates ideas of the higher good to those incapable of discovering such ideas on their own. It allows very ordinary human beings to live by a higher law and principle and to emulate a higher example than their own unaided reason would have discovered.

Perhaps the most prominent biblical resonance in Spinoza's political theory lies in his constitutionalism, with its powerful echoes of the ancient rumblings of tension over kingship. Scripture epitomizes the rationale for a state in the popular demand for a monarch to champion the cause of the people against anarchy and oppression (Judg. 21:25, 1 Sam. 8:5). But both the prophet Samuel (1 Sam. 7:11–14, 8:4–22) and the Book of Deuteronomy (17:16–17) warn of the dangers of monarchy: the amassing of wealth, wives and horses. Samuel's warning, issued at God's command, is the more explicit:

> This will be the practice of the king who will rule over you: He will take your sons and appoint them as his charioteers and horsemen, and they will serve as outrunners for his chariots. He will appoint them as his chiefs of thousands and of fifties; or they will have to plow his fields, reap his harvest, and make his weapons and the equipment for his chariots. He will take your daughters as perfumers, cooks and bakers. He will seize your choice fields, vineyards and olive groves and give them to his courtiers. He will take a tenth part of your grain and vintage and give it to his eunuchs and courtiers. He will take your male and female slaves, your choice young men and your asses, and put them to work for him. He will take a tenth part of your flocks, and you shall become his slaves. The day will come when you will cry out because of the king whom you yourselves have chosen.[86]

Maimonides, transforms these warnings into a license and a mandate,[87] but his motives are as clear as those of the ancient Israelites. Mindful of God's instructions to Samuel (1 Sam. 8:6; 9:16), he scans the horizon for some means to national redemption.[88] So he gladly assigns de jure powers to kings that the Torah warns against as de facto usurpations. But he issues no Hobbesian carte blanche and holds clear of Realpolitik and force majeure. Israel's kings must rule under the Law, observing the commandment (Dt. 17:19) to copy the scroll of the Law and read it all the days of their lives, understanding its words not by their own lights but as interpreted by the prophets and sages. Maimonides' synthesis of public law in the final book of his fourteen-volume Code nourishes the seeds of biblical constitutionalism, where royal authority arises from the popular will, not by divine right, and is offset not by popular sovereignty but by a firmer and less fickle counterweight: God's grudging understanding and consent. Biblically, it is not the mandate but the limits on sovereignty that spring from the Absolute.

The same spirit lives in Spinoza, reinforced by his own republican ideals and those of his friends.[89] It is not found in Hobbes or Machiavelli and is wholly alien to the lessons that a Filmer would father upon Scripture.

6. REASON AND EMOTION

We have seen how Spinoza's account of cognition dissolves Hume's notion that ideas cannot motivate. Ideas are as much motives for Spinoza as they are apprehensions. An affirmation, as the Stoics held, is just a special kind of appetitive act—or appetition is a special case of affirmation. But, contrary to Stoic theory, affirmation is not an accessory linking a volition to a propositional content. Every content speaks for itself: "*In mente non datur volitio, sive affirmatio, et negatio praeter illam quam idea, quatenus idea est, involvit*" (EIIP49): "There is no willing, affirming or denying in the mind, apart from that which the idea itself, as an idea, contains."

The adequacy of an idea is its warrant. For the intellect, that warrant is its appeal. So to understand an adequate idea is to affirm it, and to understand an inadequate idea is at once to see through it and to purge it. That is why adequate ideas free us and enhance our scope of action, making us more adequately the cause of our own undertakings and less the butt of events to which our passive emotions (inadequate ideas) expose us. The asymmetry of adequate and inadequate ideas is crucial. For it is not just any choice that manifests my freedom but only those choices that are grounded in adequate ideas.

We must not suppose, in the romantic manner, that emotions, as such, are personal expressions, let alone expressions of our own power. Emotions do have power, but the power of passive emotions is a power over us, not a power of ours, expressive of our own nature or fulfilling to our own being. It is in fact the power of misapprehensions, or more accurately, the power of other things over us, effective against us through the vulnerabilities opened up by our misapprehensions.

Spinoza's scheme of active and passive emotions provides a model for the reappropriation in the language of rational psychology of the ancient notion of self-mastery. Self-mastery does not mean ordering oneself around. Nor need it be construed as a battle between higher and lower selves, ego, id, and super ego. It is not a matter, as Anna Russell used to put it, of "Getting behind oneself and pushing oneself," but of recognizing who one really is and appropriating fully the goals and purposes that support one's project.

Spinoza does not deny that there are irrational motives. All sorts of motives arise in the association of ideas—guilt, spite, bigotry, remorse, censoriousness. The elegance of Spinoza's model is in the way it shows that such passions of the soul, being passions, are not genuinely ours, no matter how they might be marked with the idiosyncrasies of our personal histories. They are not expressions of the self that seeks to grow and perfect its nature—although they may readily seem such in the heat of the moment, or in bad night thoughts.

The model is rationalist but not cognitivist. It does not reduce emotions to neutral bits of fact. On the contrary, for Spinoza no cognitive content is emotively neutral. All ideas are charged with practical and speculative significance. All draw approbation or rejection and might lead us to greater or lesser realization. The metaphysics is new, and its rigor is all Spinoza's own. But the homiletics is as old as the Ethics of the Fathers: "Who is a hero? One who conquers his inclination" (Avot 4.1), and the Rambam's moral counsels:

> Power is given to every man. He may, if he wishes, direct himself toward the good and become just, or toward evil and become wicked. Do not entertain the notion of the foolish among the nations and among the mass of senseless Israelites, that God ordains from the outset of a person's creation that he will be righteous or wicked. It is not so. Every one of us is capable of growing as righteous as Moses or as wicked as Jeroboam. One can become wise or foolish, merciful or cruel, tight-fisted or liberal, and so for all the virtues and vices. . . . that is why God says, "Would that they had such a heart as this always" (Dt. 5:26), implying that the Creator does not compel or predestine human beings to do good or evil but cedes to them control of their own hearts. . . .
>
> Do not be puzzled at the thought that a person can do whatever he pleases and that his actions are left up to him. . . . Just as it was the Creator's pleasure that fire and air would ascend, earth and water descend, and the sphere revolve—and likewise that all created things behave according to the pattern He was pleased to assign them—so it was His pleasure that human beings hold in their own hands the power to choose; it was His pleasure to turn over to us all our own actions, so that without coercion or compulsion but by our own God-given discretion we would do all that a human being can do. (*Mishneh Torah*, Hilkhot Teshuvah v 1–4)

In a direct line from the Stoic idea of appropriation to the Mu'tazilite theory that our choices limit or expand our degrees of freedom, to the Maimonidean idea of delegated freedom, Spinoza makes his own the idea that human agency may grow or diminish, in part by its own wisdom. He thus sets the seal of his ontology upon the biblical idea that the consequences of our actions are visited upon us through the dynamic of our choices.[90]

7. CREATION AND ETERNITY

Maimonides, Ibn Tufayl, and Kant all address the impasse between creation and an eternal cosmos irenically, urging, in effect, that the issue need not be settled for philosophy to go forward. Maimonides holds for creation, since here God's act makes a palpable difference in the world, and since only by a volition can we humans account for the emergence of multiplicity from God's simplicity—or even avoid freezing the cosmos in a determinism so rigid as to preclude all change (*Guide* II 19). But, despite his claim that eternalist emanationism needlessly etiolates God's link to the world, Maimonides does not agree with Ghazali that Neoplatonists are atheists malgré leux. Spinoza forthrightly joins the Averroists.[91] Has he abandoned his bridging strategy? Clearly, he is no philosophical diplomatist—no Leibniz, let alone a Maimonides or Ibn Tufayl. But even on this vexed issue, we see a synthetic posture. As Genevieve Brykman argues, the divine fiat of Genesis, which figures the absoluteness and totality of creation, also mystifies that act:

> Nothing sets in clearer relief the gratuitousness of God's creative act. . . . Nothing expresses better the discontinuity between idea and achievement—a discrepancy often taken as a distinctive mark of voluntary action.[92]

The linkage of that discontinuity to voluntarism was plainly marked by the Ash'arite theologians of the *Kalām*. The issue was crystal clear to Spinoza, spotlighted by Abraham Herrera's insistent arguments for a voluntarist creationism.[93] We can see Spinoza swimming against that voluntarist tide. His aim is to mend the breach, not between creationists and eternalists but between God and nature, to prevent a stultifying mystification of the means by which transcendence is mediated into immanence. In the process, he rejects, in the interest of rational theology and theodicy, the voluntarist notion that God might have created a much better world than we know.

Updating the ancient *kalām*-style argumentation, Spinoza reasons that one substance cannot produce another (E1P3). Nor can an immaterial God give birth to a material nature. If God is its cause, the cosmos itself must be constitutive in God's Infinity. Spinoza rejects the word 'creation,' with its voluntarist connotations and its cosmic sundering of God from His work. But he retains what he takes to be essential: God is still the ultimate cause.

The strategy parallels that of Avicenna, another eternalist who held fast to the idea—or, in his case, even the word 'creation.' Avicenna's response to a predecessor like al-Razi shows us clearly what is at stake. To defend a temporal creation, Razi made matter eternal and uncreated. For the sheer origination of matter would violate Razi's atomist tenet that nothing comes

Goodman

from nothing. As Avicenna viewed the ground left by such approaches, he could only infer that too high a price had been paid. Temporal origins were preserved, but only by deeply compromising the absoluteness of creation: Matter was no longer a work of God. With a Neoplatonic model, Avicenna could produce far more welcome results. True, the world was now eternal, but matter was as much an act of God as was thought.

Spinoza similarly rejects creation as long understood by its defenders, but saves the world's absolute dependence on the divine. Indeed, he assures it, since God's causality is no external act but the reflexive activity of the necessary being, expressing Itself as Causa Sui. Where Platonists had tried to reconcile matter with the One by making it the most immediate of emanations, and where Jewish Neoplatonists had equated "relative matter," the first breath of otherness, with the divine will, Spinoza scotches the arbitrariness of that will and overcomes the ascetic anxiety about the recalcitrance of matter to the (masculine) controlling forces of form and idea. He accepts matter in its own right, as a primary expression and constituent of God, in keeping with what Santayana called Spinoza's "master thought," the "divine right of the real."[94]

It was the resultant monism that led early readers to see in Spinoza an audacious exponent of Kabbalistic themes.[95] For the Lurianic Kabbalah did strive to fold nature into the Godhead, by way of the mystic and hypostatic numbers, the *sefirot*, that were the thoughts, expressions, determinations of the Infinite. The immanentism that stirred the suspicions addressed in Warren Montag's chapter served the same ideal. So did Spinoza's treatment of time. By valorizing particulars as he does,[96] Spinoza wins a perennial goal of monists by negating the ultimacy of time: We humans, he argues, have two ways of knowing. But only one grasps things in their particularity as determinations of God's eternal essence. When we understand things in this way, not through our embodiment but by way of their eternal essences, we know them as they really are (EVP30). The move is portentous. It means that, insofar as finite, embodied beings can, we know as God knows.

From the outset Spinoza has defined eternity as existence insofar as it is conceived to follow from an eternal essence (EID8). Part of the beauty of this approach, as he puts the definition to work at the close of the *Ethics*, is in overcoming the ultimacy of time without recursion to Plato's universals, or dismissing time as an illusion. Reality at large does not change. God does not change. Reason knows things by way of their necessity—thus not temporally but, as it were, from a God's eye point of view—as Spinoza puts it, "under the aspect of eternity" (EIIP44&C). But things do change, in ways that express their eternal natures. Time, once again, as in Plato, becomes the moving image of eternity. But the Forms are not needed to mediate eternity into temporality, and the unity and absoluteness of the Ultimate is uncompromised by the recognition that its image moves. The image is no illusion. But neither is it Nature as a whole. It is an expression of God; its changes bespeak a timeless essence that is its ultimate reality and its share in eternity. That last phrase, of course, is not Spinoza's but an echo of the Mishnaic *Helek ba-'olam ha-ba*, a portion in eternity. The idea is Spinoza's gateway to the ancient rabbinic understanding of immortality.

8. KNOWLEDGE AND SKEPTICISM

Spinoza declines Descartes' rather theatrical gambit of hyperbolic doubt. Not that he was less aware of the fallibility of the senses, or of the feebleness and febrility of much that passes for reason. But his own analysis had shown him that Cartesian doubt serves only as a dialectical challenge, a hurdle for knowledge to clear. Logically speaking, the real, if concealed fulcrum Descartes needed against skepticism was the intuition of God's perfection.[97] Once it was grasped that God, being perfect, is no deceiver, the speciousness of systematic doubt was laid bare: Mere fallibility might be overcome by method. So any natural source of error was corrigible in principle. An omnipotent demon might create an undetectable deception. But if omnipotence is inseparable from perfection, an omnipotent demon—a duplicitous God—is ruled out, and knowledge can proceed in security.

So Cartesian philosophy must begin not with the isolated mind whose titanic or quixotic image so fascinated renaissance and baroque philosophers, but with the intuition of divine perfection. For intuitions are not stepwise procedures and need no external guarantor. Descartes sought artfully, even archly, to sidestep controversy over whether God would not or *could* not deceive. His carefully chosen phrase, "no deceiver," left the theologians to wrangle over grace and destiny, knowledge and error—salvation and sin. Even so Descartes needed all his skill and influence to scotch charges of Pelagianism. But the philosophical aim was won: Rational intuitions do stem from God's grace. But our trust in them needs no external reassurance. One need not know God (at least not explicitly and articulately) before one can see by His light, the natural light of reason. There is, then, no Cartesian circle. But we must start from God and the intuition of His perfection.

The new orientation appealed to Spinoza's realism, and to his impatience with anthropocentrism. Spinoza himself, as Mason shows, faced no Cartesian demon. I suspect the hypothesis would have seemed childish to him. But, if a cause can affect only things of its own nature, Spinoza had good grounds, beyond those of logic, and mere distaste, for dismissing the demon. The reasoning would expand on Aristotle's ancient argument that there is just one world: Whatever causes can affect us must connect with our

natures—and so be traceable. A cause toto caelo foreign to us can have no
impact on us, deceptive or otherwise.[98] An alien being cannot touch us; a
kindred one cannot deceive us undetectably. There may well be—for Spinoza, there *are*—(infinitely) more things in heaven and earth than are
dreamed of in our philosophies. But none that can affect us are inscrutable.

Confronting skeptics eager to ensnare the hope of knowledge in tangles
of circularity or regress, Spinoza pursues a Cartesian analogy of intellectual
to physical tools. Doubters may argue that before we can know we need a
method, which in turn demands a further method, and so ad infinitum. Similarly, it might be argued that we cannot make a hammer without tongs or
tongs without a hammer: "in this way, someone might try, vainly, to prove
that men have no power of forging iron" (*TdIE* 30, G II 13). The Midrash
uses such hammer and tongs imagery to underscore the miracle of creation.[99] But here it anchors a skeptical elenchus like the ancient Sophists'
claim that nothing is definable without a prior definition of definition, and
so ad infinitum. Descartes primes Spinoza to respond when he argues for a
fresh beginning in the search for knowledge: devising our own methods and
canons, unimpeded by inveterate suppositions and assumptions:

> Our method in fact resembles the procedures in the mechani-
> cal crafts, which need no methods other than their own, and which
> supply their own instructions for making their own tools. If, for
> example, someone wanted to practice one of these crafts—to become
> a blacksmith, say—but did not possess any of the tools, he would
> be forced at first to use a hard stone (or a rough lump of iron) as
> an anvil, to make a rock do as a hammer, to make a pair of tongs
> out of wood, and to put together other such tools as the need
> arose. Thus prepared, he would not immediately attempt to forge
> swords, helmets, or other iron implements for others to use; rather
> he would first of all make hammers, an anvil, tongs and other tools
> for his own use.[100]

A few pages on, we still discern Spinoza's careful gaze, as Descartes urges
the philosopher to focus on simple ideas:

> If one tries to look at many objects at one glance, one sees
> none of them distinctly. Likewise, if one is inclined to attend to
> many things at the same time in a single act of thought, one does
> so with a confused mind. Yet craftsmen who engage in delicate oper-
> ations, and are used to fixing their eyes on a single point, acquire
> through practice the ability to make perfect distinctions between
> things, however minute and delicate. The same is true of those who
> never let their thinking be distracted by many different objects at

the same time, but always devote their whole attention to the simplest and easiest of matters: they become perspicacious.

It is, however, a common failing of mortals to regard what is more difficult as more attractive. Most people consider that they know nothing, even when they see a very clear and simple cause of something; yet at the same time they get carried away with certain sublime and far-fetched arguments of the philosophers, even though these are largely based on foundations which no one has ever thoroughly inspected.[101]

Clearly the radicalism appeals to Spinoza, the call to independence of thought and simplicity of design. But he also takes the hint as to the affinities of skepticism with obscurantism. He turns the Cartesian case of self-made tools to his own purpose by finding the weakness of the skeptical argument in its ignoring the evolutionary possibilities:

At the start, men were able to make the easiest things with the tools they were born with (however laboriously and imperfectly). Once these were made, they made other, more difficult things more easily and perfectly. So, moving gradually from the simplest works to tools, and from tools to other works and tools, they eventually accomplished many and difficult things with little labor. Similarly the intellect, by its inborn power, makes intellectual tools for itself. Using these it acquires other powers for other intellectual works, and from these works still other tools, the power of searching further. So it proceeds by stages, until it reaches the pinnacle of wisdom.

It will be easy to see that this is so with the intellect, if we understand what the method of seeking the truth is, and what those inborn tools are, which it requires only to make other tools, so as to advance further. (*TdIE* 31; G II 13–14)

The simplest and most necessary idea, presupposed in all our thinking, is the idea of God:

the most perfect method will be the one that shows how the mind is to be directed according to the standard of the given idea of the most perfect being.

From this you will easily understand how the mind, as it understands more things, at the same time acquires other tools, with which it proceeds to understand more easily. For, as may be inferred from the foregoing, before all else there must be a true idea in us, as an inborn tool. Once this idea is understood, we understand the difference between that kind of perception and all the rest. Understanding that difference constitutes one part of the method.

And since it is clear in itself that the mind understands itself the better the more it understands of nature, it is evident, that this part of the Method will be more perfect as the mind understands more things, and will be most perfect when the mind attends to, or reflects on, knowledge of the most perfect being. (*TdIE* 38-39)

Spinoza is urging bootstrapping, but he avoids suppositiousness by acknowledging an a priori element, pure ideas, stemming ultimately from the purest, the idea of God: Our ideas win their utmost clarity when linked reflectively and articulately to the idea of God.

The gap Spinoza seeks to bridge here is that between rationalism and empiricism. He sees that sheer sensations and random experience (*experientia vaga*) can never yield scientific knowledge, with its causal explanations and judgments of necessity. Sensations, no matter how we mass them, present only "fragmentary, confused and chaotic" ideas (EIIP40S2). Pure ideas are needed to give order to our knowledge. But such ideas are not universals abstracted from particular cases. Nor are they the notions that words or customary usage may canonize. They are intuitions of the essences of things in their intimate causal relations with one another and their ultimate concatenation with the universal system of things that Spinoza identifies as God's governance.

The idea that God is the source of understanding, enlivening and actuating human awareness, is, of course, very ancient. It is voiced in Aristotle's idea of the Active Intellect:

one does not think after first thinking that one should think, or deliberate by deliberating that one should deliberate. What then could be the starting point, if not chance? But then everything would come from chance. Perhaps there is a starting point with none beyond it, something that can act as it does by being the sort of thing that it is. What we are looking for is—what is the starting point of movement in the soul. The answer is clear: as in the cosmos, so in the soul, it is God. For in a sense the divine element in us moves everything. The starting point of reasoning is not reasoning, but something greater. And what could be greater than knowledge and intellect but God. (*Eudemian Ethics* VII 14, 1248a18–29)

As in Spinoza, God's work here, in activating human thought and deliberation, is immanent. But so is the work of God that the Psalmist cites, in the lines that so inspired medieval Jewish philosophers that Ibn Gabirol took from them the title of his *Fons Vitae*: "For with Thee is the fountain of life. By Thy light do we see light" (Ps. 36:10).[102]

What Spinoza contributes is the linkage between self-understanding, the intuition of God, and the intuitive understanding of nature. For Neoplatonists, that linkage would be the work of a hypostatic Active Intellect. But Spinoza saw that one does not explain causally by renaming the effect, and he shuns the Platonic notion that the objective natures of things are mirrored in the innate ideas of the human mind. For that would seem to obviate empirical study of nature, and to hypostatize universals. What is original in Spinoza's account is the continuum, the epistemic ladder from partial to adequate knowledge that holism and naturalism make possible. But the theme that self-knowledge leads on to a knowledge of God was a favorite medieval motif, harking back to the Socratic reading of the Delphic oracle and the biblical idea of man's creation in the image of God.[103] The idea that one can (or must) learn of God from nature is again biblical, and Aristotelian. It comes clearly into focus in Maimonides' bold gloss on God's caution to Moses "thou canst not see My face" and the subsequent vision of God's back (Ex. 33:20, 23)—meaning God's act:

> Moses prays to know God's attributes when he says "Cause me pray to know Thy ways that I may know Thee," etc. (Ex. 33:13). . . . When Moses sought to know God's attributes he sought forgiveness for the nation, and this was granted. He then sought to know God in Himself, saying, "Show me, pray, Thy glory" (33:18). Whereupon his first request, "Cause me, pray, to know Thy ways," was granted: He was told, "I shall cause all My good to pass before thee" (33:19). . . . The words "all my good" allude to the arraying of all existing things before Him, of which it is said, "God saw all that He had made—it was very good" (Gen. 1:31). By the arraying of all existing things before him, I mean that he comprehended their nature and their interconnectedness, and thereby recognized the character of His governance of them, both general and particular. This is the idea referred to when it says [of Moses], "He is firmly established in all My house" (Num. 12:7), which is to say, he has a true and well-grounded understanding of the being of My world in its entirety—for unsound opinions are not firm. It follows that to comprehend these works is to "know His attributes"—through which He is known. What shows us that what was promised was grasp of His acts is the fact that that through which He is indeed encountered is a set of purely active attributes: merciful, gracious, long-suffering (Ex. 34:6–7). Thus it is clear that

the "ways," knowledge of which Moses sought and which were
consequently made known to him, are the acts which issue from
Him. The Sages call them characteristics (*middot*) and speak of
"thirteen characteristics," the term current in their usage to designate ethical traits. . . . Here it does not imply that God has ethical
traits but rather that He does acts analogous to those which
express our ethical traits. . . . Although Moses apprehended "all
His good," i.e., all His works, Scripture confines itself to the mention of thirteen "characteristics" because these are the acts which
issue from Him by way of giving existence to humankind and governing them. This was the ultimate object of Moses' request, for
his words conclude, "and know Thee, that I may find favor in Thine
eyes, and see that this nation is Thy people"—in order to govern
whom I shall require ways of acting which I shall model upon
Your actions in governing them. (*Guide* I 54)

It was Saadiah who initiated formal discussions of epistemology in
Jewish philosophy. Like Spinoza, he was dismissive of skepticism and of the
related claims of brute empiricism, systematic relativism and Sophistry like
that of the claim that every method requires a prior method, or every criterion a further criterion. Saadiah interprets the biblical phrase "self-savager"
(Job 18:4) as a piece of invective (and a compact *tu quoque* argument)
"hurled," as he puts it, in the face of those who obstruct the path of knowledge. The argument is the classic one, that skepticism is self-undermining.

Like Spinoza, Saadiah adopts an empiricism that is not averse to theory.
And, like Spinoza, he assigns tradition a secondary role, since it depends on
primary sources of knowledge in reason and experience. As Ravven notes,
Saadiah is more welcoming to tradition than Spinoza—if reliable authorities
and sound transmission are assured. He does not, as Ibn Tufayl (and Spinoza) will later do, hold suspect the very terms that tradition uses. Yet he
does not expect, as Spinoza does, that doubt will ever be entirely overcome:

Indeed it is inadmissible that any act of God could banish all
doubt at a single stroke, removing one from the laws of all created
beings, when one is a created being. One who . . . yearns that God
should make him capable of knowledge in which there is no doubt
or difficulty has asked in effect for God to make him His equal.
For the one who knows without cause or mediation is the creator
of all. (*ED* Introductory Treatise, 3)

Saadiah rests his claim that human doubt is ultimately insuperable on the
recognition that all our knowledge is temporal and mediated by causes. But
the sense of human fallibility does not make Saadiah prey to a systematic

skepticism. And Spinoza shares Saadiah's refusal to travel farther than a step or two with the pyrrhonist.

Part of Spinoza's response to efforts to herd knowledge claims into a circle or stampede them into an unbounded regress rests on his seeing that knowledge is "not like a picture painted on a screen." The self-transparency and reflexivity of knowledge—as an act and as a mode of consciousness, rather than an object—show him that one does not need to know that one knows *before* one can know. To know is already to know that one knows (*TdIE* 34; EIIP43&S; G II 14–15, 123–24). With adequate ideas, we can see why. For here to know is already to know *how* one knows (See EIIP7dem; cf. Aristotle *Post. An.* 71b 9-12).

It is this last thought that grounds Spinoza's epistemic optimism and his seemingly brash assertion that truth needs no external sign but is its own sign.[104] Our sensory awareness, mediated through our bodies, affords a positive image of the world, but one that is muddled, perspectivally canted, and pragmatically limited. Sensory data tell us not about things as they are but only about the impacts of things on our frame. The point had been made by Descartes, and by Democritus long before. Emphasizing the positive impact of external objects, the Stoics had tried to weld human subjectivity to an external objectivity with the notion of kataleptic impressions, subjective data deemed reliable because they bore the very imprint of objects upon our bodies. Descartes heeded a similar call when he first conceived of clear and distinct ideas as subjective presentations that cannot be denied. His earliest explorations into fluid mechanics (still reflected in his treatment of nerve impulses in essentially hydraulic terms) suggest that he long held to some counterpart of kataleptic impressions.[105] But the ancient Skeptics, Carneades in particular, showed that no subjective impression that purports to tell us anything about the world beyond the mind can bear its own warrant. Descartes himself, I think, saw this and shifted his search for undeniable thoughts to the contents of his own ideas. Thus the celebrated epistemic turn and the refocusing of the philosophical gaze, turning away from mere external objects in the first instance and toward self-affirmation and the idea of God's perfection.

But Spinoza did not see God as a mediator any more in epistemology than in cosmology. What our knowledge of the world requires is a rational apprehension of the natures of things, a causal account of their operations, couched in terms appropriate to those natures. This Descartes himself had shown with his example of the piece of wax: All the sensory properties, the so-called secondary qualities that Galileo (and Democritus) had bracketed, are inessential. It is extension that cannot be abstracted from the wax, just as it is thought that cannot be abstracted from my consciousness. The wax, then, *is* extension and must be understood *as* extension—ultimately, geometrically.

The mind must be understood as thought: that is, psychologically. Generalizing on this approach, we reach an Aristotelian, pluralist epistemology that shapes every method to the natures of its objects. As Jeffrey Bernstein puts it, there is no "Cartesian *mathesis universalis*,"[106] not because truth has no settled criterion but because our methods must constantly reflect the nature of the subject.

Descartes may have overstated his case in treating thought and extension as substances, but that does not erase the epistemic value of his analysis. Putting that analysis to work, Spinoza argues that understanding the natures of things will allow us to situate their behavior and dispositions in a wide-ranging (in principle, ultimately comprehensive) scheme, whose coherence is the warrant of its veracity. That is, the more internally connected our causal account of the world becomes, the less room it leaves for doubt or error and the more it lays claim to acceptance as knowledge. As the youthful Spinoza put it, "after we know the nature of body, we cannot feign an infinite fly" (*TdIE* 58).

Adequate ideas are contextual understandings. Spinoza defines adequacy without reference to truth, because adequacy will be his core epistemic test for truth. Where the Stoics had trusted an implicit causal nexus to transform subjective data into objectivity, Spinoza uses an explicit causal understanding to spring the Cartesian mind from the confines of subjectivity and extend its reach beyond the immediacy of its embodiment.

Saadiah confronts subjectivism in the context of his treatment of divine justice. For justice and truth are equated in the ancient Hebrew idiom. Spinoza is faithful to that idiom in equating essence with conatus, conatus with providence and power, and these in turn with right. The reasoning, if we spell it out, is that nature (*natura naturans*) assigns each being its due. Knowledge is a cognitive recognition of that due; justice, its moral recognition. Saadiah links realism to Jewish thinking in his commentary on Job, in the same verse (18:4) where Bildad calls the as yet unenlightened Job "self-savager." As Saadiah renders it:

> O thou self-savager in thy wrath, on thine account shall the earth be abandoned and the rock be shifted from its place?

Saadiah glosses:

> *Self-savager* refers to Job, at whom these words are hurled. For when Job said, "I have been made to suffer without offense," in their view one who said such a thing was impugning the divine decree. They said to him, *on thine account* . . . ?—"Should the whole world be abandoned just because of you? Not the whole

world, why, not even a single mountain can we shift from its place for your sake. How then can we shift the Sovereign of both worlds from His attribute of justice, and ascribe injustice to Him for your sake? No, these sufferings could only have befallen you on account of your own offenses; and such is the fate of evildoers."[108]

Saadiah holds Bildad, like Job's other comforters, to be mistaken in supposing that misfortunes befall only wrongdoers. Human ills may be trials or warnings, not just punishments. Further, the sufferings of the innocent must be recompensed, if not in this life then in the hereafter. Yet Saadiah accepts Bildad's epistemic standard. He uses what I have called "referential translucency" to countenance Bildad's epistemic argument, even while rejecting his critique of Job. Applying the rule of charity, in a strong form, to discourse embedded in Scripture, Saadiah can filter out what is to be rejected in oblique discourse, and find truth in the rest. The truth, as Saadiah sees it, is not that Job has erred in affirming his own innocence. Saadiah, unlike much of the Midrash and unlike Bahya, concedes to Job a privileged self-knowledge in the moral sphere: Job does know his own innocence.[109] But subjectivism of the sort that Bildad unfairly imputes to Job is rightly condemned. For, as Saadiah argues in his philosophical summa, one who expects reality to conform to his own notions is arrogantly reversing the epistemic poles and undermining his own position, in effect positing multiple realities and slighting the actual reality that God created.[110]

Spinoza does not accept the idea of creation—not in the transitive sense that he thinks would sunder God from the world. The divine afflatus and governance do not pass from God to the world. They act from within, in the conatus of all things. Yet Spinoza's reasoning here again seems in a way more creationist than the creationists. True he rejects creationist voluntarism. But he upholds the ubiquity of God's creativity. So, like Saadiah, he upholds the reality of the resultant creation—*natura naturata*. In this sense, he upholds, and if anything outstrips, the realism that Saadiah deems crucial in the Mosaic tradition.

9. CORRESPONDENCE AND COHERENCE

Philosophers often seem eager to force a choice between coherence and correspondence ideas of truth. Spinoza, we have suggested, sees here a nexus of means to ends. Correspondence is the goal. For Spinoza is a realist, not an idealist. He defines truth as correspondence: "A true idea must agree with its object" (EIA6). But coherence is the means. Adequacy in our ideas leads us out of solipsism and toward a grasp of things as they are in their full contextual connectedness, as apprehended ultimately, in the mind of God. I deal further with these themes in my new book *In Defense of Truth*.

10. MATTER AS ACTIVE AND MATTER AS INERT

The problem here is Aristotelian as well as biblical. Can we conceive of actions in nature as dependent on the act of God without rendering God a fifth wheel, or a meddlesome deus ex machina? Aristotelian philosophy makes God the ultimate telos and Prime Mover. Scripture, Maimonides notes (*Guide* II 48), calls even chance events acts of God. Does God's ubiquity render His acts otiose or irrelevant? Don't we have good explanations for events in the natures and volitions of finite beings? Or does divine governance require constant, or occasional interventions that obviate or vitiate the very idea of nature?

Aristotle had maintained the passivity of matter and the immanence of a divine, telic causality. Maimonides sustains the resulting overdetermination, unwilling to give up either the biblical idea of providence or the naturalism that underwrites the sciences and the arts, from craftsman to engineer, legislator, and physician. Maimonides proposes, Solomonically, that what we understand is biblically ascribed to God's wisdom; what we fail to understand, to His will. Somehow, beyond our ken, the two merge in God's ultimate unity. Spinoza carries the argument a step further. By identifying God with nature, he finds a source for the activity of all beings within themselves and leaves room for the interaffectedness of all beings of the same nature—the theme that would loom so large in Newton's world. The post-Aristotelian idea of inertia is a help: Things are active in their own right, by their own natures; and those natures are expressions of the divine. Spinoza can profit from the Maimonidean naturalization of the idea of angels as forms or forces without succumbing to the Neoplatonic model behind that idea, the notion of occult, nonnatural powers.

11. TRANSCENDENCE AND IMMANENCE

In a single poetic line Isaiah unites God's transcendent holiness (*kedushah*) with His immanent manifestation, biblically called glory (*kavod*). The epiphany that enshrines this synthesis is voiced in the words *Holy, holy, holy, Lord of hosts; the fill of all the earth is His glory* (Is. 6:3). Nature here is not set apart from God: The earth's fill is His glory.

We need to be cautious with the playfulness of words, especially when addressing issues of transcendence. Maimonides is often quoted (in English) as denying any relation between God and the world (See *Guide* I 52.4). He thus becomes a chief culprit in the radical disjunction of God from nature that Hegel took to be the identifying scar of Hebraic monotheism. But, *nisba*, the term Maimonides used here for relation, means ratio or proportion. The connotative overtones are those of genealogy—relation in the sense of kinship. *Nisba* does not have the broad abstract sense that current usage in English gives the term relation—a sense in which even the absence of a relation would be relation!

Maimonides enumerates spatial, temporal, correlative and causal classes of relational terms as inapplicable to God. Yet he specifically warrants the ascription of causal primacy to God. Indeed, he presumes it in ruling out correlative relations:

> That He is not the correlative of any of His creatures is obvious, for one of the distinguishing characteristics of correlatives is interdependence. But He exists necessarily, whereas all other things exist contingently. (*Guide* I 52.5)

So all things depend on God for their existence. Is the Rambam inconsistent here? On the contrary, he consistently affirms that God is the Creator. Indeed: "There is no way of inferring His existence, except from this world's reality taken as a whole and in detail" (*Guide* I 71, Munk 98a, *ll*. 13–14). Evidently God does bear a relationship to His creatures. He is not their correlative. Their failure to exist would not dim His reality. Temporality does not infect Eternity. Nor is there a proportion that would calibrate God's greatness against creaturely notions (*Guide* I 59, Munk 74b). Yet a causal relation is affirmed.[112] We do not, as Ken Seeskin reminds us, find the physical causality by which, say, a fire imparts its heat to an iron bar. But that is just what Spinoza meant by saying that God's causality is not transitive.

Maimonides is not content with classic emanationism. For no sheerly intellectual nexus could explain the exuberant diversity of nature—or leave room for contingent events. More probable and more plausible, he argues (*Guide* II 20–22), is a creativity that fuses what we conceive as the volitional and intellectual in God. We cannot grasp God's ultimate unity in itself—we cannot see God's face. But Scripture does image the nexus of an absolute and timeless God to His temporal, many faceted work, when it calls God the Rock of Ages,[113] standing beyond the summit of Jacob's ladder,[114] abiding at the flood.[115] Without abstract language, such images clearly propose that God is the world's ontic ground (See *Guide* I 52.4). The distinctive word *bara'*, assigned to God's creative act, conveys that act's uniqueness. Hence the absence of a naturalistic or intellectualist reduction: Creation is not the mere projection of an idea. Rather, it is the Torah's way of suggesting God's absolute transcendence while affirming God's comprehensive relevance to nature and human life.

Maimonides has no fully developed theory of the analogy of being, as deployed by Aquinas to codify and clarify the very points that the Rambam addresses. But Maimonides' appropriation of the Talmudic thesis that Torah speaks in accordance with human language does gesture in that direction.[116] With heightened assurance resulting in part from Maimonides' safeguarding of creativity against any compromise of divine transcendence, Aquinas echoes Maimonides when he insists that "God's effects have no proportion to him" (S.T., q. 2 a. 2, obj. 3) and when he accepts the license of prophetic revelation to use poetic language (S.T., q. 1 a. 9). Thomas confidently adopts the Rambam's solution to the classic problem of the disproportion of the Infinite Cause to its finite effect, arguing that even a finite effect can point beyond itself to the Infinite, although it cannot provide perfect knowledge of its creator (S.T., q. 2 a. 2, repl. obj. 3).[117]

Spinoza, of course, like the ancient Neoplatonists, spurns confinement of divine activity to a fixed temporal span. But, like Maimonides and the other medieval monotheists, he refuses to place matter beyond God's reach. He outdoes them by adopting Maimonides' idea that matter is an attribute of God but taking a realist view of this ascription. He thus boldly rejects the dualism that would sunder God from nature. His target here is Cartesian. Dualism was only a tension within Platonizing philosophies. But the Cartesian rejection of substantial forms desolated matter when it purged entelechies. Spinoza saw the implication clearly and grasped the nettle that Descartes had touched so gingerly. For Spinoza rejected even Boyle's chemical natures,[118] let alone Descartes' animal spirits, and all other mediating effluences and occult properties. A new way had to be found of integrating the cosmos. Spinoza's way was to make matter a real attribute of God—an approach long hinted by the Kabbalists, who had archly pointed to the numerical equivalence of the words *elohim*, the divine, and *ha-tevaʿ*, nature. Disdaining dualism, Spinoza celebrated what Descartes had called the union of mind and body:

> in proportion as a body is more capable than others of doing many things at once, or being acted upon in many ways at once, so is its mind more capable than others of conceiving many things at once. (EIIP13S)

Despite his bold departures from spiritualist, antiphysicalist interpretations of creation—in a way because of them—Spinoza's idea of the active power of God, *natura naturans*, retains much of the thrust of the idea of creation. It accommodates the comprehensiveness and absoluteness of biblical creation more fully than dualist accounts, which seem always to risk letting matter slip between the cracks. And the core intellectualist value in emanationism, now largely purged of the abhorrence of matter, is again given its due, in the attribute of thought and in the infinite modes: Far more programmatically than in Neoplatonism, natural relations become relations of logic, fleshing out the Neoplatonic notions of entailment and binding nature together by rational links, each with its own logic and dynamic. We might follow these as clearly as geometry, if we but knew the manifold ways in which God's essence is expressed. For, as Mason shows, Spinoza's supposed logicism is, in fact, an appeal to the underlying natures of things, not an effort to reduce natural to formal laws empty of content.

Maimonides himself never wholly rejected emanation. Indeed, he was not as skeptical of the Neoplatonic ontology as Halevi was. He made a point of affirming a tripartite world, in which angels, now construed as forms and forces, play a crucial mediating role.[119] Suitably qualified by the voluntarism that anchors his creationism, the idea of emanation allows Maimonides to achieve at least three objectives: (1) It affords a vision of the divine perfection that is the object of all the Torah's anthropomorphic imagery; (2) It projects the causal relation between God and nature in intellectual terms; (3) It picks out the human mind as the seat of the affinity between God and creation and the locus of God's special providence. For the objective correlative of Maimonides' negative theology is God's Perfection, to which we are oriented by what is intellectual in ourselves.

By naming finite perfections while excluding the privations that such names inevitably connote, the anthropomorphisms of the Torah, as Maimonides explains, systematically undermine one another and point beyond their notional referents toward the idea of God's absolute perfection (*Guide* I 47; cf. I 10). It was Neoplatonic metaphysics that taught us to understand such perfection not in wholly abstract or negative terms but concretely, in terms of intelligence—even though the purest perfection lies beyond intelligence, and so wholly beyond the determining and delimiting categories of the understanding. It is because we can conceive perfection as intelligence that the first terms Maimonides glosses in his survey of biblical anthropomorphisms are *tzelem u-demut*, image and likeness. For, as Narboni explains, Maimonides takes these to refer to human intelligence, the point of closest proximity between humanity and the divine.[120]

Spinoza dealt with matter as the tradition dealt with mind, taking it into the bosom of God. Maimonides had subjectivized both of God's chief attributes, will and wisdom, treating matter and form as God's manifestations in nature—humanly accessible (but not properly predicable) divine attributes. Spinoza, in his ardent realism and confident rationalism, made both thought and extension constitutive in God's essence. Is this an affront to transcendence? Or has Spinoza bit the bullet that earlier thinkers tried for centuries to catch in their teeth? In the light of Isaiah's epiphany, we can say that the opposition of transcendence and immanence was not the biblical idea. The chief maxim of Judaic piety, inscribed over the *bimah* of many a synagogue, is the Psalmist's admonition (16:8) to regard God in all His ineffable absoluteness as constantly before us. Anger dishonors that presence (Nedarim 22b), charity makes it manifest (Bava Batra 10a, on Ps. 17:5); so does work (Avot de R. Nathan ch. 11), or attentive dialogue on biblical themes (Shabbat 63a). God's universal presence is with children, even when things seem at their darkest (Lamentations R. 1.6.33). It is with the righteous, wherever they may be (Genesis R. 86.6). But it is alienated in the arrogant and those who ignore one another's views (Sota 5a, Berakhot 43b, Shabbat 63b). It is drawn out by honest judging and driven away, as it were, by judicial dishonesty (Sanhedrin 7a). It is manifest in a good marriage, eclipsed in a hostile one (Sota 17a).

Such homilies articulate the idea of immanence not in an ontology but in an ethos. Yet that immanence cannot be gainsaid. The God who walked in the midst of the camp of Israel (Dt. 23:15) was the same of whom the Psalmist said, "In Thy presence is the fullness of joy" (Ps. 16:11), and of whom R. Gamaliel said "There is no place on earth devoid of God's presence" (Pesikta de R. Kahana, ed. Buber, 2b; cf. Bava Batra 25a; Kidd. 31a), the same whose immanent presence is said to have accompanied Israel into exile (Mekhilta to Ex. 12.41; Numbers R. 7.10) and whose more exultant presence the Rabbis hope will one day "fill the earth from end to end" (Esther R. 1.4). The remoteness of the God of Israel is a Hegelian brickbat, a relic of ancient anti-Jewish polemics in behalf of Christian incarnationism. Emanation in Maimonides, at a minimum, makes the infinitely transcendent God of Scripture at least as immanent as He is transcendent. As Maimonides writes, professing awe at God's providence and acknowledging our incapacity to grasp its workings:

> God's separateness from the world and transcendence of it are soundly demonstrated. But there is sound proof as well of the impact of His governance and providence in every part of the world, regardless how tiny or lowly. (*Guide* I 72, Munk 104a, *ll.* 14–16)

12. FINITUDE OR INFINITUDE IN NATURE'S SCOPE OR DURATION

Spinoza's friend Johann Bouwmeester (1630–1680) translated into Dutch Ibn Tufayl's *Ḥayy Ibn Yaqẓān*, the medieval tale of a self-taught philosopher who, without the aid or interference of society, culture, language or tradition, discovers the most profound truths about God, nature and human destiny. Ḥayy Ibn Yaqẓān reaches the summit of his reasoning powers when he proves to himself that the world must be finite in size:

> He knew that the heavens and all the stars in the skies were bodies because without exception they were extended in three dimensions. . . . He wondered whether they extended infinitely in all directions or were finite, bounded at some point beyond which no extension was possible. The problem perplexed him more than a little, but ultimately his inborn talent and brilliance led him to realize that an infinite body is a pseudo-entity which can neither be nor be conceived. This conclusion was bolstered in his mind by a number of arguments that he reached quite independently in the course of his reflection.
>
> "This heavenly body," he said to himself, "is bounded on the near side, without doubt, since I can see it with my own eyes. Only the far side admits of doubt. Nonetheless I know it is impossible for it to extend forever. For if I imagine two lines beginning on this finite side, passing up through the body to infinity, as far as the body itself supposedly extends, and imagine a large segment cut from the finite end of one and the two placed side by side with the cut end of one opposite the uncut end of the other, and my mind travels along the two lines toward the so called infinite end, then I must discover either that the pair of lines really do extend to infinity, the one no shorter than the other, in which case the cut line equals the intact one, which is absurd—or else that the one does not run the full length of the other, but stops short of the full course, in which case it is finite. But if the finite segment that was subtracted is restored, the whole is finite. Now it is neither shorter nor longer than the uncut line. They must be equal then. But one is finite, so the other must be finite as well—and so must the body in which these lines were assumed to be drawn. Such lines can be assumed in any physical thing. Thus to postulate an infinitely extended physical body is fallacious and absurd."[121]

The argument was in fact an old chestnut.[122] But Ibn Tufayl caps his summary by praising "the exceptional mind which had made him aware of such a remarkable argument." The point is less to claim originality for the fictive hero than to mark a high water point of rational inquiry. For Ḥayy's visionary experience, as the story unfolds, will outstrip discursive reason. The key to the argument is the idea that finite parts cannot add up to an infinite whole.[123] Similarly, in the Kantian antinomies:

the magnitude of a quantum which is not given in intuition as within certain limits, can be thought only through the synthesis of its parts, and the totality of such a quantum only through a synthesis that is brought to completion through repeated addition of unit to unit. (*Critique of Pure Reason*, A430/B458, trans. N. Kemp Smith, 399–400)

Applying that reasoning to events, Kant's putative creationist argues:

The infinity of a series consists in the fact that it can never be completed through successive synthesis. It thus follows that it is impossible for an infinite world series to have passed away, and that a beginning of the world is therefore a necessary condition of the world's existence. (loc. cit.)

Ibn Tufayl breaks the deadlock between creation and eternity, arguing that in the end the issue, undecidable by reason, does not matter for philosophy. Creation, he suggests, is a metaphor for emanation. But, on either account (pace Ghazali), world's dependence on God is clear. Ibn Tufayl also suggests, anticipating Kant, that the impasse itself arises only out of the hubris of reason.[124] But the underlying assumption that finite quanta cannot add up to infinity is left unquestioned—as is the finitude of the cosmos.

Spinoza is convinced both of the eternal duration and of the infinite vastness of the cosmos. Again he follows the Averroists and their Greek predecessors, who held that the world must mirror the eternity of its divine source. Rejecting the notion that an infinite magnitude is a contradiction in terms, he follows Ḥasdai Crescas[125] in recognizing one of Aristotle's little self-indulgences, a question begging definition—like Aristotle's insistence on speaking of 'place' rather than 'space', so as to presume rather than prove the relativity of space. 'Magnitude' can mean a definite shape and size. But there is a more generic sense, and manipulative definitions do little to quench the intuitive appeal of the idea of infinity—whether because space itself would seem to have no boundary or because reality, in Spinoza's terms, would have no reason to corral itself in finitude.

Countering Aristotelian authority, Spinoza calls upon his holism and monism, to insist that the cosmos is not in fact composed of parts—not as conventionally conceived. As he explains to Oldenburg, there is a legitimate sense to the idea of parts: "I consider things as parts of some whole or other to the extent that their nature accommodates itself one to another so that as far as possible they agree among themselves."[126] But isolable parts are not found in nature. The aim is not to score some new verbal victory but to preserve the idea of interdependence and overcome the specious notion of mutual exclusion that Spinoza finds at the root of the familiar paradoxes about (additive) infinity. Once again Spinoza has reconceived the offending concept—not infinity, but the idea of parts. The problem arises from thinking of parts as if they were wholes:

> imagine, if you will, a small worm living in the blood, whose sight is keen enough to distinguish the particles of blood, lymph, etc., with reason to observe how each particle, on collision with another either rebounds or communicates some part of its own motion. That worm would live in this blood as we live in this part of the universe, and would consider each particle of blood not as a part at all but as a whole. He could not know how all the parts of the blood are governed by the universal nature of blood and driven to adapt to one another as the universal nature of blood requires, so that they harmonize with one another in a definite pattern. . . .
>
> All the bodies of nature can and should be conceived in the same way as we have conceived the blood. For all are surrounded by other bodies, and all are determined by one another to exist and act in a certain determinate way. . . . Whence it follows that every body, insofar as it exists modified in a certain way must be considered as a part of the universe at large, as an integrated part of the whole, not to be isolated from the rest (*cum suo toto convenire, & cum reliquis cohaerere*).[127]

The point is not that parts do not exist in any sense but that parts cannot be isolated without falsifying their nature and that of the whole. The idea is as old as Aristotle's thought that a hand is not a hand once severed from a living body,[128] as new as David Bohm's "implicate order," which Errol Harris compares to Spinoza's account:

> The whole physical universe is conceived as a single indivisible system in which every entity and process affects every other and all are coordinated and regulated by laws implicit in the structure of space time. David Bohm characterizes this conception of the world as a "holomovement" (a dynamic totality) in which an implicate order is enfolded and is immanent at every point.[129]

As Bohm writes, "whatever part, element, or aspect we may abstract in thought, this still enfolds the whole and is therefore intrinsically related to the totality from which it has been abstracted."[130] In Spinoza's terms this means that Aristotle's conception of a body part as an integrated, differentiable but un-isolable component of an organic whole must be generalized beyond Aristotle's favored biological cases. Its application is indeed universal. If parts, properly conceived, can be disengaged from their wholes only by an act of abstraction, then the very idea of parts challenges conventional ideas of quantity and undermines the classical arguments for the impossibility of an infinite magnitude.

Spinoza's conclusion seems welcome, even if his reasoning may seem problematic. Integrated parts may yet conjoin additively, and the paradoxes of infinity may lie in the difficulties we humans have in applying to the infinite categories more at home among finite things. Yet Spinoza's elenchus did overturn a rather complacent effort to show, by partitioning the infinite into finite quanta, that the cosmos must be finite. In keeping with his monism, Spinoza faults the partitioning rather than the idea of the infinite. He sides with Crescas. But, at a higher level, he chimes with Plotinus, Maimonides, and Cantor, who saw theological relevance in the idea of infinity. The idea that parts do not simply exclude one another is vital in the Hegelian outlook that inspires Errol Harris, but also in the conception of time that Bergson used to unsnarl the confusions behind the Laplacean determinism that is still widely believed to bar the way to human freedom and creativity.[131]

13. TELEOLOGY AND MECHANISM

Breaking away from his geometrical format, Spinoza inveighs against teleology in a passionate outburst in an appendix to Part I of the *Ethics*. His target, not as broad as his vehemence suggests, is the idea of a God who acts to achieve an end. Such anthropomorphism had, in fact, been excluded by Maimonides' arguments that God, being perfect, has no needs—none of the biologically rooted passions, indeed no emotions (*Guide* III 13, cf. I 46, 51–53). The Rambam had held out for some sort of divine willing, ultimately, as we have seen, to be fused with God's wisdom, at a level beyond human understanding. Divine volition was called for, on Ghazālī's grounds, to specify the particularities of creation. But if God has no needs, theistic voluntarism seems like fudging. So Spinoza is impatient to make clear, as soon as he has "explained God's nature and properties," that the one great prejudice impeding a grasp of his demonstrations and recognition of their force is the common supposition,

> that all natural things act, as men do, for the sake of an end, and that God Himself directs all things toward a definite end—as they avow to be certain. For they say that God made all things for man's sake, and man to worship God.[132]

The view was not universal among Spinoza's predecessors. Maimonides scouts it:

> Often perfect minds grow perplexed inquiring after the object of existence. Here and now I shall expose the irrelevance of this question from any point of view. (*Guide* III 13)

One of these "perfect minds" was Saadiah, who argued that the most prized of beings would naturally be found most centrally: "When we make our investigation using this criterion, we find that the goal is man" (*ED*, IV, Exordium). Small wonder that Spinoza, at the dawn of the age of Copernicus, would shun such anthropocentrism. Saadiah had written:

> When we see . . . the earth in the center of the heavens [like the yolk in the center of the egg, or the kernel in the midst of all the leaves, and the heart in the center of the body, Saadiah argues] and then find the earth in the center of the heavens, surrounded by the concentric spheres, we can soundly infer that whatever was the intended object of all this construction must be something on earth. Examining all the components of the earth, we find that earth and water are dead and animals not rational. Only man remains, and we see with certainty that he, without a doubt, must be the intended goal. (*ED* IV, Exordium)

Spinoza registers even Saadiah's persuasive language when he ascribes an air of certitude to anthropocentrists. Saadiah does argue that all things were made for man; and man, to be judged. Creation allows God's justice to act, to sanction obedience and disobedience and afford abounding opportunities for supererogation, in acts of gratitude and worship. The highest rewards are held for those who sustain their integrity and devotion, even against doubt and in the anguish of unmerited suffering.[133]

Maimonides rejects this view, despite its rabbinic roots. He condemns as unbiblical and untrue the doctrine of "the sufferings of love." For God to cause unmerited sufferings only to enhance the rewards of chosen saints is unjust and ungodly; and it is arrogant to suppose that objects as elevated as the heavenly bodies exist for man's sake. Maimonides makes good his pledge to show the impertinence of an anthropocentric teleology "from any point of view" by arguing his case on both creationist and eternalist assumptions: The eternalist, denying creation, leaves no place for an overarching telos of existence and is inconsistent in seeking one. As for the creationist, scripture may seem to give color to the notion of an ultimate purpose for nature as a whole, but the idea does not hold up:

> If this view is examined critically, as intelligent men ought to examine views, the fallacy is exposed. For the exponent of this belief has only to be asked, "This end, the existence of man—could God bring this about without all these preliminaries, or could man not be brought into being until these things were done?" If he replies that it is possible, that God could give being to man without, say, creating the heavens, he must be asked, "'What is the utility to

man of all these things which were not themselves the object but which existed "for the sake of" something that could have existed without any of them?'" Even if the universe does exist for man, and man's end, as has been said, is to serve God, the question remains: What is the object of man's serving God? For His perfection would not be augmented by the worship of all the things that He created, not even if they all apprehended Him as He truly is. Nor would He lack anything if nothing but Him existed at all. . . .

Given the belief in creation and its inevitable corollary, the possibility that causality might have been other than as it is, the absurd consequence would follow that everything that exists apart from man has no end whatever. For the sole end which all these things were purposed to serve was man, and he might have existed just as well without any of them!

For this reason, the correct view, in my judgment, in keeping with religious belief and in consonance with the theories of reason, is that all beings should not be believed to exist for the sake of man's existence. Rather all other beings too were meant to exist for their own sakes, not for the sake of something else. (*Guide* III 13)

Saadiah himself intimates such a view when he considers God's speech to Job from the stormwind. For the wild ox does not serve man or feed at his manger; rain falls on the sea, not just on plowed fields[134]—and, as the Talmud notes, it falls on the wicked and the righteous alike (Taʿanit 7a; cf. Matthew 5:45). But Maimonides' arguments, addressing both *Kalām* creationists and Aristotelian eternalists, are more systematic than Saadiah's, and his rejection of an anthropocentric teleology, in the interest of naturalism and of God's transcendence of human wishes, more forthright and consistent.

Spinoza, like Maimonides, debunks anthropomorphic and anthropocentric notions of divine intention. But he does not reject teleology per se. Thus Ravven notes the "growing consensus among scholars that Spinoza's rejection of teleology was not total but represents a higher, i.e., more sophisticated reconstruction of it."[135] Spinoza does complain that final causes reverse the causal order: "This doctrine of an end turns nature completely upside down. For it regards what is in reality the cause as the effect and vice versa" (EI, App.; G II 80/10–11). But Spinoza's alternative is not a neutral universe of mechanical causation but a universe in which purpose is made immanent, in the form of the conatus. When Spinoza substitutes appetite for an externally imposed purpose (EIVD7) and defines volition in terms of conatus (EIIIP9S), the effect is to substitute a push for a pull. Traditional final causes would seem to be counterparts of action at a distance, as if pulling at subjects from the future instead of motivating them from the present. But the conatus is goal directed. It is simply not directed toward (or by) a single, externally assigned end that beckons from a telic never-never land. Rather it pursues goals that are, in varied degrees, self-constructed, even, in some measure, self-defined.

Telic causality, then, is localized, just as efficient causality is. Indeed, as a result, the two can be equated,[136] thus achieving within nature the goal that Maimonides had sought beyond nature, of unifying the rational and purposive with the material and recalcitrant. The outcome is probably more faithful than many an account to Aristotle's original idea of final causation. For that too was immanent, and judged not just by aims but by results.[137] When the conatus, at its simplest, is assimilated to Descartes' inertia, Spinoza's story even respects the ancient affinity of final causes to the matter of their embodiment, once evident in the natural tendencies of Aristotle's elements. Here Spinoza cannot, in fairness, be said to have avoided occult principles, any more than Aristotle did.[138] But the principles now are those of value-setting natures, the groping, perfection-seeking strivings of matter toward what Teilhard called complexification.[139] Despite all mechanistic and reductive protestations, such strivings are presupposed in any account of biological adaptation or cosmic evolution. For mechanists say that the stable is simply what survives. But even in saying so they touch what nature has projected as a value—or two values—the more instrumental value of stability, and the more intrinsic value of survival.

The key to Spinoza's shift from anthropocentric teleology to local purposiveness is his recognition that "the perfection of things must be judged solely in terms of their own nature and capability."[140] But the shift was already underway in Maimonides and hinted even by Saadiah. It means moving from Stoic humanism to Neoplatonic naturalism, and again valorizing the idea of creation, here by recognizing the local worth of finite individuals and the effectual power of their agency—the very values that Spinoza is sometimes accused of slighting. As Spinoza writes to Blijenbergh:

> When you say that I make men so dependent on God that I reduce them to elements, plants, or stones, it shows that you understand my opinion very perversely and confuse the realm of intellect with that of imagination. For if you grasped purely intellectually what it is to depend on God, you would surely not think that things, insofar as they depend on God, are dead, bodily, and imperfect. Who has ever dared to speak so vilely of the supremely perfect Being? (Ep. 21; G IV 131)

Spinoza's shift to local powers and values, themselves expressive (in their measure) of a more universal, divine power and value, means a departure from an enchanted nature and a projective, even theurgical notion of God. But that shift begins in the Torah itself.

CONCLUSION

In the *Tractatus Theologico-Politicus*, Spinoza sums up what he takes to be the universal teachings of Scripture. His aim is religious. That is, it pertains to the human institution, not to the intellectual content of faith but to what we need to know in order to live with one another. Since Spinoza holds that the idea of God is open to all, he is not concerned here with the particularities of one religious tradition. In keeping with a Maimonidean suggestion (*Guide* I 46, 50, 59) he can let each inquirer find his own level of clarity and adequacy.[141] He outlines the relevant themes broadly, under seven heads:

1. God exists, is just and merciful and the exemplar of the true life.
2. God is one and unique, preeminent above all.
3. God is omnipresent, all things thus being patent to Him.
4. God is the supreme ruler, free and sovereign to rule by grace with absolute right.
5. Proper worship and obedience of God consist solely in justice and charity.
6. A life of justice and charity is the sole and sufficient path to salvation; the life of the sybarite is a life of perdition.
7. Penitence is open to sinners, among whom all humanity must be counted.[142]

Penitence is not a major theme of the *Ethics*, but the seventh point does reflect Spinoza's powerful rejection of moralism and recriminations. The aim is to derive positive and, may we say, empowering value from the sense of guilt—rather than allowing it to paralyze us.

Spinoza's summary of the core teachings of Scripture is colored by the thematic focus of the *Tractatus* on tolerance and pluralism. The core teachings are emphatically departicularized: Grace is not the sacrifice of God's son to redeem a corrupted nature; nor is favor to be wooed by ritual scrupulosity. Yet faith is of the essence, along with works, since (1) "He who does not know or believe that God exists cannot obey Him or know Him as a judge," (2) proper reverence and devotion are shown only by one who recognizes God's preeminence, (3–4) without acknowledgment of God's omnipresence one might doubt God's justice or authority, (5–6) belief that the life of justice and charity is God's will and the path to salvation is the only way of ensuring that men follow that path and not their own desires, and

(7) without trust in the possibility of penitence, men, being sinners, would despair.

The teachings are scriptural, with both testaments honed to a universalist die. Ritual is stripped away and the Christian eschaton internalized, to remove all trace of particularity:

> He who firmly believes that God forgives men's sins from the mercy and grace whereby He directs all things, and whose heart is thereby the more inspired by love of God, that man truly knows Christ according to the spirit; Christ is in him.[143]

Addressing the question of God's love, and how the Infinite can single out any person or group for special regard, Spinoza turns not to Christian theology but to his Judaic roots. Like Maimonides, he opens the door to special providence by seeing that there are no real universals. Like Saadiah, he relies on God's immanence to explain the reach of providence. The two approaches fuse when Spinoza writes, as the *Ethics* is drawing to a close:

> The mind's intellectual love of God is God's very love for Himself, not insofar as He is infinite, but insofar as He can be explained by the human mind's essence, considered under the aspect of eternity. That is, the mind's intellectual love of God is part of the infinite love by which God loves Himself. (EVP36)

Spinoza takes issue not with the particularity of providence but with crude notions of its arbitrariness and remoteness. By recognizing God's own love in the intellectual love that we feel when we long for God, we take God as our "exemplar"—without a surrogate or mediating figure. Descartes' idea of perfection, the cognitive boot-hold that allowed him to vault from the idea to the reality of God, here becomes an active principle at work in the mind, enabling us to fulfill the focal commandment: "You shall be holy, for I the Lord thy God am holy" (Lev. 19:2). As Maimonides explained, this means perfecting what is perfectible in ourselves, cementing the intellectual affinity that binds us to God.[144]

It was Maimonides who located God's providence over individuals in human intelligence, with its God-given affinity for the Divine (*Guide* III 17; I 1) and who reminded philosophers who saw providence in species alone, of Aristotle's conclusion: "that external to the mind no such entity as a species exists" (*Guide* III 18). It was Saadiah who argued, on Rabbinic authority, that Hebrew expressions like 'The Lord shall rejoice in the work of His hands' (Ps. 104:31; cf. Ps. 32:11, 64:11, 97:12) must mean that God rejoices *through* His creatures—lest we have rank anthropomorphism. As I remarked regarding such glosses:

The yearning nominally ascribed to God is transferred to Job.
. . . Rejection of anthropopathy requires not only the syntactical
boldness of transferring to humanity emotions seemingly ascribed
by Scripture to God, but also the theologically bold expedient of
finding the meanings of such ascriptions of emotion to God in
their ascription to humanity. God rejoices through the righteous,
and they are said to rejoice in God. The theme is taken up in Spinoza's doctrine that man's love of God and of his fellows is the
intellectual love by which God infinitely loves Himself. Here Saadiah's project of transposing the sense of 'love of God' from a subjective to an objective genitive is completed through the devising of
a metaphysical context in which the two senses (as in the ancient
concept of blessing) fuse and inform one another. (See Spinoza,
Ethica VP20; G II 292/15–22, 32; G II 300/22–27, 301/3, 35; G II
302/4, 36.)[145]

When Spinoza addressed immanence and transcendence, he knew that resolution of the seeming tension between them had been a project of Judaic
thought from its inception—portended in the images of Jacob's ladder and
of his wrestling with an angel. The terms that might afford a point of departure were embedded in the daily prayers of his boyhood that say of Jacob,
and so of Israel at large: "it was out of Thine own love that Thou didst
love him and out of thine own joy that Thou didst give him joy."[146] Finding
in human love the vehicle by which God's love is expressed on earth, Spinoza takes up the ancient project and offers his metaphysic as a means to
its solution.

In Ficino we read:

If God fills the world with delight and the world is filled with
delight by Him, there is a certain continual attraction between God
and the world which begins in God and passes through the world
and finally ends in God, as a circle returns to where it began. So
there is one single circle that runs from God to the world and from
the world to God and is named in three ways: insofar as it begins in
God and has power of attraction, beauty; insofar as it is transferred
to the world and fills it with delight, love; insofar as it returns to
the Creator and unites his works, delight.[147]

As Dethier remarks, Leone Ebreo "takes over this formula almost completely" and raises the very problems that Spinoza will address: How can
there be love for the inferior by the superior (indeed, the Infinite); how can a
delight, a passion, be the goal of intellectual love; how can the world be
ruled by the [immanent, goal seeking] "reductive" love of creatures for sov-

ereign beauty and not by the productive love of God for the world?[148] Spinoza's answer rests on the recognition that the "reductive" and "productive" loves are one and the same and are not passions at all, insofar as perfection remains their goal.

Divine love, the biblical *ḥesed*—grace or favor—the generosity of Plato's God, and Philo's Stoicizing *eupatheia*,[149] are active and self-determining. Thus Philo conjoins benevolence with joy (*chara*) in his conception of God's love.[150] As Lee Rice's chapter points out, Spinoza sees *generositas*, not as a passive emotion but as an expression of adequate ideas (EIIIP46). And, of course, our intellectual love of God is active rather than passive. For it is one and the same with our adequate idea of God. That is why it can be identified with the very love by which God loves Himself—and loves Himself in us.

Spinoza's conception of adequate ideas, his monism, and his recognition of the commitment inherent in any adequate idea here join hands to yield the thesis long suggested by Jewish mystics and philosophers when they sought to understand the notion that God rejoices and delights *in* His creation. The theme is broached by ancient Semitic ideas of blessing and hinted in the midrashic conceit that God's *tefillin* bear the name of Israel. The idea was touched by philosophers like Saadiah and Leone Ebreo. But none could give it the philosophical consummation of rigorous argument. That task remained for Spinoza.

✳✳✳

Returning now to our general theme: We have seen how Spinoza overcomes some of the great difficulties of classical philosophy, using a method that is synthetic rather than strictly analytic. Sometimes he uncovers false dichotomies at the base of those conundrums. Sometimes he plumps for one side of a classic antinomy but then rehabilitates the other with more adequate ideas. In all this, his thought is informed by analytic brilliance and a lambent commitment to core ideas and values of the Mosaic outlook, as articulated and disciplined by an ongoing philosophical tradition, in which Spinoza stands as a radical but creative contributor. His radicalism made his thoughts alien to his Jewish teachers, to conventional thinkers of other confessions, and even to the rare few like Leibniz who were most able to profit from them. Spinoza was probably right in guessing that his philosophical achievement could not be appreciated fully until the *TTP* had done its liberative work. He clearly erred in thinking that minds would be opened up sufficiently at any date close to his own lifetime. The trajectory marked by the philosophical work that Spinoza undertook and that the rather destructive groundclearing of the *TTP* was meant to support extends deep into the Judaic past, to the first monotheistic stirrings that we link with the name of Abraham. It extends into the future as well, on a course that future philosophers have yet to chart.

The doctrines in Spinoza's docket—combined and separated to generate a list of seven, as if to match seven ideas to the seven Noahidic commandments that the rabbinic tradition assigns to all humanity—are not just an abstract from scripture. They are also a rough agenda for the *Ethics*, which affords a philosophical interpretation for each. Spinoza does not press his own philosophical interpretations politically. Like Maimonides' 13 articles (which were also offered as a lowest common denominator, explaining how true beliefs give even ordinary Israelites a share in the understanding that opens up a portion in immortality), Spinoza's seven doctrines seek breadth without vacuity. But they are at once a social minimum and a philosophical road map to the high ground Spinoza seeks in the *Ethics*. They give access to what Spinoza thought was most universal in his philosophy and sum up what he thought most appropriable in the tradition he received. Obliquely, but undeniably, they reveal the extent of his loyalty to core elements of that tradition. Treasured up from the vastness of an ancient heritage, these elements do not dictate the contents of Spinoza's philosophy. On the contrary, his philosophy shows him what he can save, what he can deem universal and how he may interpret its key elements. But throughout that philosophy we have found Spinoza taking up the ideas and problems of his heritage and addressing them creatively, in ways that demonstrate at once how radical and how profoundly loyal he was in finding living meaning for what he took to be the tradition's central insights.

Some of Spinoza's appropriations are now of largely historical interest. His bold allegiance to eternalism has lost its éclat, as evidence of the finite age and historical uniqueness of the universe has gained credence in physics. Other ideas, notably his concepts of the mind as the idea of the body, or of truth as correspondence gleaned by way of coherence, and of thoughts as dynamic, committed, and reflexive acts—anything but pictures painted on a screen—remain to challenge philosophers and invite our further exploration.

NOTES

1. A. E. Taylor, "Some Incoherencies in Spinozism," *Mind* 46 (1937); and in *Studies in Spinoza*, ed. S. P. Kashap (Berkeley: University of California Press, 1974), 189–211, 289–309; cf. note 78 below. And see E. Curley, in *Spinoza: A Collection of Critical Essays*, ed. M. Grene (Garden City, N.Y.: Doubleday, 1973), p. 48 ad fin.

2. Cf. Lodewijk Meyer, Preface to Spinoza's *Descartes' PP* G I 29.

3. Spinoza rebukes philosophers who are lost in words (*CM*, Gebhardt 1.234–35).

4. *Emendatio* is purification and reform; thus Cicero: "*tota civitas emendari et corrigi solet continentia principium,*" *Leg.* 3.13; see Lewis and Short, *Latin Dictionary,* s.v.

5. No friend of hyperbolic doubt, Maimonides infers from our cognitive limitations a need to suspend not belief but skepticism: "do not ever categorically deny a proposition that has not been disproved" (*Guide* I 32). For order in philosophy, cf. below note 66.

6. Fabritius (1632–1697), Professor of Philosophy and Theology at Heidelberg, Councillor to Charles Louis, the Elector Palatine, and tutor to that prince's son, tactfully couched the pertinent conditions (and concerns) when he wrote, in the name of his "most gracious master," to offer Spinoza a chair in ordinary, in philosophy, at "his illustrious university": "You will have the broadest freedom to philosophize, which the Prince believes you will not misuse to trouble the publicly established religion." Well along in writing the *Ethics,* Spinoza, equally tactfully, declined: "It was never my intention to give public instruction." "If I want to find time for instructing the youth, then I must desist from developing my philosophy. I think, moreover, that I don't know within what limits the philosophizing you speak of ought to be held in order to avoid any appearance of disturbing the established religion" (Eps. 47, 48, 1673). Spinoza had not declined the blandishments of his coreligionists, and even dodged a dagger, only to succumb to the douceurs that came once the *TTP* had made him an anonymous celebrity. In the event, his choice was fortunate even by worldly standards. By 1674 Heidelberg was in French hands, the university closed, Fabritius a fugitive.

7. Even fundamentalists today invoke a wilful rather than a passive literalism.

8. See note 142 below.

9. Harry A. Wolfson, *The Philosophy of Spinoza: Unfolding the Latent Processes of His Reasoning,* 2 vols. (Cambridge: Harvard University Press, 1934).

10. Wolfson's colorful image arose in a mini-polemic: "In discussing once with a group of friends the importance of philology and of bookish learning in general for the study of the history of philosophy, I happened to remark that philosophers, after all, see the universe which they try to explain as already interpreted to them in books, with the only possible exception, perhaps, of the first recorded philosopher, and all he could see was water. 'How about Spinoza?' challenged one of the listeners. 'Was he also a bookish philosopher?' Without stopping to think, I took up the challenge, 'As for Spinoza,' I said, 'if we could cut up all the philosophic literature available to him into slips of paper, toss them up into the air, and let them fall back to

the ground, then out of these scattered slips of paper we could reconstruct his *Ethics*'" (Spinoza, vol. 1, p. 3). But as Lee Rice notes, "Transplanting a phrase or concept from one system into another does not guarantee, and often simply voids, sameness of systematic meaning" (101). Spinoza did read authors who spoke of *amor intellectualis Dei*. But, like any expression, this one acquires a distinctive meaning in its context, here, that of Spinoza's stringent conceptual demands.

11. See Idit Dobbs-Weinstein, "Maimonidean Aspects in Spinoza's Thought," *Graduate Faculty Philosophy Journal* 17 (1994): 153.

12. L. E. Goodman, *On Justice* (New Haven: Yale University Press, 1991), 198.

13. *TTP* iii, G III 57; cf. Maimonides' thesis that prophecy will be restored when Israel, returning to her land, regains the self-confidence that frees the imagination.

14. See my *God of Abraham* (New York: Oxford University Press, 1996) chaps. 1, 6, 7.

15. The Torah sanctifies life and identifies life with blood (Lev. 17:11, 14, Dt. 12:23); it bans consumption of the blood (Lev. 7:26, 17:10, 12–13, Dt. 12:16), but also demystifies it: Blood is simply to be poured out on the ground like water (Dt. 12:16, 24; 15:23).

16. Aristotle, *Cat.* 5, 3b 32–4a 1: "one man cannot be more man than another, as what is white may be more or less white than some other object, or what is beautiful may be more or less beautiful than some other beautiful object." Aristotle will speak of primary substance as more truly substance than secondary substance; and of species, more truly such than genera. But his argument that "substance does not seem to admit of variation in degree" (*Cat.* 3b) reflects both the crispness of his essentialism and his insistence on analyzing existence in terms of essence: To find that species membership does not vary in degree is to discover why particulars are privileged as substances: For here we have things that either are or are not what they are said to be, without cavil or equivocation. Plato, of course, would disagree—as would any post-Darwinian.

17. *Maqom* means 'place'; etymologically, 'standing place'—hence, ground in the ontic sense.

18. For Diodorus's Megarian agenda, see L. E. Goodman, "The Diodorean Modalities and the Master Argument," in *From Puzzles to Principles: Essays on Aristotle's Dialectic*, ed. Mui Sim (Lanham, Md.: Lexington, 1999), 15–37.

19. Al-Ghazali, *Iḥyā'ʿUlūm al-Dīn* (Revival of Religious Studies) XXXV; cf. al-Makki, *Qūt al-Qulūb* (Sustenance for the Heart) II on *al-tawakkul*, trust (Cairo, 1310 A. H.) 2.4, citing Ps. 118:8, Matt. 6:27; cf. al-Hujwiri, *Kashf al-Maḥjūb*, trans. R. A. Nicholson (London: Luzac, 1967;

1911). Ḥujwiri and Makki rely on the early Sufi al-Junayd and on pietist readings of the Hebrew, Christian, and Muslim scriptures.

20. See Bahya, K. *al-Hidāya ʾilā Farāʾiḍ al-Qulūb* (= *Ḥovot ha-Levavot, The Book of Direction to Duties of the Heart)* IV, ed. A. S. Yahuda (Leiden: Brill, 1912), trans. M. Mansoor (London: Routledge, 1973).

21. See Shlomo Pines, "Spinoza's *Tractatus Theologico-Politicus* and the Jewish Philosophical Tradition," in J*ewish Thought in the Seventeenth Century,* ed. I. Twersky and B. Septimus (Cambridge: Harvard University Press, 1987), 499–521.

22. See, e.g., *TTP,* Chap. iv, G III 64.

23. See, for example, *TTP,* chap. xviii.

24. Spinoza does complicate matters by shifting to "Christ"the purely intellectual revelatory insight that Maimonides had found in Moses. Conciliating his Christian friends and confusing our own contemporaries, Spinoza cannily removes the idea of rational revelation from any mere historical person, assigning it not to the historical Jesus but to the hypostatic Logos, in which all human wisdom is seen to share.

25. Richard Mason, The God of Spinoza (Cambridge: Cambridge University press, 1997), 27; cf. 38.

26. The idea of mystical ineffability must in part reflect how hard it is to relate unitive experience to phenomenal multiplicity and change. Any intuition is ineffable; but moral tact, or tactical reserve, may also arise with experiences whose readiest emblems and interpretations seem heterodox or unwelcome.

27. Ep. 75, to Oldenburg; in Ep. 73 pleas for miracles appeal to ignorance, "the source of all wickedness"; cf. EI App., G II 80–81/30–37; CM, 2.7, G I 261.

28. The idea of God's self-contraction, *tzimtzum,* has counterparts in myths of the *chaos* (or gap) that allowed mother earth some breathing room, when Kronos reached from her womb to castrate his father. As Scholem explains, Isaac Luria gave *tsimtsum* a liberative sense: "its literary original is a Talmudic saying which Luria inverted. He stood it on its head, no doubt believing that he had put it on its feet. The Midrash . . . refers to God as having concentrated His Shekhinah, His divine presence, in the holiest of holies. . . . to the Kabbalist of Luria's school *tsimtsum* does not mean the concentration of God *at* a point, but his retreat *away* from a point. G. Scholem, *Major Trends in Jewish Mysticism* (New York: Schocken, 1971; 1941), 260. See also S. Benin, *The Footprints of God: Divine Accommodation in Jewish and Christian Thought* (Albany: State University of New York Press, 1993).

29. E.g.: "Man mints many coins with one die, and all are alike. But the King of kings, the Holy One blessed be He, stamped every man with the seal of the first man, yet no two are alike" (Sanhedrin 4.5). The homiletic

aim is to charge witnesses with the gravity of capital cases and (as the midrash unfolds) the sanctity of each human life: "Therefore must everyone say: For my sake was the world created." The moral candor is matched by metaphysical silence: How does personhood arise? The hush is deafening.

30. For Spinoza's break with the Synagogue, see S. Nadler, *Spinoza: A Life* (Cambridge: Cambridge University Press, 1998), 116–54, and Popkin's essay in this volume.

31. See my "Matter and Form as Attributes of God in Maimonides' Philosophy," in *A Straight Path: Studies in Honor of Arthur Hyman* (Washington: Catholic University of America Press, 1987), 86–97.

32. See H. A. Wolfson, "Attributes," in *Religious Philosophy* (Cambridge: Harvard University Press, 1961), 49–68; cf. "Avicenna, Algazali, and Averroes on Divine Attributes," in Wolfson's *Studies in the History of Philosophy and Religion*, ed. I. Twersky and G. Williams (Cambridge: Harvard University press, 1973), 1:143–69.

33. Maimonides, *Guide* I 57–58; cf. Spinoza, Ep. 83; PP 11, G IV 335, I169.

34. Heidi Ravven, "Notes on Spinoza's Critique of Aristotle's Ethics: From Teleology to Process Theory," *Philosophy and Theology* 4 (1989): 18.

35. G. Santayana, "The Ethical Doctrine of Spinoza," *Harvard Monthly* (June, 1886): 147.

36. EID4. For Spinoza's realism about the attributes, see F. Haserot, "Spinoza's Definition of Attribute," *Philosophical Review* 62 (1953), repr. in Kashap, *Studies in Spinoza*, 28–42.

37. EIP14C. Zev Harvey shows how Spinoza's Hebrew Grammar found the landmarks of ontology in the elements of Hebrew syntax. But, as Spinoza saw it, we note, all the markers were misplaced: Only God is a substance, but in Hebrew 'man' is a paradigmatic substantive; matter and form are attributes, but Hebrew makes 'wise' and 'great' attributives; man is a mode, but Hebrew treats 'walking' and 'knowing' as participial, thus modal terms. The Holy tongue, then, enshrined category errors.

38. Aristotle, *De Part. An.* I 5, 644b 26–645a 25; *Metaph.* I 985a 18; Poet. 14, 1454b 1.

39. *Guide* I 63; cf. 61; see my *God of Abraham*, 58, 97.

40. Cf. A. Z. Bar-on, "The Ontological Proof—Spinoza's Version in Comparison with Those of St. Anselm and Descartes," in *Spinoza: His Thought and Work*, ed. N. Rotenstreich and N. Schneider (Jerusalem: Israel Academy of Sciences and Humanities, 1983), 108.

41. See Mason, *God of Spinoza*, 32–34; Wolfson, *Spinoza*, 1:133–34.

42. Saadiah Gaon, *The Book of Theodicy: Translation and Commentary on the Book of Job*, trans. with Commentary by L. E. Goodman (New Haven: Yale University Press, 1988), 371.

43. See Wolfson, *Spinoza*, 1:237. Cartesian matter rankled Leibniz; see my Maimonides and Leibniz," *Journal of Jewish Studies* 31 (1980): 215; M. Čapek, "Leibniz' Thought Prior to the Year 1670," *Revue Internationale de Philosophie* 20 (1966): 254.

44. Spinoza, EIIL7S; EIP33, EIII Pref, G II 75, 138.

45. Maimonides, *Guide* II 18; Ghazali, *Tahāfut al-Falāsifa* I, ed. Bouyges (Beirut: Catholic Press, 2nd ed. 1962), 50–53.

46. EIID3; Ep. 12, G IV 54/11; cf. my *Avicenna* (London: Routledge, 1992), 64.

47. Stuart Hampshire, "Eight Questions about Spinoza," in *Spinoza on Knowledge and the Human Mind*, ed. Y. Yovel (Leiden: Brill, 1994), 19.

48. Kant assigns freedom to "another causality," *Critique of Pure Reason* A444/B472.

49. See EIII Pref. Spinoza's disdain for remorse would clearly fire Nietzsche's admiration.

50. See *CM* 2.8, G I 265/18; and EIVP51S.

51. Ravven, "Notes," 24.

52. Arne Naess, *Freedon, Emotion and Self-Subsistence* (Oslo: Universitetsforlaget, 1975), 62.

53. *KV* I v, G I 40, equates *conatus* with providence; it is a drive to persist in being, but also to attain a better state (*l.* 9). In the *Ethics* "the force by which each thing perseveres in its existence is a consequence of the eternal necessity of God's nature" (EIIP45S, G II 127/21–22); this entails that "God is the cause not only of the initial existence of things but of their persevering in existence" (EIP24C).

54. See my *Jewish and Islamic Philosophy: Crosspollinations in the Classical Age* (Edinburgh: Edinburgh University Press and Rutgers University Press, 1999), 146–200.

55. Cf. Maimonides, "Eight Chapters," 5.

56. Cf. Maimonides, "Eight Chapters," 8.

57. Cf. Saadiah Gaon, *The Book of Critically Selected Beliefs and Convictions* (hereafter ED) IX 4, trans. S. Rosenblatt as *The Book of Beliefs and Opinions* (New Haven: Yale University Press, 1948), 334: "They have said that one hour of penitence in this world is more profitable than the whole of the world to come, since penitence is impossible there." Saadiah's text is *Avot* 4.17, which refers to penitence and good deeds.

58. Mason, *God of Spinoza* 67, and 63. Cf. *KV* chap. vi, 5 and chap. xvii, 5 for Spinoza's earlier view.

59. See Heidi Ravven's chapter, 210–212.

60. Thus Proclus, *Elements of Theology*, Prop. 72, Cor., ed. and trans. E. R. Dodds (Oxford: Oxford University Press, 2nd ed., 1963), 68–69, *ll.* 24–25.

61. See Moses Maimonides, *Dalālat al-Ḥāirīn, Le Guide des Égarés,* Arabic text edited with French translation by S. Munk (Paris, 1856–66; reprinted, Osnabrück: Otto Zeller, 1964) 3 volumes.

62. "Eight Chapters," 5, in my *Rambam: Readings in the Philosophy of Moses Maimonides* (New York: Viking, 1976; reissued, Los Angeles: Gee Tee Bee, 1983), 236–37.

63. Elisabeth of Bohemia, to Descartes, 16 May 1643, in John Blom, ed., *Descartes: His Moral Philosophy and Psychology* (New York: New York University Press, 1978), 106.

64. Spinoza, EV Pref, G II 279/17–19.

65. S. Hampshire, "Spinoza and the Idea of Freedom," Proceedings of the British Academy 46 (1960) 195; repr. in Grene, *Spinoza: A Collection of Critical Essays* 297.

66. Descartes to Elisabeth, Ep. 310, 28 June 1643, Anthony Kenny, ed., *Descartes: Philosophical Letters* (Minneapolis: University of Minnesota Press, 1970), 140–43.

67. It is Cartesians, not just scholastics, who "did not keep to the proper order in philosophy." For "the divine nature (which they should have contemplated before anything else, since it is prior both in nature and knowledge), they believed to be last in the order of knowledge. And the so-called objects of the senses they believed to be prior to anything else. So when they contemplated natural things they thought of nothing less than the divine nature; and when afterwards they directed their minds to contemplating the divine nature they were able to think of nothing less than those elementary fictions upon which they had built up their knowledge of natural things, which were, of course, of no help toward knowledge of the divine nature. No wonder they contradicted themselves throughout" (EIIP10C&S; cf. *KV* ii, 7 line 3 *TTP* iv, G III 67/27–29).

68. As Ravven writes, "Spinoza puts the subject into the picture. Knowledge is . . . the explanation of how the world affects me—not of how it is by subtracting me. But neither is it . . . of the me by subtracting the world," her letter of January 13, 2000.

69. To Elisabeth, 28 June 1643: "what belongs to the union of soul and body can be known only obscurely by pure intellect or by intellect aided by imagination; yet it is known very clearly by the senses." For, "the notion that everyone always has in himself without philosophizing" is that "he is one person with both body and thought so related by nature that the thought can move the body and feel things that happen to it," Kenny, *Philosophical Letters,* 141–42.

70. Aristotle, *De An.* III 7, 431a 1; cf. I 3; cf. Spinoza: "Some of the Hebrews seem to have seen this, as if through a cloud," EIIP7S, G II 90.

71. See *Midrash Tanhuma,* Va-Yiqra 11: "The body cannot exist without the soul; the soul cannot act without the body." Sanhedrin 91ab:

"Antonius said to Rabbi [Judah the Prince]: 'The body and the soul can both escape judgment. For the body can say: "It is the soul that sinned, for since the day it left me I have laid as still as a stone in the grave"; and the soul can say: "It was the body that sinned, for since the day I left it, I have flown in the air like a bird".'" The appeal anticipates Hume, and R. Judah pinions the specious dualism that underlies it: "To what can the case be compared? To that of a human king who had a lovely orchard full of fine young fruit. He posted two watchmen, one lame, the other blind." Fruit began to disappear, and the two pled their handicaps to prove their innocence, but the king said: "set the lame man on the blind man's shoulders and judge them as one." Cf. Lev. R. 4.5; *Midrash Tanhuma*, Va-Yiqra, 12; *Mekhilta*, Shirata, ed. Lauterbach, 2.21.

72. P. F. Strawson, *Individuals* (Garden City, N.Y.: Doubleday, 1963; London, 1959), xiii.

73. See Hidè Ishiguro, *Leibniz' Philosophy of Logic and Language* (Cambridge: Cambridge University Press, 1990).

74. See my *On Justice, God of Abraham, and Judaism, Human Rights and Human Values* (New York: Oxford University Press, 1998).

75. Bob Solomon once said that making love with an animal would be like talking Spinoza with a snail. Spinoza was the perfect emblem of his case.

76. TP v, 7: "If he had some good purpose, as we must believe of so wise a man . . ." Spinoza owned an octavo Machiavelli and a 1550 "Complete Works" in quarto.

77. *KV*, I v. Ravven calls the conatus an "Immanent divine essence" ("Notes," 20, citing EIIIP7; cf. 8, n. 20). Wolfson notes the Stoic roots (*Spinoza*, 2:195). Spinoza's teacher, Saul Levi Morteira, began a sermon: "Nature, the mother of all created beings, implanted in them a will or impulse to strive for self-preservation."

78. *Laetitia* is joy, not pleasure; *tristitia* is sorrow, not pain. For *dolor* and *titillatio*, Spinoza's pleasure and pain, are localized, as *laetitia* and *tristitia* are not.

79. H. G. Hubbeling writes, in *Spinoza's Methodology* (Assen: Van Gorcum, 1967), 120: "Spinoza fluctuates between two conceptions of right: right as power and right which is in accordance with reason. . . . he has the mediate position between Hobbes and Locke. The conflict that might arise from this double conception is solved by the idea that reason dictates what is in the long run more useful and gives more right. So the two conceptions are united." But if the seeming conflict is resolved, why appeal to "fluctuation"? And if the conflict is real, how is the issue resolved? Is the subordination of might to reason vitiated by the stipulation that reason yields greater power in the end?

80. See Maimonides, "Eight Chapters," 4; my *God of Abraham*, 156–60.

81. Spinoza's affirmation that self-preservation is never for the sake of another (E IV P25) anchors one end of this bridge, for there is no derivation of generosity from self-interest if self-interest is already defined in terms of generosity.

82. Cf. Maimonides, "Eight Chapters," 4. Spinoza owned Petrarch's *de Vita Solitaria.* For further parallels with Ibn Bajja, see R. Arnaldez, "Spinoza et la Pensée Arabe," *Revue de Synthèse* 89–91 (1978): 151–72; Goodman, *Jewish and Islamic,* 22–23, 109–111.

83. *TP* v, 7, G III 296–297; trans. A. G. Wernham (Oxford: Oxford University Press, 1958), 312–13.

84. As Wernham remarks, "This interpretation was adopted by Rousseau in *Social Contract* iii, 6. Some slight justification for it may perhaps be found in *Prince* xxiv; but when applied to the whole work it is quite indefensible."

85. *TP* ii, 12, G III 280; see my *On Justice,* 14–17.

86. 1 Sam. 8:11–18, Jewish Publication Society translation, in The Prophets (Philadelphia: JPS 1978).

87. Maimonides, *Sefer ha-Mitzvot,* positive commandments, no. 173.

88. See my *On Justice,* chap. 5.

89. For more on human rights in Judaism, see my *Judaism, Human Rights and Human Values;* for Spinoza's republican friendships, see Nadler, *Spinoza: A Life.*

90. Cf. *On Justice,* esp. chap. 4; *God of Abraham,* 11–12, 28–30; *Jewish and Islamic Philosophy,* chap. 6; "Moral, Metaphysical and Natural Justice" (in Portuguese), *Analise Social* (Lisbon), 4th series, 32 (1998): 263–84.

91. EIP8S2; cf. *KV,* I, ii, Art. 3, ch. 4, Art. 8.

92. G. Brykman, *La Judéité de Spinoza* (Paris: Vrin, 1972), 54; cf. Kenneth Seeskin's chapter in this volume.

93. See Abraham Herrera, *Sha'ar ha-Shamayim* III 6–7; Wolfson, *The Philosophy of Spinoza* 1:315; Brykman, *La Judéité,* 55.

94. Santayana, "Ethical Doctrine," 144.

95. See R. Popkin, "Spinoza: Neoplatonic Kabbalist?" in *Neoplatonism and Jewish Thought,* ed. Lenn Goodman (Albany: State University of New York Press, 1992), 387–409.

96. Spinoza likes to say 'singular' not 'particular.' For individuals are not mere instances of universals, and we do not know particulars only through their universals. Since such issues have receded in prominence, we may retain the more familiar usage.

97. Cf. EIIP10S, G II 93/30–36, with Meyer, in PP G I 132/31–33.

98. See Mason, *God of Spinoza,* 97–98.

99. See *Pirkei Avot* 5.9; Tosefta Eruvin ad fin.; Hagigah I ad fin.

100. Descartes, *Rules for the Direction of the Mind,* Rule 8, trans. after J. Cottingham, R. Stoothoff, and D. Murdoch (Cambridge: Cambridge University Press, 1992), 1:31.

101. Descartes, *Rules for the Direction of the Mind,* Rule 9, Cottingham et al., 33.

102. Cliché has it that the *Fons Vitae* bears no trace of its Jewish origins. But the title is such a trace, and the idea behind that title is much more than a trace.

103. See Alexander Altmann, *Studies in Religious Philosophy and Mysticism* (London: Routledge, 1969); Goodman, *Jewish and Islamic Philosophy,* 15–24.

104. *TdIE* 35; EIIP43S; cf. Moses b. Joshua, ad *Moreh Nevukhim,* ed. 1852, 14c.

105. See Stephen Gaukroger, *Descartes: An Intellectual Biography* (Oxford: Oxford University Press, 1997), 84, 270–90.

106. Jeffrey Bernstein, letter of December 23, 1997.

107. The theme is developed in my *In Defense of Truth* (Amherst, N.Y.: Humanities Books, 2001), chap. 5.

108. Saadiah Gaon, *Book of Theodicy,* trans. Goodman, 282, and my discussion ad loc.

109. See my discussion in Saadiah's *Book of Theodicy,* 60, 128–29, 377, 382.

110. Saadiah, *ED,* Introductory Treatise 2–4; I 3; Rosenblatt, *Book of Beliefs,* 13–15, 78–79.

111. See Wolfson, *Spinoza* 2:98–105; T. C. Mark, "Truth and Adequacy in Spinoza's Ideas," *Southwestern Journal of Philosophy* 8 (1977): 11–34; Spinoza's *Theory of Truth* (Ann Arbor: University of Michigan Press, 1993).

112. Maimonides distinguishes action predicates, which refer to God by way of His work, from relational predicates (in his sense), which might implicate our idea of God in our own finite categories. As Seymour Feldman shows, writers like Avicenna, Ibn Daud, Hasdai Crescas, and Joseph Kaspi found it natural to treat actions as relations; see "A Scholastic Misinterpretation of Maimonides' Doctrine of Divine Attributes," *Journal of Jewish Studies* 19 (1968): 23–39, 26, 30. The confusion over Maimonides' terminology, introduced to protect divine transcendence, continues to the present day.

113. *Guide* I 16, citing Isa. 26:4; Dt. 32:4, 32:18, 32:30; and 1 Sam. 2:2, Ex. 33:21.

114. Gen. 28:12, as glossed at *Guide* I 15.

115. Ps. 29:10, as cited at *Guide* I 11.

116. Feldman, "Scholastic Misinterpretation," (38) notes several passages in the *Guide* (I 26, 46, 47) suggestive of a theory of analogy. But the

Rambam shies away from the approach, lest it suggest too divine a creature or too creaturely a deity. He even avoids a Platonizing theory of amphiboly, which would assign to God the truest sense of positive value terms.

117. Spinoza characteristically reverses the fields when he urges that we best know the effect from its cause, not the cause from its effect.

118. See Spinoza, Eps 6, 13, etc. and Oldenburg's replies in behalf of Boyle.

119. See my "Maimonidean Naturalism," in *Maimonides and the Sciences*, ed. R. S. Cohen and H. Levine (Boston: Kluwer, 2000), 57–85.

120. Moses Narboni's Commentary on *Guide* I 1–50, in *Moshe Narboni*, ed. with French translation by Maurice Hayoun (Tübingen: Mohr, 1986), 42, Hebrew, 132; cf. 35, 125.

121. Ibn Tufayl, *Ḥayy Ibn Yaqẓān*, trans. L. E. Goodman (New York: Twayne, 1972; 2nd ed., Los Angeles: Gee Tee Bee, 1984), 128–29.

122. See Bahya, *Ḥovot ha-Levavot* I 5, trans. M. Mansoor, 117; Aristotle, *Phys.* III 4–8, *Metaph.* IX 10, *De Caelo* I 5–7; I. Efros, *The Problem of Space in Jewish Medieval Philosophy* (New York: Columbia University Press, 1917), 93; Wolfson, *Spinoza*, 1:265.

123. Cf. Spinoza EIP14S, G II 57–58.

124. See Ibn Tufayl, *Ḥayy Ibn Yaqẓān*, Goodman, 130–33.

125. See H. A. Wolfson, Crescas' Critique of Aristotle (Cambridge: Harvard University Press, 1929), 151–57.

126. Ep. 32; cf. *KV* xix, 2, G I 25.

127. Ep. 32, Gebhardt, 4.172–73.

128. *Metaph.* VII 10, 1035b 23–25; cf. *Phys.* IV 4, 211b 1–4, a passage bracketed by Ross but paralleled at *Meteor.* IV 12, 1289b 13–1290a 1 and *De Part. An.* I 1, 640b 35–641a 17. The thought was certainly available to Spinoza.

129. Errol Harris, *The Substance of Spinoza* (Atlantic Highlands: Humanities Press, 1995), 34.

130. David Bohm, *Wholeness and the Implicate Order* (London: Routledge, 1980), 172.

131. See my *God of Abraham*, chap. 8.

132. G II 77–78; for Spinoza's early placement of the point, see Mason, *God of Spinoza*, 119.

133. See my "Saadya Gaon on the Human Condition," *Jewish Quarterly Review*, n.s., 67 (1976): 23–29; Saadiah, *Book of Theodicy*, passim.

134. See Saadiah on Job 39, in Goodman, trans., 393–96.

135. Ravven, "Notes," 16.

136. Cf. Mason, *God of Spinoza*, 52–54.

137. Cf. Martha Nussbaum, *Aristotle's De Motu Animalium*: Text, Translation and Commentary (Princeton: Princeton University Press, 1978).

138. Cf. D. Lachterman, "The Physics of Spinoza's Ethics," in *Spinoza: New Perspectives*, ed. R. Shahan and J. Biro (Norman: University of Oklahoma Press, 1978), 81–89; Ravven, "Notes," 21, n. 14.

139. See Pierre Teilhard de Chardin, *The Phenomenon of Man*, trans. B. Wall (New York: Harper and Row, 1959; Paris: Editions du Seuil, 1955).

140. EI, App., G II 83; cf. *TdIE*, G II 8; 9/12–15; 12/23–24.

141. See especially *TTP* chap. iv.

142. *TTP* xiv, G III, 177.

143. I translate after Samuel Shirley, 225. Spinoza (Ep. 73 to Oldenburg) thinks of Christ as God's eternal wisdom, of which Jesus is a consummate vehicle; but he holds that a man-god makes no more sense than a square circle.

144. For Maimonides' counterpart to *intellectualis amor Dei*, see *Guide* I 39, glossing Dt. 6:5.

145. See Saadiah on Job 14:15, *Book of Theodicy*, Goodman, 256–57; and my comments, 261.

146. *Birkhot ha-Shaḥar*, in P. Birnbaum, ed., *Ha-Siddur Ha-Shalem* (New York: Hebrew Publishing Co., 1949) 23.

147. Quoted by H. Dethier, "Love and Intellect in Leone Ebreo," in Goodman, *Neoplatonism and Jewish Thought*, 373.

148. Dethier, in Goodman, *Neoplatonism and Jewish Thought*, 374; see Leone Ebreo, *Dialoghi d'Amore* III q. 3. Spinoza owned a late sixteenth-century translation under the title *Dialogos de amor*.

149. See Philo, *De Opif. Mundi* 81, *De Mut. Nom.* 129, *Abraham*.

150. Philo, *QG*, 4.188; see David Winston, "Philo's Conception of the Divine Nature," in Goodman, *Neoplatonism and Jewish Thought*, 26–27.

PART II

Metaphysics

CHAPTER 3

Love of God in Spinoza

LEE C. RICE

INTRODUCTION

Spinoza's general analysis of the emotions has been the subject of several recent studies[1] but commentators have typically neglected his treatment of love (and consequently of friendship). Some[2] have sought to position his remarks historically as a derivative or development from Descartes. Others[3] concentrate on his analysis of intellectual conversion and liberation from the passions, without attending to the implications of his approach for affective relationships in general. Still others[4] attempt to integrate his account of the affects with his general theory of individuation. Even Deleuze and other philosophers who see Spinoza as offering a source of wisdom for practical life pay little attention to his remarks on love. A rich literature has grown up around the theme of the 'intellectual love of God' (*amor dei intellectualis*) in EV. Some[5] have attempted to trace its sources in an earlier Jewish tradition. Others[6] have dealt with the problems of its consistency with the naturalism of the earlier parts of the *Ethics*. Still others have attempted to find in it Jewish or Neoplatonic mystical traditions whose consistency with Spinoza's system is open to serious doubt.[7] None have done much to connect this concept—a late arrival in the *Ethics*!—with Spinoza's earlier account of affectivity and love or with his general division of knowledge.

In EIIAx3 Spinoza remarks:

> Modes of thinking such as love, desire, or whatever affects are designated by name, do not occur unless there is in the same individual the idea of the thing loved, desired, etc. But the idea can be without any other mode of thinking.

A trivial consequence of this axiom is that affective responses are never without cognitive content. A nontrivial and less noticed consequence is that cognitive typologies will have their affective counterparts. Spinoza offers a general typology of cognition in EIIP40Schol2. The general outline of this famous tripartite division is relatively clear (at least for the first two divisions). By 'imagination' (*imaginatio*) or the first kind of knowledge, Spinoza means sensory perception as well as what we would generally ascribe to imagination (image-related thinking) in the widest possible sense. This type of knowledge (EIIP41) is not inherently clear and can lead to falsity or error in the absence of rational clarification. By reason (*ratio*), the second kind of knowledge, is intended deductive knowledge from clearly apprehended first-principles, a form of cognition that is error-free if properly conducted (EIIP42). Finally, Spinoza tells us, there is a third kind of knowledge (*scientia intuitiva*, intuition), to be discussed later (EV). This "proceeds from an adequate idea of certain attributes of God to an adequate knowledge of the essence of things." Like imagination, intuition is knowledge of individuals. Like reason, it is an adequate form of knowledge. But it is not merely knowledge of individuals through their general properties.[8]

In this paper I shall argue that we can gain a more adequate sense of Spinoza's notion of love, and particularly of the love of God, if we pursue this tripartite cognitive division as his explanation in EIIAx3 warrants. Our findings may help to clarify Spinoza's challenging idea of God's intellectual love and cast some light on what some authors call the 'Judeity' of Spinoza's philosophy.

SENSORY OR IMAGINATIONAL LOVE

Spinoza's naturalism casts thought and extension as two attributes of a single substance ('God or nature'). An important consequence of this naturalism is given at EIIP7: "the order and connection of ideas is the same as the order and connection of things."[9] One psychological consequence of this view is that mind and body are conceived not as two separate substances as in Cartesian dualism, but as dual aspects of a unified organism: Mind is a complex of mental (cognitive and affective) states parallel to the complex of particles that is body. The essence of human nature is appetitive behavior:

> When this drive (*conatus*) is related to mind alone, it is called will; when it is related to both mind and body, it is called appetite, which is nothing other than an individual's essence. . . . Further, there is no difference between appetite and desire except that desire is related to persons insofar as they are conscious of appetite. . . .

From the above remarks it is clear that we do not endeavor (*cona-mur*), will, seek, or desire something because we judge it to be good. On the contrary, something is judged to be good because we endeavor, will, seek, or desire it. (EIIIP9Schol)

There are two further primary affects in addition to conatus itself: pleasure (*laetitia*) or the transition (active or passive) of mind/body to a state of greater perfection or activity, and pain (*tristitia*) or its transition (always passive) to a lesser state (EIIIP11Schol). The greater part of EIII (through P57) is devoted to the mechanics of the affects as passive responses to the impact of our environment: this is the affective parallel to the cognitive state of imagination, and is often referenced by Spinoza as behavior according to the "common order of nature" (*ordo communis naturae*). Just as imaginational cognition contains the seeds of error, so passive affectivity contains the seeds of powerlessness (*impotentia*) in the face of an environment largely indifferent to the survival of the organism.

EIIIP13Schol introduces the derivative affects of love and hate. Love is pleasure accompanied by the idea of an external cause. Hate is pain accompanied by the idea of an external cause. The idea of a cause here need not be (and in general is not) true or adequate. If I believe that the waxing of the moon is the cause of my heightened activity, I shall love it. The truth of an idea has nothing to do with the strength of its corresponding affect, which is determined rather by its real cause, whether known or not (EIVP7).

It might be argued that a concept of love so broad as to encompass both fleeting gratification and long-term emotional attachment has little practical applicability, but such an objection confuses logical reducibility with reduction in some more sinister sense. Spinoza grants (EIIIP56) that there will be as many types of love as there are external objects to cause it. But the comprehensive philosophical psychology for which Spinoza aims does not require him to develop a complete analysis of the different types of love and hate. These types are discussed at some length in EIII and EIV. But the principal goal of Spinoza's psychological schematization is to allow us "to understand the common properties of the affects and the mind in order to determine the nature and extent of the mind's power in controlling and checking them" (EIIIP56Schol).[10]

The central moral problem with love at the imaginational or passive level is that, while consistent with the conatus of the individual (since it produces heightened activity), it remains largely outside the individual's control (because passive), and can produce side effects that are not conducive to survival. Spinoza is convinced that most of us are in bondage (*servitus*) to our affects. We typically experience love at this first level. That is, our love is not self-determined but passive. It relates to our conatus only insofar as we are a part of nature which can neither act nor exist independently of the whole. Its cognitive basis lies largely in the realm of inadequate ideas. A distinguishing feature of this common type of love is immoderation. It is frequently identified with titillation (EIVP43-P44), which is defined as an unbalanced physical or mental state. Because it is passive, it may overwhelm the powers of the body (EIVP6), to the detriment of the individual. So, while pleasure itself is always a good (EIVP41), one's love of sexual activity is harmful if its pleasure overbalances the activities by which one's essence is maintained. For the same reason, such pleasures will be unhealthy both physically and mentally. Our modern jargon would describe such tendencies as 'obsessive'. Both in the *Ethics* and in the earlier *Treatise on the Emendation of the Intellect*, Spinoza described them as a form of 'waking sleep', a phrase whose roots, according to Albiac[11] go back to Uriel da Costa and Juan de Prado.

Spinoza emphasizes the physical aspect of imaginational love, and indeed the examples that most readily come to mind are cliches of bodily or material obsession, such as ambition (EIIIDefAff44), gluttony (EIIIDefAff45), drunkenness (EIIIDefAff46), avarice (EIIIDefAff47), and lust (EIIIDefAff48). One interesting puzzle here is found in Spinoza's characterization of sexual desire (*libido*) as a form of love for the 'commingling of bodies' *(in commiscendis corporibus)*, a phrase, which typifies, though it is wider than, sexual intercourse. It is difficult to see how one may, from this definition, analytically distinguish a love based on any specific physical presence (e.g., my desire to be physically present with my dog) from sexual desire in a specific sense.[12] In any event, while Spinoza's notions of love and sexual love share many features with the later Freudian model,[13] they are clearly opposed to it insofar as Spinoza sees sexual love as a species of love in general rather than the converse.

While imaginational love can be the cause of much emotional distress (EVP20Schol), Spinoza's characterization of it is never wholly negative. Desires that do not arise from reason may be consistent with it, and may act for our good or ill (EIVApp3). The similarity of Spinoza's remarks on this point with EIIIDefAff18 suggests that Spinoza intends us to consider this type of love in much the same way as we should regard pity, an affect of pain accompanied by the idea of some ill that befalls another whom we regard as similar to ourselves (EIIIDefAff18). While harmful in itself (EIVP41), pity can move us to free its object from distress, and to that extent it may be good (EIIIP27Cor3). Similarly, if imaginational love moves us to behavior that is kind and tolerant, to which we would not otherwise be moved by reason, it is a good despite its passivity.

The fact that love at the imaginational level does not require adequate ideas of its object is a distinctive feature of the love of God at this level. Imaginational cognition arises from contact with finite sensory individuals within the limited environment in which the organism moves, and provides at best only a metaphorical knowledge of God. Frequently such knowledge casts God as judge, a governor of nature capable of directing natural events to human ends. The obsessive form of this metaphor is what Spinoza calls superstition (*superstitio*):

> So it happened that every individual devised different methods of worshipping god as he saw fit in order that God should love him beyond others and direct the whole of nature in order to serve his blind cupidity and insatiable greed. Thus it was that this misconception developed into superstition and became deep-rooted in men's minds, and it was because of this that each person strove most earnestly to understand and to explain the final causes of all things. (EIApp)[14]

It would be a gross error, however, to say that any such imaginational love of God is inherently superstitious, just as it would be an error to claim that sexual love is always obsessive. Indeed, the entire prophetic tradition is described by Spinoza in the *Tractatus Theologico-Politicus* as based upon an imaginational conception of God. Like imaginational cognition in general, it contains the seeds of error. But imaginational cognition is the basis of all human knowledge, just as affectivity (see EIIP23) and the imaginative accounts of the prophets too make their contributions in this regard. And just as scientific knowledge for Spinoza consists not in the transcendence of sensory data but rather in its controlled and rational use, so liberation from the possibility of superstition arises not from elimination of sensory love, but rather in the rational understanding and control of it.

LOVE AS RATIONAL ACTION

Although Spinoza does not develop it extensively, he also offers in the *Ethics* the concept of a different type of love based upon adequate ideas, and which may be characterized as 'self-determined'. The term he employs is *generositas* ('nobility'), which is defined (EIIIP46) as a "strength of mind that follows from affects that are related to mind insofar as it exercises understanding." Such a strength is divided into two subspecies: courage and nobility. The latter is "the desire by which each individual, according to the sole dictates of reason, endeavors to assist and befriend others" (EIIIP59S). This self-determined love is not threatened by the blindness or fragmentation of sensory imagination. If it is directed toward another human being, it includes awareness of that person's limitations and implies not only knowledge of the loved object but also adequate knowledge of self.[15]

Such reflexive knowledge is critical for the possibility of self-determined behavior (see EVP3Cor). It is also connected with freedom of mind
(*animi libertas*), a key term for Spinoza. In one discussion of marriage he
makes the strikingly egalitarian claim that the love on which it is based (for
each partner) has freedom of spirit as one of its causes (EIVApp20). This
freedom of spirit constitutes the basis in similarity on which marriage is
founded. It is also the basis for the wider relationship of friendship (*amicitia*),
about which there are numerous remarks scattered throughout the third
and fourth parts of the *Ethics*. Little research has been done as yet to unify
these remarks into a systematic Spinozist account of friendship.

One immediate consequence of the definition of love (whether it
applies to imaginational, rational, or intuitive activity) is its producing a
desire on the part of the lover to be united to the object of the love. Spinoza
is careful to point out (EIIIDefAff6Exp) that this characteristic "does not
express the essence of love." It is rather an immediate causal consequence of
love. That consequence has another, and more limited consequence: "If we
love something similar to ourselves, we endeavor as much as we can to
bring it about that it love us in return" (EIIIP33). Such a desire for reciprocation does *not* follow from the essence of love as does the desire for union,
but is caused by a perception of *similarity* to the loved object (a cognitive
feature) combined with the desire for union (an appetitive feature).

Speaking of rational love, Spinoza remarks that a person who loves
God cannot endeavor that God should reciprocate or love him in return
(EVP19). For such a desire would entail that God be affected passively, that
is, that God's essence should be other than it is (EVP19Dem). Of course, at
the imaginational level, the fact that one knows p, and that p implies q, does
not entail that one knows q. But at the level of reason and intuition, knowing a proposition entails adequate knowledge of its implications. The desire
for reciprocation of divine love is thus a basic form of what Spinoza calls
'superstition'. It operates at the level of imaginational appetite, and its cognitive correlate is an inadequate understanding of the divine nature.

Superstition and inadequate knowledge of the divine nature are not
internal features of the human mind, which has an adequate knowledge of
the essence of God, as Spinoza tells us in EIIP47. His scholium to this proposition is worth quoting:

> Hence we see that God's infinite essence and his eternity are known
> to all. Now, because all things are in and conceived through God, it
> follows that from this knowledge *we can deduce* a great many
> things so as to know them adequately and thus to form the third
> kind of knowledge. (EIIP47Schol, emphasis mine)

Deduction, of course, takes place at the level of reason, although the data
are imaginational; and an adequate understanding of the objects deduced is

a feature of intuition itself. The knowledge of God given in imagination and 'purified' (or made deductive and adequate) by reason is possible precisely because the Spinozist God is immanent rather than transcendent: "The more we understand particular things, the more we understand God" (EVP24).

Note, then, that while the love of God causes a desire for union with its object, it does not rationally induce a drive for reciprocation, although it may do so at the level of fantasy or imagination. So the notion of 'friendship with God' is an empty one, since there is no basis of similarity on which it could be logically constructed. Christianity attempts to bridge this gap with the notion of a god-man, but the notion is rooted in imagination and inherently contradictory, as Spinoza notes in writing to Oldenburg:

> As to the additional teaching of certain churches, that God took human nature upon himself, I have expressly indicated that I do not understand what is meant. Indeed and in truth, they seem to me to speak no less absurdly than one who might inform me that a circle has taken on the nature of a square. (Ep73, Nov./Dec. 1675)

One might conclude that for Spinoza there is no sense to be made of the notion of divine love. But the account that Spinoza provides of love at the level of intuition offers both a clarification and an answer. It is to this account which I now turn.

INTUITIONAL LOVE

Spinoza had characterized reason (the second kind of knowledge) in EIIP40S2, as arising from "common notions and adequate ideas of the properties of things." He initiates his discussion of intuition in EVP25 by explaining: "The third kind of knowledge proceeds from the adequate idea of certain of God's attributes to adequate knowledge of the essence of things, and the more we understand things in this way, the more we understand God" (EVP25Dem). Reason is a universal knowledge of things through their properties. It is not a knowledge of universals, for Spinoza's nominalism precludes their very existence.[16] Intuition is a direct knowledge of things through their individual essences or natures as comprehended in one or more of the divine attributes (thought or extension). Problems abound. Indeed the section beginning at EVP25 has been the subject of the most diverse interpretations in all of the secondary literature concerning Spinoza, especially the notion of eternity.[17] What is clear is that intuitive knowledge arises naturally from reason itself (EVP28), includes self-knowledge (EVP31), is a form of activity rather than passivity in relation to the environment (EVP38), and has a corporeal or physiological correlate (EVP39) no less than any other state of mind.

Since Spinoza conceives of intuitive knowledge as both active and adequate, its affective correlate, the intellectual love of God, is both wholly adequate in its causality and completely self-determined. A number of commentators[18] see an inherent ambiguity or even an outright inconsistency in the notion of *amor dei*. It has been used throughout the first four parts of the *Ethics* in its objective sense ('a love directed toward God'), and Spinoza, we are told, now trades upon the ambiguity of the genitive case to make it mean 'God's love directed at something'. But the dual meaning of the genitive (objective or subjective) has nothing to do with God or with Spinoza's Latinity. It is a feature of the English genitive no less than of the Latin. Moreover it has nothing to do with any supposed preculiarities of affectivity (love). It is equally a feature of 'idea' used with the genitive in English or Latin as well. Bennett's suggestion that Spinoza could have been confused here is not plausible, in view of the way that Spinoza underlines the difference (in EIIP17Schol) between the idea of Peter which *is Peter's mind* and the idea of Peter which is *in Paul's mind*.

But look again at the characterization that Spinoza provides of intuition in general: it proceeds from an adequate knowledge of an attribute (such as extension) to an adequate knowledge of an individual *that is a part or expression* of that very attribute. The subjective-objective features in this case, far from being muddled, become identical because of the identity of the finite individual as part of the infinite attribute.

Two further logical consequences immediately follow. Intuitive love, like intuitive knowledge, is wholly active. So both can be predicated directly of God: "God loves himself with an infinite intellectual love" (EVP35). But that very love (and knowledge) is expressed in the finite modes that comprise the nature of God: "The mind's intellectual love toward God is a *part* of the infinite love wherewith God loves himself" (EVP36, emphasis mine). EVP36Dem makes it clear that, to the extent that a finite mind (or body) is active, it comprises an actual part of the mind (or body) which is God. There is no confusion in Spinoza's exposition, but rather a conscious and straightforward accounting of the consequences of divine immanence.

It is easy and tempting to read into this transition from objective genitive to a subjective genitive some form of Neoplatonism, perhaps surreptitiously introduced by Spinoza. The case for a Neoplatonism transmitted through Kabbalistic sources is examined and rejected by Popkin,[19] and I believe quite correctly. Tempting parallels are also found in Leo Hebraeus (Judah ben Isaac Abravanel), whose *Dialoghi d'amore* were in Spinoza's personal library. The second dialogue, on the universality of love[20] builds upon the notion of a higher order of love derived from intuitive or direct knowledge.[21] There are also some possible textual parallels between Hebraeus's *Dialoghi* and the passages on intuition in Spinoza's earlier *Short Treatise*.[22]

Yet, Spinoza's mandate of the destruction of earlier drafts and notes of his own completed works, indicates that he took pains to prevent scholarly chases through the history of philosophy in pursuit of sources. He appears to have been largely successful in this endeavor. For Wolfson's famous study[23] is perhaps the best example of the patchwork approach to Spinoza, but at best it leaves us with a set of interesting but unverifiable possibilities, at worst a set of answers for which we often have no matching questions. An effort antecedent to Wolfson's traces both the metaphysics of substance in EI and the notion of 'intellectual love of God' to a patchwork of texts from Plotinus.[24]

The argument from 'x was in Spinoza's library' to 'Spinoza read x' is somewhat tenuous. The twelve volumes of the Latin Aristotle were in his library, but he himself confesses lack of familiarity with Aristotle. And, if the inference to 'Spinoza read x' is tenuous, the further claim that 'x figured in the logical development of Spinoza's system' is often far less than that.

None of the above is intended to suggest that Spinoza did not read and reflect upon philosophical sources (classical, medieval, and Jewish, as well as Cartesian) in the development of his system. It does bring forward, however, a final point. Transplanting a phrase or concept from one system into another does not guarantee, and often simply voids, sameness of systematic meaning. Terms like *amor intellectualis dei* were certainly in use in the philosophical milieux with which Spinoza was familiar. But their sense in Spinoza is determined by their systematic connections with other theoretical concepts indigenous to Spinozism. This is not a strictly 'philosophical' issue. One has only to think of the concept of 'mass' in Galileo (or Spinoza), then Newton, and finally Einstein to realize that intrasystematic connectivity is the death of transystematic synonymy. 'Mass' may have similar functions and roles to play in each of these systems of physics, but its meaning is dictated by their separate and often contrary structures.

Dethier's study[25] marks what appears to be the most one can say about possible sources of Spinozism in Hebraeus. As he notes,[26] Hebraeus's notion of intellectual love is recognition of causes external to the knower (lover), whereas Spinoza's concept references sequences of internal causes. The notion of will, and the conflict between will and intellect in the quest for salvation, is omnipresent in Hebraeus, and absent in Spinoza. Dethier goes on to suggest that the temporal aspects of Hebraeus's notion of intellectual love are missing in Spinoza, "because Spinoza holds time to be only an appearance; and an individual personality merely a transitory mode."[27] This claim, which is incorrect, is an example of the Neoplatonizing tendency in reading EV. Duration in Spinoza (not *tempus*, which is his word for the conventionality of the metric of time) is a real aspect of modal existence (not merely a specious appearance in some spurious Kantian sense) both for ideas and for their bodies; and the individual personality, while it may be transient, is the expression of an eternal essence existent in the infinite intellect, so hardly transitory. This is why Spinoza goes on in EV to emphasize the necessity of intuitive love: "He whose body is capable of the greatest amount of activity has a mind whose greatest part is eternal" (EVP39). Spinoza's immanentism shares some of the features of its Neoplatonic predecessors, but his naturalism precludes the sort of dualism that is typical in their systems, and whose presence is everywhere in the thought of Hebraeus.

It is also this very immanentism that accounts for the fact that his notion of intellectual love does not rupture the naturalistic conception of the human person, here the identity of mind and body:

> Before we proceed further, we must recall here what we demonstrated earlier, i.e., that whatever can be perceived by an infinite intellect as constituting the essence of substance pertains to one substance only, and consequently that substance thinking and extended are one and the same substance, which is now comprehended under this attribute, now under that. So also a mode of extension and the idea of that mode are one and the same thing, but expressed in two ways. Some of the Hebrews seem to have seen this, as if through a cloud, when they maintained that God, God's intellect, and the things understood by him are one and the same. (EIIP7Schol)

If Spinoza's reading of the mind of the early Hebrews is correct, then the Judeity of his concept of God is of a piece with his concept of divine love, and both are intimately related to divine immanence:

> The ideas of a purely transcendent God, of an afterlife and an afterworld, of a divine domain ontologically separate from ours, are posterior to the Bible and partly foreign to it. The biblical God is awesome, remote, and unseen, but none the less immersed in this world and in human affairs. . . . The attempts of Maimonides and other Jewish theologians to explain it away allegorically are posterior to the Bible by over a millennium and a half.[28]

Wolfson and others have claimed that Spinoza's identification of the mind and its object in God also has roots in the third book of Aristotle's *De Anima*, which was subsequently developed by both Jewish Neoplatonists and Jewish Aristotelians. Our strictures about textual sources apply as much to this claim as to any other. The autonomy of thought at the divine level is assured by the Spinozist doctrine of the independence of the attributes: the causal order of thought is self-contained. But Spinoza's naturalization of thought extends this doctrine from the divine to the finite mind, a move far outside the ambit of either Aristotelianism or medieval Neoplatonism (whether Jewish or Christian). Any causal relation between Aristotle's development of these points, however historically transmitted, and Spinoza's own reworking of them would have had to be largely unconscious on Spinoza's part. Writing to Hugo Boxel in 1674 (Ep56), Spinoza notes that Plato, Aristotle, and Socrates carry little weight with him. He sends his reader rather to the works of Epicurus, Democritus, and Lucretius. The works of Lucretius, Cicero, and Seneca are in Spinoza's personal library; and one of the basic concepts of Spinoza's own moral theory, that of *generositas*, is Ciceronian in origin and has no role in the Latin corpus of Aristotelianism.

I suspect that, were the 'Jewishness' of Spinoza's thought to have been raised as an issue to him, he would have rather regarded his approach to these themes as a liberation from the Neoplatonic and Aristotelian sources, especially of the medieval tradition, rather than a development from these. As the quotation from EIIP7 above indicates, it is the immanentism and naturalism of ancient Jewish thought to which Spinoza allies himself, rather than the frantic dualisms that he perceives as mediaeval in origin. Though perhaps personified imaginationally as separate from it, the Spinozist God resides within us and within the world of which we are a part. *Our* love *in that world* is not simply a reflection of divine love, but is that love itself. We (our actions and our relations with other individuals) can no more be separated from divine love than can that love be separated from us: they are one and the same. The consequences of this fact for a full understanding of Spinoza's notions of justice, civil society, and the moral status of the individual are awesome in number and content. While pursuit of these consequences lies beyond the scope of my topic, their existence provides eloquent testimony, not just to some of the Judaic elements from which Spinoza works, but also to the deep and underlying unity of his metaphysics and his social thought.

NOTES

1. See Gilles Deleuze, 1968, *Spinoza et le problème de l'expression* (Paris: Editions de Minuit); Alan Hart, 1990, *The Love of an Apathetic God or Blessedness* (Akron, Ohio: University of Akron Press); Genevieve Lloyd, 1994, *Part of Nature: Self-Knowledge in Spinoza's "Ethics"* (Ithaca, NY: Cornell University Press); Lee Rice, 1979, "Servitus in Spinoza: A Programmatic Analysis" in *Spinoza's Philosophy of Man*, ed. Jon Wetlesen, 179–91 (Oslo: Universitetsforlaget and New York: Columbia University Press); Lee Rice, 1985, "Spinoza's Account of Sexuality," Philosophy Research Archives

10, 1985: 19–34; Steven Barbone and Lee Rice, 1977, "Spinoza and Human Sexuality," in *Sex, Love, and Friendship*, ed. Alan Soble, 265–77 (New York: Rodopi); Amelie Rorty, 1991, "Spinoza on the Pathos of Idolatrous Love and the Hilarity of True Love," in *The Philosophy of (Erotic) Love*, ed. Robert C. Solomon and Kathleen M. Higgins, 352–71 (Lawrence: University of Kansas); and Michael Schrijvers, 1989, *Spinozas Affektenlehre* (Bern: Verlag Paul Haupt).

2. E.g., Jean-Marie Beyssade, 1990, "De l'émotion intérieure chez Descartes à l'effect actif spinoziste," in *Spinoza: Issues and Directions*, ed. Edwin Curley and Pierre-François Moreau, 176–190 (Leiden: E. J. Brill); Vincent Carraud, 1992, "Descartes et l'Ecriture sainte," in *L'Ecriture Sainte au temps de Spinoza et dans le système spinoziste*, 41–70 (Groupe de Recherches Spinozistes, Travaux et Documents, Numèro 4. Paris: Presses de L'Université de Paris Sorbonne); Edwin Curley, 1988, *Behind the Geometrical Method: A Reading of Spinoza's Ethics* (Princeton, NJ: Princeton University Press); Huan A. Garcia Gonzalez, 1992, "Poder del pensamiento y amor," in *La Etica de Spinoza: Fundamentos y'significado, ed. Atilano Dominquez*, 361–70 (Castilla-La Mancha: Ediciones de la Universidad); and Jacqueline Lagrée, 1992, "Le thème des Deux livres de la Nature et de l'Ecriture," in *L'Ecriture Sainte au temps de Spinoza et dans le système spinoziste*, 9–40 (Groupe de Recherches Spinozistes, Travaux et Documents, Numéro 4) Paris: Presses de l'Université de Paris Sorbonne).

3. E.g., Stuart Hampshire, 1973, "Spinoza and the Idea of Freedom," in *Spinoza: A Collection of Critical Essays*, ed. Marjorie Grene, 297–317 (Garden City, NY: Anchor Books); and Frans van Zetten, 1991, in *Russell and Spinoza: Free Thoughts on the Love of God* (Delft: Eburon).

4. E.g., Hampshire in "Spinoza and the Idea of Freedom," Lloyd in *Part of Nature*, Rice in "Emotion, Appetition, and Conatus in Spinoza," *Revue Internationale de Philosophie*, vol. 31 (1977): 101–16; and in "Individual and Community in Spinoza's Social Psychology," in *Spinoza: Issues and Directions*, 271–85.

5. See Gabriel Albiac, 1987, *Le synagogue vide: Les sources marranes du spinozisme*. Traduit de l'espagnol et portugais par Marie-Luce Copète et Jean Frédéric Schaub, 147–56 (Paris: Presses Universitaires de France); Mino Chalma, 1996, *Spinoza e il concetto della tradizione ebraica* (Milan: Angelis); Carla G. Calvetti, 1982, *Benedetto Spinoza di fronte a Leone Ebreo: Problemi etico-religiosi e amor Dei intellectualis* (Milan: CUSL); Ze'ev Levy, 1996, "Das Einwirken Judischer Einflusse auf Spinozas Philosophie," in *Judishche Fragen als Themata der Philosophie*, ed. Sabine Gehlhaar, 9–40 (Cuxhaven: Junghans); and I. S. Revah, 1995, *Des Marranes à Spinoza. Textes réunis par Hanry Méchoulan, Pierre-François Moreau, et Casten Lorenz Wilke* (Paris: Vrin); Yirmiyahu Yovel, 1989, *Spinoza and Other Heretics:*

The Adventures of Immanence, 126–135 (Princeton, NJ: Princeton University Press).

6. E.g., V. M. Foti, 1979, "Spinoza's Doctrine of Immortality and the Unity of Love," *Southern Journal of Philosophy* 17: 437–442; Richard Mason, 1977, *The God of Spinoza*, 51–84 (Cambridge: Cambridge University Press); and Rorty.

7. E.g., Morris Cohen, 1923, "Amor Dei Intellectualis," *Chronicon Spinzanum* 3: 3–19; Vance Maxwell, 1990, "Spinoza's Doctrine of the *Amor Dei Intellectualis*, I," *Dionysius* 14 131–156; Jean Préposiet, 1992, "*Amor dei intellectualis*,' in *La "Etica" de Spinoza: Fundamentos y significado*, 488–92; and Nathan Rotenstreich, 1977, "Conatus and Amor Dei: The Total and Partial Norm," *Revue Internationale de Philosophie* 31: 117–134.

8. See Rice, "Mind Eternity in Spinoza."

9. For the epistemic difficulties of this 'psycho-physical parallelism' see Michael Della Rocca, 1996, *Representation and the Mind-Body Problem in Spinoza* (Oxford: Oxford University Press).

10. There is also a second source of divergence in the types of love that is rooted in Spinoza's nominalism (see Rice, "Le nominalisme de Spinoza" *Canadian Journal of Philosophy* 24: 19–32): the desire (and hence general affective responses) of one individual will differ from that of another just as their essences differ (EIIIP7Schol). Although a discussion of the 'phenomenology' of love would make his account more comprehensive, it also is not central to his preoccupations in the *Ethics*.

11. Albiac, 409–415.

12. See Barbone and Rice, "Spinoza and Human Sexuality."

13. Rice, "Spinoza's Account of Sexuality"; Rice, "Freud, Sartre, Spinoza: The Problematic of the Unconscious," *Gionarle di Metafisica*, n.s. XVII: 87–106.

14. The claim that the conception of God as creator, judge, and intervening governor arises from inadequate knowledge and misdirected human appetite has been traced by Revah (375–80) to Juan de Prado and Ribera, two other members of the Jewish community in Amsterdam whose writings are roughly contemporaneous with those of Spinoza. See also Albiac: 327–33.

15. Schrijvers: 169–72

16. See Rice, "Le nominalisme de Spinoza."

17. See Rice, "Mind Eternity in Spinoza."

18. E.g., Bennett: 369–72

19. Richard Popkin, 1992, "Spinoza, Neoplatonic Kabbalist?" in *Neoplatonism and Jewish Thought*, ed. Lenn E. Goodman, 387–409 (Albany: State University of New York Press).

20. Leone Ebreo [Judah Abravanel], 1929, *Dialoghi d'amore, hebräis-che Gedichte, herausgegeben mit einer Darstellung des Lebens und des Werkes Leones con Carl Gebhardt*: 75–153 (Bibliotheca Spinozana, Tomus III. Heidelberg: Carl Winters Universitätsbuchhandlung).

21. See esp. Ebreo, 1937, *The Philosophy of Love (Dialoghi d'amore)*, trans. F. Freideberg-Seeley and J. H. Barnes, introduction by Cecil Roth, 109–119 (London: Soncino Press).

22. See P. Pozzi, 1990, "L'intendere come 'puro patire' nella *Korte Ver-handeling*," in *Dio, l'uomo, la liberta: Studi sul "Breve Trattato" di Spi-noza*, ed. Filippo Mignini, 235–64 (L'Aquila: Japadre Editore).

23. *The Philosophy of Spinoza*.

24. Emile Lasbax, 1926, *La hiérarchie dans l'univers de Spinoza*, 2d ed. (Paris: Vrin. [First edition, 1910]).

25. Hubert Dethier , "Love and Intellect in Leone Ebreo: The Joys and Pains of Human Passion," in *Neoplatonism and Jewish Thought*, 353–86.

26. Dethier, 362.

27. Dethier, 363.

28. Yovel, 167.

CHAPTER 4

Spinoza's Metaphysical Hebraism

WARREN ZEV HARVEY

Spinoza was not only an accomplished philosopher but also an accomplished Hebraist. It is sometimes said that he was the first modern philosopher. He himself seems to have thought he was the first true Hebrew grammarian. In the following brief comments, I wish to explain in what sense Spinoza seems to have seen himself as the first true Hebrew grammarian, and to raise the question of the relationship between his Hebraism and his metaphysics.

Rabbi Judah Halevi, the great twelfth-century Hebrew poet, wrote in his philosophic dialogue, the *Kuzari*, II 68, that Hebrew has shared the fate of the Jews, "becoming impoverished with their impoverishment, shrinking as they dwindled." We lack words today, he explains, but the biblical authors had ample names for "nations, species of fish, stones," etc.[1] Spinoza makes the same point in the *Theologico-Political Treatise*, Chapter vii, citing the loss of "words for fruits, birds, fishes."[2]

He also makes a related point. The ancient Hebrew speakers, he notes, left no discourses on the principles of Hebrew, "neither dictionary nor grammar nor text-book on rhetoric." Without a thorough knowledge of Hebrew, he insists, we cannot properly understand the Bible.[3] Thus, the problem posed by the shrinkage of Hebrew and the absence of grammars is grave. The obvious remedy would be for someone to write a Hebrew grammar. But how would one go about doing this? How could one retrieve Hebrew? How could one go beyond the limited number of words and phrases that happen to be preserved in the Bible?

In his unfinished *Compendium of the Grammar of the Hebrew Language*, composed toward the end of his life, Spinoza declares: "There are many who have written a grammar of Scripture, but none of the Hebrew language."⁴ Since according to its title his *Compendium* is a grammar of the Hebrew language, Spinoza apparently saw it as being the first true grammar of the Hebrew language, and not merely another grammar of Scripture. Elsewhere in the *Compendium*, he remarks that he will not treat of a certain fine point concerning the cantillation accents (namely, the *ga'ya* preceding a *zarqa*), since it is not relevant for those "who desire to speak Hebrew, not cantillate it."⁵ He evidently wrote the *Compendium* for those who desire to speak Hebrew. Occasionally, he refers to his own experience with spoken Hebrew in the Portuguese Jewish community of Amsterdam. Thus, after giving the forms of the Imperative, he remarks that they are "imperious," and not used in the presence of superiors or equals, but instead "we are accustomed to make use of the future."⁶

He did not imagine he could retrieve lost Hebrew vocabulary (e.g., words for fruits, birds, fishes), but was convinced that he could reconstruct lost grammatical forms by way of analogy. For example, he reconstructs unattested forms of the infinitive (e.g., for *huf'al* verbs), and unhesitatingly asserts: "I have no doubt the Hebrews had . . . all the forms of the infinitive I have mentioned."⁷ In his note in the *Theologico-Political Treatise* on the word *nabiʾ* (prophet), he confidently distinguishes between Hebrew meaning and biblical usage: *nabiʾ* means "translator" in Hebrew, although in the Bible it is always used in the sense of "prophet" (i.e., one who translates God's revelations to the people). He then reconstructs the supposed development of the verb *nbʾ* (to translate), through *nobeb* (cf. Zechariah 9:17), to *nib* or *nub* (e.g., Isaiah 57:13; Proverbs 10:31), basing himself resourcefully on the analogy of *bzʾ* (to divide, cf. Isaiah 18:2, 7), *bzz* (to spoil), and *buz* (to contemn).⁸

His insights into the foundations of Hebrew are bold and fascinating, if often controversial or eccentric. They make a serious contribution to Hebrew philology.⁹ He is aware that many of his insights were unknown to previous grammarians, whom he often criticizes. For example, in setting down one of his distinctive views about Hebrew grammar, he remarks: "Because the grammarians did not notice this, they considered many words to be irregular which according to the usage of the language are most regular, and they were ignorant of many things that are necessary to know for eloquence in the language."¹⁰ Spinoza seems to have believed he was the first person in centuries to understand Hebrew properly.

Spinoza's view of himself as a consummate authority on Hebrew is clearly illustrated in his aforementioned note in the *Theologico-Political Treatise* on the word *nabiʾ*. After endorsing Rashi's interpretation, he rejects that of Rabbi Abraham ibn Ezra, remarking that he "did not know the Hebrew language so exactly." Now, Ibn Ezra, whom Spinoza lauds elsewhere for his pioneering critical approach to the Bible, was not only an exegete and philosopher but also a Hebrew poet and grammarian. Not everyone would feel competent to judge his Hebrew deficient.[11]

Often in the *Theologico-Political Treatise* Spinoza attacks biblical interpretations of previous commentators and defends his own interpretation by an appeal to the rules of Hebrew grammar.[12] In such passages, he proves himself a perceptive exegete and an astute Hebraist.

Not only did he criticize the Hebrew of postbiblical grammarians and commentators, but he even faulted that of the biblical writers. Thus, after observing that the Hebrew verb lacks several tenses and moods found in other languages, he complains:

> Although all the tenses and moods . . . could have been supplied, with ease and even with the greatest elegance, by definite rules deduced from the fundamental principles of the language, the writers of old showed complete disregard for such rules, and indiscriminately used Future for Present and Past, and contrariwise Past for Future, and furthermore used Indicative for Imperative and Subjunctive, to the great detriment of clarity.[13]

In other words, Spinoza thought that he could rewrite the Hebrew Bible so as to improve its elegance and clarity.

Spinoza lets us hear his opinion about the quality of the Hebrew styles of the different prophets, which according to him varies with "the learning and capacity of the prophet." He contrasts the "cultured" Hebrew of Isaiah and Nahum with the "unrefined" Hebrew of Ezekiel and Amos, and suggests a comparison of Isaiah 1:11–20 with Amos 5:21–24. He also suggests comparing Jeremiah 49 with Obadiah, and Isaiah 40:19–20 and 44:8–28 with Hosea 8:6 and 13:2.[14] As he criticized Ibn Ezra, so he criticized Ezekiel, Amos, Obadiah, and Hosea.

Obviously Spinoza had very high standards of Hebrew style. It is unfortunate that we do not have a specimen of his own Hebrew writing.[15]

While the *Compendium* is a technical Hebrew grammar, replete with declensions and conjugations, it has an intriguing metaphysical dimension. Spinoza is concerned to understand the relation of language to the world, or to the speakers' perception of the world. He explains grammatical phenomena by reference to the presumed mentality of the ancient speakers of Hebrew. For example, he explains the causative (*hif'il*) form of the verb as reflecting the Hebrew habit of referring everything to the *causa principale*.[16] He explains the absence of a present tense in Hebrew as reflecting the Hebrews' view that time is a line in which every present point is both the end of the past and the beginning of the future.[17] Grammatical gender is explained by the tendency of all people, but especially the Hebrews, to personify nature.[18] The presence of many homonyms in Hebrew is explained by the fact that the Hebrews were not much bothered by ambiguity.[19]

Moreover, there are striking parallels between what Spinoza writes in his *Compendium* about Hebrew and what he writes in his *Ethics* about God or Nature. The substantive noun (i.e., the proper noun or the common noun) and the infinitive ("a pure unadulterated noun") correspond to *substantia*, adjectives and verbs to *attributa*, participles and adverbs to *modi*. The noun in the *Compendium* plays a role similar to that of God or Nature in the *Ethics*. By a noun (*nomen*) Spinoza understands "a word by which we signify . . . something that falls under the intellect" (*sub intellectum cadit*), that is, things, attributes, modes, relationships, actions. He holds that in Hebrew not only substantive nouns and infinitives, but also adjectives, participles, verbs, adverbs, and even prepositions, are truly genera of the noun. All Hebrew words, according to him, have the force of nouns, "except a few interjections and conjunctions and one or two particles." He was a noun-intoxicated grammarian. Substantive nouns, he explains, name things (*res*); adjectives (or adjectival nouns) name *attributa* of things; and participles (or participial nouns) name *modi* of things.[20] The word *ish* (man) is given as an example of a substantive noun naming a thing; *hakham* (learned) and *gadol* (big) are given as examples of adjectives naming attributes; and *yodea*ᶜ (knowing) and *holekh* (walking) are given as examples of participles naming modes. The examples of the adjectives and the participles recall the divine attributes of *cogitatio* and *extensio*. As for *ish*, it is used in medieval Hebrew philosophic texts to designate the macrocosm.[21] In the *Ethics* there is God as substance, God's attributes, and God's modes; in the *Compendium* there are substantive nouns, nouns naming attributes, and nouns naming modes. It is not surprising to hear that Spinoza had intended to write a Hebrew Grammar in the manner of his *Ethics*, that is, *more geometrico*.[22]

Spinoza's Hebrew Noun of Nouns is the Tetragrammaton (*YHVH*). He explains it in accordance with the ontological interpretation of Ibn Ezra and Maimonides. According to this interpretation, it is derived from the root *hyh* (to be), and refers to pure Being. In Spinoza's words, it designates "a Being who has always existed, exists, and will always exist"; that is, it designates "the absolute essence of God, without reference to created things."[23] In other words, it designates *Deus sive substantia*. How amazing that Spinoza, so critical of medieval philosophic interpretations of Scripture (see *Theologico-Political Treatise*, chapters vii and xv), should unabashedly embrace the most blatant and famous of such interpretations! Now, since he did not believe that the ancient Hebrews had true knowledge of God (see ibid., chapters ii and iii), how could he have imagined that they had a word designating "the absolute essence of God"?[24] He must have thought that there was more philosophical wisdom in the Hebrew language than among the Hebrew speakers. He must have held some potent metaphysical presuppositions about the Hebrew language.[25]

The most conspicuous example of Spinoza's adopting a medieval philosophic interpretation of a Hebrew word appears in the climactic conclusion of the *Ethics*. He affirms there that the Scriptural term "glory" (Hebrew: *kabod*) designates *amor Dei intellectualis* or *beatitudo*. Like his interpretation of the Tetragrammaton, his interpretation of *kabod* is borrowed from Ibn Ezra and Maimonides. Its direct source is Maimonides' exegesis of Isaiah 58:8 in his discussion of the intellectual love of God in *The Guide of the Perplexed*, III 51.[26] Spinoza's statements about *kabod*, no less than about the Tetragrammaton, presuppose that ancient Hebrew somehow contained the highest philosophic truths.

In view of the parallels between the *Compendium* and the *Ethics*, it has often been asked: Is Spinoza's *Compendium* merely his projection of Spinozism onto the Hebrew language?[27] Perhaps it may also be asked with some justification: Is Spinoza's *Ethics* merely his projection of the Hebrew language onto God or Nature?[28]

NOTES

1. Judah Halevi, *Kuzari*, trans. Hartwig Hirschfeld (New York: Schocken, 1964), 124–25. Cf. Abraham ibn Ezra, *Commentary on the Pentateuch*, Genesis 2:11 ("families, provinces, animals, birds, stones"). See Isadore Twersky, *Introduction to Maimonides' Code* (New Haven: Yale University Press, 1980), 325–29.

2. *TTP* vii, 106.20–24. Page and line references to the *TTP* are to G III. Quotations from the *TTP* are based on Samuel Shirley's English translation: *Theological-Political Treatise* (Indianapolis, Ind.: Hackett, 1998).

3. *TTP* vii, 106.16–20. "Bible" includes the New Testament, whose Greek bears the imprint of Hebrew (100.6–7; 110.30–34).

4. *Compendium Grammatices Linguae Hebraeae* vii, 310.10–12. Page and line references to the *Compendium* are to G I. Quotations from the *Compendium* are based on Maurice J. Bloom's English translation: *Hebrew Grammar: A Concise Compendium* (New York: Philosophical Library, 1962); cf. the French translation by Joël Askénazi and Jocelyne Askénazi-Gerson, *Abrégé de grammaire hébraïque* (Paris: Vrin, 1968). Spinoza completed thirty-three chapters of the first part of the *Compendium* (on phonetics, alphabet, morphology); the second part (on syntax) remained unwritten.

5. *Compendium* iv, 300.22–25. Spinoza had originally agreed with Halevi (*Kuzari* II 72, 126) that the cantillation accents express nonverbal

communication (e.g., raising the voice, winking, hand movements), but changed his mind (*Compendium* iv, 294.30–295.20).

6. *Compendium* xiii, 344.30–345.1 (*futurum usurpare solemus*). The custom is preserved in current Israeli Hebrew.

7. *Compendium* xiv, 348.9–10; cf. xii, 341.26–27; xix, 360–361. On Spinoza's analogism, see Ze'ev Levy, "The Problem of Normativity in Spinoza's Hebrew Grammar," *Studia Spinozana* 3 (1987): 390; A.J. Klijnsmit, "The Problem of Normativity Solved," ibid., 4 (1988): 305–14.

8. *TTP* i, 15.6–16, and Note 1, 251. Cf. *Compendium* xxxi, 392.6–12.

9. Jacob Gruntfest, "Spinoza as a Linguist," *Israel Oriental Society* 9 (1979): 103–28, writes that Spinoza's "originality as a language analyst is manifested in his new classification of the parts of speech in Hebrew," which is "unique in the entire history of Semitic philology" (117). Although in his day nothing was known about the development of Semitic languages, Spinoza's "analytic mind and perceptive intuition" enabled him to present a classification that "reveals the special historical development of Hebrew in a concise and schematic matter" (127–28). "[H]e deserves a place of honour in the history of Semitic and general linguistics" (128). Cf. M. Ben-Asher, "Spinoza's *Compendium of Hebrew Grammar*" (in Hebrew), in *Baruch Spinoza*, ed. Z. Levy, M. Strauss, and A. Yassour (Haifa: University of Haifa, 1978), 187–96; A. J. Klijnsmit, "Amsterdam Sephardim and Hebrew Grammar in the Seventeenth Century," *Studia Rosenthaliana* 22 (1988): 144–64; and Isaiah Teshima, "Spinoza's Hebrew Grammar and the Medieval Dispute on the *Sheva*," lecture delivered at the 13th World Congress of Jewish Studies, August 2001.

10. *Compendium* v, 303.4–10. Cf. xvi, 355.17–19: "Most grammarians think . . . But they are mistaken."

11. *TTP* i, Note 1, 251.7–10. See viii, 118.20–120.32.

12. He denounces "the commentators," who "corrupt the language," and cites as an example an old Rabbinic exegesis of II Chronicles 22:2 adopted by Rashi and others, according to which Ahaziah's reign is dated from the beginning of Omri's (*TTP* ix, 134.25–135.1). Regarding II Samuel 6:2, he rejects the reading of Rashi and David Kimhi, arguing that Hebrew does not use the infinitive (*le-ha'alot*) in the sense they require (*TTP* ix, 136.2–8, and Note 19, 258–59). Regarding Numbers 27:19, 23, he remarks that all the commentators he has seen (e.g., Rashi) have not understood that the verb *ṣvh* is used here in the sense of "appoint" (cf. I Samuel 13:14, et al.), not in that of "command." He overlooked Nahmanides' interpretation (*Commentary on the Pentateuch*, Numbers 27:19), which is the same as his, and which also cites I Samuel 13:14 (*TTP* xvii, 208.3–6, and Note 37, 265–266).

13. *TTP* vii, 107.22–32.

14. *TTP* ii, 33.29–34.9; but cf. *Compendium* xxiv, 373.5–10, where Isaiah (19:6) is criticized for using the form *he'eznihu* instead of *hoznehu* or

huznehu. Regarding Isaiah and Ezekiel, see Maimonides, *The Guide of the Perplexed*, trans. Shlomo Pines (Chicago: University of Chicago Press, 1963), III 6, 427 (on BT *Hagigah* 13a). At *Kuzari* II 68, 125, Halevi praises the Hebrew of Psalms, Job, and Isaiah.

15. Richard H. Popkin conjectured that Spinoza was the author of a 1658 Dutch-to-Hebrew translation of Margaret Fell's Quaker tract, *A Loving Salutation*, and marshaled impressive supporting evidence (see Popkin and M. A. Signer, *Spinoza's Earliest Publication?* [Assen: Van Gorcum, 1987]). However, the Hebrew of the translation lacks the grammatical precision we must expect of Spinoza. Nonetheless, if the young Spinoza did have contact with the Quakers, he may have been consulted by the translator. This would explain some features of the translation, such as the use of philosophic terms like *'esem* (lines 52, 50), *hanhagah kelalit* (line 288), and *bilti ba'al takhlit* (lines 97, 681), and allusions to Ibn Ezra's *Commentary on the Pentateuch*, Genesis 3:24 (lines 404–05), Maimonides' *Guide* III 51, 621 (line 549), and Albo's *Book of Principles*, ed. and trans. Isaac Husik (Philadelphia: Jewish Publication Society 1946), IV 40, 393–94 (line 54).

16. *Compendium* xii, 341.18–26. Cf. *TTP* i, 16–17, 23–24; and cf. also Maimonides, *Guide* II 48, 409–12.

17. *Compendium* xiii, 343.11–17. Cf. my "The Term *Hitdabbekut* in Crescas' Definition of Time," *JQR* 71 (1981): 44–45.

18. *Compendium* v, 304.17–21.

19. *Compendium* xi, 336.25–30. Ambiguities caused no confusion among the Hebrews, "as long as their language flourished" (xiii, 344.20–25).

20. See *Compendium* v, 303.3–304.2. Regarding verbs (naming *attributa*) and adverbs (naming *modi*), see Gruntfest, "Spinoza as a Linguist" (above, n. 9), 121–22; cf. Askénazi, Introduction to *Abrégé* (above, n. 4), 24. Spinoza's description of the parts of speech fits Hebrew alone. Not only does it not fit Latin and other European languages, but it does not fit Aramaic, Arabic, and other known Semitic languages; see Gruntfest, 126–27. Since Jacob Bernays, "Über die Grammatik Spinozas," in C. Schaarschmidt, *Des Cartes und Spinoza* (Bonn: Koschny, 1850), 195–203; reprinted in Bernays, *Gesammelte Abhandlungen* (Berlin: Hertz, 1885), vol. ii: 342–50, students of Spinoza's Grammar (e.g., A. Chajes, S. Rubin, J. M. Hillesum, N. Porges, as well as Askénazi, Ben-Asher, Gruntfest, and Klijnsmit) have been engaged by its connection to his metaphysics; but cf. Harry Austryn Wolfson, *The Philosophy of Spinoza* (Cambridge: Harvard University Press, 1934), vol. i: 54–55.

21. *Compendium* v, 303.20–22. Cf. EIP14C2, G I/56 (*rem extensam et rem cogitantem, vel Dei attributa esse, vel affectiones attributorum Dei*). Cf. Klijnsmit, "Amsterdam Sephardim and Hebrew Grammar" (above, n. 9) 161. See Maimonides, *Guide* I 72, 184, in Samuel ibn Tibbon's Hebrew translation: "this whole of being is one *ish*." On Spinoza's view of the

human being as microcosm, see Wolfson, *Spinoza*, vol. ii: 384, s. v. "Microcosm—and macrocosm."

22. Spinoza, *Opera Posthuma* (Amsterdam, 1677), editor's preface.

23. *TTP* ii, 38.21–25; xiii, 155.7–13. See Ibn Ezra, *Commentary on
the Pentateuch*, Exodus 3:14–15; Maimonides, *Guide* I 61–64, 147–57. Cf.
Askénazi, Introduction to *Abrégé*, 25–27.

24. Spinoza repeatedly states that the ancient Hebrews, including the
prophets, had only common (*vulgares*) ideas about God; for example, *TTP*
ii, 37.10–18; iii, 48.2–8; xiv, 173.4–7; xv, 180.23–32. In Epistle 73 (to Oldenburg), G IV/307.8–11, he attributes a metaphysical view of his to "the
ancient Hebrews," but this statement may ultimately be one about the
Hebrew words *maqom* (space, place) and *kol* (all); cf. Wolfson, *Spinoza*,
vol. i: 296–97. It is of course possible that Spinoza believed that *prebiblical*
Hebrews had true ideas about God.

25. Askénazi prefaces his Introduction to Spinoza's Grammar with a
provocative quotation from Rashi (*Commentary on the Pentateuch*, Genesis
2:23): "the world was created in Hebrew" (Introduction to *Abrégé*, 13).
Geneviève Brykman, *La judéité de Spinoza* (Paris: Vrin, 1972), 123, wonders if "for Spinoza Hebrew is not *la langue par excellence*"; that is, the one
that most corresponds to the world and is most fit to express true ideas.

26. EVP36S, G II/303. Compare Maimonides, *Guide* III 51, 628, with
TTP v, 71.13–27 and Note *. See my "The Biblical Term 'Glory' in Spinoza's *Ethics*" (in Hebrew), *Iyyun* 48 (1999): 447–49 (English summary in
49 [2000] 111). Wolfson, *Spinoza*, vol ii: 311–25, cites other pertinent texts.

27. This was in effect the critical opinion of Bernays (above, n. 20);
but cf. Askénazi, Introduction to *Abrégé*, 14.

28. If Spinoza's metaphysics was Hebraic, should he not have written
the *Ethics* in Hebrew? This option was unavailable since his intended audience did not read Hebrew. Jacob Klatzkin, the Hebrew translator of the
Ethics (1924), held that although Spinoza wrote his philosophy in Latin, he
conceived it in Hebrew; see my "Portrait of Spinoza as a Maimonidean,"
Journal of the History of Philosophy 19 (1981): 154–55.

CHAPTER 5

Maimonides, Spinoza, and the Problem of Creation

KENNETH SEESKIN

Although Judaism is committed to belief in one God, it is also committed to the belief that God is separate from everything else. In a nutshell, monotheism is not pantheism.[1] It is not the belief that God is equal to the world but the belief that God stands over and against the world. As Isaiah (45:6) says, everything is as nought before God. Nor is monotheism only a claim about heavenly arithmetic. Belief in a single pagan god like Athena or Poseidon would not be monotheistic. For one deity that resembles other things is one among many. In a monotheistic religion, God is one in a stronger sense—utterly alone and unique.

The usual way to explain God's uniqueness and separation is to invoke creation. If God created heaven and earth, then everything owes its existence to God, while God owes existence to nothing. Thus, Maimonides claims that belief in creation is a "pillar of the Law" (*Guide* III 50)[2] and was regarded as such by Abraham, the pillar of the world:

> However, when the pillar of the world grew up and it became clear to him that there is a separate deity that is neither body nor a force in a body and that all the stars and the spheres were made by Him, and he understood that the fables upon which he was brought up were absurd, he began to refute their doctrine and to show up their opinions as false; he publicly manifested his disagreement with them and called in the name of the Lord, God of the world— both the existence of the deity and the creation of the world in that deity being comprised in that call. (*Guide* III 29)[3]

It is well known that Spinoza rejects the idea of creation in *Ethics* I and seeks to replace it with an eternal universe where will and purpose, as the scholastics understood them, play no part. His rejection is part of his overall strategy of replacing the scholastic world view with a naturalistic theology consistent with the science of his day. I want to examine Spinoza's position in the light of his disagreement with Maimonides and argue that the differences between them are still worth talking about.

GOD AND CREATION IN MAIMONIDES

Let us begin with the idea that creation is the primary way to account for separation. Here Mainonides makes no compromise. "There is," he insists, "absolutely no likeness in any respect whatever between Him and the things created by Him."[4] It follows that the difference between God and creatures is not a matter of degree but of kind: "Everything that can be ascribed to God . . . differs in every respect from our attributes, so that no definition can comprehend the one thing and the other."[5] In another passage, Maimonides goes so far as to say that it is *not* true that God's existence is more durable than ours, God's life more permanent, God's power greater, and God's knowledge more perfect.[6] For to say that it is would imply that there is a measure of comparison between us and God, that it makes sense to rank God's perfection on the same scale as ours. Even words like 'existence', 'unity', 'knowledge', 'life', and 'power' are completely equivocal when applied to us and to God. According to Maimonides, a mustard grain has more in common with the outermost sphere of the universe than we do with God.

So rigorous is Maimonides on this point that he denies any sort of relation between God and other things. Following Aristotle, he argues that relation implies correlation and therefore some degree of mutuality: if x is the father of y, then y is the son of x.[7] Thus relation can join only things of the same species. To use Maimonides' example, one finite intellect can be greater than another, and one color can be darker than another, but there is no possibility of a relation between the intellect and color, because they have nothing in common; nor of a relation between a hundred cubits and the heat of a pepper, nor between clemency and bitterness. All such comparisons are category mistakes. But in Maimonides' opinion, a relation between a necessary being and a contingent one, between creator and creation, is no better.

The problem is that as we normally understand it, causality is a relation. Echoing the standard view of the time, Maimonides writes (*Guide* II 22):[8] "there subsists necessarily a certain conformity between the cause and its effect."[9] Behind this remark is the view that causality is best understood as the transmission of an attribute from the cause *to* the effect, from fire, say, to an iron bar. The cause, in other words, establishes itself in the effect, from which it follows that the effect must bear some trace or reflection of the cause. But this is exactly what Maimonides denies between God and the world, since God, in his view, is utterly unique. The result is that whatever creation is, it cannot be a connection in which an attribute is passed from one thing to another.[10] If creation is ex nihilo, there is nothing for an attribute to be passed to.

To see this point in another way, one need only realize that causality presupposes temporal succession: The attribute is in *a* and gets passed to *b*. According to Mainonides, time is not absolute: it is an accident dependent on motion (*Guide* II 13).[11] It follows that if motion is created, time must be created as well. If time is created, it is impossible for creation to take place *in* time as a process with a beginning, middle, and end.[12] In Maimonides' words (*Guide* II 13): "God's bringing the world into existence does not have a temporal beginning, for time is one of the created things."[13] Rather than a temporal process, creation is an instantaneous act.

Without temporal succession or similarity between creator and creation, any analogy between God's bringing the world into existence and fire passing heat to an iron bar fails. In Kantian terms, the principle of causality has meaning and application only with reference to the sensible world. So any attempt to reach beyond the sensible world with causal reasoning constitutes a misuse of reason.

What then is creation? One does not have to read very far in medieval philosophy to see that any number of suggestions were put forward. Some thought that God created the world from preexistent matter, as a potter shapes clay; some, that God created the world out of the divine substance; some, that the world emanated from God in a manner the medievals attributed to Aristotle but that actually derives from Plotinus; some, that creation is completely ex nihilo. Unfortunately, Scripture is of little help. For the word for creation in Genesis 1: 1 (*bara*) applies only to God's creation of the world, not to the human creation of artifacts. The obvious implication is that we cannot rely on our everyday experience to form a conception of God's act of creation. As Genevieve Brykman observed, the absoluteness and totality of the act of creation have the effect of mystifying it. It is as if creation is the work of God and we, its beneficiaries, have no hope of grasping its nature. Not surprisingly the Rabbis regarded creation as an esoteric topic, not to be discussed in public.[14]

A good way to approach Maimonides' discussion of creation is to see it as a corrective to some of the sloppy thinking of his time. As he indicates (*Guide* I 71),[15] philosophers have been discussing creation for three thousand years and have still not reached a resolution. He castigates the Mutakallimun for confusing demonstration with dialectical or sophistic argument.[16]

Although he himself makes use of their arguments, he frequently warns the reader that his task is not to prove that creation occurred but to show that it is possible, or reasonable as an object of belief.[17] The simple truth is that the issue of creation is too speculative for anyone to reach a definitive conclusion.

Thus Maimonides argues that we cannot use our knowledge of the world as it is at present to infer anything about its origin. According to *Guide* II 17[18]:

> No inference can be drawn in any respect from the nature of a thing after it has been generated, has attained its final state, and has achieved stability in its most perfect state, to the state of that thing while it moved toward being generated.

In other words, we cannot look to the production of artifacts or to animal or vegetable reproduction to furnish a model for how God created the world. Nor can we use the argument that because everything that is generated has a material cause, creation has a material cause. While everything in nature proceeds from and eventually passes into prime matter, Maimonides argues that there is no reason to suppose that prime matter is a factor in creation.[19] On the contrary, there is good reason to suppose that it too is created from nothing.

Similar doubts apply to the theory of emanation. According to this view, the emergence of the world from God is a necessary and eternal process grounded in divine thought: God is engaged in perfect self-conscious reflection and generates the first intelligence. The first intelligence thinks about itself and God and generates the outermost sphere of the cosmos and the second intelligence. The second intelligence thinks about God and the first intelligence and generates another sphere and another intelligence. The process is repeated until we reach the Active Intellect, which is the last intelligence in the heavenly realm. From there the forms of the sublunary realm are generated and with them, human intelligence.

Overall the theory of emanation sought to explain how a complex material world can emerge from a simple and immaterial God through a series of intermediaries. But Maimonides objects that it is a failure. Underlying his objection is an assumption that he claims (*Guide* II 22)[20] is accepted by Aristotle and "all who have philosophized"—that it is impossible for anything but a single simple thing to proceed from a single simple thing.[21] It may be reasonable to suppose that a simple intelligence should proceed from God or that one intelligence should proceed from another intelligence. But even with a thousand intermediaries we would still wind up with something simple. How, then, can a sphere, which is a composite of matter and form and contains a star that is also a composite, proceed from God or any of the heavenly intelligences?

In short, there is no causal process to explain the emergence of a complex world from a radically simple God. While emanation is superior to mechanical causation in that it does not require physical contact between cause and effect, it breaks down because it too presupposes a basic similarity between them.[22] With his usual disdain for the imagination, Maimonides warns the reader not to try to think about creation in visual images. As Lenn Goodman once argued, we must put Cecil B. deMille movies and Nova broadcasts completely out of our mind.[23]

Why should a person believe in creation at all? Aside from religious reasons—the prophets proclaim it and the Law presupposes it—Maimonides' main defense is to invoke the particularity argument of the Mutakallimun. If the world were eternal and proceeded from God by a necessary causal process, we would expect the motion of the heavenly bodies to be regular and uniform. Each sphere would impart motion to a smaller sphere, which means that all heavenly bodies would move in the same direction, with the furthest ones moving faster than the closer ones. But observation does not confirm this expectation. Thus *Guide* II 19:

> For we see that in the case of some spheres, the swifter motion is above the slower; that in the case of others, the slower motion is above the swifter; and that, again in another case, the motions of the spheres are of equal velocity though one be above the other.[24]

In effect the argument from particularity asks why we have this arrangement of things rather than a more orderly one. The crux of the argument is that there is no available scientific answer and little likelihood of finding one.

Maimonides' response is that the motion of the heavenly bodies is consistent with a will that created them for a purpose but not with a necessary causal process.[25] Behind this claim is the assumption that there is a distinction between an act of will and the content willed in the act.[26] Thus a simple being can will complexity and remain simple; an immutable being can will change and remain immutable. If, for example, God wills from all eternity that one thing will happen today and a different thing tomorrow, in Maimonides' opinion, this does not imply a change in God's essence.[27] So, unlike causality, acts of volition do not imply any similarity between the agent and what it produces. Volition can offer a better way to understand the emergence of complexity and particularity.

Yet here too there is a qualification: while God had a purpose in making a certain number of heavenly bodies and having them move in particular ways, Maimonides insists we cannot understand that purpose. According to *Guide* II 19[28]: "For we say that there is a being that particularized, just as it willed, every sphere in regard to this motion and rapidity; but we do not know in what respect there is wisdom in making these things exist in this fashion." The idea is that while the motion of the heavenly bodies appears to be regular in the sense that we have a good idea where Mars or Jupiter are going to be, from Maimonides' standpoint, the regularity cannot be adequately explained by scientific principles. To say that the heavens reflect will and purpose is to say that their order and arrangement could be different from the one we observe. In the absence of a scientific explanation, Maimonides thinks, there is no reason to suppose otherwise.

Again it should be emphasized that Maimonides does not regard this argument as a demonstration. Since it is based on our inability to understand why the heavenly bodies behave as they do, it can do nothing more than tip the scales in the direction of creation. Although he admits (*Guide* II 24)[29] that it is possible that someone may find a scientific explanation for what seems obscure to him, it is safe to say that he did not consider this very likely. On the preceding page, he claims that "regarding all that is in the heavens, man grasps nothing but a small measure of what is mathematical. . . ."[30] In fact Maimonides is so skeptical of astronomy that he opts for an instrumentalist view, according to which the goal of astronomy is not to say what is really happening but merely to save the phenomena. Even Aristotle, in Maimonides' opinion, had to rely on guesswork.

Where does this leave us? Maimonides' theology is based on the conviction that while we know *that* God is, we will never be in a position to know *what* God is.[31] In many ways, his view of creation is similar: although we have grounds for believing *that* creation occurred, we will never be in a position to say *how*. In fact most of what we know about creation is negative: it does not resemble a causal process, it does not take place in time, it does not require a material cause, it cannot be explained by emanation, and nothing is gained by trying to represent it with visual images. The best we can do is to say that it is an instantaneous act undertaken by a unique agent.

We should keep in mind, however, that since the essence or defining characteristics of the Creator are beyond our comprehension, we cannot say much about how the Creator confers existence on something while remaining completely separate from it. The *how* of creation remains a mystery. In connection with the Book of Job, Maimonides tells us: "The purpose of all these things is to show that our intellects do not reach the point of apprehending how these natural things that exist in the world of generation and corruption are produced. . . ."[32] Based on his repeated warnings against pressing human reason beyond its limits, one gets the impression that we would be better off leaving the *how* of creation alone.

As for the *that* of creation, Maimonides asserts two things: (1) creation is possible, and (2) the Law presupposes it. By the latter he means that if God can act spontaneously in bringing us into existence, it makes sense to suppose that God is free to offer commandments and grant redemption. Thus the appropriate response to creation is not to try to puzzle out the details of how it all happens but to feel gratitude in the face of a cosmic mystery: the fact that we are here at all. Since the prescribed way to express this gratitude is by Sabbath observance, it is hardly surprising that Maimonides maintains that Sabbath observance and the prohibition against idolatry are each equivalent to the sum total of all the other commandments.[33]

My reading of Maimonides' views is complicated by the fact that he wrote in an esoteric fashion designed to hide his intentions behind a trail of hints and clues. The extent of his esotericism has been debated from the moment the *Guide* appeared. Some, like Samuel ibn Tibbon and Moses of Narbonne, maintained that the argument from particularity is not convincing, so that given the naturalistic tone of the rest of Maimonides' philosophy, he either was or should have been a proponent of eternity.[34] In modern times, this view has been put forward by Isaac Husik,[35] Shlomo Pines,[36] and Zev Harvey.[37] Husik, to take one example, objects that if the Aristotelians have no explanation for the order and arrangement of the heavenly bodies, Maimonides, who invokes the will of God, does not have one either. To people who think the *Guide* is deeply esoteric, this is exactly what Maimonides wanted us to see. In other words, he wanted us to see the emptiness of necessity. I do not accept this interpretation. But, if true, it would make Maimonides a forerunner of Spinoza rather than an opponent.

Still we should not lose sight of the fact that others, like Albo[38] and Abravanel,[39] claimed that Maimonides' arguments for creation were convincing and reaffirmed that belief in creation ex nihilo is a central dogma of Judaism. At *Guide* II 13, Maimonides *says* that he is committed to a creation that is both ex nihilo and de novo. But, under the circumstances, what he says and what he means could be very different. I have argued in another context that Maimonides' esotericism has been overemphasized and that when one takes into account the difficulty of the issues and the need to discuss them in a dialectical fashion, one will see that his exposition is as clear as it can be.[40] But the fact remains that the proper way to read Maimonides on the subject of creation has been a central topic in Jewish philosophy for centuries.

SPINOZA'S CRITICISM

Enter Spinoza. With the arrival of modern science, the argument from particularity collapsed and with it the idea that astronomy would never achieve the status of a rigorous science. Since Maimonides himself allowed for such a possibility, Spinoza could feel perfectly justified in seeing Maimonides' appeal to voluntarism as an argument from ignorance, an attempt to have will and purpose do a job that can only be done by adequately understood cause and effect. We saw that even some of Maimonides' contemporaries criticized the argument, and they were still operating in a geocentric universe. But Spinoza's criticism runs deeper. If, as Maimonides asserts, God has nothing in common with the world, then it is impossible for the world to be understood *through* God. If it cannot be understood through God, then, according to *Ethics* IP3, God cannot be its cause.

In one respect, Maimonides would agree. We saw that creation is not a causal connection and does not link the world to God in a way that heat links an iron bar to fire. But when it comes to what creation is and how it does link God to the world, Maimonides can say only that creation is a unique act whose details are beyond our comprehension. Since principles that apply to the world as it is at present have no bearing on creation, all we can say is that there is nothing contradictory in supposing that God created the world ex nihilo. If there is nothing contradictory, there is no rational barrier to accepting it. Spinoza's objection is that once again Maimonides substitutes a form of unknowing for an adequate understanding. Unless the divine nature serves as a cause from which to infer an effect, it adds nothing to our understanding of the world. If it adds nothing to our understanding of the world, there is no rational basis for accepting it.

Students of Kant will see in Maimondes' account of creation the outline of Kant's defense of the freedom of the moral subject. According to Kant, we do not—indeed cannot—understand freedom; all we can know about freedom is that it is a presupposition of moral action and then allow for the possibility of its being thought.[41] Reason, as he goes on to say in the *Groundwork of the Metaphysic of Morals*[42] would overstep its bounds if it undertook to say how freedom is possible, for we cannot explain something unless we can subsume it under laws given in a possible experience. Since freedom cannot be subsumed under laws of this type, all such explanations fail. But reason would also overstep its bounds if it were to say that because freedom cannot be subsumed under natural laws, it cannot be thought and therefore cannot be presupposed. Thus the primary strategy for defending freedom is negative: show that the arguments of those who oppose it are defective.

Spinoza's reply is that we cannot think something unless we have a clear idea of what it is. Appeals to volition only complicate the issue by dragging in the confused notions of the will that were promulgated in the scholastic tradition. The question remains: What is meant by calling God the creator of the world? Either the world and God have something in common, in which case God is the cause of the world, or they do not, in which case it is possible to understand the world without referring to God at all. If the former option destroys God's transcendence, the latter empties the idea of God of any explanatory power.

Maimonides' reply to Spinoza would be to accept a version of the second horn of the dilemma and proclaim it an honest assessment of the human condition. Since Maimonides offers several versions of the cosmological argument, he must believe that the idea of God explains something. In brief God is needed to explain the motion of the spheres and the existence of contingent beings. The first of these considerations is patterned on Aristotle's account of the prime mover and seeks to show that only an incorporeal being separate from the outermost sphere of the cosmos can account for the continual rotation of the heavenly bodies. The crux of the argument is the assumption that anything corporeal is finite and therefore cannot be the source of eternal motion. The second argument holds that if all beings were contingent, eventually everything would perish and nothing would exist. If nothing exists, nothing can be generated, and the universe would not exist. Both arguments have obvious parallels in Aquinas.

But, in keeping with the rigors of negative theology, Maimonides formulates the conclusions of his argument as a string of denials. The argument from eternal motion establishes the existence of a being that is immobile, atemporal, indivisible, unchangeable, and separate from the thing whose motion it explains.[43] The argument from necessity establishes the existence of a being who is necessary in the sense of being uncaused, incomposite, and neither a body nor a force in a body.[44] The problem is the transition from God to the world: How can the idea of an immobile, atemporal, indivisible, being help us understand motion from place to place? How can the idea of an immaterial being help us understand the existence of a material world?

If any version of the cosmological argument works, it must be the case that the world is conceived through God. Maimonides argues that we know that eternal motion cannot be caused by a corporeal being and that contingent beings must eventually perish. But our understanding of the emergence of eternal motion or contingent being is severely limited. Just as emanation theorists cannot explain how we get from a simple God to a complex world, Maimonides cannot explain how we get from a God beyond human comprehension to a world within it.

According to Wolfson, Spinoza faces a similar problem.[45] If God is infinite and eternal, and if, as Spinoza insists, the cause must resemble the effect, how is it possible that an infinite and eternal God can be the cause of finite modes? According to EIP28, a finite mode can be determined to exist and to act only by another finite mode; thus everything that follows from the absolute nature of an attribute of God is infinite and eternal. On Wolfson's interpretation, Spinoza can say only that God is the proximate cause of the infinite modes that follow immediately from the divine nature and the remote cause of finite modes. While there may be an infinite succession of finite modes, we still face the question of how finitude arises.

If Wolfson is right, Spinoza is in the same predicament as the emanation theorists, because he tries to get from an infinite cause to a finite effect by appealing to a series of intermediaries. But if intermediaries do not work in one case, why should they work in another? If an infinite cause can never produce a finite effect, how can the introduction of additional causes solve the problem? We may ask whether Maimonides' appeal to creation 'ex nihilo' is any worse an explanation of finitude than Spinoza's, or whether either thinker has an explanation of finitude at all.

Maimonides argues that our experience of the world gives us reason to believe in the existence of a being who brings finite things into existence but remains separate from them. When asked to say what that being is, he typically takes refuge in skepticism:

> Glory then to Him who is such that when the intellects contemplate His essence, their apprehension turns into incapacity; and when they contemplate the proceeding of His actions from His will, their knowledge turns into ignorance; and when their tongues aspire to magnify Him by means of attributive qualifications, all eloquence turns to weariness and incapacity! (*Guide* I 58)[46]

Not only does Maimonides believe this, he considers it the height of piety. So there is no possibility of a geometric method explaining the nature of God in a precise way. Nor is there any possibility of moving from an understanding of what God is to an understanding of how God acts.

Told that his position results in a sizable loss of explanatory power, Maimonides would say that this result is inevitable, given that God cannot be defined and that creation has no correlate in human experience. In fact the very relevance of experience is questionable, since creation is not a spatial or temporal phenomenon. Why, then, should we expect to understand it? From Spinoza's perspective, all Maimonides has done is take a vice—ignorance—and turn it into a virtue, indeed, the ultimate virtue. Thus Maimonides (*Guide* I 59)[47] claims that Moses was the wisest of humankind because, more than anyone else, he realized that we can approach God only through negation. But the idea that an unknowable God created a world in an unknown fashion and endowed it with an unknown purpose is what Spinoza terms "the sanctuary of ignorance." The pursuit of knowledge cannot tolerate miracles or mysteries. The problem with creation is not so much that it is false as that it is empty.

Once the idea of creation is undermined, so too is the idea of a God separate from the world. Where Maimonides insists that God has no positive attributes and cannot be defined, Spinoza (EIIP47) counters that: "God's infinite essence and his eternity are known to all." There is, as Richard

Mason points out, no possibility of esotericism in Spinoza.[48] Even more controversial is Spinoza's claim that one way in which God's essence or perfection manifests itself is through the attribute of extension. Still under the sway of Neoplatonism, Maimonides saw matter as filthy, disloyal, and the root cause of ignorance and disobediance. Like most of his contemporaries, he assumes that everything extended must be finite and divisible.[49] As Spinoza (EIP15) rightly says: "they think that corporeal substance, insofar as it is substance, is made up of parts, and so they deny that it can be infinite, and consequently that it can pertain to God." Once again Spinoza (EIP13) argues that this assumption is false, that God, though extended, is infinite and indivisible. His argument takes us back to the similarity between cause and effect. Since extension expresses some degree of reality, we have to account for it. If it were not an attribute of God, there would be no way to explain how it was produced by God and thus no way to account for an obvious feature of experience.[50]

Spinoza contends (EIP18) that God is not only a cause but the immanent or indwelling cause of all things. The separation of things from God is a metaphysical absurdity. From Maimonides' perspective, Spinoza's alternative is not as clean as it appears because the distinction between proximate and remote causes introduces a degree of separation, even if Spinoza does not want to call it that. What is more, the price Spinoza pays for making God a cause at all is that the God of Scripture, the God who hid the divine face from Moses (Ex. 33), completely disappears. From Spinoza's perspective, it is questionable whether anything significant has been lost. For if this idea of God lacks explanatory power, there is little reason to hold on to it.

AFTERMATH

Although modern science destroyed the argument from particularity, in our time science provides ample reason to doubt that the world is eternal. To be sure, the idea of a cosmic explosion ten to twelve billion years ago is a long way from Maimonides' suggestion that God created the world with will and purpose. But the problem of inferring something about origins based on a knowledge of present conditions remains the same. Can we extrapolate from visible phenomena to a point with infinite temperature, pressure, and density without causing significant changes in categories like space, time, and causality? Or more radically: Do these categories even make sense when we are talking about a time zero 'prior' to the explosion that set everything in motion?[51] In a recent publication, Steven Weinberg cites Maimonides and goes on to say: "I am not trying here to argue that the universe undoubtedly has some finite age, only that it is not possible to say on the basis of pure thought that it does not."[52] In a word, a finite beginning is thinkable. A follower of Spinoza would no doubt reply that even if it is thinkable, the big bang of modern physics is not the mystification proposed by Maimonides, not a 'something I know not what' but a theoretical possibility based on clearly defined concepts and a considerable degree of explanatory power.

I invoke modern cosmology not to argue that it solves the problem for us but to suggest that despite the resources at our disposal the dispute between Maimonides and Spinoza is still alive. Both thinkers accepted the transmission theory of causality. Both were rationalists who called attention to what they regarded as misuses of reason. But what one thinker sees as a misuse the other sees as a model of restraint. Are we justified in appropriating an idea much of whose content we cannot understand? There is an obvious respect in which the answer is no. Why clutter our conceptual landscape with empty boxes? But suppose we can offer a systematic explanation for why we cannot understand it, why no experience we can have will allow us to answer the questions we have posed. Suppose, in other words, that there are reasons for saying that natural causation does not set the limits for what is rational to believe. What then?

As noted above, Kant sides with Maimonides. He agrees that creation has no sensuous manifestation and can be considered a causal connection only by analogy.[53] He also agrees that to give up the idea of a creating God would be tantamount to giving up theology altogether.[54] His solution is to say that God is the creator of things only to the extent that they are regarded as noumena. In this way, his position amounts to the claim that one supersensible being is responsible for the existence of other supersensible beings in a manner that is unknown and unknowable. In Kant's terms, creation has no theoretical employment; if it has any relevance to science, it is strictly as a regulative idea.

The mention of noumena and phenomena tells us everything we need to know about the price Kant paid for his acceptance of creation. For Kant too has to concede a sizable loss in explanatory power. One can easily imagine Spinoza repeating his "sanctuary of ignorance" criticism. In the end, people cling to creation because without it, we may have a necessary being, a being with infinite attributes, even a being who inspires love; but, in the eyes of traditional theists, we do not have God. We do not have a being we can praise for the fact that we are here. Creation, in other words, is the primary way traditional theists think about God. It establishes God's dominion over the world, where all things owe existence to God. Since we have no absolute right to this gift of existence, we have grounds for viewing the God who gives it as merciful or generous. With mercy and graciousness, we get the foundation of an entire theology. It follows that once the opening sequence of Genesis is accepted, even as a mystification, the rest of traditional theism becomes a form of commentary. To Spinoza commentary on a mystification is still mystifying.

NOTES

1. Cf. Hermann Cohen, *Religion of Reason out of the Sources of Judaism*, transl. Simon Kaplan (1972; reprint, Atlanta: Scholars Press, 1995), 44–45. Although Cohen links Spinoza with pantheism, Richard Mason, *The God of Spinoza* (Cambridge: Cambridge University Press, 1997), 31–32, does a good job in explaining why this characterization cannot be true. Mason's position is derived from Alan Donagan, *Spinoza* (New York: Harvester Wheatsheaf, 1998), 90.

2. All quotations from *the Guide of the Perplexed* are taken from the Pines translation published by the University of Chicago Press. For "creation of the world in time," I suggest we substitute "creation *de novo* [*huduth*]." For the importance of creation, also see *Guide* II 25, 328–29; III 32, 531; III 50, 613.

3. Pines, 516.

4. *Guide* I 35, Pines, 80.

5. *Guide* I 35, Pines, 80.

6. *Guide* I 56, Pines, 130.

7. See Aristotle, *Categories* VII 3.

8. Pines, 317.

9. Cf. Aquinas, *Summa Theologica* 1, IV 2.

10. Maimonides does say that God is the efficient cause of the world at *Guide* I 69, Pines 176–77. But clearly this is a context where he is speaking loosely. What he says is that he does not *disagree* with those philosophers who hold that God is an efficient, formal, and final cause. But sensing that this admission might lead to a misunderstanding, he goes on to affirm that there is no analogy between God's causality and the causality of things endowed with matter. In fact the whole discussion of I 69 is described as provisional.

11. Pines, 281.

12. That is why Pines' translation of *huduth* as "creation in time" is highly misleading. A better translation would be "creation *de novo*." See Note 2 above.

13. Pines, 282.

14. *Hagigah* 11b, 13a.

15. Pines, 180.

16. *Guide* I 74, Pines, 180.

17. See, for example, *Guide* II 17, Pines, 298.

18. Pines, 295.

19. *Guide* II 17, Pines, 296-97.

20. Pines, 317.

21. For further discussion of this argument, see Arthur Hyman, "From What Is One and Simple Only What Is One and Simple Can Come to Be," in *Neoplatonism and Jewish Thought,* ed. Lenn Goodman(Albany: State University of New York Press, 1992), 111–35. Note, however, that on the basis of *Guide* II 12, Harry A. Wolfson, *The Philosophy of Spinoza* (1934; reprint, New York: Schocken Books, 1961), 1: 88–89 attributes the theory of emanation to Maimonides. Although it is true that Maimonides praises the theory in this chapter, his criticism of the theory at *Guide* II 22 indicates that he accepts it to explain human knowledge and prophetic awareness but not to explain creation.

22. On this point, see Plotinus, *Enneads* 5 I 7 and 5 II 1.

23. Lenn Goodman, *God of Abraham* (New York: Oxford University Press, 1996), 238.

24. Pines, 307.

25. Although Spinoza talks about God's decrees (e.g., EIP33), it is clear that God cannot decree something in Maimonides' sense; that is, God cannot act for a purpose. When Spinoza speaks of the "laws of his own nature" (EIP17), he clearly means some kind of necessity. On the question of the laws of nature in Maimonides and Spinoza's attempt to break with Maimonides, see David R. Lachtermann, "Laying Down the Law: The Theological-Political Matrix of Spinoza's Physics," in *Leo Strauss's Thought,* ed. Alan Udoff (Boulder and London: Lynn Rienner Publishers, 1991), 138–41.

26. This seems to be the point Maimonides is making at *Guide* II 28, 300–01, when he says that willing one thing now and a different thing later does not imply a change in the essence of the will. Or, as Aquinas (*Summa Theologica* 1 XIX 7) puts it, to will change is not the same as changing the will. For further discussion, see Kathryn Tanner, *God and Creation in Christian Theology* (Oxford: Basil Blackwell, 1988), 72–79.

27. Pines, 308.

28. Pines, 327.

29. *Guide* II 18, Pines, 301.

30. For more on Maimonides' views on astronomy, see Menachem Kellner, "On the Status of Astronomy and Physics in Maimonides' *Mishneh Torah* and *Guide of the Perplexed,*" *British Journal for the History of Philosophy* 24 (1991): 453–63.

31. On this point, see *Guide* I 52, 115, where Maimonides takes it as a given that God cannot be defined. Also see *Guide* I 58.

32. *Guide* III 23, 496.

33. *Mishneh Torah* 3, Laws of Sabbath Observance, XXX 15.

34. For discussion of Ibn Tibbon, see Aviezer Ravitzky, "Samuel ibn Tibbon and the Esoteric Character of the *Guide of the Perplexed*," *AJS Review* 6 (1981): 87–123, as well as Idit Dobbs-Weinstein, "The Maimonidean Controversy," in *History of Jewish Philosophy*, ed. Daniel H. Frank and Oliver Leaman, (London: Routledge, 1997), 342–43. For Moses of Narbonne, see M. Hayoun, "L'Epitre du libre-arbtre de Moise de Narbonne," *Revue des Etudes Juives* 141 (1982): 139–67, as well as *La Philosophie et la theologie de Moise de Narbonne* (Tübingen: Mohr, 1989), esp. 139.

35. Isaac Husik, *A History of Medieval Jewish Philosophy* (1916; reprint New York: Anthenum, 1976), 275.

36. Shlomo Pines, "Translator's Introduction," *The Guide of the Perplexed* (Chicago: University of Chicago Press, 1963), cxxviii–cxxix.

37. Warren Zev Harvey, "A Portrait of Spinoza as a Maimonidean," *Journal of the History of Philosophy* 20 (1981): 151–72, as well as "A Third Approach to Maimonides' Cosmology-Prophetology Puzzle," in *Maimonides: a collection of Critical Essays*, ed. Joseph Buijs (University of Notre Dame Press, 1988) 71-81.

38. J. Albo, *Sefer ha-Iqqarim: Book of Roots*, ed. and transl. Isaac Husik (Jewish Publication Society, 1946), 1: 117. For a recent discussion of Abravanel's position, see Seymour Feldman, "Abravanel on Maimonides' Critique of the Kalam Arguments for Creation," *Maimonidean Studies* 1 XIX: 15–25.

39. Abravanel, *Principles of Faith (Rosh Amanah)*, transl. Menachem Kellner (Rutherford, N.J.: Associated University Presses, 1982), 34–36.

40. See Kenneth Seeskin, *Searching for a Distant God* (New York: Oxford University Press, 2000), 177–88.

41. Kant, *Critique of Pure Reason*, B xxix.

42. Kant, *Groundwork for a Metaphysic of Morals*, 458–59.

43. *Guide* II 1, 246.

44. *Guide* II 1, 248.

45. Wolfson, *Spinoza*, 1: 388–92.

46. Pines, 137.

47. Pines, 137–38.

48. Mason, *God of Spinoza*, 3.

49. See the introduction to Part Two of the *Guide*, premises 1 and 22.

50. For the historical background to this argument, see E. M. Curley, *Behind the Geometrical Method* (Princeton, N.J.: Princeton University Press, 1988), 25–27.

51. On this issue, see Alan H. Guth, *The Inflationary Universe* (Reading, Mass.: Addison-Wesley Publishing Co., 1997), 86–87: "If one continues

the extrapolation backwards in time, one comes to a point of infinite density, infinite pressure, and infinite temperature—the instant of the big bang explosion itself, the time that in the laconic language of cosmologists is usually called '$t = 0$.' It is also frequently called a *singularity*, a mathematical word that refers to the infinite values of the density, pressure, and temperature. It is often said—in both popular-level books and textbooks—that this singularity marks the beginning of the universe, the beginning of time itself. Perhaps this is so, but any honest cosmologist would admit that our knowledge here is very shaky. The extrapolation to arbitrarily high temperatures takes us far beyond the physics that we understand, so there is no good reason to trust it. The true history of the universe, going back to '$t = 0$,' remains a mystery that we are probably still far from unraveling."

52. Steven Weinberg, *Dreams of a Final Theory* (New York: Pantheon, 1992), 174.

53. Kant, *Critique of Practical Reason*, 102–03.

54. Kant, *Critique of Practical Reason*, 100.

CHAPTER 6

"That Hebrew Word"

Spinoza and the Concept of the Shekhinah

WARREN MONTAG

Beginning in 1666, the consistory of the Reformed Church of Amsterdam, a body of Church elders whose task it was to safeguard the morals of the community and to watch for signs of the heresy and atheism that, it was feared, were everywhere to be found in the too tolerant city, directed its attention to a group of thinkers inspired, if not directed, by Spinoza. Church records reveal that on June 10, 1666, the clergyman Pieter Leupen reported to the consistory that brothers Johannes and Adriaan Koerbagh, the latter of whom was one of Spinoza's closest friends, had expressed to him "very heretical and unhealthy opinions"[1] concerning certain key articles of faith. Nor were the transgressions limited to matters of belief: Adriaan not only regarded the sacrament of marriage as a form of superstition but lived his belief fully, producing a child out of wedlock and acknowledging the child as his own without the slightest sign of remorse or repentance. For reasons that are not entirely clear, Johannes alone was summoned before the consistory and questioned about his beliefs. Whether from prudence or lack of conviction, he allowed his interrogators to persuade him that perhaps some of his opinions were wrong and that he would be well served to return home and reconsider them.

Within a year, however, the consistory received information from unnamed sources that Johannes Koerbagh continued to hold "defamatory" opinions about, among other things, the Holy Scripture, and that he had publicly defended "pernicious and abominable theses."[2] Although the consistory demanded that the municipal authorities take action to safeguard "the honor of God, his church and state,"[3] nothing was done. Even when

131

Adriaan Koerbagh's scandalous *Bloemhof*[4] (or *Flower Garden*) appeared in February 1668, the authorities deemed it imprudent to arrest the author, fearing certain unspecified "inconveniences." The *Bloemhof* is an extraordinary and thoroughly Spinozist work. Nominally, it is a list of philosophical and theological terms in the Dutch language aiming to establish a native vocabulary in place of the foreign terms that dominated earlier speculative writing. In fact, it is nothing less than a treatise on how to translate supernatural notions into the language of nature and to rethink the transcendent as the immanent. Koerbagh thus practices the form of critique that Spinoza used so effectively, a critique that operates through translation and substitution rather than through direct confrontation. At the beginning of chapter iii of the *TTP*, a work that was certainly in progress, if not complete by the time of the *Bloemhof*'s publication, Spinoza, for example, explains that by the phrase "God's direction" he means "the fixed and immutable order of nature" and by "God's help," "whatever man—who is also part of nature acquires for himself to help to preserve his own being."[5] In a similar way, Koerbagh, who insists on reading the Old Testament in Hebrew, informs us that "Jehovah" signifies in the original "that which is, or Being."[6]

Undeterred by the outcry that greeted the *Bloemhof*, Adriaan Koerbagh rapidly produced another book, *Een Ligt, schynende in Duystere Plaatsen* (*A Light Shining in Dark Places*). The new work was even more outspokenly heretical in its treatment of such central notions of the Christian faith as the Trinity, Jesus, Heaven, and Hell. The printer to whom he entrusted the manuscript, located in Utrecht, was so alarmed and offended by its matter, that he ceased work midway through the book, refused to finish the text and promptly reported the contents to the city bailiff, who in turn relayed the charges to his counterpart in Amsterdam. Initially, both the consistory and the municipal authorities believed Johannes to be the author of both texts. For how, they wondered, could Adriaan, a jurist and physician, have mastered Hebrew? When it was determined that Adriaan was indeed the author of the two treatises, an order was issued for his arrest. On July 17, 1668, he was arrested in Leyden and conveyed in shackles to Amsterdam.

Three days later his interrogation began, undertaken by a group of municipal council members, together with the Grand Bailiff of Amsterdam. They had before them several copies of the *Bloemhof* as well as a copy, half in print, half in manuscript, of *Een Ligt*.[7] The interrogation was carefully recorded in its entirety[8] and published with a few omissions both in the original Dutch and in German translation by Jacob Freudenthal in his *Die Lebensgeschicte Spinozas*. Insistently the questioners keep returning to Spinoza. Did Spinoza help write Koerbagh's books? Did Spinoza share his opinions? Koerbagh, while admitting that he frequented Spinoza's company and discussed many things with him, steadfastly maintained that the opinions in his book were his alone. The interrogators were not satisfied. A passage from page 664 of the *Bloemhof* was read to him. It states that the notion of the immaculate conception of the Savior Jesus contradicts both Scripture and nature. The question, already asked many times, was repeated in an even more pointed form: Did Koerbagh not speak to Spinoza about this matter? The answer: No.

Why were the municipal councilmen so interested in Spinoza? He had published nothing and had engaged in no public expression in word or deed that threatened Church or state. The record of Koerbagh's interrogation suggests some interesting possibilities: "Question: did he understand Hebrew? Response: only with the help of a dictionary. Question: what was the meaning of the Hebrew word *Schabinot*? Response: I do not know and must look it up in Buxtorf's Lexicon." Whatever relations he may have had with others, Koerbagh "affirms never to have spoken of this doctrine with Spinoza."[9]

There is much that is curious about these few elliptical lines. First, it is clear that the interrogators' concern with the possibility that Koerbagh may have been able to read Hebrew does not derive simply from a fear that he will contest the authorized translations of the Bible, carrying out a reformation within the reformation. Nor is their fear that the Hebrew text may not correspond to what they know to be the true meaning and perfection of the word of God (a fear that Spinoza's *TTP* will fully justify in a mere two years). Rather, the authorities seem to fear the importation of certain Hebrew or, more accurately, Jewish doctrines. And although the interrogators mention only a Hebrew word (*het hebreeus wort*), Koerbagh replies, despite having asserted his ignorance of the word, that he never spoke with Spinoza about this "doctrine" (*dees leer*). What exactly is this word or doctrine that appears so threatening to the good burghers?

Unfortunately, this seemingly simple question poses a number of difficulties. Meinsma and Freudenthal, both of whom reproduce the Dutch text of the interrogation record, spell the word differently: Meinsma, *Schabunot* and Freudenthal, *Schabinot*. No Hebrew word corresponds to either spelling, clearly indicating an error either of transcription or of the interrogators themselves. The editors of the recent French translation of Meinsma's *Spinoza en zijn Kring* suggest that the word should be read *Hag Shavuot*,[10] a reference to the Feast of Weeks. While the word certainly bears a resemblance to the transcribed term, it seems questionable that the councilmen would be interested in a festival that in no way comprises a *leer* or "doctrine." Freudenthal offers a different interpretation, which he simply inserts into the German translation of the Dutch transcript without justification or explanation: Schabinot is actually the Hebrew word "*Schekhina*" (which denotes God's indwelling or presence in the world), a doctrine, indeed, and one with a long, complex history with which Spinoza's most heretical utterances can be connected. In fact, it is this word, the one word that attracted the attention of Koerbagh's interrogators, that, in the eyes of the guardians of public virtue, Spinoza brought, like the plague, into the heart of purest Christendom. A century and a half before Hegel's commentary in the *History of Philosophy*, it is in the anonymous records of the civil authorities of Amsterdam, that Spinoza emerges as a kind of contagion, the non-European, unchristian, atheistic Other, incapable of being assimilated into the social order and thus an ever-present danger that must be eradicated. They could not, yet, reach Spinoza (whose personal motto was *caute* or caution); they could, however, destroy those whom he had infected and who did not hesitate publicly to express unhealthy doctrines. Koerbagh was sentenced to ten years in prison, followed by banishment from Holland, Zealand, and West Friesland. Within a year he was dead.

What was at stake in the doctrine of Shekhinah that excited the interest of the municipal authorities, activated a juridical process and aroused the coercive power of the state? On the face of it, their concern seems so misplaced that it might be imagined that they not only misspelled the word, but thoroughly misunderstood its meaning as well. Precisely what authorizes us to entertain Freudenthal's suggestion (given that the matter will probably never be definitively settled) that the word that so interested the councilmen was, in fact, *Shekhinah*? Why would an inquiry into heresy or, more accurately, in this case atheism and libertinism, concern itself with a Hebrew term that denotes God's presence or indwelling? One of the few twentieth-century Spinoza scholars to take an interest in these obscure proceedings was Lewis Feuer, whose stimulating and provocative account, while erroneous in certain particulars[11] nevertheless offers the beginning of a justification of Freudenthal's interpolation:

> It is especially significant that the magistrates cross-examined the unfortunate Koerbagh concerning the doctrine of the Schekhina, with which they tried to link Spinoza's name. The doctrine of the Shekhinah is the Talmud's closest approximation to a theory of the immanence of God in the world. Shekhinah literally means "dwelling"; its use connotes the presence of God everywhere. . . . The Shekhinah was a Talmudic form of pantheism. The interrogation of Koerbagh tried to elicit whether he had been persuaded by Spinoza to import into Dutch thought a doctrine of Jewish pantheism. The inquiry thus took on something of the character of an investigation into un-Dutch activities and modes of thought.[12]

Writing in the 1950s, Feuer (himself tainted by a Leftist past), could not help alluding to a certain resemblance between the anti-Jewish suspicions of Koerbagh's persecutors and those of the members and supporters of the House Un-American Activities Committee. And while Feuer's definition of Shekhinah as "a Talmudic form of pantheism" is only the most schematic beginning of an explanation of the Dutch authorities' interest in an obscure Hebrew word, it nevertheless points to something important: What Feuer (and many others before him) quite imprecisely call "pantheism" allows him to establish a connection between certain strains in Jewish theology and philosophy and Spinoza's theses concerning God, found in their most comprehensive form in Part I of the *Ethics*.

Feuer rightly links the term Shekhinah to the Talmud. Indeed, some commentators have argued that the term first appears in the Talmud (as a noun derived from the verb, "to dwell") as a way of conceptualizing God's presence in the world, a presence that is only metaphorically expressed in the scripture, often in materialized or personified forms, such as God's light, God's face, God's gaze etc. and is closely linked to the idea of the Holy Spirit. But apart from a few passages there is little that is terribly pantheist in the use of the term. Rather, it evokes an anthropomorphized image of God who confers or withdraws his presence at will, often in response to human actions. We find nothing in the Talmudic doctrine of the Shekhinah that could alarm the guardians of Amsterdam's theologico-political order.

It is, of course, not with the Talmud that the term is today most often associated but rather with the Kabbalah, i.e., with Jewish mysticism rather than with either the normative rabbinic tradition or Jewish philosophy. More precisely, the term Shekhinah is associated with the Kabbalah's pre-eminent work, the *Zohar*. This only further complicates the matter. For while Spinoza, as Sylvain Zac notes, rarely refers to the Talmud, he mentions the Kabbalah only once and then in an utterly negative way. In chapter ix of the *TTP*, after presenting the correct method of scriptural interpretation, Spinoza curtly dismisses as absurd mystical explanations of gaps and breaks in the text of scripture and reserves his greatest scorn for the interpretations of the "Kabbalistic triflers": "*Legi etiam et insuper novi nugatores aliquos Kabbalistas, quorum insaniam, nunquam mirari satis potui*";[13] "I have read and am acquainted with certain Kabbalistic triflers whose madness never ceases to astonish me."[14] Here he speaks of the Kabbalistic method of the interpretation of scripture: specifically, the practice of discerning in the lacunae and faults in the Scripture, signs of the most profound mysteries and the most powerful secrets: "there are many who deny the possibility of any fault having occurred even in other texts; they maintain that God by some singular act of providence has preserved all the sacred books uncorrupted. They say that the variant readings signal mysteries most profound; they contend that the same is true of the 28 cases of asterisks in midparagraph, and that great secrets lurk even in the markings above the letters."[15] What Spinoza objects to then is the tendency on the part of these Kabbalistic triflers to devalue the text in its actuality (which for Spinoza is all that exists) as mere appearance, a surface concealing a reservoir of hidden meaning. Such a procedure, which adds to Scripture what is not to be found in it, is nothing more than a negation and denial of the text. It can never produce a knowledge of Scripture. Thus, what Spinoza criticizes in the work of "certain Kabbalistic triflers" is precisely their transcendentalism, their refusal, in the case of Scripture, of what is, in favor of the excess of meaning that lies behind, beyond or beneath the text itself.

Spinoza does not condemn the Kabbalah itself, or even those who have written on the Kabbalah in general, only "certain" or "some" (*aliquos*) of them. In fact, in opposition to what certain Kabbalistic triflers have said about scripture,[16] a significant number of passages in the *Zohar* and in the works of certain of its most illustrious commentators exhibit a view of God's relation to the world that, in the words of one writer, seem to lead to "something very similar to the constitutive elements of Spinoza's doctrine."[17] Leibniz himself in the *Theodicy* reports approvingly another's argument that "Spinoza revived the ancient Cabala of the Hebrews."[18]

Henry Walter Brann[19] (following Dunin-Borkowski's interesting and provocative arguments in *Der Junge de Spinoza*) maintains that there are at least two indirect but identifiable references to Kabbalistic thought in Spinoza's work, both connected to what his age found most disturbing about his philosophy. Further, as Gabriel Albiac reminds us, a number of commentators, including Spinoza's contemporaries, Leibniz and Johann Georg Wachter, noted striking resemblances between the *Ethics* and that masterwork of seventeenth-century Kabbalism, Abraham Cohen de Herrera's *Puerta del Cielo*. While there is no evidence that Spinoza read Herrera's text, it would be surprising if he did not possess at least a secondhand knowledge of its contents. Not only did Herrera spend much of the last thirty years of his life in Amsterdam (where this descendent of a prominent Marrano family formally "returned" to Judaism), but his work was enthusiastically consumed by those who dominated the world in which Spinoza was educated, including Menasseh ben Israel, Saul Morteira (according to Dunin-Borkowski the *Puerta* was "*ein lieblingsbuch Manasses und Morteiras*"),[20] and Isaac Aboab, who translated the work into Hebrew in 1655. Further, the *Puerta del Cielo*, irrespective of its significance for Spinoza, was regarded as an important philosophical text long after its author's time: Hegel regarded it as one of the three main "sources of high cabalistic wisdom."[21]

What authorizes us to speak of a relation between Herrera's reading of the Kabbalah and Spinoza's philosophy? The *Puerta*, which is composed of a series of propositions, begins with a definition of the *Ensof*, or the Infinite, which, as Dunin-Borkowski remarks, resembles Spinoza's definition of substance at the opening of the *Ethics*: "Let it be affirmed that there exists an uncaused and necessary first being which is eternal and absolutely perfect,"[22] which infinite and first being he will call the Ensof. In keeping with his Neoplatonic orientation, Herrera argues that between the infinite and the finite, the perfect and the imperfect, the spiritual and the corporeal are interposed certain *"medios,"* emanations from the Ensof, through which that inferior realm of being known as nature is produced and governed.[23] To denote these, he uses the Kabbalistic term *sefirot*. In Proposition XI of Book I, Herrera directly criticizes the notion of creation, arguing that such a notion implies a separation in time and space between that which creates[24] and that which is created. Instead, he suggests that we think of the Ensof "as an immense sun that radiates innumerable rays or lights, containing everything within itself, in the form of what we have called attributes, names or numbers" (*sefira* literally means number or numeral).[25]

It may well be that the first reader not simply to connect Herrera and Spinoza (as both Leibniz and Wachter had) on the question of the relation between substance and the attributes, but to actually produce a Herrerean reading of Part I of the *Ethics*, was Hegel himself. Hegel argued that from the sixth century onward, philosophy "has its sphere within the Christian world, for Arabians and Jews have only to be noticed in an external and historic way."[26] In order to justify his rigorously linear conception of history Hegel must, paradoxically, abandon strict chronology: he places Herrera, a seventeenth-century Spanish Jew, (and the Kabbalah in general) in the category of Greek thought of late antiquity, that is, in a period before philosophy took its place within the sphere of Christianity. It is precisely Spinoza's link to this mode of thought that is not only premodern, but premedieval, that renders him troublesome to Hegel, a figure difficult to place in the temporal and spatial grid that Hegel applies to the history of philosophy. While Spinoza's thought may appear to belong to modern European philosophy insofar as it drives Cartesian philosophy to its logical conclusions, Hegel insists that even Spinoza's response to Descartes can be understood only in the light of the fact that Spinoza was a Jew. Spinoza's rejection of dualism in particular is "an echo from Eastern lands." It is thus, necessarily, an echo from the past, an "Oriental theory" that Spinoza has imported into Europe. In *The Science of Logic* Hegel compares Spinoza's notion of the substance-attribute relation to what he calls "the Oriental conception of emanation," which he presents as if it were a recapitulation of that "Oriental" text, the *Puerta del Cielo*: The emanations of the absolute "are distancings from its undimmed clarity; the successive productions are less perfect than the preceding ones from which they arise. The process of emanation is taken only as a happening, the becoming only as a progressive loss."[27]

Hegel here succinctly restates the main points of the conclusion to the *Puerta*, which consists precisely of twenty-five *"razones"* or arguments by

which Herrera attempts to "prove that the *Ensof*, the first cause, is neither
one of the *sefirot* nor all of them together" but is prior to, greater and more
perfect than any or all of its emanations. Among Herrera's arguments: "The
Ensof is one; the *sefirot* are multiple. . . . The *Ensof* is simple; the *sefirot* are
complex. . . . The *Ensof* is infinite; they are limited. . . . The *Ensof* is
uncaused; they are caused. . . . It has existed *ab eterno* without them; they
could not exist without it."[28] Through a careful selection of certain passages
and the suppression of others, Hegel arrives at a reading of the *Ethics* that
has been called (with perfect justification) Kantian but which can just as
plausibly be understood as Herrerean. Hegel, driven by his need to make
Spinoza Eastern and Oriental, reads Spinoza through the lens of Herrera's
"high Kabbalism." Pierre Macherey has analyzed in detail the peculiarities
of Hegel's interpretation of the substance-attribute relation as presented in
Part I of the *Ethics*: substance is prior logically as well as chronologically to
its attributes; it is as independent of them as they are dependent on it, instituting a hierarchy of being. Moreover, the attributes are the necessarily dim
and degraded reflections of substance in the consciousness of human beings,
effectively rendering substance unknowable, ungraspable except through its
intermediaries.

Are we then to conclude that, to the extent that Hegel erred in finding
in Spinoza the Oriental or Jewish "conception of emanation," Spinoza must
then have broken not simply with the Jewish *imperio in imperium*, but with
the history of Jewish philosophy and theology? *To come to such a conclusion would be to falsify both the history of Jewish thought and Spinoza's
work itself.* Albiac has shown that emanation and a hierarchical conception
of being[29] sharply differentiate Spinoza's philosophy from Neoplatonism.
Yet the approach Spinoza does take is linked to the very stratum in the
Zohar that commentators have traditionally called pantheist. The inadequacy of the term lies precisely in the fact that it obscures the distinction
between immanence and emanation. Of course, no one has more to tell us
about this filiation than does Spinoza himself.

In 1675, Henry Oldenburg wrote to Spinoza to encourage him to publish what must have been the *Ethics*, which he regarded (apparently at Spinoza's prompting), as an attempt "to elucidate and moderate those passages
in the *TTP*, which proved a stumbling block to readers." The stumbling
block: those passages "which appear to treat in an ambiguous way of God
and Nature which many people consider you have confused with each
other."[30] In addition, Oldenburg reports that "they say you are concealing
your opinion with regard to Jesus Christ, Redeemer of the World, sole
Mediator for mankind, and of his Incarnation and Atonement, and they
request you to disclose your attitude clearly on these three heads."[31]

Spinoza's response is striking. He begins by displacing the question at hand: his critics accuse him of undermining the Christian faith, but he responds by asking what in his work undermines the "practice of religious virtue."[32] We note not only the substitution of practice for faith, but also that of "religious virtue" for Christianity. Spinoza now directly addresses what will be the most persistent theme of the theological critics of the *Ethics*: "I entertain an opinion on God and Nature far different from that which modern Christians are wont to uphold. For I maintain that God is the immanent cause, as the phrase is, of all things, and not the transitive cause. All things, I say, are in God and move in God, and this I affirm together with Paul and perhaps together with all ancient philosophers, though expressed in a different way, and I would even dare to say, together with all the ancient Hebrews, as far as may be conjectured from certain traditions, although these have suffered much corruption."[33]

Spinoza, of course, has engaged (successfully, in this case) in a bit of sleight of hand: he makes out that the notion of God as immanent cause is simply a different way of saying what Paul had said, namely that all things are in and move in God. By equating these views, he suppresses what is really at stake, the fusing of God and Nature to which Oldenburg alludes. What worries the "reasonable and intelligent Christians" for whom Oldenburg is kind enough to act as interlocutor is not that all things are in God, participating, to varying degrees, in the divine essence. It is rather their sense that the God of the *TTP* is purely coextensive with nature and in no way transcendent of it. The *Ethics* of course would not quiet the doubts of Christian readers. It would, by developing to their logical conclusion what remained mere hints in the *TTP*, be universally understood as the most systematic treatise of atheism. To read the *Ethics* to the letter is to see that the very notion of God as the immanent cause leads Spinoza to oppose Herrera's Neoplatonic theory of the relation between the *Ensof* and the *sefirot* point by point. God does not exist prior to the world, nor substance prior to the attributes. Substance is not greater than the attributes and does not exceed them in any way. On the contrary it consists of them and they are infinite. There is no primal simplicity and unity that degenerates into complexity and diversity, nor spirit that through intermediary existences will give rise to matter. If it is true that Paul, all the ancient philosophers, and all the ancient Hebrews affirmed that all things are in God, is Spinoza alone in asserting that God is in all things and nowhere else?

Not if we take him at his word. We have seen that the function of the twenty-five "*razones*" with which Herrera concludes the *Puerta del Cielo* is precisely to separate the *Ensof* from the *sefirot* and to make the former prior to the latter in a clearly hierarchical relation, giving the primacy to spirit over matter. Spinoza, of course, utterly rejected the separation of spirit and matter or of thought and extension, arguing that "the order and connection of ideas is the same as the order and connection of things."[34] It is all the more significant, then, that at this precise point in the *Ethics* Spinoza declares his debt to "Certain Hebrews who seem to have seen as if through a cloud (*quasi per nebulam*) that God, God's intellect and the things known by him are one and the same." He thus attributes to these Hebrews the notion that spirit and matter are, not parallel (to use a term often associated with Spinoza but which fundamentally distorts his position) but the same. Further, the specific manner in which he restates their position renders God's intellect, in which everyone participates as a part of nature, inseparable from, the "same as" the things it knows. *As if this were not enough, Spinoza moves beyond even the phrase that so shocked his contemporaries, his equation "God, or Nature," to redefine nature as a plurality, as the indefinite plurality of "things": God is the infinity of things.*

Commenting on this passage, Brann identifies Moses Cordovero (a sixteenth-century commentator on the *Zohar*, whose discussion of the *Ensof-sefirot* relation has much in common with Spinoza, even if, like Herrera, he reaches opposing conclusions) as the source of Spinoza's phrase, citing a passage from the *Pardes Rimonim*: "The creator . . . is himself the perception, the perceiving and the perceived."[35] While this passage certainly resembles that in which Spinoza summarizes the positions of the Hebrews in question, Brann fails to note that in the remainder of the extract, despite his apparent agreement with Spinoza's philosophy on the inseparability of God and nature, Cordovero will begin with this premise only to reach a conclusion utterly opposed to Spinoza's, a conclusion, moreover that cannot, strictly speaking, be derived from the proposition that precedes it: "He is the archetype of all being and all things are in him in their purest and most perfect form so that the perfection of the creatures just consists in the existence by which they find themselves united with the primary source, and to the extent that they withdraw from him, they descend from his perfect and exalted state."[36]

However unsatisfactory Brann's reading (or lack of reading) of Cordovero may be, he has nevertheless performed a valuable service: He has allowed us to see that Spinoza has read the Hebrews to whom he refers by *drawing a line of demarcation through* their arguments, making visible an antagonism that animates even (or perhaps especially) the most "mystical" texts. For it is precisely these texts, more than any others, that insist upon God's presence in the world to such an extent that there exists an ever-present danger that God will become confused with the world, abolishing any form of transcendence and with it any meaningful distinction between the divine and the mundane, spirit and matter. Spinoza's reading of this tradition allows us to understand the way in which the conclusion to Herrera's *Puerta* constitutes a defense against a repressed "immanentism" internal to Kabbalistic speculation. Spinoza liberates this element and gives it free play. Thus, Proposition 15 of Part I of the *Ethics* sounds perfectly familiar to readers of the *Zohar* and its commentaries and is a version of a notion repeatedly expressed throughout this literature: "Everything which is, is in God and can neither be nor be conceived without God." Spinoza, however, draws from this passage (which is again closely related to Cordovero's and to the view that Spinoza attributed to certain Hebrews) a conclusion directly opposed not only to Cordovero's and to Herrera's but to the entire "emanationist conception" (to use Hegel's phrase). In opposition to the hierarchy organized according to the degree of distance from God, the *Ensof*, or the One of Neoplatonism, Spinoza's immanent cause is, as Gilles Deleuze has argued, "equally present in all things," equally immanent and never removed, separated or distant. This does not lead, as Hegel argued, to a suppression of all difference and the emergence of an undifferentiated bad infinity. It leads rather to a rehabilitation of the material and the corporeal, once thought to be external to and unworthy of the divine nature, and to the realization of a "horizontal" diversity that can no longer be conceived in the form of a vertical hierarchy of substances: soul/body, spirit/matter, heaven/earth, infinite/finite, one/many, unity/diversity, potential/actual. Substance consists of or is its attributes. They express substance, but substance does not preexist those expressions.

But the scholium to Proposition 15 yields even more: it is here perhaps more than anywhere in the *Ethics* that Spinoza discusses not simply the content of his philosophy but its form, or to use a metaphor in keeping with the passage itself, its strategic and tactical resources. In particular, Spinoza employs a phrase that Louis Althusser has never allowed us to forget: "*Quare telum, quod in nos intendunt, in se ipsos revera conjiciunt*" ("the weapon they have aimed at us, they have really turned against themselves"). Althusser reads this as the key to Spinoza's philosophy. He attributes to Spinoza a more active role, however, than the phrase suggests. It is not so much that the enemy has unwittingly turned his weapon upon himself, as that Spinoza operates by systematically appropriating and then turning against the enemy its own weapons. Thus, Spinoza opposes every form of transcendence and teleology in the name of rather than against the notion of an eternal, infinite, omniscient, and omnipotent God. It is through God that he leads us to conceive the irreducible materiality of the world and to reject as irreligious superstition any attempt to explain this world by looking beyond it. One of the most important weapons he appropriated from and turned against superstition was the notion of Shekhinah, the notion of God's presence not beyond or outside the material world, but throughout it.

In his discussion of the passage cited above, Albiac[37] selects from Karppe's commentary five passages from the *Zohar* [38] that explicitly reject any separation between the *Ensof* and the *sefirot* and which thus tend to undermine the hierarchical relation that Herrera's conclusion insists upon: "Everything is one and everything is Him, everything is one thing without distinction or separation."[39] Among the passages, which Karppe adduces to show the Pantheistic or even Spinozist strain in the *Zohar*, one in particular stands out. It carries out a concerted destruction of the hierarchical distinction between God and nature, spirit and matter. The great equalizer in this case is not death or the void, to which all will return, but rather the Shekhinah, or God as the immanent cause of all that exists: "Thus, the inferior and superior worlds are equally close to the body of the Shekhinah and they are joined and united into one body; and thus all is one body and God is on high and below, and the breath from on high animates all things and everything is one body and as the Scripture says: Holy, Holy, Holy, the universe is filled with his glory."[40]

Spinoza's praise of the Jewish thinkers who saw, albeit through a cloud, allows us to see through the clouds that continue to envelop some of the most important texts in the history of Jewish philosophy. We can see not only that these texts are heterogeneous, but that they are traversed with conflict, often straining to deny what they themselves have demonstrated. Spinoza has read these texts carefully, as carefully and rigorously as he read the Scripture itself. If we follow his pathway through these works we will find that his assertion that he did not invent the notion of the immanent cause is surely right. This pathway begins in that misty region where the *Ensof* cannot rigorously be separated from the *sefirot*, where the Shekhinah like breath, like light, like water, fills all things, overturning every hierarchy natural or human, if indeed such a separation can endure its unceasing flow. Spinoza then followed this pathway to the concept of an immanent cause, the very "confusion of God and nature" that Oldenburg feared. The gentlemen of the consistory of the reformed church of Amsterdam were not as ill-informed as it might appear. They understood perfectly well not only the provenance of the ideas that their informants attributed to the apostate Jew, but also the destructive consequences of these ideas (which Spinoza insisted could be realized only in practice) for every form of human servitude, including and perhaps especially that which represented itself as true Christian morality. If they erred, it was only in thinking that the effects of this Hebrew doctrine, dispersed throughout the world with the Hebrew language itself, effects to which the most pious utterances could paradoxically give rise, could be mastered by imprisoning a few individuals, as if these were the source of the heresy.

Finally, if as we have argued this element is inseparable from the history of Jewish theology and philosophy, we can only conclude that this history, far from exhibiting the homogeneity of a tradition that could only be accepted or rejected in toto, is instead marked by insurmountable internal conflict. This would explain why Spinoza's excommunication is not a single, datable event but must regularly be reenacted: his work compels us to see the irreducible pluralism of Judaism in its historical actuality. There are, of course, those today who like the *Hakhamim* of seventeenth-century Amsterdam dream of ridding themselves once and for all of the heretic Spinoza, hoping thereby to restore Judaism to its authentic nature. Were they to succeed in eliminating its discordant and even subversive elements, they would have finally abandoned the historical reality of Judaism once and for all, and substituted something else, something far poorer, in its place.

NOTES

1. K. O. Meinsma, 1983, *Spinoza et son cercle*, translated by S. Roosenburg and J.-P. Osier, 339 (Paris: Vrin).
2. Meinsma, *Spinoza et son cercle*: 356.
3. Meinsma, *Spinoza et son cercle*: 358.
4. Adriaan Koerbagh, 1668, *Een Bloemhof van allerley lieflijkheyd sonder verdriet* (Amsterdam: Universieit Brussels, Centrum voor de Studie van de Verlichting [Based upon the first edition]).
5. Spinoza, *TTP* iii: 89.
6. Meinsma, *Spinoza et son cercle*: 332.
7. Adriaan Koerbagh and Jan Koerbagh, 1974, *Een ligt schijendee in juystere plaatsen* (Brussels: Vrije).
8. Included in Meinsma, *Spinoza et son cercle*: 355–77.
9. Meinsma, *Spinoza et son cercle*
10. Meinsma, *Spinoza et son cercle*: 381.
11. Here and elsewhere in *Spinoza and the Rise of Liberalism* (1964. Boston: Beacon Press) Lewis Samuel Feuer's historical narrative is not always supported by the evidence he cites. For example, Feuer ignores the difficulties posed by Freudenthal's interpretations, as well as the alternative posed by Meinsma, and simply asserts that "it is significant that the magistrates cross-examined the unfortunate Koerbagh concerning the doctrine of the Shekhinah (109)," a statement that could easily mislead the unwary reader.
12. Feuer, *Spinoza and the Rise of Liberalism*: 110.
13. Spinoza, *TTP* x; G IV/136.
14. Spinoza, *TTP* x: 180.
15. Spinoza, *TTP* x: 180.
16. Recall in this connection that Spinoza argues in chapter vii of the *TTP* that the method for interpreting nature and that for interpreting scripture are one and the same.

17. S. Karppe, 1901, *Etudes sur les origines de la nature du Zohar*: 411 (Paris: Alcan).

18. G. W. Leibniz, *Theodicy*, 79 (Chicago, Illinois: Open Court).

19. Henry Walter Brann, 1977, "Spinoza and the Kabbalah," in *Speculum Spinozanum* (Boston: Routledge).

20. Stanislaus (Graf von) Dunin-Borkowski, 1910, *Der junge de Spinoza: Leben und Werdegang im lichte der weltphilosophie*, 188 (Münster: Aschendorff) Hegel demonstrated an acquaintance with the works of the "speculative Israelite, Rabbi Abraham Cohen Irira"[19] in his *Lectures on the History of Philosophy*.

21. Dunin-Borkowski, *Der junge de Spinoza*: 395.

22. Spinoza, EIP1

23. Spinoza, EIP10.

24. There is nothing in the *Puerta* that would allow us to speak of an anthropomorphized Creator.

25. Abraham Cohen de Herrera, 1987, *Puerta del Cielo*, 108.

26. G. W. F. Hegel, 1974, *Lectures on the History of Philosophy*, 3 vols., vol. 3: 1 (New York: Humanities Press).

27. G. W. F. Hegel, *The Science of Logic*, 538-539 (New York: Humanities Press).

28. Herrera, *Puerta del Cielo*, 262

29. Gilles Deleuze, 1974, *Expressionism in Philosophy: Spinoza*, translated by Martin Joughin (New York: Zone Books).

30. Spinoza, 1995, *The Letters*, translated by Samuel Shirley, letter 71 (Indianapolis, Ind.: Hackett Publishing Company, Inc.).

31. Spinoza, *The Letters*, letter 71.

32. Spinoza, *The Letters*, letter 73.

33. Spinoza, *The Letters*, letter 73.

34. Spinoza, EIIP7.

35. Brann, "Spinoza and the Kabbalah," 111. This is a phrase and concept originating in Aristotle's *De Anima*.

36. Brann, "Spinoza and the Kabballah," 111.

37. Gabriel Albiac, 1997, "The Empty Synagogue," in Montag and Stolze, ed. *The New Spinoza*, 130 (Minneapolis: University of Minneapolis Press).

38. Re'uven Margaliot, ed., 1964, *Sefer ha-Zohar*, 3 vols. 4th ed. The Great Assembly, Book III. Jerusalem.

39. Margaliot, *Sefer ha-Zohar*: III 290ab.

40. Margaliot, *Sefer ha-Zohar*: III 43ab.

PART III

Theology and Epistemology

CHAPTER 7

Maimonides, Spinoza, and the Book of Job

EDWIN M. CURLEY

I invite you to reflect with me on the meaning of the Book of Job and of Maimonides' comments on it in the *Guide to the Perplexed*. This exercise in interpretation offers the pleasures inherent in any attempt to decipher a difficult text, a pleasure doubled here by the fact that we have two difficult texts. Maimonides' discussion of the Book of Job is at least in some ways as puzzling as the work it analyzes.

But philosophers have a special reason to try to solve the puzzle of these texts. They treat, in an uncompromising way, a difficulty for theism which, as Hobbes remarked, has shaken the faith, not only of ordinary people, but also of philosophers, and even of the saints themselves: why do bad things happen to good people? This is clearly one of the main perplexities Maimonides hopes to resolve in the *Guide*.

Those are no doubt reasons enough to do what we are about to do. But students of Spinoza have a further motive for pursuing this inquiry. It appears that the main reason Spinoza turned to philosophy, and to the new philosophy of Descartes, was that he was disillusioned with the theology taught in the synagogue.[1] It appears also that his *Theological-Political Treatise* (*TTP*), although published only in 1670, recapitulates the essence of the lost defense of his opinions which Spinoza wrote when he was excommunicated fourteen years earlier.[2] Since Maimonides is very much under attack in the *TTP*, it seems fair to regard him as a prime example of the kind of theology Spinoza was rebelling against in 1656. And though Spinoza has very little to say explicitly in the *TTP* about Maimonides' interpretation of the Book of Job, it seems likely that in reflecting on the Book of Job and on Maimonides'

147

analysis of Job we will be engaging in the kind of reflection Spinoza went through at a critical stage of his development. At least I hope you will find that conjecture plausible by the time we finish.

***

Let's begin by recalling the broad outlines of the story. We can divide Job, the book, into three main parts:

1. a prose prologue, consisting of two chapters,
2. a poetic dialogue, running from the beginning of Chapter 3 through verse 6 of Chapter 42, and so constituting by far the greatest part of the story; and
3. a prose epilogue, consisting of the remaining 11 verses of Chapter 42.

It's also natural to subdivide that long second part into three parts of its own:

2a. the dialogue between Job, Eliphaz, Bildad and Zophar in Chapters 3–31,
2b. the intervention of Elihu, in Chapters 32–37; and
2c. God's address to Job from the whirlwind, in Chapters 38–42: 6, making a total of five parts in all.

The prose prologue characterizes the hero of the story as a man "blameless and upright"[3] who lived and prospered in the land of Uz. The prologue then shifts to a scene in heaven, where the Satan[4] appears before God, who asks him what he has been doing. The Satan replies that lie has been roaming the earth. God says to the Satan:

> Have you marked my servant, Job? There is none like him on earth, a blameless and upright man, who fears God and shuns evil. (1:8)

To this the Satan replies:

> Does Job fear God for nought? Have you not hedged him round, him and his household and everything he has? His efforts you have blessed, and his property has increased in the land. Just reach out and strike what he has, and he will curse you to your face. (1:9–11)

God takes up the challenge, giving the Satan permission to afflict Job with various evils, so long as he does not touch Job's person. So the Satan destroys Job's livestock, and his servants, and his children. But Job accepts these afflictions and refuses to curse God:

> Naked I came from my mother's womb, and naked shall I return there; the Lord gave, and the Lord took away; blessed be Yahweh's name. (1:21)

The same scenario is then repeated, except that in the second dialogue with the Satan God gives him permission to touch Job's person, so long as he spares Job's life. The Satan then inflicts "loathsome sores on Job from the sole of his foot to the crown of his head" (NRSV 2:7). But still Job remains faithful to God. His wife says to him:

> Do you still maintain your integrity? Curse God and die. (2:9)

To which Job replies:

> You talk like a foolish woman. Shall we accept good from God and not accept evil? (2: 10)

Then three friends come to comfort him, Eliphaz, Bildad, and Zophar. They sit with him on the ground for seven days and seven nights, and no one speaks, "for they [see] that his anguish [is] very great" (2:13).

At this point there is an abrupt shift, both in literary style and in content. The characters begin to speak in poetry. Job, whose conduct up to this point has justified traditional talk about his patience, now curses the day he was born. His friends, often called his comforters, begin now to blame the victim—he should not complain; he must have sinned in some way, or he would not be so afflicted, since God is just. Job defends his innocence and demands to be told his fault. He can no longer calmly accept his afflictions. This kind of dialogue runs from Chapter 3 to the end of Chapter 31, and constitutes the first of three subdivisions in the poetic dialogue.

In Chapter 32 a new character appears, Elihu, a young man who criticizes the friends for failing to confute Job, and undertakes to do so himself. Whether he has anything to add to what they have said, or whether there are any interesting differences among the three friends,[5] are questions we must defer until later. Elihu goes on for six chapters, without any response from Job. This is the second subdivision of the poem. Then God speaks to Job out of a whirlwind, in a long series of rhetorical questions:

> Who is this that obscures counsel with words void of knowledge?
> Gird your loins like a hero, I will question you and you tell me.
> Where were you when I founded the earth? Tell me if you know so much. (38:2–4)

The poem continues in this vein for four chapters; they do not to respond directly to Job's challenge by identifying his sin, but emphasize God's power and knowledge, contrasting it with Job's weakness and ignorance. The poetic section then concludes with Job submitting once again to God:

> I know that you can do all things, and that no purpose of yours
> can be thwarted . . .
> I talked of things I did not know, wonders beyond my ken

I had heard of you by hearsay, but now my own eye has seen you;
So I recant[6] and repent in dust and ashes. (42:2–6)

Here the poetic portion of the book ends, and God, in prose, chastises Eliphaz, Bildad and Zophar for not speaking the truth about him, as Job did (42:7). He does not mention Elihu, but then Elihu is not mentioned anywhere in the book outside those six chapters where he speaks. Nor is there at the end of the work any reference to the Satan or his challenge. God simply restores Job's fortunes, giving him twice as much as he had before.[7] The final word is that Job continued to live for another 140 years, and saw his children, and his children's children, "to four generations," until he finally died, "old and satisfied with life" (42: 17).

If you have a fresh memory of this book, you will know that in retelling this story I have left out much interesting detail. My aim has been to set the stage for philosophical discussion and interpretation, without, so far as possible, prejudging the questions the narrative may occasion. I have alluded to certain oddities in the story—the differences in perspective between the prose and poetic parts of the story, the mysterious appearance and disappearance of Elihu late in the poetic dialogue, the absence of the Satan at the end. Such puzzles may make a modern reader suspect multiple authorship. But Maimonides seems not to consider that possibility, and for now I shall follow his example.

***

Maimonides' discussion of Job is contained in two chapters of the *Guide*, III 22 and 23.[8] Before analyzing it, however, we need to look first at III 17. The discussion of Job occurs in the context of a general discussion of the problem of providence. In III 17, Maimonides says that there are, all told, five kinds of opinion people have about providence, all of which are "ancient," in the sense that they have all been around since the time of the prophets (464/282). When he comes later to the Book of Job, he will identify Job, Eliphaz, Bildad, and Zophar with one or another, each with a different one of these five opinions. So we need to lay out these various possibilities.

The first opinion, which Maimonides identifies as that of Epicurus, is that

> there is no providence at all; that everything [both in the heavens and in the sublunary world] happens by chance and in accordance with the way things were predisposed, there is no one who orders, governs, or is concerned with anything. (464/282)

This is the one opinion Maimonides does not identify with any participant in the dialogue of the Book of Job.[9] It is also the one opinion he says definitively is "inadmissible," since Aristotle has demonstrated that "it cannot be true that all things should have been generated by chance—, and that, on the contrary, there is someone who orders and governs them."

Students of Aristotle may protest at the idea of finding a defense of divine providence in his works.[10] After all, they may say, the God of Book Lambda of the *Metaphysics* is thought thinking about itself and only about itself (1074b 15–34). So it cannot order and govern all things. Later we will find Spinoza complaining that Maimonides reads Greek philosophy into Scripture; here we might rather complain that he reads Scripture into Greek philosophy.

In a way Maimonides addresses this objection when he goes on to describe the position he ascribes to Aristotle, the second of the five opinions he discusses in III 17. On this view God does not watch over everything, but only over certain things. His concern for individuals extends only as far as the realm of the spheres; in the sublunary world he is concerned only with species, not with individuals. It appears that Maimonides owes this reading of Aristotle to a treatise by Alexander of Aphrodisias *On Providence*, written originally in Greek and surviving only in an Arabic translation.[11] Maimonides apparently thinks Aristotle held this view because the Greek philosopher observed order at the level of individuals only in the realm of the spheres, and only at the level of species in the sublunary world. "Order" here seems to mean continuous subsistence without any corruption or change (III 17, 466/283). What happens to individuals in the sublunary realm, on this reading of Aristotle, is to be ascribed to chance,[12] not to the governance of one who governs.

The next two opinions Maimonides discusses he associates with two schools of Islamic theologians, the Ashʿarites and the Muʿtazilites. The Ashʿarites react strongly against the idea that anything might happen by chance. Everything that happens happens through the will of God. They interpret this dictum in a way which entails a denial of the effectiveness of finite causes. "It is not the wind which causes the leaves to fall, for every leaf falls through an ordinance and a decree of God" (467/283). On the Ashʿarite view,

> if we see that an excellent man who was devoted to God's worship has been killed through torture, we should say: He [i.e., God] has willed this. And in this there is no injustice, for according to them, it is permissible for God to punish one who has not sinned and to reward a sinner with benefits. (467/284)

The permissibility of God's punishing the innocent (like their denial of the effectiveness of finite causes) stems from the Ashʿarite conviction that anything else would be incompatible with God's omnipotence. That is to say, if a finite cause were to be truly effective, or if God were to be bound by justice to reward the virtuous and punish the ungodly, that would imply that God's power was not absolute. The Ashʿarites were voluntarists about right and wrong, who held that sin consists in disobedience to the will of God, with the consequence that it is impossible for God's acts to be unjust, regardless of what their specific nature is.[13]

Maimonides does not reject the Ashʿarite view as unequivocally as he rejects Epicureanism. He does not say that it has been demonstrated to be false. But he does say that it involves "great incongruities,"[14] which constitute a burden for the people who accept it. One incongruity is a point on which they agree with Aristotle: that there is an equality between the fall of a leaf and the death of a human individual (466/283). Of course they understand that equality differently than Aristotle does. For them both events happen as a result of the will of God. For Aristotle (as interpreted by Maimonides) both happen by chance. Maimonides rejects the equality. He finds it repugnant to say that there is no difference between the fall of a leaf and the death of a human individual or between a spider's devouring a fly and a ravenous lion's devouring a prophet. Other incongruities in the Ashʿarite position are that they deny free will and contingency, and that their position entails that the Law is "quite useless," since the man to whom it is addressed lacks the ability either to do or not to do what it commands or forbids. (467/284).

The fourth opinion Maimonides discusses he identifies with the Muʿtazilites, who hold that man does have free will (in the sense of an ability to act of his own accord), and that the commandments and prohibitions, rewards and punishments, of the Law are "well ordered" (467/284). All God's actions follow from his wisdom, injustice is not permissible to him, and he does not punish a man who does good. So far, you might think, this is a position congenial to that of Scripture, and indeed the Muʿtazilite view is also represented within Jewish thought, as Maimonides is aware.[15]

But the Muʿtazilites also hold (with the Ashʿarites) that God has knowledge of everything which happens to individuals, both in the human realm and in the nonhuman. God knows "the falling of this particular leaf and . . . the creeping of this particular ant, and . . . His providence watches over all the beings" (468/284). The Muʿtazilites do, it seems, allow, as consistent with God's justice, that a person might be born with an infirmity without having sinned or that an excellent man might perish. This happens, they say, not as punishment, but as a benefit, though we may not be able to understand what the benefit consists in. In the case of the excellent man who perishes, it is presumably that he may have a greater reward in the life to come. In the case of the man born with the infirmity, it is apparently that it is better for this individual to be infirm than for him to be sound in body, though we may not be able to understand why.

One thing Maimonides finds particularly objectionable in the Mu'tazilite view is that they extend divine providence even to animals other than man. So if a mouse, which has not sinned, is devoured by a cat, this is because God's wisdom has required it, and the mouse "will receive compensation in the other world for what has happened to it." Still more serious, however, is the charge of self-contradiction. To hold both that God knows everything and that man has the ability to act, Maimonides claims, leads to self-contradiction, "as the slightest reflection should make clear" (469/285).

The fifth opinion, that of the Law of Moses, is that man has an absolute ability to act, and indeed, that all species of animals move in virtue of their own will. It is also a principle of the Law that God cannot be unjust, where this is held to entail that the benefits and calamities which come to men are deserved, though we may be ignorant of the way in which they are deserved. I will call this, for short, the Mosaic position. It is also, apparently, the Maimonidean position, though we will subsequently encounter some grounds for doubting whether or not we should ascribe it to him.

Maimonides does not claim that he has demonstrative knowledge that the Mosaic position is correct (471/286). He accepts it, he says, because this clearly appears to be the teaching of Scripture. And sometimes his acceptance sounds grudging, as when he says that the Mosaic position is "less disgraceful than the preceding opinions and nearer than they to intellectual reasoning."[16]

One reason for preferring the Mosaic position to the others, apparently, is that, as Maimonides interprets the teaching of the Law, the doctrine of a divine providence coordinating good and evil with desert applies at the level of individuals only to humans. Regarding members of other species in the sublunary realm, Aristotle is right and the Law agrees with Aristotle. It is not the case that "this particular leaf has fallen because of a providence watching over it; nor that this spider has devoured this fly because God has now decreed and willed something concerning individuals." Maimonides says that he

was impelled to adopt this belief by the fact that I never found in the book of a prophet a text mentioning that God has a providence watching over one of the animal individuals, but only over a human individual. The prophets are even sometimes astonished because providence watches over human individuals—man being too insignificant for providence to watch over him . . .[17]

So he will cite, among other verses, one from Elihu in Job:

For his eyes are on man's conduct,
He sees his every step,[18]

but also the familiar question of the Psalmist:

What is man that thou art mindful of him?[19]

The idea is that, since humans barely qualify as objects of God's concern, nonhuman individuals certainly will not qualify. Maimonides dismisses scriptural texts which might suggest a divine providence extending even to the animals, for example,

He gives to the animals their food,
and to the young ravens when they cry. (*Psalms* 147:9)

These show only a concern for species, not one for individuals.

The argument that God's providence does not extend to individual members of nonhuman species is essentially an argument from silence. But it does help to explain why Scripture permits us to kill animals and use them for our own ends, and I do not find this limitation of God's providence to human individuals outlandish as a reading of Scripture (472–473/287).

Toward the end of III 17, however, Maimonides suggests, apparently as a further specification of the Mosaic position,[20] an additional limitation on God's providence. On this view, God's providence is selective even within the human species—God is more concerned with the welfare of the wise than with that of the ignorant:

I believe that providence is consequent upon the intellect and attached to it. For providence can only come from an intelligent being, from One who is an intellect perfect with a supreme perfection. . . . Accordingly everyone with whom something of this overflow is united will be reached by providence to the extent to which he is reached by the intellect. (474/288)

I take this to mean that God will have some concern for every human being who achieves some measure of participation in the overflow (or emanation) from the divine intellect, but that God's concern will be less for those whose degree of participation is less, and nonexistent for those who do not participate at all.[21] I take it that participation to any degree requires some knowledge of God, and that rationality alone is not sufficient.[22] The ignorant cannot expect a nice correlation of benefits and calamities to desert; the wise can. I propose to call this "the intellectualist position," since it seems, prima facie, to be a view distinct from the Mosaic position. Though Maimonides apparently regards what I am calling the intellectualist position as the proper way to understand the Mosaic position, I find his arguments to that effect perfunctory and unconvincing.[23]

The intellectualist position has a fair claim to being Maimonides' final word on the general subject of divine providence, and knowledgeable interpreters of Maimonides often take it to be just that.[24] I would like, for the time being, to leave open the following questions:

1. Whether the intellectualist position is, in fact, Maimonides' final word on the issue of providence?
2. Whether Maimonides honestly believes that the intellectualist position is the proper way to understand the Mosaic position? and
3. Whether there is any plausibility at all in regarding the intellectualist position as being, in fact, a legitimate way of understanding Scripture?

If the answer to the first two of these questions is "yes," and the answer to the last question is "no," then that would be a confirmation of Spinoza's general criticism of Maimonides as a Hellenizer of Scripture. Whether or not the intellectualist position is one we can really describe as a Platonic or Aristotelian speculation, the preference it gives to intellectual excellence over moral excellence does seem at first blush more Hellenic than Hebraic in spirit.[25] But since the answer to the third question seems to me to be "no," I hesitate to answer "yes" to the second. And I also have doubts about the right way to answer the first. Some of my reasons will emerge from our consideration of what Maimonides has to say about Job, but I can indicate one reason now.

Much earlier in the *Guide*, in I 72, Maimonides had made a preliminary, and rather skeptical declaration on the subject of providence:

The governance and the providence of Him, may He be exalted, accompany the world as a whole in such a way that the manner and true reality of this accompaniment are hidden from us: the faculties of human beings are inadequate to understand this. On the one hand, there is a demonstration of His separateness, may He be exalted, from the world and of His being free from it, and on the other, there is a demonstration that the influence of His governance and providence in every part of the world, however small and contemptible, exists. (193/119)

Here we have Maimonides the precursor of Kant, denying knowledge in order to make room for faith.[26] Except, of course, that when Kant claims that the exercise of pure reason leads to antinomies, he actually gives you what purport to be demonstrations of the contradictory propositions, whereas Maimonides merely claims that the demonstrations are available, and leaves it as an exercise for the reader to find them.

When Maimonides comes back to the discussion of providence in III 17, he makes no mention of this earlier skeptical view and it is a fair question how the two parts of the *Guide* are supposed to be related. Here is one possible answer: in the earlier passage, when Maimonides claims that God is demonstrably separate from the world, he is claiming the demonstrability of either the Epicurean view or the Aristotelian view (Epicureanism if we take "the world" to refer to the whole of the physical universe, Aristotelianism if we take it to refer only to the sublunary realm); when he claims that God's providence demonstrably extends to every part of the world, he is claiming the demonstrability of either the Ashʿarite or the Muʿtazilite view (since the universality of God's providence is common to both positions and they disagree only about how to reconcile this with God's justice). If the first demonstration is sound, it presumably destroys both the Ashʿarite and Muʿtazilite positions (since it proves the falsity of their common element). If the second demonstration is sound, it presumably destroys the Epicurean and Aristotelian positions (since its conclusion is inconsistent with the weaker Aristotelian position, a fortiori it destroys the Epicurean view). The mutual destruction of these views leaves the field clear for Maimonides to affirm the Mosaic position on grounds of faith.

I say that's a possible answer, in the sense that I can imagine someone saying that. But I don't think it's a very satisfactory answer. After all, the Mosaic position, insofar as it affirms the compromise view that God's providence extends only to part of the world and not to all, is inconsistent with the conclusions of each of the alleged demonstrations. So you might better say: if either of these demonstrations actually works, then the Mosaic position must be false, and given Maimonides' view that we must interpret scripture in such a way that it is consistent with what philosophy can demonstrate (*Guide* II 25, 327–29/199–200), then if either of the demonstrations works, any scriptural passage we might appeal to as prima facie supporting the Mosaic position would have to be interpreted so as not to actually support it. Faith is deprived of its basis. Before we ever enter into the interpretation of Job, we have reason to find Maimonides' position highly problematic.

***

The intellectualist position appears to offer the following simple solution to the problem of undeserved suffering: if a person is morally virtuous, but lacking in intellectual excellence, he cannot expect his well-being to be proportioned to his moral virtue. God does not care that much about moral virtue; what he values is intellectual excellence. This somewhat brutal way of stating the position will make it clear, I hope, why I find it unattractive philosophically, and hence, why I need some persuading that it is Maimonides' ultimate answer to the problem of people like Job.

Of course, if Maimonides held that moral and intellectual virtue were necessarily connected, so that you could not have either one without the other, the notion that providence is proportionate to intellectual excellence would be less problematic. Sometimes Maimonides does seem to hold that there is such a connection between moral virtue and intellectual excellence.[28] But if this is his considered view, then it excludes the possibility of dealing with Job in the way he seems to want to in III 22:

> The most marvelous and extraordinary thing about this story is the fact that knowledge is not attributed in it to Job. He is not said to be a *wise* or a *comprehending* or an *intelligent man.* Only moral virtue and righteousness in action are ascribed to him. For if he had been *wise*, his situation would not have been obscure for him. . . .[28]

Job's problem, it appears, is that he is one of those "ignoramuses who observe the commandments,"[29] that is, someone who is scrupulous in his observance of the Law (1:5), but whose belief in God is based only on hearsay, not on philosophical argument (42:5). Such people are too remote from God to merit his consistent concern for their well-being.

One thing to note about this passage, though, is the concluding counterfactual. Maimonides does not say that if Job had been wise, his situation would have been different (i.e., he would not have suffered the calamities he did). He merely claims that Job would have understood his situation (i.e., presumably, he would have understood why he suffered those calamities). So this passage does not represent a straightforward application of the intellectualist theory of providence to the case of Job.

To understand what is going on in Maimonides' discussion of Job, I think we need first to ask ourselves why it is divided into two chapters. Does this merely reflect Maimonides' preference for keeping his chapters relatively short, or is there some deeper rationale for the division of the material?

＊ ＊ ＊

Maimonides begins the first of his chapters on Job by claiming that the story "is a parable intended to set forth the opinions of people concerning providence." In support of this Maimonides cites the opinion of "some of [the Sages]," that is, the wise men of the Talmud, who have said that "Job never existed." He is careful to note that other sages believe Job did exist, and that the story told of him did happen, though they differ as to when and where these events occurred, whether it was in the days of the patriarchs, or in those of Moses, or in those of David, or in the postexilic period. Maimonides seems to think this disagreement about the time and place confirms the view of those who hold the story to be a parable.

What is at stake in this dispute? I take it that the issue is how much of the story we should believe to be true. Maimonides writes that whether Job ever existed or not, "cases like his always exist,[30] and that they cause "all reflecting people" to become perplexed and to turn to one or another of the five opinions about providence (486/296). Someone who holds the story to be a parable will hold that only the most general features of the story are descriptive of any sequence of events which ever occurred. Suppose we rewrote the story, stripping it of all proper names:

> Once upon a time there was a man who was blameless and upright and who prospered for a long time. Then one day calamity befell him without there being any evident reason why he should deserve to suffer . . .

This would be sufficient to generate perplexity in anyone who believes in God, who believes that God is aware of what happens to individuals in the world, and who believes that God has the power and the disposition at least to intervene in those happenings, to prevent bad things from happening to good people.

Maimonides writes that even those who believe that Job really existed take certain aspects of the prose prologue to be a parable. He mentions specifically, "the discourse of Satan, that of God addressed to Satan, and the giving-over [of Job to Satan]." Anyone "endowed with intellect" recognizes that that part of the story is a parable, though Maimonides remarks that

> it is not a parable like all others, but one to which extraordinary notions *and things that are the mystery of the universe* are attached. Through it great enigmas are solved, and truths than which none is higher become clear.[31]

In the remainder of this chapter Maimonides focuses primarily on the role of Satan in the story, whom he takes to be (or at least to be presented in the Book of Job as) the cause of Job's misfortunes (487/297). The picture he presents of Satan is one that modern scholarship would reject as anachronistic: Satan[32] is not a member of God's court carrying out one of its functions but an adversary of God's, who leads men astray.[32]

At the end of III 22, Maimonides comments, astonishingly, that he has "analyzed and explained the story of Job up to its ultimate end and conclusion."[34] But he has not, at this point, said anything at all about the dialogue between Job and his friends, or God's answer to Job, or Job's final submission to God, or the restoration of Job's prosperity. Those subjects Maimonides reserves for the following chapter:

> I want, however, to explain to you the opinion ascribed to Job and the opinion ascribed to each of his friends, using proofs that I gleaned from the discourse of each of them. You should not, however, pay attention to the other dicta rendered necessary by the

order of the discourse, as I explained to you in the beginning of this Treatise. (490/299)

This last appears to be a warning that what is to follow may contain certain contradictions, and hence encourages a Straussian reading of the text.[35]

* * *

Guide III 23, proceeds on the assumption that the story is not a parable: "if it is supposed that the story of Job happened . . ." And it seems to take the notion that the story happened in a stronger sense than had been allowed before. Previously we were told that even those who believed that Job existed (i.e., who thought the story was not a parable) rejected as a literary fiction the prologue's depiction of God as wagering with the Satan on Job's integrity and giving the Satan permission to afflict him. Now *one* consequence of taking the story not to be a parable is that God is understood to be the cause of Job's misfortunes:

> the first thing that occurred was a matter on which there was general agreement between the five [Job, Eliphaz, Bildad, Zophar, and Elihu], namely, that everything that had befallen Job was known to Him, may He be exalted, and that God caused these misfortunes to befall him. (490/299)

This is indeed a point on which Job and his four friends agree. It is also a point that the biblical narrative endorses. After the first round of calamities God points out to the Satan that Job

> still holds fast to his integrity, though you incited me against him, to destroy him without cause. (2:3)

The Satan may have instigated Job's destruction and been its proximate cause, but God accepts responsibility for it as well.[36]

I observe further that the intellectualist solution to the problem of undeserved suffering will apparently not work on this hypothesis. That is, if God caused Job's misfortunes, then we cannot explain them by saying that God concerns himself consistently only with the wise and leaves the ignorant largely to chance. That, I take it, is why the remark about Job's possessing moral virtue, but not intellectual excellence, occurs in III 22, not III 23. It would be inconsistent with the hypothesis under which III 23, is conducted.

The rest of III 23, consists in a discussion of the various participants in the dialogue, most of whom are identified with one or another of the five positions on providence described in III 17. Maimonides acknowledges that there is a good deal of repetition in the dialogue and that it may seem hard to distinguish the participants' perspectives.[37] But he insists that it is possible.

The remainder of the first paragraph describes Job's position in the dialogue: that he is righteous, that he has suffered terribly, and that his fate shows that God treats the righteous and the wicked equally. In the heat of his suffering Job charges God with contempt for the human species and with having abandoned it. There follow three paragraphs describing, respectively, the positions of Eliphaz, Bildad, and Zophar. These three all agree that (in the end, at least) God rewards the righteous and punishes the wicked, but Maimonides undertakes to find differences among them. In ¶5 he claims that Job's position is the Aristotelian one, Eliphaz's the Mosaic position, Bildad's the Mu'tazilite position, and Zophar's the Ash'arite position. Then comes a long paragraph dealing with Elihu, in which Maimonides argues that, though he may seem merely to repeat the views of the other three friends (of whom he is highly critical for their failure to confute Job), he does add one new idea: that Job may hope for an angel to intercede on his behalf. The chapter concludes with a paragraph on God's answer from the whirlwind.

These various identifications are extremely interesting. To say that Eliphaz represents the teaching of the Law is neither surprising nor problematic. To say that Bildad is a Mu'tazilite may be slightly surprising, but is supported with plausible scriptural evidence.[38] The claim that Zophar is an Ash'arite seems much more difficult to make out.

Prima facie Maimonides' identification of Zophar as an Ash'arite is inconsistent with the previous assertion (491/299) that all three of the friends agree that people suffer if and only if they have sinned. The scriptural evidence Maimonides offers in support of his new view might more aptly be taken as evidence for the old. He cites the following passage:

> 11:5 [Would] that God would speak, and open His lips against thee;
> 11: 6 And that He would tell thee the secrets of wisdom, that they may teach thee doubly
> 11-7 Canst thou by searching find out God? Canst thou find out the Almighty unto perfection?

What Zophar says here, essentially, is that man cannot understand why God does what he does. Insofar as Zophar suggests that God has a reason for afflicting Job, which Job might understand if only God would reveal it, he denies that God might afflict Job without cause. Note also that Maimonides omits that part of 11:6 in which Zophar says that God exacts of Job "less than thine iniquity deserveth." On this evidence, Maimonides has no case that Zophar is an Ash'arite. Moreover, there is a more plausible candidate for representing the Ash'arite position in God himself. At any rate, that is one natural way of reading God's answer to Job in chapters 38–41.[39] More of this anon.

The most interesting case, though, is that of Job. Absolutely nothing is said to show that Job is an Aristotelian in the sense of holding that God exercises a providence over individuals among the spheres and over species in the sublunary world. Prima facie, the only sense in which it can be said that Job is an Aristotelian, on the evidence presented in the paragraph describing his views, is that he denies that God has any concern to adjust welfare to desert among individuals in the sublunary realm. And, of course, that's a point of agreement between Aristotle and the Epicureans. So we might just as well say that Job is an Epicurean.

That would not be a nice thing to have to do. Job, after all, is not merely a character in a dialogue, whose views need not be ascribed to the author of the dialogue. He is a character whose views are pronounced by God himself, at the end of the dialogue, to be correct. Immediately after Job repents, God turns to Eliphaz and rebukes him:

> My anger burns against you and your two friends, for you have not spoken the truth of me, as did Job, my servant. (42:7, repeated with some variation in 42:8)

To his credit Maimonides faces this problem squarely. After citing the passage just quoted, Maimonides reports that

> the Sages, in order to find an excuse for it, say *A man is not to be blamed for [what he does when] suffering,* meaning that he has to be excused because of his great suffering. (492/300)

Maimonides observes that "this kind of speech does not accord with the parable." I think we may agree that the Sages' solution is inadequate. Job's suffering may excuse his words, but praising him for speaking the truth goes beyond mere excuse, and Job's suffering gives God no reason to fault Eliphaz and his friends for defending the idea that God afflicts only those who deserve it.

Maimonides' solution to the problem of God's praise of Job is that by the end of the dialogue Job had given up his mistaken views and had demonstrated that they were mistaken. This view,

> [viz., that God treats the righteous and the wicked equally, because he has contempt for the human species and has abandoned it] was such as arises at the first reflection . . . especially in the case of one whom misfortunes have befallen, while he knows of himself that he has not sinned . . . For this reason this opinion is ascribed to Job. However, the latter said all that he did say as long as he had no true knowledge and knew the deity only because of his acceptance

of authority, just as the multitude adhering to a Law know it. But
when he knew God with a certain knowledge, he admitted that
true happiness, which is the knowledge of the deity, is guaranteed
to all who know Him and that a human being cannot be troubled
in it by any or all the misfortunes in question. While he had
known God only through the traditional stories and not by way of
speculation Job had imagined that the things thought to be happiness, such as health, wealth and children, are the ultimate goal.
For this reason he fell into such perplexity and said such things as
he did . . . (492–93/300–301)

So the opinion of Job which God approves is not the Aristotelian opinion he had expressed through most of the dialogue, but an insight he comes
to only after God has appeared to him, when he realizes that what he had
taken to be evils befalling him were not really evils, not, at any rate, by
comparison with the good he was finally granted. In support of this Maimonides quotes Job's final lines:

I had heard of Thee by the hearing of the ear;
but now mine eye seeth Thee,
wherefore I abhor myself and repent of dust and ashes.[40]

He glosses the last line:

wherefore I abhor all that I used to desire and repent of my being
in dust and ashes.

How satisfactory a solution is this?

I find this to be in some ways an attractive reading of Job. It seems to
make plausible sense of the concluding verses of the poetic dialogue. And it
is preferable to the solution of the Sages in that Maimonides does have
available a response to the question: what is wrong with what Eliphaz, Bildad, and Zophar have been saying? Their problem is not that they defended
God's justice, but that they misconceived the nature of good and evil. They
thought, as Job had before his enlightenment, that such things as the loss of
wealth, of family, and of health, were evils. So while they may have been
right to say of God that he does not afflict man with undeserved evils, they
were wrong to grant that Job was suffering evils.

This line of thought would combine naturally with what we have previously called the intellectualist position. On that conception of providence,
merit is determined by intellectual excellence, not by moral virtue; if we
add that knowledge of God is the greatest good man can attain, by comparison with which any other human good is of no consequence, then there
will be a necessary correlation between merit and well-being; coming to

know God by speculative reasoning is one of the criteria of intellectual excellence; so anyone who achieves intellectual excellence necessarily possesses the highest good.

Maimonides' solution, if this is indeed his solution, does have some awkward consequences, though. The prose epilogue represents Job as being blessed in the end by having all the things he had lost restored to him. If these things are not true goods, this is no blessing. But perhaps Maimonides would reply that the story of Job is one of those parables in which not every detail "adds to the intended meaning," some being included either "to embellish the parable and render it more coherent or to conceal further the intended meaning."[41]

More seriously, this solution requires us to say of Job, prior to his revelation from God, that the misfortunes which befell him were of no importance by comparison with his separation from God. I think that trivializes those misfortunes in a way not true to the spirit of Job. In III 22, Maimonides says, more realistically I think, that, though some people may be able to bear the loss of their fortune, and others the loss of their children, "no one endowed with sensation" can bear patiently the kind of pain Job had to endure (487/297).

It would also seem to distort the narrative to say that Job was abandoned to the natural order, when it was by God's choice that the Satan was permitted to inflict those sufferings on him, or to say that Job ultimately achieved knowledge of God "by the way of speculation" (Pines, 493), or by "research" (Friedlander, 300), when Job's ignorance of God was repaired by a direct revelation from God, and not the kind of arduous intellectual discipline Maimonides usually seems to think is necessary for speculative understanding. Moreover, if the position of Eliphaz is the position of the Law, then any rejection of the position of Eliphaz is a rejection of the position of the Law, in spite of the fact that Maimonides represents himself as an adherent of the Law.[42] Perhaps these are minor difficulties, but they do seem to me to be difficulties. The ultimate test, however, is whether this reading of God's praise of Job in the prose epilogue is consistent with what God says when he addresses Job in chapters 38–41. It is to that passage that I now turn.

※※※

On any reasonable interpretation of Job which does not dismember the text,[43] God's answer to Job out of the whirlwind must be the key to the meaning of the work as a whole.[44] I've already suggested that I think one natural way of understanding that answer is to give it an Ash'arite reading. Let me elaborate that idea.

God does not respond directly to Job's challenge. He does not identify any sins Job has committed which would justify his punishment. How could he, given the repeated insistence in the prose prologue on Job's being without fault? Not only had the narrator said that Job was "blameless and upright" (1: 1), so had God Himself (in 1: 8 and again in 2: 3). I take it that the initial situation has not been changed by anything which occurs in the course of the dialogue, that is, that Job has not become wicked merely by protesting that he is and has been innocent. What he has said about himself in the dialogue has been true, so I do not think he commits the sin of pride in saying it.[45]

God addresses to Job a series of rhetorical questions which emphasize his impotence and ignorance, by contrast with God's power and knowledge. God does not explicitly affirm his own omnipotence and omniscience, but that affirmation is contextually implied, as Job's response acknowledges:

> I know that you can do all things;
> No purpose of yours can be thwarted.[46]

The implication would appear to be that God's omnipotence makes it legitimate for God to do as he will with Job, whether Job has disobeyed an antecedent divine command or not. To say this is to give an Ash'arite reading of Job. It is also to agree with Hobbes: God's irresistible might gives him the right to afflict men at his pleasure.[47]

How does Maimonides read God's answer to Job? He says he takes the speech to be intended to show

> that our intellects do not reach the point of apprehending how these natural things that exist in the world of generation and corruption are produced in time and of conceiving how the existence of the natural force within them has originated them. They are not things that resemble what we make. How then can we wish that His governance of, and providence for, them should resemble our governance of, and providence for, the things we do govern and provide for? (496/303)

That is, Maimonides invokes his doctrine of equivocal predication to deal with the problem of undeserved suffering. The term "providence," applied to God, does not mean what it does when applied to man. There is nothing in common between the two uses of the term except the term itself. If a man knows this, he will be able to bear "every misfortune lightly" (497/303).

It is an interesting feature of Maimonides' discussion that he does not explicitly identify the answer he attributes to God with any of the five positions on providence he had previously distinguished. On the plausible assumption that those five positions were supposed to exhaust the possibilities, we must ask: can we see the divine answer as corresponding to one of those five positions?

Prima facie we can immediately exclude both the Mu'tazilite position and the teaching of the Law. Both of these positions are committed to holding that (in the end, at least) God distributes good and evil to individual humans in proportion to their desert. But if that were true of God, then we could say that the term 'providence' is applied to God in the same sense in which we might use it in reference to a wise and just human ruler. And while I find the doctrine of equivocal predication rather mysterious, one thing it seems to imply is that we cannot truly say of God that he is just in the same sense a human ruler might be said to be just: It is not true that God sees to it that individual well-being is proportioned to desert.

Now, it *may* be possible to reconcile the teaching of the Law with the doctrine of equivocal predication by interpreting the Mosaic position in an intellectualist way. So we might say: Look, the problem with claiming that God is provident in the same sense in which a human ruler might be provident is not that God does not distribute well-being to individuals in proportion to their merit. The problem is that God's conceptions of well-being and merit are quite different from ours; He recognizes that knowledge of Himself is the greatest gift he can bestow on his creatures, and He recognizes that only the intellectually excellent are worthy of that gift. So although there is a superficial similarity between God's providence and human providence, it is merely superficial.

Still, I think the Ash'arite position gives a better expression to Maimonides' theory of equivocal predication. If we adopt the compromise solution outlined above, blending equivocal predication with the intellectualist interpretation of the Mosaic position and Job's 'Aristotelian' valuation of contemplation, we do see an analogy between the meaning of "providence" when it is applied to God and its meaning when it is applied to humans. Providence does, in each case, consist in proportioning well-being to merit. Divine providence differs from human only insofar as it presupposes different conceptions of well-being and merit. And even those conceptions are not totally different from the human conceptions, just more restrictive. It seems perfectly consistent with human conceptions of well-being and merit to regard knowledge of God as *a* good, though not *the* good, or to regard intellectual excellence as *a* ground of merit, though not *the only* ground of merit. So on the compromise position the difference between human and divine providence does not seem to be total.

But Maimonides' doctrine of equivocal predication, as I understand it, does involve a complete difference between the meaning of terms applied to God and the meaning of the same terms as applied to humans:

> The terms "knowledge," "power," "will," and "life," as applied to
> Him . . . and to all those possessing knowledge, power, will, and

life, are purely equivocal, so that their meaning when they are predicated of Him is in no way like their meaning in other applica-
tions. (I, 56, 131/79)

It seems to me that this total disparity of meaning is better expressed by saying that it is consistent with God's providence that there should be no connection at all between well-being and merit as human beings would conceive
these notions, that God's justice does not require Him to relate well-being to
merit in any way. He may act quite arbitrarily and still be just. And after all,
isn't that just what God admits to doing when he says to the Satan, "You
incited me against him, to destroy him without cause" (2:3)?

There is, however, a price to pay for this interpretation too. I think it's a
better reading of Job. But it does reinstate a view of divine providence which
Maimonides characterizes as a mistake Job first made and then corrected (III
23, 492/300). What Job argued during the dialogue was that God treats the
wicked and the righteous equally, that to judge by his actions he is indifferent
to questions of desert. For most of the dialogue Job sounds like an Epicurean.
But so far as I can see, the Ash'arites (and Maimonides, when he is availing
himself of the theory of equivocal predication) really agree with that part of
the Epicurean view. Where they differ from the Epicureans is in assigning an
all-powerful agent as the cause of man's misfortunes, not chance.

Where does this leave us? At this stage of my reflections on Maimonides, I find it very hard to decide what his final word is on providence
in general or on the Book of Job in particular. It does seem that his position
on this issue is implicitly, if not explicitly contradictory, in that he suggests
two different and incompatible solutions to the problem of undeserved suffering. I am inclined to think that the contradiction is one he was astute
enough to recognize. So I also think, with Strauss,[48] that we should identify
one of these solutions as his exoteric doctrine and the other as his esoteric
doctrine. I would guess that the intellectualist position (or the intellectualist interpretation of the Mosaic position) is his exoteric doctrine, and the
Ash'arite position is his esoteric doctrine. I realize that the intellectualist
solution is the one Maimonides suggests more frequently than he does the
Ash'arite solution, particularly in the concluding chapters of the *Guide*. But
I have come to think Strauss was right to advocate the following rule for
dealing with Maimonides' contradictions:

Of two contradictory statements in the *Guide* that statement which
occurs least frequently, or even which occurs only once, was considered by him to be true.[49]

While this may seem a rather mechanical principle, which reverses all
normal canons of textual interpretation, it seems inescapable given the following statement from the Introduction to Part I:

My purpose is that the truths be glimpsed and then again concealed, so as not to oppose that divine purpose which one cannot possibly oppose and which has concealed from the vulgar among the people those truths especially requisite for His apprehension. (6–7/3)

But, of course, any estericist interpretation of the *Guide* must be highly controversial, and ultimately unprovable. I can well imagine the young Jewish students in Amsterdam arguing for hours over the right way to understand Maimonides on this issue, and spending many more hours arguing about whether Maimonides, as they severally interpreted him, was right in his interpretation of Scripture.

✳✳✳

For the Spinozist it is a piece of rare good fortune that we have available some fairly direct evidence about how these matters were discussed in the Amsterdam synagogue. In 1632 one of Spinoza's teachers, Menasseh ben Israel, published a work called *The Conciliator*,[50] in which he attempted to explain *all* the apparently contradictory passages in Scripture. His premise was that since the Bible is "in the highest degree true, it cannot contain any text really contradictory of another" (ix). Of the various prima facie contradictions he finds either within Job itself or between Job and other Scriptural texts, the most interesting deals with Job's denial of a life after death. So far we have not had any occasion to consider this, since it is an aspect of Job Maimonides does not discuss in the *Guide*.[51] But it is noteworthy that, of the five solutions Maimonides canvasses, the only one to invoke the idea of compensation in the life to come is the Muʿtazilite view Maimonides rejects.

Menasseh begins by citing the following, prima facie contradictory, Scriptural verses:

I Sam. 2:6. The Lord killeth and maketh alive, he bringeth down
to the grave and bringeth up.
Job 7:9. So he that goeth down to the grave shall not come up.

He acknowledges that the verse from Job is only one of many in Scripture which appear to deny the resurrection of the dead, and he refers the reader to his treatise on the subject for a full explanation of the others. But he does offer an explanation of Job's statement in *The Conciliator*:

Moses, who wrote the Book of Job, introduces him as suffering much affliction, and considering himself innocent, so that he doubted and disbelieved the interposition of Divine Providence, attributing everything, even resurrection, to the influence of the planets. (II, 41)

This is interesting for a number of reasons. Note

1. that Menasseh takes Moses to be the author of the Book of Job, whereas Maimonides grants that it may have been written as late as the postexilic period;

2. that Menasseh appears to doubt Job's innocence, representing this as an idea Job had (in spite of the fact that both the narrator and God testify to Job's innocence), whereas Maimonides never questions Job's innocence;

3. that Menasseh also seems to have rejected Maimonides' contention that Job is an Aristotelian, making him, instead, a believer in astrology; where this idea comes from I do not know.

In all these respects Menasseh disagrees with Maimonides. As he continues, however, he follows Maimonides in ascribing to Eliphaz the Mosaic position, to Bildad the Muʿtazilite position, and to Zophar the Ashʿarite position. (He does not use these labels, but his brief descriptions of the three positions match those of Maimonides quite closely.) Then he presents his solution to the problem of Job's (apparent) mortalism:

> Moses, therefore, being desirous of treating on Divine Providence in this Book, by interlocutors, and giving reasons pro and contra, as usual in such discussions, therefore, no notice can be paid to Job denying, or his apparent denial of resurrection; for we find him at the conclusion repentant, saying, "O Lord, I have heard of thee by the hearing of the ear, but now mine eye seeth thee, therefore I abhor myself and repent me in dust and ashes." (II, 41)

Menasseh seems here to accept the view that the Book of Job is "a parable intended to set forth the opinions of people concerning providence"; he is not content simply to say that Job is a character in a dialogue, whose views are not necessarily those of Scripture itself. Though he does not call attention to God's endorsement of Job's statements, he does implicitly deal with that problem as Maimonides had, by calling attention to Job's repentance and the consequent ambiguity as to just what opinion of Job's God is endorsing. Menasseh's use of the recantation, though, is different from Maimonides': the opinion Job recants must be his denial of resurrection, not his affirmation that in life as we experience it the innocent often suffer and the wicked often prosper.

The logic of this analysis would seem to lead to a Muʿtazilite solution of the problem of Job: "the upright sometimes experience misfortunes and troubles, that their reward in the next world may be increased.[52] Though this is a reading of Job which seems natural enough if you focus on the prose prologue, it is difficult to defend if you take into account the prose epilogue, where God rejects the opinions of all three of the friends.

I think Menasseh's reading of Job is also difficult theologically. The Mu'tazilite idea is that Job is being tested: though at the beginning of his afflictions he has been without sin, it has to that point been too easy for him to be virtuous—the depth of his integrity can be fully demonstrated only if he persists in his loyalty to God even though he does not receive a reward for it, but instead suffers terribly in spite of it; by demonstrating the depth of his integrity, Job earns an even greater reward than he would have merited without this trial.

But to whom, on this view, is Job's integrity to be demonstrated? For Saadiah the answer is fairly clear. It cannot be to God, since his foreknowledge makes it unnecessary to test his creatures.[53] Had God not permitted the Satan to afflict Job, *He* would still have known how Job would have responded to such a trial. The test must be intended to demonstrate Job's integrity to someone else, the obvious candidate being the Satan, whom Saadiah takes to be a man (54–158), representative of Job's many neighbors, who envied him his prosperity, and thought he did not deserve it, since he served God, they thought, only out of self-interest (159). But it seems rather hard on Job that he (and his family) should have to suffer so to prove a point to these other people. Is this not to treat Job as a means only, and not as an end in himself? And is afflicting an innocent man with grotesque suffering really an effective way to teach people that he is disinterestedly loyal to God? None of Job's friends seems to have drawn the intended conclusion, persisting, until corrected by divine revelation, in their belief that Job must have done something terribly wrong. It would have been fairer to Job if God had resorted to that revelation earlier. Perhaps the difficulty of understanding God's action on Saadiah's interpretation of Job is one reason Menasseh hesitates to accept the textual evidence that Job must be conceived as innocent. The tendency of theists to find some fault with Job is strong.

Menasseh makes no mention of Elihu or of God's address to Job from the whirlwind, but concludes by mentioning another way of dealing with the problem of Job's denial of the resurrection of the dead:

> Maimonides solves it in another manner, saying that this verse of Job, and similar ones, treat only of the ordinary course of nature, for he who dies does not naturally awake or rise again from the grave; he does not, therefore, impugn resurrection, for that will be a future miracle that will surpass the natural order of things. By which the doubt is also resolved.[54]

This completes Menasseh's reconciliation of the contradiction from which he began. I'm afraid that it is characteristic of his treatment of prima facie contradictions in Scripture. He is content if he can come up with one way of reconciling them; if he is aware of more than one, he may simply give the alternatives without feeling obliged to justify a preference for one over the other. Menasseh is a very learned man whose work drew high praise from his contemporaries,[55] but his attempts to reconcile scriptural contradictions often seem rather casual. Whatever difficulties Spinoza may have had with Maimonides' treatment of Job, I suspect he recognized it to be superior to Menasseh's.

***

Maimonides is clearly an important figure in the *Theological-Political Treatise*. Spinoza frequently cites him, always for purposes of disagreement. His general complaint in the *TTP* about the religious thinkers of his day is that they teach nothing but

> Aristotelian and Platonic speculations. Not to seem to constantly follow pagans, they have accommodated Scripture to these specu-
> lations. It was not enough for them to be insane with the Greeks, they wanted the prophets to rave with them. This clearly shows that they do not see the divinity of Scripture even through a dream. (Preface, §§18–19, G III/9)

Maimonides appears to be Spinoza's historical paradigm of that misconceived Hellenization of Scripture. So when Spinoza is defining his own method for the interpretation of Scripture in *TTP* vii, it is Maimonides he takes as the representative of the principal alternative methodology, which requires you first to know the truth before you can determine what Scripture is saying. He quotes at length a passage from the *Guide*, in which Maimonides writes that he does not deny the eternity of the world merely because of the scriptural texts which appear to teach that the world was created:

> The texts indicating that the world has been produced in time are not more numerous than those indicating that the deity is a body.
> (*Guide*, II 25, 327/199, cited at *TTP* vii, 76, III/113–14)

If we had a philosophical demonstration of the eternity of the world (as we have for God's incorporeality), we would be obliged to interpret figuratively the texts indicating creation in time (as we do those indicating God's corporeality). It would not be difficult to do this; but it is not necessary, since Aristotle's attempt to demonstrate the eternity of the world is inconclusive.

This does seem to illustrate an attitude toward the biblical text which fails to respect its integrity. Whatever you think Maimonides' final word on Job is, our examination of him certainly supports the claim that he reads Scripture in terms of Platonic or Aristotelian speculations. Insofar as he advocates the Mosaic position, he does so by understanding it in terms of Greek ideas about the value of contemplation and intellectual excellence. And even when he seems to be adopting an Ash'arite view of providence, which you might think not particularly Platonic or Aristotelian, he develops those ideas in the context of a negative theology which evidently goes back at least to Plotinus, and perhaps to Plato's *Parmenides*. The God who emerges from this theology seems very remote from the personal God of the Bible. However you understand Maimonides on this issue, arguably he hellenizes Scripture or emphasizes its divergent tendencies.

Still, I want to argue, Spinoza's final evaluation of Maimonides may not be as negative as this would suggest. To say that Maimonides reads Scripture in a Greek way is not necessarily to say that he reads Greek ideas into Scripture. Perhaps those Aristotelian and Platonic ideas are there in the text. I think, in fact, that's a plausible thing to say, so long as we restrict ourselves to the Book of Job and certain other books like it. I think each of the two views of providence to which Maimonides seems drawn has some support in the text of Job. I'm inclined to think the Ash'arite view is a better reading of the text than the Mosaic/Aristotelian view. But neither seems to me crazy as an interpretation of Job.

Spinoza does not offer an extended discussion of the Book of Job in the *TTP*. He does, however, make a number of brief, but suggestive comments. The first of the three passages I shall consider occurs toward the end of Chapter 11, where Spinoza is arguing that God accommodated his revelations to the prophets' intellectual capacities and opinions and that the prophets could be ignorant about speculative matters, though not about practical matters:

> Concerning the reasonings by which God showed Job his power [*potentiam*] over all things—if it is in fact true that they were revealed to Job, and that the author was concerned to narrate a history, not (as some believe) to embellish his conceptions—we must say the same thing: that they were adduced according to Job's power of understanding [*ad captum Jobi*], and to convince him only, not that they are universal reasons for convincing everyone.[56]

What is most interesting in this passage, though also quite puzzling, is its implicit critique of the reasoning in Job. Job is convinced by reasons which are not suitable to convince everyone. Indeed, Spinoza suggests that the reasons which convinced Job would not have convinced someone whose power of understanding was greater.

It is tempting to see in this a critique of the Book of Job, as read by voluntarists like Calvin and Hobbes (and Maimonides?): in Job God claims that his omnipotence gives him the right to inflict suffering on Job without cause; but this is a primitive view of the relation between power and right, which a more sophisticated understanding would reject. But this seems a dubious reading of the passage, since Spinoza himself appears later in the

TTP to embrace the voluntarist ideas which this reading would have him criticize. This occurs when he argues that

> nature, considered absolutely, has the supreme right [*summum jus*] to do everything in its power, i.e., that the right of nature extends as far as its power [*potentia*] does. For the power of nature is the power itself of God, who has the supreme right over all things. (*TTP* xvi, 3, III 189/17–21)

It's difficult to see how someone who holds this could legitimately criticize the teaching of Job, as interpreted by the voluntarists.

Perhaps the solution is that Spinoza is criticizing not the inference from absolute power to absolute right but the reasoning by which absolute power is established in the first place. (He does, after all, speak of the reasonings by which God showed Job his *power* over all things, not his *right* over all things.) When God speaks to Job out of the storm-wind, he does not offer reasons from which Job could legitimately infer that God can do all things. He addresses a series of rhetorical questions to him, challenging him to say, for example, where he was when God founded the earth, or whether he has ever commanded a morning, or whether he can tie Pleiades' fetters, or whether he knows when the ibex gives birth. If Job answered these questions, he would presumably say "I didn't exist then," or "no, I haven't," or "no, I can't," or "no, I don't know." Perhaps Spinoza's criticism is that, although the suggested answers might well be correct, Job should not infer from his ignorance and incapacity that there is a personal being who possesses the power and knowledge he lacks, who can, in fact, do the things Job can not, and knows the things Job does not. This is a conjecture, no more. But it seems more coherent with the rest of Spinoza's philosophy than the first suggestion does.

Spinoza returns to the Book of Job briefly in Chapter iii of the *TTP*, in connection with the claim that the Jews are God's chosen people. Here he uses the example of Job to argue that far from favoring the Jews, God is equally well disposed to all nations. Both reason and Scripture show this, and he cites Job 28:28,

> Behold, the fear of the Lord that is wisdom,
> To turn from evil is understanding,

as one of several scriptural passages which are supposed to establish his point. Job, Spinoza argues, was a Gentile,[57] yet he was most acceptable to God, because he surpassed everyone in piety and religion.

When Spinoza returns to the topic of Job later in the *TTP*, he begins by noting the controversies which have existed about this book and about the person of Job:

Some people think that Moses wrote this book, and that the whole story is only a parable. Certain Rabbis in the Talmud hand down this view, and Maimonides too is favorably inclined towards it in his *Moreh Nebuchim*. Others believed the story to be true. Of these, some thought that this Job lived in the time of Jacob, and that he married Jacob's daughter, Dinah. (*TTP* x, 16, III/144)

Then he reports Ibn Ezra's opinion, that the Book of Job was not written originally in Hebrew, but was translated into Hebrew from another language,[58] commenting that

I wish he had shown us this more convincingly, for if he had, we could infer that the Gentiles too had sacred books. So I leave the matter in doubt. Nevertheless, I do conjecture that Job was a Gentile whose heart was very constant, and whose affairs at first prospered, then went very badly, and finally went very favorably. For Ezekiel 14:14 names him among others [as a righteous man]. And I believe that the changes in Job's fortunes, and the constancy of his heart, gave many people an occasion for arguing about God's providence—or at least gave the author of the dialogue of this book an occasion to argue about it. For both the content and the style seem to be, not those of a man suffering among the ashes, but of a man reflecting at leisure in his study. (§§17–18)

Here Spinoza, possibly following Hobbes,[59] aligns himself with those who think, on literary critical grounds, that the story of Job is a parable, though (like Hobbes) he will allow that the story probably has some historical basis, in the sense that there was a person of that name, to whom roughly those things happened.

Most significantly, perhaps, Spinoza is attracted to the hypothesis that Job is a Gentile book. Here is how he concludes his discussion:

I would believe, along with Ibn Ezra, that this book really was translated from another language, because [the author] seems to aspire to the poetic art of the Gentiles. For twice the Father of the Gods calls a council, and Momus, here called Satan, criticizes God's words with the greatest freedom, etc. But these are only conjectures, and are not sufficiently firm. (§18)

In the end Spinoza declines to flatly affirm that Job is a Gentile book, but it is clear what he would say, if forced to make a judgment.

What is the significance of this issue? In the first instance, of course, it bears on the question "In what sense are the Jews God's chosen people?" If other peoples had sacred books, then God's revelation was not to the Jews alone, even before the advent of Christianity. But it is possible to see in this issue a broader significance: if Job is a Gentile book, then there is no particular reason to expect its theology to be consistent with the dominant Jewish one. Spinoza's concluding remarks suggest that the Book of Job reflects, indeed, a Gentile, polytheistic theology, with God as "the father of the Gods," and Satan as Momus, a figure from classical mythology noted for his fault finding. There is then no particular reason to expect the Book of Job to be consistent with the dominant theology of the rest of the Hebrew Bible. Is this what Spinoza intends to suggest?

I think quite possibly it is. If we could press Spinoza on his interpretation of Job, and get candid answers from him, what we might find him saying is this: Job is a book whose meaning is very obscure. But the kind of interpretation you're apt to get in the synagogue—which says that Job was just being tested, and that if he passed the test by demonstrating that he really was serving God disinterestedly, his unmerited sufferings would be compensated in the afterlife—that interpretation is hopeless both as a reading of the text and as a theodicy. There are better readings of the text available in the Jewish tradition, specifically in Maimonides, where what Ibn Ezra suggested is tacitly admitted—that the theology of the Book of Job is heterodox, that we have to either conceive God as caring only about intellectual excellence and not about moral virtue, or else regard him as a purely arbitrary ruler, who has no concern for proportioning well-being to merit in any way. This last way of reading Job is probably the best, but adopting that interpretation requires you to realize that the theology of Job is radically different from what you get in *most* of the rest of the Hebrew Bible.

We can only say "most of the rest" because Job is not without parallel in the Bible on the issue of providence. If you accept the theology of Job, then you will say, with Solomon:

> All this I laid to heart, examining it all, how the righteous and the wise and their deeds are in the hand of God; whether it is love or hate one does not know. Everything that confronts them is vanity, since the same fate comes to all, to the righteous and the wicked, to the good and the evil, to the clean and the unclean, to those who sacrifice and to those who do not sacrifice. As are the good, so are the sinners . . . This is an evil in all that happens under the sun, that the same fate comes to everyone. Moreover, the hearts of all are full of evil; madness is in their hearts while they live, and after that they go to the dead.[60]

Solomon's view is equivalent to Epicureanism, a view that has resonances in the theology of Job: there is no proportioning of well-being to merit in this life; there is no life to come in which we might hope that things would be corrected; Solomon, like the author of Job, will express this in terms of a kind of theism, saying that everything happens by the will of God, but so long as God is conceived as acting completely arbitrarily, there is no meaningful difference between that kind of theism and the Epicurean doctrine that everything happens by chance.

We should not be surprised to find a contradiction this fundamental in the Bible. After all, does not Maimonides warn us that one reason why books or compilations contain contradictory statements is that someone "has collected the remarks of various people with differing opinions, but has omitted citing his authorities and has not attributed each remark to the one who said it" (Pines, 17)? He cites the Talmud as an example, but he might equally well have cited the Bible itself. The idea current in the synagogue of Spinoza's day—that Moses wrote both the Pentateuch and the book of Job—can only be defended by profoundly misunderstanding the meaning of Job.

This view has consequences which go beyond the immediate issue of theodicy. Once we recognize the impropriety of conceiving God as proportioning well-being to merit, we will recognize also that we cannot any longer conceive of God as a lawgiver, who rewards the obedient and punishes the disobedient, and that the whole notion of a natural (moral) law, and of sins being committed in the state of nature, is without foundation (cf., *TTP* xix, 8). But to pursue those consequences would take us out of theology and into politics. That is a story for another day.

NOTES

An earlier version of this article appeared in a French translation in *Architectures de la raison*, ed. Pierre-Francois Moreau (ENS editions, 1996). In the interim I have profited from comments by Steve Nadler and the editors of this volume, to make substantial improvements. I'm especially grateful to Robert Sharples for sending me bibliographic references and unpublished work of his on Alexander of Aphrodisias.

1. Cf. the preface written by Spinoza's close friend, Jarig Jelles, for the edition of his posthumous works:

> from his childhood on the author was trained in letters, and in his youth for many years he was occupied principally with theology; but when he reached the age at which the intellect is mature and capable of investigating the nature of things, he gave himself up entirely to philosophy. He was driven by a burning desire for knowledge; but because he did not get full satisfaction either from

his teachers or from those writing about these sciences, he decided to see what he himself could do in these areas. For that purpose he found the writings of the famous René Descartes, which he came upon at that time, very useful.

This document is given in F. Akkerman, *Studies in the Posthumous Works of Spinoza* (Gronihgen: Krips Repro Meppel, 1980), 216–17.

2. See Bayle's article on Spinoza in his *Historical and Critical Dictionary*, reprinted in Pierre Bayle, *Ecrits sur Spinoza,* ed. F. Charles-Daubert and P. -F. Moreau (Paris: Berg International Editeurs, 1983), 22.

3. 1: 1. Unless otherwise indicated, I follow the translation by Marvin Pope, in the Anchor *Job* (Doubleday, 3rd ed., Garden City, NY: 1973). I also consult the King James (KJV) and Revised Standard Versions (RSV), as given in *The Interpreter's Bible*, vol. VI, ed. with commentary by Samuel Terrien (New York: Abingdon, 1954), the translation of the Jewish Publication Society (JPS), as given in the Soncino *Job* (2nd ed., by Rabbi Dr. Victor Reichert, with revisions by Rabbi A. J. Rosenberg, London, Jerusalem, New York: Soncino Press, 1985), the New Revised Standard Version (NRSV), as given in the *New Oxford Annotated Bible,* (Oxford: Oxford University Press, 1991), the translation by Norman Habel in *The Book of Job* (Philadelphia: Westminster Press, 1985), and the new JPS translation, as given in *Tanakh: The Holy Scriptures* (Philadelphia: JPS, 1985).

The KJV at this point has "perfect and upright," a rendering against which the Soncino commentary protests, on the ground that "such a designation the Jewish mind would only accord to God. What the word connotes is 'without moral blemish, blameless, innocent, serving God without ulterior motives.' Job is presented to us as a man of complete human integrity." Other commentators who would apparently allow the use of the term "perfect" seem to mean no more by it than what the Soncino commentary allows. Cf. Pope, 6, and *The New Jerome Bible Commentary*, (Englewood Cliffs, NJ: Prentice Hall, 1990), 469 (cited as NJBC).

4. On the use of the definite article, see Pope (9–10): ". . . the term is a title and not yet a proper name. The figure here is not the fully developed character of the later Jewish and Christian Satan or Devil . . . The Satan is one of the members of the divine court and comes with other attendants to present himself at the celestial court and report on the fulfillment of his duties . . . The Satan was a kind of spy, roaming the earth and reporting to God on the evil he found therein . . ." The NJBC concurs, 470. The later conception of Satan with which that in Job *is* here contrasted would be one in which Satan is the leader of the forces of evil in the world, who tempts man to sin that he may have companions in his rebellion against God. Cf. *Harper's Bible Dictionary* (San Francisco: Harper and Row, 1985), 908–09 and Milton's *Paradise Lost.*

5. Pope remarks that "attempts to find progression in the debate and subtle differences in the character and personality of the three friends are labored and unconvincing" (Anchor, *Job*, lxxv).

6. The Hebrew does not supply an object for the verb and translations fall into two main groups, those which offer something equivalent to Pope's translation (e.g., "I abhor my words" (JPS), "I repudiate what I said" (Samuel Rolles Driver, George Buchanan Gray, Charles Briggs (Editor), Alfred Plummer (Editor), (Edinburgh: TTT Clark, 1995) and those which follow the lead of the KJV ("I abhor myself," followed by RSV and NRSV).

7. So 42:10 says. And indeed Job does get double the number of sheep, camels, oxen, and donkeys. But the numbers of sons and daughters are not doubled.

8. In citing *The Guide to the Perplexed* I generally follow the highly regarded translation by Shlomo Pines (University of Chicago Press, 1963), 2 vols. Cf. the comments by Marvin Fox, in *Interpreting Maimonides* (Chicago: University of Chicago Press, 1990), 47–54. Occasionally I suspect that Pines may be misleading. In such cases, lacking Arabic, I consult and cite as possible alternatives the renderings of M. Friedländer (Mineola, NY: Dover, 1956), S. Munk, *Le guide des égarés* (Paris: A. Franck, 1866), and Lenn Goodman, in *Rambam: Readings in the Philosophy of Moses Maimonides* (New York: Viking, 1975). Page references are to Pines first, and then to Friedländer.

9. Maimonides does, however, ascribe this opinion to "those in Israel who were unbelievers," citing Jeremiah 5:12, "They have spoken falsely of the Lord, and have said, 'He will do nothing. No evil will come upon us, and we shall not see sword or famine'" (NRSV). So the claim that all five opinions are ancient is safe. Note that Maimonides does not ascribe this first position to any passage in Scripture where the author is speaking propria persona and not representing the views of others. (He might have cited Ecclesiastes 9:1–6.)

10. From Charles Touati, I learn that there was a controversy about the correctness of this reading of Aristotle among Maimonides' medieval successors. See his "Les deux théories de Maïmonide sur la providence," in *Prophètes, Talmudistes, Philosophes* (Paris: Cerf, 1990), 189 n. I am indebted to Steve Nadler for calling my attention to Touati's work.

11. See Pines's introduction, lxv–lxvii, and his "Un texte inconnu d'Aristote en version arabe," in *Archive d'histoire doctrinale et littéraire du moyen age* 31 (1956): 5–43, 34 (1959): 446–49 (repr. in vol. 11 of Pines's *Collected Works*, [E. J. Brill, Jerusalem and Leiden, 1986], 157–200). H. J. Ruland has translated this treatise into German (*Die arabischen Fassungen zweier Schriften des Alexander von Aphrodisias aber die florsehung und aber das liberuin arbitriuni*, diss. Saarbi-Ocken, 1976). See also the discussion by Robert Sharples, "Alexander of Aphrodisias on Divine Providence:

Two Problems," in *Classical Quarterly*, n.s., 32 (1982): 198–211. I understand from Sharples (personal communication) that there should be an Italian translation out by now (S. Fazzo and M. Zonta, *Alessandro dAfrodisia, Sulla Provvidenza*, [Milan: Rizzoli]). But I am indebted for most of my knowledge of the treatise to course materials Sharples communicated to me in 1995. He regards the basic ideas in Alexander's treatise as "authentically Aristotelian."

12. The view Maimonides ascribes to Aristotle in III 17 (Whatever happens to individuals in the sublunary realm happens by chance) seems patently inconsistent with the view he ascribes to him in II 20 (No natural things come about by chance). More of this later.

13. In III 17, Maimonides does not explain why (according to the Ash'arites) we should not seek reasons for God's actions, but in III 23, he does: "The point of view of justice or a requirement of wisdom should not be sought in whatever the deity does, for His greatness and true reality entail His doing what He wills . . ." On Ash'arite voluntarism see George Hourani, *Reason and Tradition in Islamic Ethics* (Cambridge: Cambridge University Press, 1985), 118–23, and Oliver Leaman, *An Introduction to Medieval Islamic Philosophy*, (Cambridge: Cambridge University Press, 1985), 123–43.

14. Goodman: "outrageous consequences."

15. See *The Book of Theodicy, Translation and Commentary on the Book of Job*, by Saadiah ben Joseph Al-Fayyumi, trans. by L. E. Goodman (New Haven: Yale University Press, 1988). For Maimonides' awareness of Saadiah's position, see the passage cited below in n. 17 ("some of the latter-day Gaonim"). It is unclear, however, whether Saadiah embraces the extension of divine providence to nonhuman animals. Cf. p. 138, n. 31.

16. Pines, 471. But perhaps the appearance of grudging acceptance is an artifact of the Pines translation. Friedländer here reads: "The principle which I accept is far less open to objections, and is more reasonable than the opinions mentioned before" (286). Munk reads: "L'opinion que j'admets offre moins d'invraisemblance que les opinions précédentes et s'approche davantage du raisonnement de l'intelligence." Goodman: "This view I accept is less beset with unfortunate consequences than those I have already described and more capable of winning the assent of reason."

17. See 472/287. Cf. 471/286: "Our Law is exclusively concerned with the circumstances of human individuals; and in ancient times the story of this compensation accorded to animals has never been heard in our religious community, nor was it ever mentioned by one of the sages. But some of the latter-day Gaonim . . . have heard it from the Mu'tazila and have approved it and believed it."

18. Job 34:21, cited on 472/287.

19. Psalms 8:4. There is an ironic allusion to this verse in Job 7:17–21, interesting (among other reasons) because the context suggests not merely that Job does not welcome God's attention, but also that God's interest in him would be more understandable if he were (not a mere man) but "the Sea or the Dragon" (7:12).

20. Cf. 474/288: "This is the opinion that to my mind corresponds to the intelligible and to the texts of the Law."

21. In comments on an earlier draft of this paper the editors of this volume commented that this sentence presupposed "a more anthropomorphic/anthropopathic God than Maimonides'" (citing *Guide* III 28). But this, in fact, is one important reason why I don't think that the position I describe here represents Maimonides' last word on the subject. See below, 163ff.

22. "Accordingly, divine providence does not watch in an equal manner over all the individuals of the human species, but providence is graded as their human perfection is graded" (III 18, 475/289). In III 51, Maimonides is more specific about what "grading" implies:

> Providence always watches over an individual endowed with perfect apprehension, whose intellect never ceases from being occupied with God . . . an individual endowed with perfect apprehension, whose thought sometimes for a certain time is emptied of God, is watched over by providence only during the time when he thinks of God . . . [the] withdrawal [of providence when he is occupied with something else] is not like its withdrawal from those who have never had intellectual cognition . . . [the latter are] like one who is in darkness and has never seen light . . . the reason for an individual's being abandoned to chance so that he is permitted to be devoured like the beasts is his being separated from God. (624–26/388–89)

23. For example, in III 19, 475–76/289–90, Maimonides cites various passages in which God promises to watch over Abraham, Isaac, Jacob, Moses, and Joshua, and cause them to prosper. But nothing in the passages cited suggests, what Maimonides would need to show, that these men were selected for special favor because of their intellectual excellence (or a combination of intellectual excellence and moral virtue). "With regard to providence watching over excellent men and neglecting the ignorant," Maimonides cites I Samuel 2:9, "He will keep the feet of his holy ones, but the wicked shall be put to silence in darkness, for not by strength shall man prevail," which seems rather to indicate that moral virtue is the sole criterion for divine providence. The Hebrew term translated by "holy ones" in Pines is *hasidim,* which is rendered "saints" (KJV) and "faithful ones" (RSV,

NRSV). According to the *Interpreter's Bible,* "it includes in it an element of love, but the fundamental element is loyalty, and usually it is loyalty to an agreement" (Vol. III, 885).

24. Maimonides reaffirms this view vigorously at the end of the *Guide* (see particularly III 51 and 54). Oliver Leaman seems to take this to be Maimonides' last word on providence in *Moses Maimonides* (*London, New York:* Routledge, 1990), 120–28 (but see 170–71 for a more subtle reading), as does Fox, *Interpreting Maimonides,* 192–93, 218–19, 314–15 (but see 203–04 for a passage suggesting an Ash'arite solution). Perhaps Touati's 'second maimonidean theory of providence' is a version of what I am calling the intellectualist position, though he seems to stress direct knowledge of God more than intellectual excellence in the broad sense.

25. As to whether it is a Hebraic view, see Fox, 172 (commenting on the view, expressed in the *Guide,* III 27, 511, that the ultimate perfection of man is "to become rational in actu"): "This doctrine might be expected to trouble any thoughtful reader . . . If one were to ask within a normal Jewish setting what it is to be a good man or a good Jew, the answer would almost certainly focus on moral virtues and/or the fulfillment of God's commandments."

As to whether it is Hellenic, we might cite the following passage from the *Nicomachaean Ethics:*

> If the gods have any care for human affairs, as they are thought to have, it would be reasonable both that they should delight in that which was best and most akin to them (i.e., intellect) and that they should reward those who love and honor this most, as caring for the things that are dear to them and acting both rightly and nobly. And that all these attributes belong most of all to the wise man is manifest. He, therefore, is the dearest to the gods. (X, viii, 1179a24–30, Ross trans., rev. by Urmson, cited by Touati, 189 n)

I find this passage curious both in its own right, and in relation to other Aristotelian passages. Aristotle begins with a conditional, whose antecedent he does not affirm (and whose antecedent seems inconsistent with the theology of Book Lambda). He concludes with a claim which seems to require the truth of that antecedent. I suppose that he is seeking support for his high valuation of contemplation in popular beliefs which he himself does not accept.

As further evidence of the difference between Aristotle's view and that of the Hebrew Bible, we might note that earlier in chap. viii, Aristotle finds it absurd to think of the gods as behaving justly, in the sense of making contracts and performing what they have promised (1178b10).

26. Cf. Fox, 82–84.

27. III 22, 489–90/298: "Good inclination is only found in man when his intellect is perfected." This would make moral virtue entail intellectual excellence. That intellectual excellence entails moral perfection seems implicit in the claim that our love of God is proportionate to our knowledge of him (III 51, 621/386).

28. III 22, 487, translator's emphasis. Cf. Leaman's comment on this passage: "The account of Job only arises because Job is not very bright" (Moses *Maimonides*, 125).

29. III 51, 619. Friedländer's translation seems less disparaging of those who observe the commandments: "the multitude that observe the divine commandments but are ignorant" (384). Munk has "Les ignorants qui s'occupent des pratiques religieuses."

30. This is somewhat surprising, since Maimonides holds elsewhere that "an individual cannot but sin and err" (III 36, 540/332), a view encouraged by the Psalmist: "They have all gone astray, they are all alike perverse; there is no one who does good, no, not one" (Ps. 12:3). We might interpret the claim that cases like Job's always exist to mean that there are always some people who approximate blamelessness and who nevertheless suffer calamities out of all proportion to their fault. I think this is consistent with the passage from the *Guide* III 36, if not with the Psalm.

31. III 22, 486/296; the phrase in italics is an allusion to the Talmud, though Pines reports that the passage alluded to is a discussion of the vision of Ezekiel, not the story of Job.

32. Pines's translation always uses "Satan" as a proper name; Friedländer uses "the adversary."

33. In III 22, see 487/297 and 489/298, and cf. II, 30, 356/217.

34. So Pines, 490. Similarly Goodman. Friedländer: "I have *fully* explained the idea contained in the account of Job . . ." (298, my emphasis). Munk reads: "Je crois maintenant avoir exposé et éclairci à fond l'histoire de Job."

35. Pines's annotation at this point refers us to the introduction to Part I, presumably to pages 17–18 (= Friedländer 10–11), where Maimonides lists seven reasons why contradictions may be found in a book, and indicates that one of the reasons why contradictions may be found in his book is the need to conceal some parts of his teaching regarding obscure matters from the vulgar.

36. Cf. David Clines: "In reminding the Satan that he 'urged' Yahweh to 'destroy' Job, Yahweh is by no means repudiating responsibility for Job's former trial (Peake), nor giving him credit for instigating the experiment (Pope). Rather Yahweh invites Satan's agreement to the apparent success of the experiment in which the Satan and Yahweh have together been

implicated" (*Word Biblical Commentary, Job 1–20* [Dallas, TX: Word Books, 1989], 43).The commentary of Norman Habel (*The Book of Job, a commentary*, 94–95) seems to concur. The prose epilogue flatly ascribes responsibility for Job's misfortunes to God (41: 11).

37. He goes so far as to say that "if now you consider the discourse of the five in the course of their conversation, you may *almost* think that *whatever one of them says* is *said also by all the others . . .*" (491, my emphasis). This would be reasonable as regards Eliphaz, Bildad, Zophar and Elihu, but is hard to accept (even giving due weight to "almost") when Job is included. The paradox is also present in Friedländer: "When you consider the words of the five who take part in the discussion, you will easily notice that things said by one of them are also uttered by the rest" (299). Munk reads: "Si l'on considère les paroles que les cinq hommes échangent dans leur dialogue, on serait tenté de croire que ce que dit l'un, tous les autres le disent également . . ." Similarly Goodman.

38. Maimonides cites Job 8:6–7, which contends that, if Job really is innocent, God will compensate him in the future for his undeserved suffering. What Bildad says there, however, makes no explicit appeal to compensation in an afterlife.

39. It was Hobbes's reading of God's answer (*Leviathan* chap. xxxi, 16, 236–37 in the Hackett edition). It is also a good Calvinist reading. See his *Sermons on Job,* esp. Sermon 5, emphasizing Job 1:21, "The Lord gave, the Lord took away, blessed be the name of the Lord."

40. Here I follow the translation of 42:5–6 given in the Pines translation, which is closer to the KJV (and RSV and NRSV) than to the Pope translation.

41. Introduction to Part 1, 12/6-7. At the end of III 23, Maimonides writes that he has summed up all the notions of the Book of Job, "nothing being left aside except such matters as figure there because of the arrangement of the discourse and the continuation of the parable, according to what I have explained to you several times in this Treatise." (497/303). I don't believe Maimonides ever does mention the restoration of Job's prosperity.

42. It may, however, be necessary to take Maimonides' professed adherence to the point of view of the Law with a grain of salt for independent reasons. The contradiction he claims to identify in the Muʿtazilite position does not involve any doctrine peculiar to the Muʿtazilite view, but only doctrines which are shared between the Muʿtazilites and the adherents of the Law (that man has free will and that God knows everything). See 469/285 and 485/295. On the other hand, III, 20, 482–83/293-94, seems to take back the claim that the Muʿtazilite position is contradictory.

43. On one interesting theory of the formation of the book, in the original narrative Job maintained his patience throughout, though (in a section now lost) his friends urged him, as his wife had done, to "curse God

and die." (H. L. Ginsberg, "Job the Patient and Job the Impatient," *Conservative Judaism* 21/3 (1967):12-28) This would completely alter the significance of God's rebuke of the friends and praise of Job. But if the poetic dialogue is, as this hypothesis assumes, a later addition, we still have to reckon with the fact that whoever joined the poetic dialogue to the prose narrative and whoever judged the result worthy of inclusion in the canon apparently thought the composite work told a coherent story.

44. In "Maimonides, Aquinas, and Gersonides on Providence and Evil" (*Religious Studies* 20(1984):335-351) David Burrell criticizes Maimonides (and Gersonides) for mislocating the dramatic center of the work in the speech of Elihu, rather than the address from the whirlwind. Since Maimonides has to stretch to find anything new in what Elihu says, I hesitate to ascribe this view to him.

45. *Pace* Samuel Terrien, *Interpreter's Bible,* III 899. In conversation Eric Sward suggested a way of defending the claim that Job is guilty of pride in claiming to be innocent: we might so define pride that you commit the sin of pride merely by holding highly favorable beliefs about yourself without adequate evidence, even if the beliefs are true. On this view, Job commits the sin of pride, not by falsely believing that he is without fault, but by believing in an innocence no human can know himself to possess. This is an interesting conception of pride. But if that had been the point of God's answer, then it would seem that it should have focused, not on Job's ignorance of the operations of nature, but on his ignorance of himself.

46. 42:2. The Qumran Targum has an interesting variant at this point: "I know that you are able to do all, and power and wisdom are unlimited for you." See the Anchor *Job,* 349. This explicitly affirms both oninipotence and omniscience, whereas the Masoretic Text is explicit only about omnipotence.

47. *Leviathan* xxxi, ¶5, pp. 235–36 in the Hackett edition. If it is possible to translate 41:11 as in the RSV ("Who has given to me that I should repay him? Whatever is under the whole heaven is mine."), the Ash'arite/Calvinist/Hobbesian reading would be strongly confirmed, but there seems to be no consensus about that translation.

48. My agreement with Strauss is only of a general, methodological kind. So far as I can see, he is never explicit about the nature of Maimonides' esoteric teaching regarding providence. See "The Literary Character of the *Guide,*" in *Maimonides: A Collection* of *Critical Cssays,* ed. Joseph Buijs (Notre Dame, Indiana: University of Notre Dame Press, 1988), 50–51 and "How to Begin to Study the *Guide,*" *liv–lv,* in the Pines edition of the *Guide.* As Fox remarks somewhere, Strauss' discussion of Maimonides seems itself to be an instance of esoteric writing, as well as a discussion of it.

49. "The Literary Character," 48. I would not, however, hold that the Ash'arite view is one which occurs only once in the *Guide.* It seems to me to

surface also in III 53, where Maimonides writes that "every benefit that comes from Him . . . is called *hesed*," that is, an act of "beneficence toward one who has no right at all to claim this from you" (p. 631/392). I take this to imply that God cannot be under any obligation to man.

50. First published in Spanish, in Frankfurt, and subsequently in Latin. My page references are to the English translation by E. H. Lindo, 2 vols. (London, 1842).

51. Maimonides does allude to Job's denial of the resurrection of the dead, pointing out that some of the sages of the Talmud accused Job of blasphemy because of it (III 23, 492/300). But when he discusses the excuse other sages made for Job ("A man is not to be blamed for what he does when suffering"), he treats this as if the blasphemous opinion to be excused were that God treats the righteous and the wicked equally, and not the denial of resurrection. Perhaps Maimonides' avoidance of this issue is one reason why some who denied resurrection claimed his authority for doing so, in spite of the fact that he had explicitly included the life-to-come as one of the essential articles of Judaic faith. See Maimonides' *Essay on Resurrection*, in *Crisis and Leadership: Epistles of Maimonides.*, trans. Abraham Halkin, comment by David Hartman (Philadelphia: Jewish Publication Society, 1985), 217.

52. This is how Menasseh characterizes Bildad's position, II, 41. When Maimonides describes Bildad's position, he does not claim (nor would the text he cites permit him to claim) that the compensation is in the afterlife.

53. See the Goodman edition, 155: "God foreknew that the angels would never disobey Him, and it is not possible for what contravenes His foreknowledge to take place. For if things were to take place contrary to what we have supposed, God would have foreknown that instead." In *Guide* III 24, Maimonides considers the notion of a trial, though in connection with the Abraham-Isaac story, not the story of Job. He finds that to be the strongest scriptural case for the theory that God sends calamities to an individual, without their having been preceded by sin, in order that the individual's reward might be increased. He agrees with Saadiah that God's foreknowledge precludes conducting a trial so that God will know the individual's virtue. On his account, the purpose of Abraham's trial was that the people of the religious community should know what the love and fear of God require of them, and that they must take a prophetic revelation as true even if it comes to them in a dream or vision.

I suppose Maimonides might say something analogous about Job. The first purpose seems relevant, even if the second is not. But it seems a harder thing to say in the case of Job than in the case of Abraham. The way the story of Abraham is usually told at least, Abraham did not have to sacrifice Isaac; he had only to show himself willing to do so. So he does not actually have to suffer the loss of his only son, whom he loves. But Job has to suffer all the calamities the Satan had planned for him. If this is to show the community what the love and fear of God require of you—that you should remain loyal to God no matter how he treats you—that may be counterproductive, generating more doubt than piety.

Both Saadiah and Maimonides assume that God has what later came to be called "middle knowledge," that is, knowledge of counterfactual conditionals in which the consequent describes the free actions of God's creatures, such as "If David stayed in Keilah, Saul would besiege the city." (The example comes from I Samuel 23:1–14.) Middle knowledge is controversial. Robert Adams denies that God has it, essentially because Adams does not understand what the truth conditions for such counterfactuals would be. (See his "Middle Knowledge and the Problem of Evil," *American Philosophical Quarterly* 14[1977]:109–17.) I think the Saadian-Maimonidean intuition that God must have middle knowledge is sound, and have argued this in a paper-in-progress called "Some Problems About the Coherence of (Christian) Theism."

54. II, 41. Menasseh is referring here, not to anything Maimonides says in the *Guide,* but to the position he takes on the resurrection of the dead in the *Essay on Resurrection*, 225–27. Saadiah deals with Job 7:9 in a similar way (Goodman edition, 209).

55. Lindo cites the following testimonial from *Rees's Cyclopedia:* "This work shews that its Author had a profound and intimate acquaintance with the Old Testament Writings, and it procured for him the esteem and admiration of all the learned, as well Christians as Jews. It was recommended to the notice of Biblical Scholars by the learned Grotius" (vii).

56. *TTP* ii, Bruder section 55; G III, 43/13–19.

57. This is apparently an insecure inference from the fact that Job lived in the land of Uz. Cf. David Clines: "The name [Uz] . . . does not mean that Job necessarily *is* a foreigner, for most Jews of the exilic period and beyond . . . lived outside (the borders of Israel, and the patriarchs themselves . . . were almost as often to be found outside the land as within it. The Book of Job simply does not say whether or not Job is an Israelite" (*Word Biblical Commentary, Job 1–20,* 10). Nevertheless, Cline also comments that Job's designation as an inhabitant of Uz "signifies that the action has a horizon which is not peculiarly Israelite . . . by leaving open the question of his race the book effectively makes his experience transcend the distinction between . . . Jew and non-Jew." This would vindicate the point Spinoza is making.

58. Initiating a controversy which is still going on. See Pope, xlix–l.

59. *Leviathan,* chap. 33, ¶12, takes the fact that the bulk of Job is written in verse as evidence that the book is not a history but a philosophical treatise on the problem of evil: "Verse is no usual style of such as either

are themselves in great pain, as Job, or of such as come to comfort them, as his friends, but in philosophy, especially moral philosophy in ancient time, frequent."

60. Ecclesiastes 9:1–3, cited twice by Spinoza in the *TTP*, in vi, 32 (111/87*)* and in xix, 7 (III/229). In each case Spinoza accepts the traditional ascription of Ecclesiastes to Solomon. The former passage also cites Ecclesiastes 3:19–20, denying the immortality of the soul: "The fate of humans and the fate of animals is the same; as one dies, so dies the other. They all have the same breath, and humans have no advantage over the animals, for all is vanity . . ."

CHAPTER 8

Spinoza's Rupture with Tradition— His Hints of a Jewish Modernity

HEIDI M. RAVVEN

Near the end of the *Ethics*, in Book V in the Scholium to Proposition 39, Spinoza articulates for the reader the optimal ethical, bodily, and emotional state. Reflecting on the process of transition and transformation that leads to this perfected condition, he writes:

> In this life, therefore, we mainly endeavor that the body of childhood, as far as its nature allows and is conducive thereto, should develop into a body that is capable of a great many activities and is related to a mind that is highly conscious of itself, of God, and of things, and *in such a way that everything related to its memory or imagination should be of scarcely any importance in comparison with its intellect*, as I have already stated in the scholium to the preceding proposition.[1]

Blessedness is characterized as a progression or developmental progress that diminishes the influence of Memory and Imagination in one's cognitive and affective life. If we look at the preceding Scholium, as Spinoza directs us, we find that he there contrasts the part of the human mind that survives and that which perishes with the body. That which perishes, he says, is "of no account compared with the part of it that survives."[2] And lest we assume that Spinoza is simply reiterating some standard account of the separation of mind from body in death, I call to your attention what I and others have called his "materialism,"[3] a doctrine that Spinoza evokes immediately following this Scholium both in Proposition 39 and its Scholium, already quoted above. Proposition 39 reads:

187

He whose *body* is capable of the greatest amount of activity has a
mind whose greatest part is eternal.[4] (my emphasis)

This is no standard Neoplatonic doctrine of the mind's separation from the
body as a necessary condition of its final intellectual perfection. Rather it
points to the expression of the body-as-itself-already-perfected. It is *that*
which survives. Now the precise details of Spinoza's doctrine of immortality,
notoriously elliptical, are not our present concern. The questions I raise here
are, these: First, what is the nature of the imaginative thinking that is to be
muted in the course of a lifetime? Second, what is the content of the memories to be forsaken or at least rendered less poignant? Third, and more basi-
cally: Why does Spinoza maintain that memories ought to be less significant
over the course of a lifetime, rather than accumulating, as we usually think
of them, older people having a wealth of memories upon which they may
reflect and focus and the young having but few? I think we can get a handle
on how Spinoza would answer these questions by examining what he says
about Imagination and Memory in the *Ethics*,[5] glancing from time to time
also at what he says about them in the *Tractatus Theologico-Politicus*.

Spinoza envisions the rational control and management of the imagination as vital in the institution and maintenance of a free democratic society.
Moreover, he regards imaginative ideas as informing the highest cognition,
intuitive knowledge, giving rise to the perfected ethical life that is its expression.[6] Nevertheless it is Spinoza's treatment of the imagination in its initial
unexamined and unreformed condition that I will address here. This paper
will focus exclusively on the initial imaginative condition that is to be tran-
scended and leave to another occasion Spinoza's account of how imaginative ideas can and ought to be (rationally) reformed and transformed.

In EIIP17S Spinoza states his definitions of the terms 'image' and the
'Imagination':

> To retain the customary words, the affections of the human Body,
> whose ideas present external bodies as present to us, we shall call
> images of things (*imagines*), even if they do not reproduce the [NS:
> external] figures of things. And when the Mind regards bodies in
> this way, we shall say that it imagines.[7]

Thus, first of all, to imagine is to maintain as existent a certain external
thing[8] insofar as one's body registers its presence, having been affected by it.
Now any time the body registers that affected condition, the mind maintains as present that external thing, even if that thing is not, or is no longer,
present, Spinoza writes.[9] The imaginative idea indicates and makes a claim
about the constitution of one's own body, Spinoza argues, more than it

articulates the external thing. Moreover, ideas are never corporeal images, Spinoza emphasizes, but intellectual acts.[10] They make propositional claims[12] and are more like beliefs according to Edwin Curley. Nevertheless, Spinoza is quick to point out that the imagination as such does not err. "I should like you to note," he writes, "that the imaginations of the mind, looked at in themselves, contain no error; i.e., the mind does not err from the fact that it imagines."[12] Error enters in, Spinoza goes on to explain, insofar as no additional idea excludes the existence of the imaginative claim of the presence of an object. For the imaginative idea is simply expressive of the actual (true) state of one's body, as manifesting the condition that it had when affected by that object, and it expresses that state without error. Spinoza has just reminded us at the beginning of this Scholium that he had already demonstrated that the human body exists just as we sense it (EIIP13C) and that, therefore, "we must not doubt experience."

We can already note that memory is inherent in the operation of the imagination. For whenever the body, for whatever reason, manifests a certain state expressive of the presence of a certain object, it brings to consciousness the mental idea of, and claims the presence of, the external object with which that bodily state had been in the past *associated*, even if that object is not in fact then present:

> Although the external bodies by which the human body has once been affected may no longer exist, the mind will regard them as present whenever this activity of the body is repeated. (IIP17CDem)[13]

While Spinoza does not explicitly identify this simple imaginative task of perception and recognition as involving memory and recollection, he no doubt has Descartes' *Passions of the Soul* in mind. For Descartes had argued that the recollection of an initial association is exactly what is involved in understanding the relation of mental states to external objects.[14] Spinoza, not surprisingly, goes on in the next Proposition and its Scholium to introduce a principle of Imaginative Association that operates as a function of Memory and Recollection.[15] The imagination works by remembering and recalling how experience has happened to link together various temporally contiguous bodily conditions:

> The mind imagines (preceding Cor.) any given body for the following reason, that the human body is affected and conditioned by the impressions of an external body in the same way as it was affected when certain of its parts were acted upon by the external body. But, by hypothesis, the human body was at that time conditioned in such a way that the mind imagined two bodies at the same time.

Therefore, it will now also imagine two bodies at the same time, and the mind, in imagining one of them, will straightway recollect the other also. (IIP18D)[16]

In the Scholium that follows immediately upon this Spinoza tells the reader that now,

we clearly understand what memory is. It is simply a connection of ideas involving the nature of things outside the human body, a connection that occurs in the mind parallel to the order and connection of the affections of the human body.[17]

In EIIIP16 Spinoza will introduce another way that imaginative association works in addition to temporal contiguity: The mind, in imagining, associates things that are similar with each other.

Spinoza points out the role of imaginative association in *linguistic* recognition in EIIP18S. He makes the point in explaining the proposition that puts forth the principle of the imaginative association of *things* perceived at the same time. He writes:

For example, from thinking of the word '*pomum*' (apple) a Roman will straightway fall to thinking of the fruit, which has no likeness to that articulated sound nor anything in common with it other than that the man's body has often been affected by them both; that is the man often heard the word '*pomum*' while seeing the fruit.

Thus he must mean that the principle is widely applicable beyond the association and recollection of things perceived at the same time: It clearly includes the association of language and things and I would suggest also of psychophysical states with states of affairs.

Descartes considered the linking of the mental and physical states of a person as contingent (because it reflects the link between mind and body). But for Spinoza the mental state simply *is* an alternative expression of the same physical state. Descartes writes, for example (*PA* II, ¶¶107–08, 365–66):

Our soul and our body are so linked that once we have joined some bodily action with a certain thought, the one does not occur afterwards without the other occurring too . . .

For it seems that *when our soul began to be joined to our body*, its first passions must have arisen on some occasion when the blood . . . was a more suitable fuel than usual for maintaining the heat which is the principle of life. This caused the soul to join itself willingly to the fuel, i.e., to love it.

Spinoza follows Descartes in holding that imagination reflects our past experiences. It is its component of recollection which is open to modification for both—for Descartes by an act of will and for Spinoza by the correction and expansion of knowledge. In neither case is imagination—or its concomitant affects—dispensed with but rather rationally reformed.

Harry Wolfson[18] suggests that, like Descartes, Spinoza reduces what the medievals designated 'the internal senses'—in contrast with the five external senses—to two, Imagination and Memory. For Spinoza, however, unlike for Descartes, Wolfson holds that the two become interchangeable as indicated by his use of the phrase, "imagination or memory,"[19] on several occasions (EIIP40S; EIIIP2S; and EVP34S, the last passage is the one quoted above on the first page of this chapter). And this is no doubt because the act of having an object present to oneself in awareness in fact involves recollection. In recollection, a certain physical condition of one's body is evoked. It is recalled in association with the memory of a certain external object. The recollection also brings forth memories of other objects, chronologically linked with the first, or identical, or similar to it. For Spinoza, imagination essentially grasps one's own bodily state (although occasioned by the impinging of an external object). Everything else is a memory associated with it and triggered whenever imaginative perception is engaged. So perception and memory are aspects of the same cognitive process. They are not fully discrete cognitive events. Even the recognition of an object, on this analysis, necessarily involves the memory of one's first encounter with that object. It is informed by the memory of the first association of a particular bodily state with its occasioning object. And it is also informed by the memory of the other objects that were present at the time and even by thoughts of objects not then present but similar to them.

Hence Spinoza's insistence that the imagination functions passively,[20] "for it is not within the free power of the mind to remember or forget anything."[21] Imagination is not the creation at will of fantasies of nonexistent objects—flying horses and centaurs—but is the least voluntary kind of thinking. For it is driven by memories and associations beyond one's control or even rational understanding.[22] Imagination is our helplessness in the face of how past experiences exercise a continuing domination over the present. Spinoza further remarks that:

> the mental decision that is believed to be free is not distinct from imagination and memory, and is nothing but the affirmation which an idea insofar as it is an idea, necessarily involves (Pr. 49, II). So these mental decisions arise in the mind from the same necessity as the ideas of things existing in actuality.[23]

The passivity of the imaginative mind has important implications for Spinoza's account in the *Tractatus Theologico-Politicus* of how common cultural

memories, mediated by the two great imaginative forces shaping and trans-
mitting a common ethos, Language[24] and Religion, dominate the individual.
That the imagination is a type of thinking that triggers an entire constellation
of associations suggests that it reawakens a whole context and brings with it
all sorts of related contexts. Every moment pricks and calls forth cascading
memories.

It is not surprising then that Spinoza argues that time is a product of
the imagination.[25] He writes, "it is in the nature of reason to perceive things
under the aspect of eternity *sub quadam specie aeternitatis*,"[26] but "nobody
doubts that time . . . is a product of the imagination."[27] "It is in the nature
of reason to regard things as necessary,"[28] but the temporally bound imagination leads us to regard things as contingent[29] and, we might add, also as
historical. Imagination, is, essentially a historical kind of thinking, in contrast with the timeless truths of philosophy and science. Similarly, imagination is essentially local. For imaginative associations are emergent from and
inextricably expressive of one's own locus of awareness. As Spinoza puts it:

> We conceive things as actual in two ways: either in so far as we
> conceive them as related to a fixed time and place, or in so far as
> we conceive them to be contained in God and to follow from the
> necessity of the divine nature. (EVP29S)[30]

Imaginative thinking is never solipsistic for it provides real access to
one's own narrow world or context. Imaginative associations are inextricably tied to a local world and bring that world as baggage to all that is new.
The imagination always constructs the world through the prism of one's
own bodily and biographical experience, operating cumulatively and not in
isolated fragments. Since it perceives via one's arbitrary and contingent, yet,
contextually driven, associations it is accurate and yet at the same time,
highly biased. We have seen that the mind, in imagining, does not err insofar as it restricts itself to presenting to itself passively actual data derived
from the body's present and past experiences. Nevertheless, in so doing, it
does not think *adequately*. For it does not adequately know the external
object.[31] Nor, for that matter, does it know its own body adequately.[32]

> Whenever the human mind perceives things after the common
> order of nature, it does not have an adequate knowledge of itself,
> nor of its body, nor of external bodies, but only a confused and
> fragmentary knowledge. (EIIP29Cor)[33]

The kind of personal autobiographical construction of knowledge that imagination provides is inadequate not insofar as the material reality it expresses
is in fact itself not real—for it *is* real. But it is partial and hence potentially
misleading. "Inadequate and confused ideas follow by the same necessity as

adequate or clear and distinct ideas,"[34] for both reflect and express empirical experience. Yet the explanatory notions that the mind constructs through the cognitive operations of the imagination—namely, the "imaginative universals" derived by generalizing from personal associations—are both false and biased.[35] The common order of nature as we experience it is thus 'real'—that is, empirically derived. But that does not make it the causal order of science:

> Those notions called 'universal', such as 'man', 'horse', 'dog', etc., arise when so many images are formed in the human body simultaneously (e.g., of man) that our capacity to imagine them is surpassed, not indeed completely, but to the extent that the mind is unable to imagine the small[36] differences of individuals . . . and imagines distinctly only their common characteristic in so far as the body is affected by them. . . . The mind expresses this by the word 'man', and predicates this word of an infinite number of individuals. . . .
>
> But it should be noted that not all men form these notions in the same way; in the case of each person the notions vary according as that thing varies whereby the body has more frequently been affected and which the mind readily imagines or calls to mind. . . . Each will form universal images according to the conditioning of his body.[37]

Some current theories in cognitive science of how universal categories are formed by the mind take a page from Spinoza so to speak. George Lakoff, in *Women, Fire, and Dangerous Things*,[38] argues that recent research in a number of cognitive sciences, especially anthropology, linguistics, and psychology (xiv), on the nature and development of conceptual categories has shown that (xii) "our bodily experience and the way we use imaginative mechanisms are central to how we construct categories to make sense of experience":

> On the traditional view, reason is abstract and disembodied. On the new view, reason has a bodily basis. The traditional view sees reason as literal, as primarily about propositions that can be objectively either true or false. The new view takes imaginative aspects of reason—metaphor, metonymy, and mental imagery—as central to reason, rather than as a peripheral and inconsequential adjunct to the literal. (xi)

According to the 'the new view,' Lakoff argues that thought is (xiv–xv): (1) "embodied," (2) imaginative," (3) "has gestalt properties and is thus not atomic," and (4) "has an ecological structure," which means that such processes as "learning and memory, depend on the overall structure of the conceptual system and on what the concepts mean. Thought is thus more than just the mechanical manipulation of abstract symbols." Lakoff suggests (xvi) that on his model in contrast with the purely procedural one, "meaningful thought and reason essentially concern the nature of the organism doing the thinking—including the nature of its body, its interactions in its environment, its social character, and so on." Although Spinoza certainly tries to show that the imaginative construction of universals can and ought to be overcome, many of the other characteristics that Lakoff mentions here as always obtaining are also found in rational thought by Spinoza, because of its embodiment. For in Spinoza all thinking fulfills the desires of the organism; rational thinking, and not only imagination, has a gestalt quality generating scenes and not atomic facts; and rational and intuitive thinking are never confined to the mechanical manipulation of abstract symbols for Spinoza.

Imaginative cognition is the sole source of error, and one of the forms that error takes is personal or cultural biases.[39] In explaining how categories are formed by the mind, Spinoza introduces his famous threefold categorization of cognitive processes; and he divides the first, most primitive, kind of cognition according to the two ways that it forms imaginative universals, one idiosyncratic and personal and the other social and cultural:

> From what has been said above, it is clear that we perceive many things and form universal notions:
>
> 1. from individual objects that have been presented to us through the senses in a fragmentary and confused manner without any intellectual order (see Cor. Pr. 29, II); for that reason I call such perceptions 'knowledge from casual experience'.
>
> 2. from symbols [or 'signs', *signis*]. For example, from having heard or read certain words, we recollect things and form certain ideas of them which are like them and through which we imagine the things (Sch. Pr. 18, II).
>
> Both of these ways of regarding things I shall henceforth refer to as 'knowledge of the first kind', 'opinion', or imagination.[40]

Spinoza here introduces the cultural component of imaginative cognition: One may perceive through the prism of one's own past experience via the categories or 'templates'[41] that are emergent from, and expressive of, one's own memory and that are triggered by all memories and perceptions.[42] But some templates are held in common and available through language and culture. These are common not because they are natural or scientifically true. They are not the *common notions* but instead are the products of a common inheritance—namely, the heritage of a given language and culture.

These are the (linguistic) signs or symbols[43] that are transmitted through hearing and reading, that is, tradition.[44]

De Deugd[45] and Curley[46] deëmphasize and even deny the symbolic character and social construction of the imaginative categories. In their concern to prove Spinoza's understanding of and commitment to the empirical contribution to adequate knowledge, they privilege the atomism of sense perception and play down the associative character of its construction of a world view that is typically built up through false inferences and biased categories. Yet such operations of the imagination take up far more room in the texts than does the reliability of perceptual simples! De Deugd (22) denies without argument that Spinoza's use of opinion and signs is of any import. He makes that denial a methodological principle of his entire treatment:

> The term 'opinion', despite its Platonic overtones, seems to carry little significance of its own. . . . There are no indications that any special significance must be attached to this term going beyond the very general description of Spinoza's first kind of knowledge. . .
>
> In addition it is worth noticing that the terms 'hearsay' and 'hearing' scarcely play any part in the elaboration of the Spinozistic epistemology.

At the end of his study (246), De Deugd concludes that imagination "is the continuous stream of sense perception . . . It is a non-verbal 'stream of consciousness', consisting only of sense perception and needing no verbalization." Yet Spinoza insists that language is included in imagination, as is all of the symbolic. The imagination is not just empirical impingement and memories of that impingement. Rather imagination works by its own, non-rational, rules of association; and, as we shall see, it also suppresses unpleasant images and favors pleasant ones. It makes (false) causal inferences and explanations. These processes are hardly reducible to some mere stream of consciousness. De Deugd treats (245) imaginative ideas as correlates of corporeal images, that is "mental pictures." But Spinoza repeatedly denies this, emphasizing that ideas, even imaginative ones, are acts of thinking!

Curley, similarly, interprets imagination as atoms of sense perception. He goes so far as to deny (34) that Spinoza's designation of imagination as including knowledge from 'hearsay' or 'report' includes any knowledge based on authority, even arguing that Spinoza's knowledge from report and knowledge on authority are mutually exclusive! He writes:

> It is, as the comparison with the parrot [from *Short Treatise* II, 1] might have told us, a very simple *stimulus-response situation*. Indeed, I suspect that once you introduce the notion of authority you get

something which is not knowledge "from report" at all. For to say
that the reporter is taken to be an authority implies a judgment on
his reliability as a truth-teller. If this judgment is supported by evidence—if we take the reporter's word because we have found him,
or people like him to be trustworthy in similar situations in the
past—then I think Spinoza might want to classify this as knowledge from vagrant experience.[47] (My emphasis)

This, I think, is to misunderstand Spinoza: First, if a person were literally
like a "parrot" responding to a stimulus one would repeat utterances as if
they were random, meaningless squawks. Spinoza's first kind of knowledge,
however, has the person in question adopting and following the rule (i.e.,
the meaning) to which the "squawks," so to speak, refer. Spinoza could
hardly deem a mere parrot performance as a form of "knowledge" or treat
it in any way as something that involves belief. But Spinoza is categorizing
beliefs and levels of understanding, for the person in question is able to
understand the rule in a rudimentary way after hearing it. Mere mimicking
would preclude even the little understanding it takes to notice the difference
between the general articulation in language of a rule and a particular instance of its application. For even the most rudimentary cognition presupposes some grasp of the referential quality and the generality of language.

But a person who follows a rule by rote does not understand the rule in
any other than its literal, surface sense—just enough to apply it, but without
understanding why one does so, why the rule works, or even whether it in
fact can be expected to work. For "he still governs his actions according to
this rule," (albeit) "without having had any more knowledge of the rule of
three than a blind man has of color," Spinoza writes here. Thus, the parrot
simile (and the blind man, too) must refer to one who adopts wholesale and
uncritically the beliefs—and rules—(not the noncognitive, nonreferential
performance) of others. But that is to accept them—to believe them, adopt
them on authority, to have one's mind filled with them and not merely one's
outward behavior. Thus, even though this first kind of knowledge represents
a very rudimentary cognitive condition, it is, nevertheless, not quite as primitive as that of the literal parrot to whom no cognitive understanding (i.e.,
the acquisition of a belief content as a result of hearing and understanding
and following the meaning of language, of linguistic utterances, and applying that meaning in specific instances) of even the most basic kind, but only
literal behavioral mimicking, is attributable.

Moreover, it is simply not true, as Curley argues, that, according to Spinoza, knowledge on authority would imply that "we take the reporter's
word because we have found him, or people like him to be trustworthy in
similar situations in the past." Knowledge on authority—that is, accepting

and adopting uncritically others' claims as one's own—is not a matter of the individual's personal determination according to prior evidence of who is a historically reliable "truth-teller." Curley's analysis amounts to thrusting upon Spinoza a prevalent, but naïve (and false), twentieth-century Anglo-American notion of how knowledge on authority operates: It is deemed optional and every piece of it is open to adoption or rejection. Some of us, today, might (naïvely and mistakenly) assume that authoritative knowledge—and even cultural transmission—is something each individual examines and voluntarily chooses to adopt piecemeal, item by item, fact by fact, according to some standard of reliability—either of the knowledge itself or of the person reporting it—which each person brings to it. Spinoza, however, makes it clear in the *Tractatus Theologico-Politicus* that he knew better.

The account of religious tradition in the *TTP* makes absolutely clear that the imagination fills the mind through the passive introjection of the common order of imaginative associations—primarily those of language and culture but also those originating in (random and idiosyncratic) personal experience, as well. (Spinoza follows Maimonides' *Guide to the Perplexed* in his account of the imaginative nature of prophecy, that is, religion, and also of language. The imaginative character of both phenomena includes their conventionality—a point on which Spinoza also follows Maimonides.) Spinoza's later, mature account of the first stage of knowledge exposes it as a naïve and uncritical passive posture toward the world as constructed by language, culture and random experience. Thus, the individual is, to begin with, not a tabula rasa, judging each piece of knowledge prior to its adoption by some critical standard. Rather, one is at first mentally filled with the imaginative world of a culturally specific language and tradition. One takes in the world indirectly at first, according to the way it has been imaginatively constructed—that is, interpreted—by others and on their authority. Confirming our account is Wolfson's demonstration of the linguistic origins of Spinoza's terminology of Hearsay or Report. For while the terms literally mean 'hearing' or 'telling,' they are used in Hebrew to mean and refer to Tradition. As Wolfson (II: 132) shows, Spinoza's classification of knowledge follows Saadiah's by including as a special and additional category of knowledge, Knowledge from Hearsay or Tradition. Thus, while Wolfson's linguistic argument shows these terms to refer to knowledge on authority here in the *Ethics*, the later extensive elaboration of this stage in the *TTP* as that of the adoption of religious cultural tradition on authority leaves no doubt in the matter.

That the imagination constructs universals rooted in a particular location, time, and culture, indicates that the imagination is a source of common beliefs and attitudes and not only of differences and conflicts.[48] In Part III of the *Ethics*, Spinoza also devotes considerable space to explaining how the imagination is driven, paradoxically perhaps, in its basic desire to further the self, to construct *common* emotions and emotional attitudes. Language captures the common imaginative categories that arise in this way and transmits them intra-culturally and cross-generationally. From Spinoza's example of how a painful personal experience might give rise to a general prejudice, a negative ethnic stereotype, for example, we can see how an experience might be held in common and enshrined in an imaginative linguistic category—Nigger, Kike, etc. Spinoza says:

> If anyone is affected with pleasure or pain by someone of a class or nation different from his own and the pleasure or pain is accompanied [i.e., by imaginative association] by the idea of that person as its cause, under the general category of that class or nation, he will love or hate not only him but all of the same class or nation.[49]

Language thus reinforces common cultural biases inherent in the categories by which we construe the world. Once again "Opinion" involves the incorporation into one's imaginative universals—which are formed from the ongoing mass of data—of some common beliefs. Knowledge from "signs" designates the integration of received linguistic and cultural categories into one's personal generalizations from sensual memory. Arbitrary personal generalizations and common beliefs generate together imaginative universals: "Opinion" integrates one's own isolated and random experiences into the cultural universals conveyed by language and by cultural practices—Spinoza says that one picks them up through "hearing" and "reading." Together the two historical aspects of the imagination—one predicated on personal memory and the other on the symbolic rendering of collective memory—make one's mind a reflection of its immediate world and also of the social world with its common memories. The imagination, thus, continuously renders the mind an ongoing product of its environment. The imagination creates common experiences, through shared emotions. It also integrates disparate experiences through a common language and culture.

Imaginative thinking is driven by its essential affectivity, that is by its desires, and not only by its cognitive passivity.[50] Spinoza proposes that imaginative ideas are sources of pleasure and pain,[51] because they express the changes in the condition of one's body as it is affected by external bodies. Spinoza defines the emotions as just such imaginative ideas—or the internal component (and not the representational component) of imaginative thinking:

> An affect . . . is an imagination, insofar as [the affect] indicates the constitution of the body.[52]

The primary emotions of pleasure and pain register a person's increased or decreased activity in both mind and body as one entity. Activity designates an enhancement, and passivity a diminishing, of the power of the conatus, that is, of the capacity for self-determination.[53] The conatus is desire for self. All the emotions are variations of the conatus and composed of its three basic states, pain, pleasure, and desire.

> 3. By emotions (*affectus*) I understand the affections of the body by which the body's power of activity is increased or diminished, assisted or checked, together with the ideas of these affections.[54]

In an emotion, we register the presence—accurately or not—of an external object and feel pleasure or pain according to whether it has enhanced or diminished our capacity for self-determination. Our judgments about the causes of our pain and pleasure are implicit in the ideas of the affections and thus are themselves components of our emotions.[55] The affects are emotional attitudes towards objects. As such, emotions are subject to both error and distortion. They err because they depend in part on an associative component that is often arbitrary, idiosyncratic, or held on authority, rather than truly explanatory and predictive. They are subject to distortion because we prefer pleasure to pain and hence deceive ourselves with wishful thinking, the sources of the traditional motives of hope and fear.

Spinoza firmly maintains the affective character of thinking: The mind as well as the body, because it is in identity with the body, is essentially desiderative and a source of pleasure,[56] and its thinking serves the purpose of its own conatus, that is, of its own self-furthering.[57] Thus we try to entertain pleasurable thoughts and, even further, we desire to have pleasurable beliefs about ourselves:

> We endeavor to affirm of ourselves and of an object loved whatever we imagine affects us or the loved object with pleasure, and, on the other hand, to negate whatever we imagine affects us or the loved object with pain.[58]

Hence, the imaginative mind as far as it can is wont to bring to mind the thoughts that give it pleasure and to avoid systematically those that are painful (or even merely non-pleasurable).[59] Yet it is generally at the mercy of the externally impinging common flow of things and of its past associations with them, so it can never (*pace* Descartes) exercise exclusive control over its own thoughts. Spinoza never tires of reminding us that "human power is very limited and is infinitely surpassed by the power of external causes."[60] Despite the mind's desires and our deepest preferences, reality intervenes. None but the most deluded of us lives in a hallucinatory world of our own making.

Yet even if the mind were able to bring to its awareness only those imaginative ideas that give it pleasure and to exclude from awareness painful realities, the pleasures derived would still be incomplete and inadequate. For they would be passive pleasures and thus mixed with pain. Imaginative ideas are by definition "passive transitions."[61] They thus diminish our self-determination, even though the mind, in recalling them, "endeavors to imagine those things that increase or assist the body's power of activity."[62] Pleasure is the expression of an increase in one's capacity for self-determination and a decrease in the sense of being at the mercy of external forces. Yet, paradoxically, Spinoza warns us that many of the events that make us feel empowered in this way themselves depend on external circumstances. Hence they are "passive transitions" to greater activity. So the enhanced self-determination they promise is at best partial, certainly unreliable and, more often than not, illusory. The imaginative life simply cannot bring us the control over our lives that it seems to promise. For here the pursuit of self-determination proves self-defeating. It results in less, not more, independence from external circumstance.

The imaginative life, then, is thus seductive and corruptive. For imagination always holds out the promise of more pleasure than it can deliver. Hence Spinoza's General Definition of (passive) Emotions is: "A *confused* idea whereby the mind affirms a greater or lesser force of existence of its body or parts of its body than was previously the case, and by the occurrence of which the mind is determined to [i.e., desires to] think of one thing rather than another" (my emphasis).[63] Unexamined pleasure and pain do not turn out to be accurate indicators of enhanced self-determination at all. Spinoza points out that they are not just slightly off at times but wildly inaccurate. For pleasure and pain can be indirectly or accidentally [*per accidens*] occasioned by *anything whatsoever*! Anything whatsoever can be associated by similarity or temporal contemporaneity with something that causes us pleasure or pain. Hence anything whatsoever can be recalled as a source of any emotion.[64] In imaginative thinking pleasure is pursued and pain is avoided according to the rules of associative memory. And associative memory includes cultural tradition.

What Spinoza seems to be saying is that we (consciously or unconsciously, implicitly or explicitly)[64] hold plausible causal explanations of why we feel pleasure and pain based on the idiosyncrasies of our narrow experience and of our imaginative cultural narratives, when in fact they are at best partial and generally highly arbitrary. They often systematically ignore all the painful countervailing evidence . . . yet we tend to treat these interested and partial explanations as reliably predictive of what will offer us self-determination (and hence pleasure) in the face of the onslaught of the environment. Imaginative Association is a source of error and bias *first of all* because it masquerades as causal explanation when it really only grasps the correlations that it forges between external world and internal states. We naively assume that the objects that prompt the bodily states that produce in us their corresponding imaginative ideas are both adequately expressed in these ideas and adequately explained by them. This is a major theme of *Ethics* Part III. Spinoza further says of these "ideas of affections" that they "are like conclusions without premises," because they do not grasp the true causal relatiions between the body and external objects. The problem is compounded because we not only *act* on this buried, that is, unconscious, mistaken explanatory system, but we are loath to part with it, because of the recollections of pleasures it provides. These pleasures, although they are in part illusory, dispose us to wish and hope for more of the same. This is the *second* problem with the imagination, namely, its interestedness. Our false hopes explain our reluctance to assess honestly the partial data and inadequate inferences—from association—that *are* available to us.

The problem reminds me of a recent incident with our Turkish Angora cats, Moxie and Vashti, who spend each night in the garage. One morning the cats would not come out of the garage, no matter what we offered them. During the night they had caught a mole. Their eyes were now glued to the space beneath the garage door and we could not budge them. They were, no doubt, waiting for another mole to scamper in. The memory of intense pleasure and an arbitrary (unlikely to be repeated) individual association had corrupted their minds. They had mistakenly formed a causal (and hence predictive) link between the door opening and the idea of prey, where there was only an incidental correlation. And, their thinking was driven not only by memory and association but also by the pleasure principle! For their pleasure was so great that one incident had raised their hopes and given them an illusion of mastery. They now knew how to capture moles! As Spinoza suggests, this kind of associative and affective memory is highly influenced by temporal proximity:[66] A week later, the cats more or less ignored the garage door and were reluctant even to go into the garage. Most of us, in Spinoza's estimation, function for much of the time at a similar primitive level of cognition—a level we share with animals, although the associations involved in the human version are widened through language and culture.

Charles Rycroft's account of Freud's doctrine of the Pleasure Principle, in *A Critical Dictionary of Psychoanalysis*,[67] would seem to fit Spinoza's characterization of imaginative thinking:

> Pleasure Principle According to Freud (1911, 1917), the psyche is initially actuated solely by the pleasure or *pleasure-pain principle*, which leads it to avoid pain or unpleasure aroused by increases in instinctual tension and to do so by hallucinating the satisfaction necessary to reduce the tension. Only later, after the ego has developed, is the pleasure principle modified by the reality principle,

which leads the individual to replace hallucinatory wish-fulfill-
ment by adaptive behaviour.

Unlike Freud, Spinoza does not have a doctrine of instinctual tension or of
full-blown hallucination. Nevertheless, Spinoza, like Freud, argues that in
imaginative thinking beliefs are driven far more by hope (and fear) than by
a realistic assessment of what even associative thinking would lead one to
believe. The imaginative mind is deflected (and corrupted) from the integrity
of even the partial local truths of personal memory and culture by its pursuit of pleasure and its avoidance of pain.[68]

We can now understand Spinoza's insistence on the domination of the
imaginative mind by the emotions of Hope and Fear. These emotions also
essentially characterize Superstition and even Religion.

We are so constituted that we are ready to believe what we hope
and reluctant to believe what we fear, and that we over-estimate
and under-estimate in such cases. This is the origin of Superstition
(*superstitiones*), to which men are everywhere a prey.[69]

Hope and fear, emotions characteristic of a weak mind,[70] impede self-determination, leaving a person vulnerable to external, social control. Religious
authorities exercise control over the masses by inspiring hope and fear of
imagined rewards and punishments. Yet they can thereby act to further the
social good—although at a cost to personal autonomy—when they so induce
in the multitude the desire to do what is in the public interest. For "not by
hope alone, but also and especially by fear of incurring dreadful punishment
after death, . . . [the multitude is persuaded] to live according to the commandments of the divine law."[71] Spinoza suggests that "it is not surprising
that the prophets, who had regard for the good of the whole community,
and not of the few, have been so zealous in commending humility, repentance, and reverence,"[72] emotions of important social utility but expressive
of personal passivity.

It is an irony of the imaginative life that the desires and the emotions
that most sway one's beliefs in response to the pleasure-pain principle, and
are thus those that are driven by the conatus to pursue one's own self-interest in its crudest and most selfish form, turn out to be those that also serve
to bring the individual into conformity with social utility. For the emotions
that most compromise one's beliefs and desires, fear and hope, while indeed
generative of unremitting competition and rivalry, also foster conformity,
making possible a primitive communal life. Human beings in the throes of
Spinoza's version of the imaginative life, in keeping with Hobbes' grim
assessment of humanity, are overcome with extreme and often vicious emotions.[73] Nevertheless, they are not in a condition of a war of all against all.

Instead, they are parties to an unstable kind of conformity, a conformity that can be seen to arise first from common associations based in common memories, common language, and common texts—that is, a common tradition. This is a primitive form of the group mind. The common desires, hopes, and fears instituted in tandem by both the legal and religious systems of reward and punishment contribute to the formation of the social body. The imagination in both its forms, cognitive and affective, is a powerful socializing force.

The emotions in general express not the individual considered in isolation but instead the individual's active or passive relation to its environment. The imaginative affects are the emotions whose cognitive component is contributed by imaginative association. Being passive they are called passions. The imaginative affects primarily focus upon social relationships and upon the social arena as a whole for their satisfaction, essentially registering the increase or decrease in an individual's self-determination. According to Spinoza, several factors contribute to the external social determination of the passions and detract from our self-determination. *First*, the passive emotions are, by definition, directed at external objects and invest those external (generally human) objects (by imaginative association) with affective power over oneself and one's emotions. Objects of love and hate thus become extensions of the self that must be either placated or destroyed to bring about one's own pleasure. *Second*, passive emotions, Spinoza argues, are, in and of themselves, contagious. This is Spinoza's famous doctrine of the Imitation of the Affects: Human beings, realizing their fundamental similarity to each other (by the imaginative association of similars), pick up each other's emotions, and the greater the similarity perceived the greater the contagion—hence, the emotional closeness of ethnic groups, for example, and also the origin of the imaginative universal, 'humanity'. *Third*, we human beings have a general tendency (following from the first and second points) to desire that our passions be confirmed and shared by others. Our desire that our feelings be held in common by as many people as possible is a condition of our being able to maintain them unconflictedly[74] or even at all. So we endeavor both to please others, seeking their approval, and also to dominate them, seeking their compliance.

These three factors underlie the tendency of the passions to group expression. They also undergird society, as a necessary but insufficient condition of the formation of group identity. For the one thing that a person in the throes of the passivity of imaginative affects cannot do is remain independent of social forces, that is, of the beliefs and emotions of others. Hence, in Spinoza's estimation the passive emotions cannot express the relative condition of a person's self-determination considered in isolation, independently of others, even though the conatus, of which the emotions are specifications, by definition, aims at self-determination. Self-assessment and its emotional expression is always manifested via, and also is, in part, an expression of, extant social relationships! Our affective responses are always mediated by the emotions of others, to both our own shifting states of pleasure and pain, and also to the objects of the world that affect us. Thus our passions are always necessarily, according to Spinoza, in part determined by the social web in which they arise.

Let us examine in more detail how the social contribution to the external determination of the passions works. Regarding the *first* point, namely, that the imaginative affects are directed at external objects and invest those external objects with power over one's emotions, Spinoza writes:

> He who imagines that what he loves is being destroyed will feel pain. If however, he imagines that it is being preserved, he will feel pleasure.[75]

And conversely,

> He who imagines that a thing that he hates is being destroyed will feel pleasure.[76]

This principle is at the very heart of Spinoza's analysis of the passive emotions. For Love and Hatred are not two emotions among many, but the most basic manifestations of the three primary affects of Desire, Pleasure, and Pain. In the Definitions of the Emotions at the end of Part III, Spinoza summarizes his theory of emotion. All the various emotions are variants of Desire, since Desire is "the very essence of man in so far as his essence is conceived as determined to any action from any given affection of itself."[77] The essence conceived generally as the power of self-determination is the conatus.[78] Pleasure and Pain manifest the increase or decrease in the power of the conatus[79] and thus are really direct expressions and manifestations of desire, that is, affective motivation. The passions of Love and Hate are simply pleasure and pain *imaginatively associated with* external objects as causes.[80] Pleasure and pain are the primary and basic constituents of which all other emotions are secondary variations, either as direct variants of either pleasure and pain or of love and hate.

It is the nature of the passive emotions to be occasioned by the presence—or the imagined presence—of objects *imaginatively associated* with the changes in the affections of the body. All emotions are directed at objects and include the implicit judgment that the object of the emotion is its cause. In the passions, the causal judgments are false or incomplete, insofar as they are determined by imaginative associations to which the mind is passive. In the active emotions, the judgments are not only true but also rationally generated and hence self-determined. We invest ourselves *in* objects, seeing them as extensions of ourselves because we infer (sometimes rightly and sometimes wrongly) our dependence upon them to ensure our pleasure. Spinoza explains further that our dependence has an additional dimension: Our pleasure and pain not only depend on the presence or absence, well being or diminution, of objects with which they are imaginatively associated. They are also affected by the *emotions* of the object.

When the objects of love are people, we not only care about their presence and their condition but we also take on their emotions. The passions are thus contagious from lover to lover through emotional identification with the person whom one loves.

> He who imagines that what he loves is affected with pleasure or pain will likewise be affected with pleasure or pain, the intensity of which will vary with the intensity of the emotion in the object loved.[81]

The circle of affection begins to spread out from the individual conatus to the object of its love, and then even further, in accordance with the principle, The Friends of your Friend are your Friends but his Enemies are your Enemies.

> If we imagine that someone is affecting with pleasure the object of our love, we shall be affected with love towards him. If on the other hand we imagine that he is affecting with pain the object of our love, we shall likewise be affected with hatred toward him.[82]

From here, it is a short leap to the *second* factor contributing to the rise of group passions, the Imitation of the Affects. We can expect—although Spinoza does not state this outright—that the greater the similarity perceived between oneself and others, the greater the emotional contagion. This psychological mechanism functions as an extension to similars of a love one feels for a certain person. The imagination associates in memory people similar to ourselves and recalls them together, giving rise to an imaginative extension or projection of our own emotions to those like us. But in addition, emotional contagion can arise even from an initial emotional neutrality.[83] We ourselves need not entertain an emotion at all to take on the emotions of others whom we imagine to be similar to ourselves. Spinoza's principle is this:

> From the fact that we imagine a thing [i.e., person] like ourselves, towards which we have felt no emotion, to be affected by an emotion, we are thereby affected by a similar emotion.[84]

Emotional contagion is thus not just the projection of our own affects upon others but the direct introjection of their emotions for no other reason than their imagined similarity to us! In this Spinoza offers the starkest statement of what we can infer is the origin of the Group Body and Mind. As a corollary, Spinoza infers the extraordinary difficulty of remaining independent of such profound and pervasive group pressures:

> If we imagine that someone loves, desires, or hates something that we love, desire, or hate, that very fact will cause us to love, desire, or hate the thing more steadfastly. But if we imagine he dislikes what we love, or vice versa, then our feelings will fluctuate.[85]

This general principle of the Imitation of the Affects leads to what I shall call Spinoza's General Law of Social Conformity. This is the *third* factor that contributes to the development of the common emotions and the Group Mind and Body: We desire that our passions be confirmed and shared by as many people as possible:

> We also endeavor to do whatever we imagine men to regard with pleasure, and on the other hand we shun doing whatever we imagine men to regard with aversion.[86]

Spinoza informs us in a note to this proposition that those in question here and in what follows are "men for whom we have felt no emotion."[87] In other words, this is a general principle of social conformity that does not arise from personal attachments or aversions. While this can result in a general humanitarian sentiment, Spinoza remarks that it is far more often expressed as Ambition, "especially," he says, "when we endeavor so earnestly to please the multitude that we do . . . things to our own hurt or another's hurt."[88] Hence our pervasive desire for fame, the adulation of the masses. Spinoza defines Ambition as "the immoderate desire for honour."[89] Ambition is not the same as kindliness (humanitas). For the desire to please everyone not only can be rather ruthless, as Spinoza indicates, but in addition it is as much the desire to dominate as to please. Spinoza defines Ambition here as the "conatus to bring it about that everyone should approve of one's loves and hates."[90] "Everyone," he says, "endeavors, as far as he can, that what he loves should be loved by everyone, and what he hates should be hated by everyone."[91] In the *Tractatus Politicus*,[92] Spinoza even calls Ambition "the main motive of man." And at the end of Part III of the *Ethics*, he says of Ambition that it is "the desire whereby all emotions are encouraged and strengthened; and thus this emotion can scarcely be overcome. For as long as a man is subject to any desire, he is necessarily subject to this one."[93]

So Spinoza regards the urge to social conformity as overwhelming and pervasive and even ruthless. It is the conatus operating at its most primitive and imaginative. This is Spinoza's counterpart to the Hobbesian 'war of all against all'. For at the end of the Scholium to IIIP31 about Ambition, Spinoza writes:

> So we see that it is in everyone's nature to strive to bring it about that others should adopt his attitude to life; and while all strive equally to this end they equally hinder one another, and in all seeking the praise or love of all, they provoke mutual dislike.

While the overall impression here is rather Hobbesian, Spinoza has introduced an important departure from Hobbes both in his understanding of human nature and in his assessment of the resulting social condition. The first departure from Hobbes is that the striving for self-determination takes place not directly by everyone pursuing his interests as if he were alone on earth but then, sort of unexpectedly, bumping into others who hinder him because they are engaged in the pursuit of conflicting, competitive desires. In Spinoza's version, competitive desires are directed by human beings at each other instead of primarily at things, at scarce resources, as Hobbes would have it. Thus the human core desire is not acquisitive but rather emotional: We strive for emotional and attitudinal confirmation. It is a primitive *social* desire, one that creates both ongoing conflict but also unstable conformity. The desire for confirmation is Spinoza's second departure from Hobbes. It is, Spinoza remarks, particularly evident in children.[94]

Spinoza's doctrine of Ambition shares important features with Hegel's account of the basic human desire for Recognition. Hegel argues that we all desire to find ourselves mirrored in another. For Hegel, such competitive desires result in a battle for domination that ends, like Spinoza's ambition, in unstable postures of domination and submission.[95] When read carefully, the passages in the *Ethics* that we have been discussing are more reminiscent of Hegel's Lordship and Bondage in the *Phenomenology* than they are of Hobbes' atomic antagonisms—and this despite Hegel's debt to Hobbes. Both Hegel and Spinoza find the potential for more rational social relations in this primitive social moment. For Hegel Lordship and Bondage brings to our awareness the *possibility* of a society in which individual self-determination and group purposes might be reconciled, "the I that is We and the We that is I."[96] Spinoza proposes informing the social glue of imaginative association and emotional contagion with rational content, namely, with democratic and pluralistic principles and institutions. Such an imaginative ruse, he implies, is a necessary condition of the establishment of the rational society, the modern liberal polity.

> Nothing is more advantageous to man than man. Men . . . can wish for nothing more excellent for preserving their own being than that they should all be in such harmony in all respects that their minds and bodies should compose, as it were, one mind and

one body, and that all together should endeavor as best they can to preserve their own being, and that all together they should aim at the common advantage of all. From this it follows that men who are governed by reason, that is men who aim at their own advantage under the guidance of reason, seek nothing for themselves that they would not desire for the rest of mankind; and so are just, faithful and honourable.[97]

For a stable society to be a realizable goal, there has to be another way to establish agreement than mere emotional irrationality. In the final two books of the *Ethics*, Spinoza shows us how to emerge from the irrational investment in others and in the multitude that obtains in the most primitive imaginative life. Spinoza contrasts the two possible kinds of community in the Appendix to E4 in his collection of the rules of right living, no. 7:

> A man is bound to be a part of Nature and to follow its universal order; but if he dwells among individuals who are in harmony with man's nature, by that very fact his power of activity will be assisted and fostered. But if he be among individuals who are by no means in harmony with his nature, he will scarcely be able to conform to them without a great change in himself.[98]

Spinoza warns us here that more often than not a person cannot but conform to social pressures. One pays the price—that of one's own integrity—in the bargain. For "it needs an unusually powerful spirit to . . . restrain oneself from imitating [others'] emotions."[99]

We can now understand Spinoza's claim in the *Tractatus Politicus* that people in society are led by common passions, most often by common hopes and fears. For the irrational forces of the imagination, rather than any rational agreement about how best to benefit the society as a whole, bring about group solidarity.

> Since men . . . are led more by passion than by reason, their natural motive for uniting and being guided as if by one mind is not reason but some common passion; common hope, or common fear, or a common desire to avenge some injury . . . But since all men fear isolation . . . they desire political society by nature, and can never dissolve it entirely.[100]

The imagination functions both cognitively and affectively as the powerful socializer of the individual.

Mihaly Csikszentmihalyi, the University of Chicago psychologist, defines socialization as "the transformation of the human organism into a person who functions successfully within a particular social system."[101] He continues:

The essence of socialization is to make people dependent on social controls, to have them respond predictably to rewards and punishments. And the most effective form of socialization is achieved when people identify so thoroughly with the social order that they no longer can imagine themselves breaking any of its rules.[102]

Spinoza's imaginative associative system of cultural linguistic meaning and the system of social rewards and punishments function together to create just such powerful and interwoven forces of socialization. The cognitive and affective operations of the imagination bring about a primitive form of group life and group mind, or morals. While it can and should be transformed in the name of freedom and reason, the full transcendence of the binding ties of the imagination is open only to the few and never to a society as a whole.

In the *Tractatus Theologico-Politicus*, Spinoza analyzes religion as an imaginative socializing force that contributes to the creation and maintenance of the primitive community. Its form of ethics uses as its means of suasion the coercive but imaginary reward system of fear of and hope for the afterlife. Spinoza points out that Religion's suasive power to engender obedience makes it indispensable to the state. For the state, unlike the individual, can never depend on reason as its foundation.

The object of knowledge by revelation is nothing other than obedience and so it is completely distinct from natural knowledge in its purpose, its basis and its method, . . . these two have nothing in common, . . . they each have a separate province that does not intrude on the other.[103]

In the *TTP*, Spinoza argues that the consummate use of the imagination is in Religion. For, paradoxically, the imaginative authority of religion can be used to help gain public support and legitimacy for rational government and political freedom. It is the irony of the public arena that the authority of religion and its mechanisms of suasion can be invoked, albeit with considerable restraint, to incur enthusiastic *obedience* to a system of government that fosters self-determination and *independence of mind*. The imagination can thus be called into the service of a form of government that Reason independently commends as the one that best supports human freedom. The historical model that Spinoza chooses to illustrate the proper social function of the imagination, that is, of religion, in the democratic and just society is the ancient Jewish commonwealth as he finds it described in the Hebrew Bible.

The democratic society in which freedom of conscience and of speech are encouraged is a necessary social condition of the independence of mind that Spinoza envisions as the *summum bonum* but it is not its sufficient condition. The burden of the last two Parts of the *Ethics* is to demonstrate to the reader how the powerful, albeit vital, socializing forces of the imagination—including religion and tradition—can be loosened by philosophy and even overcome, so that a measure of freedom therefrom can be gained. In the highest stage of cognition, Intuition, the images and associations of the imagination and memory are not suppressed or lost but rationally reconfigured. We are no longer passive to their hold over us. For the meaning of the past is transformed by the widest possible perspective and the fullest explanatory grasp. It is through this rational, self-determined prism that memories are now reexperienced. The unexamined past in its rude initial form—which I have shown to be both biased and corruptive—loses its affective tyranny over the mind and a new, freer, yet still emotionally fecund, relation to memory and tradition develops. Yet the joys of self-understanding are open only to the few and can never be a reliable basis for community and politics.

Hence we discern here a parallel: Both the *Ethics* and the *Tractatus Theologico-Politicus* delineate the cognitive and affective coercive power of the imagination to shape the individual to social demands, leaving Reason carefully distinguished as the source of a hoped for independence. By reading the *Ethics* closely we have derived the major doctrine of the *Tractatus*. The *Ethics*, and not only the *TTP*, is a book about the emotionally and cognitively seductive and coercive—yet necessary—hold of the community upon us through memory and tradition. One of Spinoza's aims in the *Ethics*, we now realize, is to distinguish precisely the operations of the religious mind from the rational mind with a view to enabling the reader to dispel the imagination's seductive and corruptive power. It is now also apparent that a major purpose of not only the *TTP* but of the *Ethics*, too, is the separation of imagination from reason, and hence of religion from philosophy. If we now look back at Spinoza's doctrine of the liberation of the mind from imagination and memory, we understand its wider significance: Spinoza's *Ethics*, perhaps even more than the *Tractatus*, is one of the deepest articulations, and also one of the most thorough analyses, of the modern posture as an irreversible rupture with Tradition and the traditional community. Yet that rupture finds legitimacy and adequate expression only for the few, in the philosophic life.

I shall end with a comment on the importance of the religious imagination and of the western memory of ancient Israel in the service of social justice and democracy. Spinoza makes it clear in his political works that the *public* arena, unlike the personal one, can never dispense with religion as a primitive imaginative moral educator and instrument of social cohesion. Religion, ideally, should use its powers of suasion to gain obedience to a democratic civic life that honors freedom of speech and conscience, that is, to political institutions and values in accord with reason. It ought to channel its imaginative powers in the service of instituting and maintaining a political life more rational and free than its means. Spinoza chose the biblical Mosaic polity to illustrate the point:

> Although the right and power of government . . . are quite extensive, there can never be any government so mighty that those in command would have unlimited power to do anything they wish. . . . As to the question of how, in spite of this, a state can be formed so as to achieve constant stability, I have already said that it is not my intention to discuss this. Still, in pursuing this theme, I shall draw attention to the means of achieving this end which Moses of old learned from divine revelation; then we shall consider the course taken by the history of the Jews, from which we shall eventually see what are the most important concessions that sovereign powers should make to their subjects to ensure the greater security and prosperity of the state.[104]

Spinoza proposed that the Mosaic constitution serve as the *model*[105] of the ever-necessary, but generally corrupted, function of the religious imagination in politics. For the first biblical constitution in the wilderness used imaginative suasion to inspire reverence and hence engender a willing obedience to the collective authority and will of the people in placing the public good over private advantage. That is to say, Moses used imaginative suasion and institutional rewards to institute what reason itself, independently, recommends—namely, a democratic constitution with extensive checks on the exercise of sovereignty.

> Reason and experience tell us quite clearly that the preservation of the state depends mainly on the subjects' loyalty and virtue and on their steadfastness in carrying out orders, but the means whereby they should be induced to persevere in their loyalty and virtue are not so readily apparent. For all, both rulers and ruled, are but men, and as such prone to forsake duty for pleasure. Indeed those who have experienced the fickleness of the masses are almost reduced to despair; for the masses are governed solely by their emotions, not by reason; they rush wildly into everything, and are readily corrupted either by avarice or by luxurious living. . . .
>
> To guard against all these dangers, to organize a state in such a way as leaves no place for wrongdoing, or better still, to frame such a constitution that every man, whatever be his character, will set public right before private advantage, this is the task, this is the toil.[106]

The ancient Hebrew commonwealth, Spinoza suggests, ought to serve the constitutionalists of his own day and thereafter as a model for modern political society. For it granted considerable power and freedom to the people even as it set the interests of the community above those of individuals or subgroups. The original Mosaic state was in principle, an egalitarian,[107] federalist,[108] and even partially socialist,[109] direct democracy[110] with extensive checks and balances and a wide division of power (especially between the religious and political authorities),[111] an independent judiciary,[112] legal transparency,[113] and a citizen army.[114] This ancient society, Spinoza points out, promoted and defended freedom of conscience, only regulating actions and not beliefs.[115] The description Spinoza offers of the earliest Hebrew commonwealth in the *TTP* is in accord with the central features of the ideal constitution that Spinoza later set out in the *Tractatus Politicus*. He even suggested that such a constitution might befit his beloved Netherlands. Hence, in the final analysis, Spinoza envisioned, and hoped for, the reshaping of Holland—and of all modern polities—along the general lines of the democratic political constitution of the original Jewish commonwealth. That constitution, as encouraging independence of mind as its cardinal virtue, was not (and could not have been) successful in its own time and in a people still imbued with the experience of slavery. Spinoza portrays biblical society as having devolved into a more authoritarian form of polity even before democracy could be given a fair trial. Yet in introducing the ancient Jewish commonwealth as the model government, Spinoza seems to have hoped that finally, in modernity, its time had come.

NOTES

I wish to thank Lee C. Rice and Lenn E. Goodman for their helpful comments and suggestions on earlier drafts of this paper.

1. EVP39S; Van Vloten and Land, vol. 1: 270; Shirley, 223. All references to Spinoza's works will be to the J. Van Vloten and J. P. N. Land *Benedict de Spinoza opera quotquot reperta sunt.* edition of *Benedict de Spinoza: Opera*, 3rd ed., 4 vols. (The Hague Martinus Nijhoff, 1913). Translations of the *Ethics* will be from *Baruch Spinoza: The Ethics and Selected Letters*, trans. Samuel Shirley and ed. Seymour Feldman (Indianapolis, Ind.: Hackett, 1982), unless otherwise noted.

2. EVP38S; Van Vloten and Land, vol. 1: 268; Shirley, 222.

3. See, for example, my articles "Spinoza's Materialist Ethics: The Education of Desire," in *International Studies in Philosophy* XXII, no. 3 (1990): 59–78, and "Spinoza's Individualism Reconsidered: Some Lessons

from the *Short Treatise on God, Man, and His Well-Being*," *Iyyun: Jerusalem Philosophical Quarterly*, no. 47 (July 1988): 265–92. See also Andrew Collier's recent paper, "The Materiality of Morals: Mind, Body and Interests in Spinoza's *Ethics*," in *Studia Spinozana* 7 (1991), devoted to "The Ethics in the *Ethics*": 69–93.

4. EVP39; Van Vloten and Land, vol. 1: 269; Shirley, 222.

5. There have been a number of scholarly treatments of Spinoza's account of the imagination in the *Ethics* to which I would like to draw the reader's attention: Michele Bertrand's *Spinoza et l'imaginaire* (Paris: Presses Universitaires de France, 1983); R. G. Blair's "Spinoza's Account of Imagination," in *Spinoza: A Collection of Critical Essays*, ed. Marjorie Grene (New York: Anchor Books, 1973); Edwin Curley's "Experience in Spinoza's Theory of Knowledge," also in Marjorie Grene; P. Cristofolini's, "Imagination, joie, et socialite chez Spinoza," in *Spinoza: Science et Religion* (chap. 5), ed. R. Bouveresse (Paris: Vrin, 1988); C. De Deugd's *The Significance of Spinoza's First Kind of Knowledge* (Assen: Van Gorcum, 1966); Fatma L. Haddad-Chamakh's "L'Imagination chez Spinoza," in *Studi sel Seicento e sull'immaginazione*, ed. P. Cristofolini (Pisa: Scuole Normale Superiore di Pisa: 1985); Agnes Meur's "Spinoza et l'imaginaire," in *Raison pressente* 81 (1986); Nocentini's "Spinoza, le projet éthique et l'imaginaire" in *Bulletin de l'association des amis de Spinoza* 23 (1989); Y. Yovel's "The Ethics of 'Ratio' and the Remaining 'Imaginatio'," in *La Etica de Spinoza: Fundamentos y significado* (chap. 20), ed. A. Dominguez (Madrid: Castilla-La Mancha, 1992). And cf. Don Garrett's "Truth and Ideas of Imagination in the *Tractatus de Intellectus Emendatione*," in *Studia Spinozana* 2 (1986); S. Hutton's "The Prophetic Imagination: A Comparative Study of Spinoza and the Cambridge Platonist, John Smith," in *Spinoza's Political and Theological Thought*, ed. C. De Deugd (New York: North Holland Publishing Co., 1984); H. Laux's *Imagination et Religion chez Spinoza: La potentia dans l'histoire* (Paris: Vrin, 1993); F. Lucash's "Ideas, Images, and Truth" in *Philosophical Quarterly* 6 (1989); S. Preus's "Spinoza, Vico, and the Imagination of Religion," in the *Journal of the History of Ideas* (1989); H. Zellner's "Spinoza's Puzzle," in *History of Philosophy Quarterly* 5 (1988). See also D. L. Sepper's *Descartes's Imagination: Proportion, Images, and the Activity of Thinking* (Berkeley: University of California Press, 1996).

6. The second project mentioned here is the subject of Michele Bertrand's *Spinoza et l'imaginaire*. Bertrand argues persuasively that Intuitive Knowledge, knowledge of the third kind (K3), includes a liberated form of imagination resulting from the autonomous self. On the whole, I agree with this position and call the reader's attention in this regard to Spinoza's position that images always mediate emotions (E III P18 & S) and therefore for knowledge of the third kind to have affective expression it

must be mediated by images. I argued, similarly, a number of years ago, in "Spinoza's Materialist Ethics: The Education of Desire," that Spinoza's ethics is centrally concerned with transforming external causes of the passive emotions to internal ones and reattaching the images from the external and partial to the internal and inifinite. It is desire that develops insofar as its aim is activity—a point Vance Maxwell also argues in his disseratation *Substance and A Priori Knowledge: A Spinozan Epistemology* (Toronto: University of Toronto Press: 1974), and also in his article "Spinoza's Doctrine of the *Amor Dei Intellectualis* I" in *Dionysius* 14 (December 1990), 131–56.

Maxwell has argued persuasively and at great length in his dissertation that Spinoza's three stages of cognition also mark the continuous development, the ongoing progress, of the reformation of the imagination. Maxwell further argues in the dissertation that the body per se is active insofar as its actions are caused by itself; and they are caused by itself when and insofar as it enacts its own rational (self-caused) ideas. The scientist and the mathematician, for example, generate images in the rational order because they result from their own active and rational praxis. Maxwell argues that the body itself becomes (more) active in generating rational actions, so to speak, in its higher endeavors of science, art, and mathematics, and then its self-reflection in (higher/reformed) imagination perceives (creates images of) its now reformed order. Thus, in this imaginative awareness (of the reformed body) passive awareness and active generation coincide in content—as Maxwell also argues they do in common notions.

Yirmiahu Yovel, in his discussion of imagination in his article, "The ethics of 'ratio' and the remaining 'imaginatio'" argues that there is a semi-*ratio* (semi-rational state) in which imagination serves the interests and purposes of reason. In political society, this serves to render the multitude obedient to the moral conclusions of reason but through the irrational means of imagination and memory. And in the *Ethics* this is something that the individual imposes on oneself, "an inner authority commanding obedience," by which one uses the imagination to make oneself obedient to reason. Yovel bases this view on EVP10 & S. Yovel speaks of Spinoza as "reshaping the imaginatio in the image of ratio." This is a reference to the moral maxims to be memorized.

7. Van Vloten and Land, vol. 1: 92; Curley, *Collected Works*, vol. 1: 465.

8. In *De Anima*, III, 3, 428a Aristotle defines the imagination as "the process by which we say that an image is presented to us." See the Loeb Classical Edition, W. S. Hett, MA, trans. (Harvard, 1964), 158/159.

9. Van Vloten and Land, vol. 1: 92; Shirley, 78.

10. EIIP48S; Van Vloten and Land, vol. 1: 113; Shirley, 96.

By ideas I do not mean images such as are formed at the back of the eye . . . but conceptions of thought.

Yirmiahu Yovel ("The Ethics of 'Ratio'": 243) remarks that Spinoza's "ideas are actual mental states and acts."
11. EIIP49S; Van Vloten and Land, vol. 1: 117; Shirley, 99:

Nobody is deceived insofar as he has a perception, that is, I grant that the imaginings of the mind considered in themselves, involve no error (see Sch. Pr. 17, II). But I deny that a man makes no affirmation in so far as he has a perception. For what else is perceiving a winged horse than affirming wings of a horse?

See also here (Shirley: 97) where Spinoza writes, "an idea, insofar as it is an idea, involves affirmation or negation."
Aristotle also claims that imaginations make propositional claims that are true or false. In *De Anima* III, 3, 428a (158/159), he writes:

The [imagination] is one of those faculties or states of mind by which we judge and are either right or wrong.

12. EIIP17S; Van Vloten and Land, vol. 1: 91; Shirley, 78.
13. EIIP17S; Van Vloten and Land, vol. 1: 91; Shirley, 78.
14. Descartes cites among other examples of the arbitrariness and particularity of people's associations "the strange aversion of certain people to . . . the smell of roses" or "the presence of a cat," *Passions of the Soul* (henceforth, *PA*), II, ¶ 136, 376. All quotations are from *The Philosophical Writings of Descartes*, trans. John Cottingham, Robert Stoothoff, and Dugald Murdoch, vol. 1 (Cambridge: Cambridge University Press, 1985).
15. Jonathan Bennett, *A Study of Spinoza's 'Ethics'* (Hackett, 1984), 278–79, points out that the doctrine of the 'association of ideas' was "a commonplace in the seventeenth century and thereafter, was prominent in Locke's philosophy and pivotal in Hume's. Spinoza uses it a lot. He gets from it a thesis about association and imaginings in (2p18s) and uses it in his theory of general terms (2p40s1), in relating imagination to contingency and to time (2p44c1s, 3p11s, 4p13), and in devising techniques for achieving greater mental freedom (5p10s, 12, 13)."
16. Van Vloten and Land, vol. 1: 92; translated after Shirley, 79.
17. Van Vloten and Land, vol. 1: 92–93; translated after Shirley, 79.
18. Harry A. Wolfson, *The Philosophy of Spinoza*, two volumes in one (1934; reprint, New York: Meridien Books, 1958), 2: 80 and 84. (Henceforth this work will be cited as Wolfson.)

19. The 'or' in question is 'sive', the term that Spinoza also uses in the phrase "God or Nature" to indicate their interchangeableness and equivalence.

C. De Deugd, *The Significance of Spinoza's First Kind of Knowledge*, 203, also points out that Spinoza uses the terms 'imagination' and 'memory' "as all but interchangeable and in some cases synonymous." R. G. Blair, in "Spinoza's Account of the Imagination," suggests (326) that on Spinoza's account, "one cannot imagine without remembering" and Yovel often speaks interchangeably of 'imagination' and of "imagination and memory" in "The ethics of 'ratio'" (e.g., 243, 247).

20. EIIIP1; Van Vloten and Land, vol. 1: 122.

21. EIIIP2S; Van Vloten and Land, vol. 1: 125–26; Shirley, 108.

22. In the *Treatise on the Emendation of the Intellect* where Spinoza treats of the fictive capacity of the imagination at length (50–65), his major point seems to be that the more we know the less we can imagine in the sense of 'pretend' or 'feign' that things are other than as they are. In the imagination, the mind is not creative but passive. De Deugd (76) identifies four main characteristics of the fictive imagination in the *TdIE*:

In the case of coining fictitious ideas:
(1.) the mind perceives many things simultaneously;
(2.) the mind cannot produce anything new;
(3.) the mind is passive and possesses no creative power;
(4.) fiction is limited not by fiction but by understanding.

23. EIIIP2S; Van Vloten and Land, vol. 1: 125–26; Shirley, 108.

24. See also, *TdIE*, 88–89, where Spinoza says that words are imaginative.

25. This issue is addressed most recently in Michael Della Rocca's *Representation and the Mind-Body Problem in Spinoza* (Oxford: Oxford University Press, 1996).

26. EIIP44 Cor. 2; Van Vloten and Land, vol. 1: 110; Shirley, 93.

27. EIIP44S; Van Vloten and Land, vol. 1: 109; Shirley, 93.

28. EIIP44 Cor. 2 Dem; Van Vloten and Land, vol. 1: 110; Shirley, 93.

29. EIIP44S; Van Vloten and Land, vol. 1: 110; Shirley, 93.

30. Van Vloten and Land, vol. 1: 264; Shirley, 218.

31. EIIP26Cor; Van Vloten and Land, vol. 1: 97.

32. EIIP27; Van Vloten and Land, vol. 1: 98.

33. Van Vloten and Land, vol. 1: 99; Shirley, 84.

34. EIIP36; Van Vloten and Land, vol. 1: 102; Shirley, 87.

35. In the *Ethics* (e.g., E I Appendix; Van Vloten and Land, vol. 1: 72; Shirley, 62), Spinoza indicates explicitly that these are universals constructed by the *imagination* whereas elsewhere, although clearly suggesting the contrast with "real entities" (*entia realia*) he yet calls them "entities of reason"

(*entia rationis*). (See, for example, *Short Treatise* I, X.) See Wolfson (I: 438) on this point and also De Deugd, chapter 3, Section 5: "Entities of Imagination" (40–44).

36. I am grateful to Lee C. Rice for pointing out that 'small differences' is a more apt translation of "parvas differentias" here than Shirley's "unimportant differences."

37. EIIP40S1; Van Vloten and Land, vol. 1: 105–06; Shirley, 89–90 (my emendation).

38. *Women, Fire, and Dangerous Things: What Categories Reveal About the Mind* (Chicago: University of Chicago Press, 1987).

39. EIIP41; Van Vloten and Land, vol. 1: 107.

40. EIIP40S2; Van Vloten and Land, vol. 1: 16; Shirley, 90 (with some emendations).

41. 'Templates' is a term from psychoanalytic psychology. In *Between Therapist and Client: The New Relationship*, rev. ed. (New York: W. H. Freeman and Company, (1997), Michael Kahn includes a brief section in chapter 2: "The Discovery of Transference," titled, "The Theory of Templates," where he defines the term (25):

> In our earliest relationships we establish templates, patterns, into which we tend to fit all of our subsequent relationships, or at least all of our *important* subsequent relationships. If I had a warm and supportive relationship with my father [for example] it is likely that I will tend to see male authority figures in a positive light.

Kahn attributes this theory of templates to Freud in his 1912 essay, "The Dynamics of Transference," in J. Strachey, ed. and trans., *The Standard Edition of the Complete Psychological Works of Sigmund Freud* (London: Hogarth), 12: 97–108.

Now Spinoza clearly does not have patterns of *relationship* in mind. But he does have in mind categories that we acquire early in life through salient memories and via which we interpret subsequent events and objects.

42. EIIP49S; Van Vloten and Land, vol. 1: 115; Shirley, 97.

> The essence of words is constituted solely by corporeal motions, far removed from the concepts of thought.

43. That Spinoza uses "signs" to refer to language we may infer from the following evidence brought forth by Wolfson (vol. II: 137):

> The term "sign" in the sense of words heard or written, and hence of the ideas formed of them, has been ascribed to Occam, from whom it has been suggested, Spinoza borrowed it. But there is a passage in Aristotle which may be considered the source of Occam

as well as of Spinoza. "Spoken words, says Aristotle, "are the signs (*symbola*, *signa* in the Latin translation accessible to Spinoza) of mental experience, and written words are the signs of spoken words" [*De Interpretatione*, I, 16a, 3-4]. Similarly Hobbes speaks of names as the "signs" of our "conceptions" [*Elementa Philosophiae*, Pars I, Cap. 22, §5, p. 15]. What is more significant still is the fact that Hobbes calls them arbitrary (*arbitraria*) signs in contradistinction to natural (*naturalia*) signs.

G. H. R. Parkinson also holds that by "sign" Spinoza means words. See his essay, "Language and Knowledge in Spinoza," in Grene, *Spinoza: A Collection of Critical Essays*, 79–80.

For an extended treatment of Spinoza's doctrine of the imaginative character of prophecy as referring to its figurative and symbolic language and also to its institution of social conventions, see my essay, "Some Thoughts on What Spinoza Learned from Maimonides about the Prophetic Imagination," in *The Journal of the History of Philosophy* vls. xxxix, nos. 2 and 3, April and July 2001.

44. Warren Zev Harvey's essay in this volume lends further support to the claim that Spinoza viewed the distinctive aspects of a language in terms of the cultural peculiarities of a people—namely, of the Hebrews, in the case of the *Compendium of Hebrew Grammar*. Because he regarded both tradition and language as products of the imagination, Spinoza linked the epistemic prism of a people with its linguistic expressions.

It is interesting that Saadiah stresses, as Curley does, the reliability of the authoritative transmitters of knowledge, and that, like Curley, he considers this kind of knowledge not to be at the bottom of the scale and also to depend upon an independent account of its reliability in the particular case. Saadya in this way aims to guarantee the reliability and truth of the biblical text. Spinoza's in his own account however, instead, places this kind of knowledge—from authoritative Report or traditional authority—at the bottom of the scale. Thus, the way that this knowledge must operate, according to Spinoza, given both its status as the lowest and its failure to assess and assure its reliability in any independent way—a procedure that Spinoza clearly states enters in only at the next stage—suggests an implicit and incipient radical critique of (general and biblical) tradition and of cultural authority—a critique that Saadya tried to head off at all costs and that Curley (and De Deugd), perhaps inadvertently, tries to expunge from the Spinozist text.

Dennis Slepper comes to similar conclusions about Descartes's Imagination to the ones I have come to regarding Spinoza. He writes (7):

Phantasm in the fullest sense turns out to be something that is not just an image of corporeal things but also *words* and *intellectual memories that are biographically and historically situated.*

45. See *The Significance of Spinoza's First Kind of Knowledge.*

46. See "Experience in Spinoza's Theory of Knowledge."

47. "Experience," 34.

48. For a discussion of Spinoza's theory of the imaginative character of language, see David Savan's essay, "Spinoza and Language," in Grene, *Spinoza: A Collection of Critical Essays,* 60–72. Savan argues that Spinoza maintains the "radical inadequacy of words" (64). Also, see G. H. R. Parkinson's response to Savan, in "Language and Knowledge in Spinoza," immediately following (73–100), in which Savan's claim is challenged.

49. EIIIP46; Van Vloten and Land, vol. 1: 154; Shirley, 131.

50. In EIIIP14 Dem (Van Vloten and Land, vol. 1: 132; Shirley, 113), Spinoza explains how the emotions follow the rule of the association of images of the imagination:

> If the human body has once been affected by two bodies at the same time, when the mind later imagines one it will straightway recollect the other too (Pr. 18, II). Now the images formed by the mind reflect the affective states of our body more than the nature of external bodies (Cor. 2, Pr. 16, II). Therefore if the body, and consequently the mind (Def. 3, III), has once been affected by two emotions, when its is later affected by the one, it will also be affected by the other.

51. I will follow Shirley's translation of *laetitia* and *tristitia* by 'pleasure and pain' rather than Curley's 'sadness and joy' or Bennett's (253–54) 'pleasure and unpleasure'. The benefit of the Shirley translation is that, as Bennett (254) suggests, it captures the joint physical and mental character of the states in question (as Curley's 'joy' and 'sadness', for example, do not). Bennett, however, wishes to further link his formulation to that of Freud with which it has much affinity:

> This good word [namely, 'unpleasure'] is listed in the OED, with examples where it has the kind of meaning I am giving it. Its principal twentieth century use is when 'pleasure' and 'unpleasure' are used to render Freud's *Lust* and *Unlust.* That is a comforting precedent, since Spinoza's polarity is like Freud's, and in a current German translation of Spinoza (Jakob Stern's) the terms *laetitia* and *tristitia* are rendered by the Freudian *Lust* and *Unlust.*

Yet, Lee Rice has pointed out (private communication) that Bennett herein confuses the matter rather than clarifying it. For while 'pleasure and pain' capture Spinoza's claim that the absence of *laetitia* does not imply the presence of *tristitia* and vice versa, the German *Lust* and *Unlust* are contradictories and so the absence of *Lust* is *Unlust*. 'Unpleasure' would seem to be wider than 'pain' covering both neutrality and pain. But neutrality would hardly seem to be encompassed within Spinoza's *tristitia*. So I will stick to the Shirley translation even if 'pain' perhaps connotes a harsher meaning or higher threshold.

    52. EIVP9Dem; Van Vloten and Land, vol. 1: 190–91; Curley, 551.

    53. EIIIDef.2; Van Vloten and Land, vol. 1: 121; Shirley, 104.

    54. EIIIDef.3; Van Vloten and Land, vol. 1: 121; Shirley, 104.

    55. For a more extended treatment of the cognitive component of emotions, see my paper, "Spinoza's Materialist Ethics."

    56. EIII Preface; Van Vloten and Land, vol. 1: 121.

    57. EIIIP9; Van Vloten and Land, vol. 1: 128; Shirley, 110:

> The mind, both in so far as it has distinct ideas and in so far as it has confused ideas, endeavors to persist in its own being over an indefinite period of time, and is conscious of this conatus.

Cf. the autobiographical introduction to the *TdIE*. Spinoza says that his painful and despairing emotional state began to lift precisely when he focused his thinking upon explaining the causes of his malady. The joyous beatitude that contemplation provides goes back, of course, to Aristotle's *Nicomachean Ethics*, XII and the Neoplatonic (and Renaissance Platonic) appropriation of that concept. Nevertheless, Spinoza's rational psychological explication of the Aristotelian-Neoplatonic-Renaissance viewpoint is, as far as I know, unique as is his generalization—and general explanation—of the affective charge of thinking.

    58. EIIIP25; Van Vloten and Land, vol. 1: 138 - 139; Shirley, 119.

    59. EIIIP13 & C; Van Vloten and Land, vol. 1: 131; Shirley, 113.

    60. EIV Appendix no. 32; Van Vloten and Land, vol. 1: 243; Shirley, 201.

    61. EIIIP11 S; Van Vloten and Land, vol. 1: 129–30; Shirley, 111.

    62. EIIIP12; Van Vloten and Land, vol. 1: 130.

    63. EIII, General Definition of Emotions; Van Vloten and Land, vol. 1: 180; Shirley, 151.

    64. EIIIP15; Van Vloten and Land, vol. 1: 132.

    65. Lenn Goodman points out that "the association, being passive and irrational need not proceed by way of some conscious process of reasoning."

    66. EIVP9; Van Vloten and Land, vol. 1: 190; Shirley, 160.

An emotion whose cause we think to be with us in the present is stronger than it would be if we did not think the said cause to be with us.

67. 2nd ed. (Penguin, 1995), 135.

68. Lee C. Rice, in "Freud, Sartre, Spinoza: The Problematic of the Unconscious," in *Giornale di Metafisica*, Nuova Serie, XVII (1995): 87–106, puts forth a strong argument that Spinoza holds a doctrine of the unconscious—and of unconscious ideas—and that it is one that could be seen as both clarifying Freud's account and also defending it against Sartre's criticisms. On Rice's reading (104) of Spinoza,

> An idea ceases to be conscious when it conflicts with a mental state which is affectively stronger than it; and an idea enters the conscious field provided that either (1) it is consistent with the existing field, or (2) it is of sufficient strength to "annul" or repress that which conflicts with it in this field. This is why no emotion can be checked or destroyed except by an emotion contrary to it which is also affectively stronger. (E4P7)

Hence, for Spinoza (104), "self-consciousness [is] a fundamentally affective response, and the presence or absence of mental states *in consciousness* a matter of their relations with a given present field of affective responses." Hence also, I would add, Spinoza's materialism—what Rice calls (105) his "behaviorism," which latter I suspect might be taking Spinoza's claim of the materiality of causes in psychological explanation a bit too far.

69. EIIIP50S; Van Vloten and Land, vol. 1: 156; Shirley, 133.

70. EIVP47 & S; Van Vloten and Land, vol. 1: 217; Shirley, 182.

> P47: The emotions of hope and fear cannot be good in themselves.
>
> S: . . . These emotions indicate a lack of knowledge and a weakness of mind, and for this reason, too, confidence, despair, joy and disappointment are also indications of our weakness. For although confidence and joy are emotions of pleasure, they imply a preceding pain, namely, hope and fear. Therefore the more we endeavor to live by the guidance of reason, the more we endeavor to be independent of hope, to free ourselves from fear, and to command fortune as far as we can, and to direct our actions by the sure counsel of reason."

71. EVP41S; Van Vloten and Land, vol. 1: 271–72; Shirley, 224. The Stoic tradition attested in Seneca (see, e.g., *Seneca: Letters from a Stoic* (*Epistulae Morales ad Lucilium*), selected and translated with an introduc-

tion by Robin Campbell, [Penguin (1969]) mounts a critique of the social servitude and anxiety induced by 'fear and hope', keeping people in a state of both unease and thralldom (see, e.g., Letters V & VI: 38, 39).

72. EIVP54S; Van Vloten and Land, vol. 1: 221; Shirley, 185.

73. EIIIP28; Van Vloten and Land, vol. 1: 141; Shirley, 121.

We endeavor to bring about whatever we imagine to be conducive to pleasure, but we endeavor to remove or destroy whatever we imagine to be opposed to pleasure and conducive to pain.

74. EIIIP31; Van Vloten and Land, vol. 1: 143; Shirley, 123.

75. EIIIP19; Van Vloten and Land, vol. 1: 135; Shirley, 116.

76. EIIIP20; Van Vloten and Land, vol. 1: 136; Shirley, 116.

77. EIII Definition of the Emotions, no. 1; Van Vloten and Land, vol. 1: 167; Shirley, 142.

78. EIIIP7; Van Vloten and Land, vol. 1: 127; Shirley, 109.

79. EIII Definition of the Emotions, nos. 2 & 3; Van Vloten and Land, vol. 1: 167–68; Shirley, 142.

80. EIII Definition of the Emotions, nos. 6 &7; Van Vloten and Land, vol. 1: 169; Shirley, 143–44.

81. EIIIP21; Van Vloten and Land, vol. 1: 136; Shirley, 117.

82. EIIIP22; Van Vloten and Land, vol. 1: 137; translated after Shirley translation, 117.

83. See also, EIIIP27C1; Van Vloten and Land, vol. 1: 140; Shirley, 120:

If we believe that someone for whom we have felt no emotion, affects with pleasure a thing similar to ourselves we shall be affected by love towards him. If on the other hand, we believe that he affects the said object with pain, we shall be affected with hatred towards him.

84. EIIIP27; Van Vloten and Land, vol. 1: 139; Shirley, 119 –20.

85. EIIIP31; Van Vloten and Land, vol. 1: 143; My emendation of the Shirley translation, 123.

86. EIIIP29; Van Vloten and Land, vol. 1: 142; Shirley, 121.

87. Van Vloten and Land, vol. 1: 142; Shirley, 121.

88. EIIIP29S; Van Vloten and Land, vol. 1: 142; Shirley, 122.

89. EIII Definition of the Emotions no. 44; Van Vloten and Land, vol. 1: 178; Shirley, 150.

90. EIIIP31S; Van Vloten and Land, vol. 1: 144; Shirley, 123.

91. EIIIP31 Cor; Van Vloten and Land, vol. 1: 144; Shirley, 123.

92. *TP* vii, 6; Van Vloten and Land, vol. 2: 37.

93. EIII Definition of the Emotions no. 44 Explication; Van Vloten and Land, vol. 1: 178–79; Shirley, 150.

94. EIIIP32S; Van Vloten and Land, vol. 1: 145; Shirley, 124.

95. *Phenomenology of Spirit*, trans. A. V. Miller, with an analysis of the text and foreword by J. N. Findlay (Oxford: Oxford University Press, 1979), "B. Self-consciousness, iv. The Truth of Self-certainty and A. Independence and dependence of self-consciousness; Lordship and Bondage" (esp. 109–19).

96. *Phen.* §177; Miller, 110.

97. EIVP18S; Van Vloten and Land, vol. 1: 197; Shirley, 165.

98. Van Vloten and Land, vol. 1: 238; Shirley, 197.

99. Appendix to E4 no. 13; Van Vloten and Land, vol. 1: 239; Shirley, 198.

100. *TP* vi, §1; Van Vloten and Land, vol. 2: 24–25; Wernham:, 315.

101. *Flow*, 17.

102. *Flow*, 17.

103. See, e.g., *TTP*, Pref; Van Vloten and Land, vol. 2: 91; Shirley, 55.

104. *TTP* xvii; Van Vloten and Land, vol. 2: 271; Shirley, 252.

105. For a detailed account of the status of ethical and political models according to Spinoza and also of Spinoza's use of the biblical commonwealth as just such a model, see Michael Rosenthal's essay in this volume.

106. *TTP* xvii; Van Vloten and Land, vol. 2: 271; Shirley, 252–53.

107. *TTP* xvii; Van Vloten and Land, vol. 2: 283; Shirley, 265.

108. *TTP* xvii; Van Vloten and Land, vol. 2: 278; Shirley, 259.

109. *TTP* xvii; Van Vloten and Land, vol. 2: 283; Shirley, 265.

110. *TTP* xvii; Van Vloten and Land, vol. 2: 274; Shirley, 255–56.

111. *TTP* xvii; Van Vloten and Land, vol. 2: 280; Shirley, 262.

112. *TTP* xvii; Van Vloten and Land, vol. 2: 280; Shirley, 262.

113. *TTP* xvii; Van Vloten and Land, vol. 2: 280; Shirley, 262.

114. *TTP* xvii; Van Vloten and Land, vol. 2: 280–81; Shirley, 262.

115. *TTP* xvii; Van Vloten and Land, vol. 2: 274; Shirley, 256.

CHAPTER 9

Why Spinoza Chose the Hebrews

The Exemplary Function of Prophecy in the Theological-Political Treatise

MICHAEL A. ROSENTHAL

INTRODUCTION

In 1664 Ferdinand Bol produced a large painting for the Magistrate's Chambers (*schepenkamer*) in the Amsterdam Town Hall entitled "Moses Descends from Mount Sinai with the Ten Commandments."[1] Bol depicts Moses as he is described in Exodus 34:29–30: face shining and eyes wide with awe, descending with the tablets of the Law. From the position of the tablets, we can infer that this is Moses' second descent from Sinai. The first time Moses was greeted by the sight of the Hebrews dancing around the Golden Calf, the idol they had erected in his absence (Ex. 32:19). Other contemporary artists, among them Rembrandt, depicted Moses at this moment holding the tablets high above his head in anger, ready to smash them in disgust. But in Bol's painting, we see Moses holding the tablets before his chest, preparing to show a far more reverent crowd the Law God has just given them.[2] Below Moses are the people of Israel, who are attentive and bathed in his heavenly light. Having already been brutally punished for their idolatry (Ex. 32:26–35), all the figures below Moses look up to him in awe, except for one who looks down at the ground. If the painting itself does not provide certain evidence for the identity of this figure, we can turn to the marble frieze commissioned by the Amsterdam burgomasters to be set underneath the painting.[3] At its center, the frieze depicts the frenzied scene around the Golden Calf, and at its periphery, the increasingly debased forms of

225

behavior (singing, dancing, gambling, fighting, fornicating) that occurred as a result. The draped and bearded figure who leads the worship of the idol at the focal point of the frieze is most likely the same as the figure bowing down in the painting. It is Aaron the high priest, who had succumbed to the demands of the people and fashioned the idol (Ex. 32:4) and now contritely avoids looking directly at Moses. Indeed, the drama of the painting is focused in the tension between these two figures, counterposed along a diagonal axis of light: Moses bearing the law, and Aaron the high priest bowing down before him. The painting, as we shall see, was commissioned by the Magistrates to make a specific point: the welfare of the people requires that the priests, the interpreters of the law, submit to the authority of the state and its founding principles.

We know, from two letters, that Spinoza was working on something resembling the *Tractatus Theologico-Politicus* in 1665, a year after Bol's painting was finished and hung in the Town Hall. He probably had begun work before then.[4] Although the medium is obviously different, Spinoza's book shares some key features with Bol's painting. First, they share a common subject, the Hebrews; and more specifically, the portrayal of Moses as the lawgiver. For while Spinoza treats a great range of biblical topics in the *TTP*, the role of Moses as founder of the state is clearly the central one. Second, Bol's painting and Spinoza's text share a historical moment. Not only are they composed at roughly the same time and place but they address the same fundamental issues: the ongoing struggle between the Dutch Reformed Church and the state, and by extension, the struggle between the republican States party and the monarchist Orange party. Third, Spinoza and Bol (or at least the authorities who commissioned his work) both clearly understood that, to be effective, political argument must move beyond purely rational discourse. They attempt to appeal to the masses through an interpretation of an imaginative example.[5]

Why should this example taken from Scripture be relevant to Spinoza's situation, let alone to our own? Although all Spinoza scholars have noted his use of ancient Israel in the *TTP*, their interpretations have varied. Some have argued that Spinoza used the ancient Hebrews only as an example of "a rude and barbarous way of life"; they are not models to be imitated but "antagonists of the Moderns."[6] But while I agree that Spinoza is trying to overturn a sacred view of history and replace it with one more secular, I do not think that Spinoza rejects the use of the Hebrew example altogether. Important work has also been done in tracing Spinoza's relation to his medieval predecessors, particularly Maimonides, and to his liberal successors in the enlightenment.[7] But here I would like to concentrate on a more immediate context: politics and political theory in seventeenth-century Netherlands. Some have insisted that Spinoza adopted this example solely for external reasons, because it belonged to his ostensible political enemies, the Calvinist clergy, and he simply wanted to subvert their use of it.[8] Yet, as I hope to show, that approach pays too little attention to the constructive use Spinoza makes of the example. In sympathy with those who are sensitive to the context in which Spinoza writes and the use he makes of his historical exempla,[9] I will argue that Spinoza uses his analysis of the function of prophecy and religion among the ancient Hebrews to illustrate and resolve a deep theoretical problem in the Hobbesian social contract theory as he sets it forth in the *TTP*. For what Spinoza needs to explain is how self-interested individuals in the state of nature are willing to surrender their natural rights and create a sovereign power to which they become subject in civil society. The history of the Hebrews is an example of just how that transition is managed, through the prophetic appeal to divine authority and through the institutionalization of religion in the life of the state.

But even if prophecy solved the Hebrews' dilemma, we still must ask how the Hebrew theocracy can be relevant to the Dutch republic, or to our own secular age?[10] The deeper relevance of the ancient Israelites' story must transcend the specificity of their historical situation. It must tell us something about the constitution of society and the nature of political discourse itself.[11] I think that what makes the Hebrews exemplary in this broader sense is the function of prophetic language, which appeals to an imaginative narrative that claims universal authority in order to justify a particular set of institutions.[12] That is, when the prophets called the Hebrews 'chosen', they were performing a function essential to any society: using the imagination to transcend individual interests and create a common standard of judgment and behavior. When Spinoza and Bol chose the Hebrews as their subjects, they were performing a function analogous to that of the prophets, appealing to and interpreting the collective imagination of a people in order to exhort them to right public conduct.

In what follows, I will make four basic points: First, I will take what Spinoza says in the *Ethics* about an exemplar of human nature as a clear and basic indication of what the purpose of an exemplar is: to transform value from an individual and subjective utility to a universal and objective standard. Second, I will argue that the function of prophecy in the foundation of the state is essentially to provide an exemplar, but on a political (not ethical) level; that is, to persuade the individual that personal interest is best fulfilled through submission to the state's authority. Third, I will show how the history of the Hebrew state exemplifies the tension inherent in an exemplar between its particular imaginative origins and its universal claims. Fourth, I will argue that Spinoza's account of the use and misuse of prophecy in ancient Israel spoke directly to the Dutch of Spinoza's time and speaks indirectly to the political theorists of our own time.

THE ORIGIN AND FUNCTION OF AN *EXEMPLAR* IN THE *ETHICS*

Spinoza defines "good" and "evil" in the opening definitions of Part IV of the *Ethics*: "By good I shall understand what we certainly know to be useful to us" (EIVD1); "By evil, however, I shall understand what we certainly know prevents us from being masters of some good" (EIVD2). The striking feature of these definitions is their apparent relativity. What is useful and therefore good to one person may not be useful and good to another. This, of course, raises an immediate problem about the use of these value terms. For if they are to be meaningful socially they must apply not only to the experience of a single individual but to others as well. Spinoza is well aware of this difficulty and for further explanation refers the reader back to the Preface of Part IV, in which he discusses the idea of an exemplar of human nature,[13] whose purpose is to bridge the gap between subjective value and objective value.[14] The role of such an exemplar is exactly parallel to that of prophetic language in the *TTP*: it provides a bridge for the transition from personal interest or utility to general interest.

An exemplar of human nature belongs to a broader category of exemplary ideas, each of which creates a standard for making value judgments. Let us, for example, take a look at the origin of a judgment about something's perfection. To judge the perfection of a thing, one must have some idea of the end for which it was made. Spinoza thinks that he can discern the origin of the notion of perfection in the Latin etymology of the word itself (*perficere* from *per* + *facere*): "If someone has decided to make something, and has finished it, then he will call his thing perfect—and so will anyone who rightly knows, or thinks he knows, the mind and purpose of the Author of the work" (EIVPref; G II 205). The idea is that when something is complete, and the end of the Author or maker of the work is realized, then it can be said to be perfect. In Spinoza's own example, when a man desires to build a house, he will consider it perfect when it is complete according to his original plan. Of course, one who does not know the intentions of the author will be unable to judge whether the work is imperfect or perfect. So a judgment of value relates to a specific work and its relative stage of completion.

When people wish to make judgments about things whose authors' intentions remain unknown, the need arises for broader categories that subsume specific judgments under more general ideas. That is precisely the structure of an exemplary idea: it is a universal idea that functions as a model, on the basis of which a value judgment may be made. Although the idea of an end is no longer readily apparent, it is still very much present as the universal idea towards which things do or should tend. As Spinoza writes:

> But after men began to form universal ideas, and devise *exemplaria*
> of houses, buildings, towers, etc., and to prefer some *exemplaria* of

things to others, it came about that each one called perfect what he saw agreed with the universal idea he had formed of this kind of thing, and imperfect, what he saw agreed less with the *exemplar* he had conceived, even though its maker thought he had entirely finished it.[15]

In this way, the meaning of "perfect" changes from a literal judgment of completeness, to a more abstract judgment of conformity to a universal idea. This move allows an individual to judge the perfection of a thing, whether or not he actually knows the intention of its maker. For now the judgment is not whether a specific intention has been realized but whether the thing realizes an abstract degree of exemplification, under which the particular intentions have been subsumed. One person can thus judge the house of another, not on the basis of the owner's original plan and whether it is complete or not, but on the basis of an idea of what a house as such should be like. Universal ideas not only group diverse things under a single category but also warrant judgments of their relative perfection. An exemplar is the abstract "end" towards which things of a certain kind should tend if they were to become perfect; it is the standard which they should imitate and by which they should be judged.

The same process occurs in a judgment about whether something is "good" or "bad." As we have seen, Spinoza originally defines these terms from the point of view of individual utility. But obviously what is useful to one person at a given time and place may not be so to another. Thus "one and the same thing can, at the same time, be good, and bad, and also indifferent. For example, Music is good for one who is melancholy, bad for one who is mourning, and neither good nor bad to one who is deaf" (EIVPref). If the value terms 'good' and 'bad' are to mean something more than mere subjective utility, it is necessary to find a basis for this kind of judgment that transcends the particular judgment of the individual. That is the specific purpose of an exemplar of human nature. So, after the apparently "subjective" definitions of good and evil in IVD1 and D2, Spinoza points the reader back to the preface, where he says, "I shall understand by good what we know certainly is a means by which we may approach nearer and nearer to the model of human nature that we set before ourselves. By evil, what we certainly know prevents us from becoming like that model" (EIVPref). Exemplars can serve as a bridge from "subjective" to "objective" value, because they are formed not on the basis of an individual judgment but on the basis of a universal idea. In this light, when an individual judges something (or someone's actions) as good, he is making a judgment based on a model that applies to all things or actions of that kind, and therefore has some injunctive force.

However, the universal idea upon which an exemplar is constructed is itself open to question. Spinoza distinguishes between ideas that he calls "common notions," which "are the foundations of our reasoning," and "ill-founded" "axioms, *or* notions, [that] result from other causes" (EIIP40S1). Universal ideas belong to the second category. "Common notions" are "equally in the part and in the whole, [but do] not constitute the essence of any singular thing" (EIIP37), but universal ideas (despite their name) are the confused product of a single mind that has been affected by the ideas of many external bodies.[16] Thus a universal idea is derived not from the reflective comparison of the ideas we have of different bodies but from "fortuitous encounters with things" (EIIP29S) that are superimposed one upon the other through the equally haphazard workings of memory.[17] A universal, then, is not an adequate idea, or the clear and distinct foundation of reason, but an inadequate idea; it is nothing more than a mutilated and confused image of the external world.[18]

Since it is an image, a universal idea is always at bottom the product of a subjective experience of the external world.[19] So it can never attain the universal status, to which, in name at least, it aspires. Some images are certainly more frequent or more vivid than others. But that only explains why some images become the central features of these general ideas, not why they are rightly described as universal. For, as Spinoza emphasizes, "these notions are not formed by all [men] in the same way, but vary one to another, in accordance with what the body has more often been affected by, and what the imagination recollects more easily" (EIIP40S1). Someone might think that 'Man' refers to a single, universal species, but when descriptions are given, the term's extension will vary, depending upon which features of bodies have most vigorously or frequently affected the subject. One person will understand "an animal of erect stature," another will say "an animal capable of laughter," and so on (EIIP40S1). Such definitions may be useful as an aid to memory, but as a means towards scientific truth or as a way to overcome the subjectivity of value judgments they are flawed.[20] The very appearance of universality in which such terms are draped obscures their origins as judgments made by individuals in particular circumstances. Our specious universals appear as natural categories, discovered rather than invented. But, like teleological explanations of nature, they are really impositions upon the natural world of human categories produced by the imagination. Since exemplars are not common notions derived from adequate ideas but are ill-founded constructs of the imagination, these so-called "beings of reason" are perhaps more aptly named "beings of the imagination."[21] For the sake of gaining an appearance of objectivity, we can easily confound exemplars based upon universal ideas with real natural categories, but we can never really escape their origins in the subjective domain of imaginative experience.

The need for exemplars should now be clear. They are "notions we are accustomed to feign" (EIVPref) in order to compare and judge individuals of the same kind according to a single standard. But it should also be clear that insofar as they are based on universal ideas that are ultimately derived from the imagination, they fail in their purpose of defining an objective and certain standard of value. It remains an open question to what extent these exemplars, "beings" more of the "imagination" than of "reason", can lead us to an ethical life in Spinoza's sense—that is, a life governed by reason.[22] But in another guise, that of prophecy, exemplars will play a critical role in the political sphere, where the imagination and the passions, according to Spinoza, necessarily dominate.

THE ORIGIN AND FUNCTION OF PROPHECY IN THE *TTP*

Prophecy, as Spinoza analyzes it, has both the structure and the function of an exemplar. It is an inadequately conceived universal idea that serves to guide human judgment and conduct. Although prophecy originates in the particular situation of the prophet and uses highly imaginative language, it claims universal authority because it appeals to God as its source. Despite the theologians who "have accommodated Scripture to [Aristotelian and Platonic] speculations" (Pref., ¶18, III 9), the true purpose of prophecy is not speculative but ultimately practical: It exhorts men to "right conduct" in their affairs. It creates a standard to judge human actions and serves as a model to be imitated.

Spinoza explains the idea of the chosenness or "election" of Israel by God in terms of the exemplary function of prophecy. The prophets called their people chosen in order to exhort them to conduct that the people would believe was approved by God, a universal authority. And, to the extent that the people followed the exhortations of their prophets and adhered to a single standard of right conduct, they saw visible proof of their chosenness in the positive results of social cohesion, which became a further incentive to follow the prophets, thus reinforcing the original standard of conduct. The exemplary structure of prophecy uniquely suits it to solve the problem that arose for the ancient Hebrews in the Sinai desert, a problem equivalent to that of the theoretical state of nature.

In the *TTP*, Spinoza examines in great detail how Moses was able to found the Israelite state. When the Hebrews were cast out of Egypt into the desert they had no constitution of their own: "they were no longer bound by the legislation of any other nation, so that they were permitted to enact new laws as they wished" (v, ¶26, III 74).[23] Yet "they were quite incapable of ordaining legislation wisely and retaining the dominion in their own hands, as a body," since "Almost all of them were crude in their understanding and weakened by wretched bondage (v, ¶27, III 75). Moses, aware that his people were unable to take control of their own destiny, realized that "dominion had to remain in the hands of one person only, who would command the others and compel them by force, and who would prescribe laws and afterwards interpret them" (v, 27, III 75). But how could Moses alone compel his people, in the face of their divergent interests, to obey him? Even if he could gather enough support to use physical force, he would not achieve his long-term aims. For the "obstinate temperament of the people . . . would not allow itself to be compelled by force" (v, 28, III/75). Peaceful means were necessary if the state were to endure. So, Moses invoked divine authority, first to ensure his own power;[24] then, to institute the state.[25] Moses overcame the lawless condition of the Hebrews by instituting a state founded on religious practices and ceremonies. His commonwealth was a successful theocracy whose nominal king was God.[26] That alone, for Spinoza, was the purpose of Sinai, and was what entitled the ancient Hebrews to be called a chosen people.

We have already noted the situation of the ancient Hebrew nation once they had left the slavery of Egypt under Pharaoh. They were no longer subject to the laws of any other nation and were free to choose a new set of laws and institutions for themselves.[27] Spinoza describes their situation in these juridical terms: "For after they had been freed from the intolerable oppression of the Egyptians, and had not attached themselves to any mortal by any contract, they again acquired their natural right to do everything they could, and each of them could decide anew whether he wanted to keep it, or to surrender it and transfer it to someone else" (xvii, 26, G III 205). But why could they not just decide their future rationally among themselves? Using concepts developed in his analysis of "natural and civil right" in the previous chapter, Spinoza suggests that the difficulties the Hebrews faced in their task were juridically and psychologically equivalent to those faced in the "state of nature."[28] The dilemma they faced was that, although each person had the natural right to make his or her own decision, the exercise of that right would prevent the institution of a civil society.

The problem results from the fact that most people are led not by reason but by their appetites and passions. In the state of nature, an individual lives according to his natural right. That is, an individual has "the supreme right . . . to exist and act as it is naturally determined to do" (xvi, 4, III 189). But most people are not determined to live according to the dictates of reason; "on the contrary," Spinoza emphasizes, "they are all born ignorant of everything" (xvi, 7, G III 190). Consequently, the exercise of natural right in the state of nature is determined "not by sound reason, but by desire and power" (xvi, 7, G III 190). If people were led by reason, they would quickly realize that mutual aid and cooperation afford the most beneficial course of action; but since they are led by their desires, they are brought instead to division and conflict.[29] For "according to the laws of appetite each person is drawn in a different direction" (xvi, 14, G III 191). Since all people have a natural right to act according to their individual appetites, no one has any obvious reason to compromise the effort to satisfy individual desires. Indeed, in the state of nature, each person "is permitted, by supreme natural right, to want and to take, in whatever way, whether by force, by deception, by entreaties, or by whatever other way is, in the end, easier" (xvi, 8, G III 190). The "obstinacy" of the Hebrews was anchored in the exercise of each individual's right to live as he or she wished. Without the intervention of Moses' divine revelation, the inevitable result would have been conflict and distrust.

In Spinoza's view, Moses understood what needed to be done to forestall the disintegration of the state of nature into conflict and chaos: he needed "to so establish a political authority that there is no room left for deception, indeed, to so establish everything that everyone, no matter what his mentality, prefers the public right to the private advantage" (xvii, 16, G III 203). Moses also realized that an appeal to disinterested reason would not move the Israelite masses, who were led by desire and appetite. Spinoza, in fact, denies the possibility of the masses ever acting on the basis of anything but personal advantage: people must therefore somehow be led to act for the public good through their own self-interest. Since "no contract can have any force except by reason of its utility," it is entirely rational for an individual to break a contract (whether private or social) when it no longer serves his purpose (xvi, 20, G III 192).[30] Hence, whoever hopes to persuade the unruly masses that cooperation is in their best interest must be aware of what Spinoza calls the "universal law of human nature," that "between two goods, each person chooses the one he judges to be the greater, and between two evils, the one which seems to him lesser" (xvi, 15, G III 192). To this iron law of self-interest, Spinoza adds one important rider: the individual chooses "the one which seems to the person choosing to be greater or lesser, and not that things necessarily are as he judges them to be" (xvi, 15, G III 192). According to Spinoza, not only did Moses understand the underlying logic of self-interest that governs human behavior in the state of nature, but he also understood that the appearance of self-interest was as important as its reality. His strategy was to manipulate the appearance of self-interest until it was in line with real public interest. Moses appealed to revelation as the source of his views because prophetic revelation spoke to the situation of the people in language that they could readily understand and that directly appealed to their individual self-interest while using it in service of the community.

Spinoza defines prophecy as vivid imaginative language used by a person (a prophet) to exhort the ignorant masses to right conduct. The Prophets "perceived God's revelations only with the aid of the imagination, i.e., by the mediation of words or of images, the latter of which might be either true or imaginary" (i, 43, G III 27). God communicated to the prophets either through a "true voice," as he did to Moses alone, or through "visible forms and symbols," that often appear in a dream, such as Joshua's vision of an angel with a sword. Spinoza does not think that the prophets had any super-human capacity: "the Prophets were endowed, not with a more perfect mind, but instead with a power of imagining unusually vividly" (ii, 1, G III 29). Since the people were ignorant of its causes, they misinterpreted the richness of prophetic language as an indication of its supernatural origin. Thus "the Prophets were said to have the Spirit of God because men were ignorant of the causes of Prophetic knowledge, wondered at it, and on that account, were accustomed to refer it to God—as they did all other abnormal phenomena—and to call it the knowledge of God" (i, 42, G III 27–28). It is this very misunderstanding of prophecy which paradoxically explains its success in guiding conduct. For, although the prophet speaks in language that addresses a particular set of circumstances it is understood by its audience to have universal authority. Only so can it function effectively to define right conduct, not only for the individual but for everyone.

Because there are no prior rules of conduct in the state of nature, each interaction between individuals has an uncertain outcome. A person can never be sure whether or not he will be deceived by another, or even whether he will live or die. This uncertainty produces a constant affective vacillation in the individual between hope that things will turn out in his self-interest and fear that they will not. Indeed, the wretchedness of the state of nature is such that people have good reason to presume that things will not turn out in their favor. As Spinoza remarks in the opening sentences of the preface to the *TTP*, men "are often reduced to such straits that they can bring no plan into operation, and since they generally vacillate wretchedly between hope and fear, from an immoderate desire for the uncertain goods of fortune, for the most part their hearts are ready to believe anything at all" (Pref., 1, G III 5). This affective quandary provides fertile ground for both prophecy and superstition.[31]

Prophecy can address a person's self-interest, not by way of the abstract principles of reason, but by a direct appeal to the passions. Since, "by natural right each person can act deceptively, and is bound to stand by the contract only by the hope of a greater good and fear of a greater evil" (xvi, 23, G III 193), each person is interested in finding out what concrete expectations he has for an outcome that would justify his abiding by the contract. A person will listen to prophecy because he or she desires above all to have a consistent set of expectations about the results of his or her actions, and prophecy appears to provide that certainty through its status as the word of God. It regulates hopes and fears by locating them in a larger scheme of things, governed by an omnipotent being who responds to human choices with various passions (anger, care, etc.). In this way, what works for one individual can be seen to work for another, and a pattern of stable interactions emerges.[32] Prophecy satisfies a person's narrowly conceived self-interest in the state of nature, ending, or at least regulating the vacillation between hope and fear. But it also serves the general interest by establishing a standard of conduct that all can be expected to, and indeed do, imitate.

Therefore, when Moses called the Hebrews chosen he was not merely describing their relation to God but exhorting them to a way of life that would mold them into a nation The Israelites were a lawless band of people, cast out into the desert, thrown back into the state of nature. But Moses, gave them a law and founded a nation by placing their particular experience in the framework of a divine plan in which they played a special role. He recast their bad fortune as the founding principle of their society.[33] His idea appealed to the particular experience of each person and yet provided a broad basis on which to build institutions and practices that would coordinate the interactions among self-interested individuals. In effect the people were transferring their natural right to the authority of Moses, but they believed they were giving it to God. "God alone, then, held political authority over the Hebrews, and this authority alone, by the force of the covenant, was rightly called the Kingdom of God, and God was rightly called also the King of the Hebrews" (xvii, 30, G III 206). The anthropomorphic conception of God, as a ruler who made a covenant and guided his people in history, made it easy for individuals to transfer their hopes and fears concerning other people to their relationship with God. Moses was not interested in teaching the people, with their "childish understanding," about the nature of God, but only about His plan for their conduct, their rights and responsibilities to Him. He ritualized the people's relationship with their God using ceremonies and practices, and in this way the worship of God meant the establishment of institutions through which the founding principles of the state were secured.

Spinoza is quick to point out that the sense in which the ancient Hebrews were chosen was unique to them. For "the Laws of the Old Testament were revealed and prescribed only to the Jews" (iii, 22, G III 48). So, we might think that their story would be useful to others only if they too were of "primitive" understanding and predisposed to believe in an anthropomorphic God, miracles, and the like.[34] But before we dismiss the history of the ancient Hebrews we need to recognize that it is not just the content of prophecy itself that is exemplary but the structure of prophecy and its function in the state. Spinoza is not trying to eliminate the use of prophetic language, for he realizes that it would be impossible as long as people are driven by their appetites and passions and think through the medium of the imagination alone. Rather, he seeks to attack and undermine a misuse of exemplary language that is plainly illustrated in the narrative of the Hebrews.

PROPHECY AND SUPERSTITION

Although prophecy performs a crucial function in the creation and maintenance of the state, a danger lurks in the exemplary language of prophecy itself: People can easily mistake the appeal to divine authority for an appeal to the truth. That precisely is the difference between religion and superstition, in Spinoza's view.[35] Both religion and superstition originate in the uncertainty and affective vacillation characteristic of the state of nature. And both have the same immediate purpose: to guide wretched, self-interested individuals in their behavior. But while religion uses the prophetic language of revelation for the sake of teaching knowledge about right conduct alone, superstition uses prophetic language to lay claim to the truth about nature itself. Religion stays within the epistemological limits of prophetic language; superstition oversteps them. The result, at least in the scriptural history of the ancient Hebrews, is that while the prescriptions of religion are based upon devotion to God and produce a relatively stable society, the prescriptions of superstition are almost invariably based upon the fear of an earthly king and produce conflict.

We can see how superstition develops out of prophetic language if we recall what Spinoza says about exemplars in the *Ethics*. The purpose of an exemplar is to establish an objective standard of value, by appeal to a universal idea. But this universal idea often proves to be epistemologically inadequate. It claims to represent the ideal or model of all things of a certain kind, but it might represent only a particular image or a series of particular images blurred together. For example, an exemplar of human nature might look as if it were a rational concept common to all, while it is in fact an imaginative construct reflecting the particular situation and experience of its creator. To fulfill its function—to create a standard of value and conduct—an exemplar of human nature trades on its *appearance* of universality so as to be accepted in practice by the multitude. Thus, even as Spinoza underlines the need and desire for such an exemplar, he is also careful to point out the errors to which its underlying epistemological weakness can lead. Most importantly, he warns against imagining that exemplars and the values attendant on them are found in, or are products of, nature itself. They are just human constructs made in order to compare things, to judge relative value, and to emulate in one's actions. As soon as those who use an exemplar exceed its epistemic and practical limitations—using it to explain nature itself, rather than simply as a guide to conduct—it tends to fail in its original purpose. Moreover, certain people, realizing that the masses are ignorant and easily manipulated, eagerly misuse these exemplars to gain power for themselves.

What the misuse of an ethical exemplar and the misuse of prophetic language have in common is a misapplication of teleological thinking to nature. In the Preface to Part IV of the *Ethics*, Spinoza reiterates his critique of cosmic teleology articulated in the Appendix to Part I: "Nature does nothing on account of an end. [. . .] What is called a final cause is nothing but a human appetite insofar as it is considered as a principle, or primary cause, of some thing." But, since men imagine nature to act as they do, on account of an end, "when they see something happen in nature which does not agree with the model they have conceived of this kind of thing, they believe that Nature itself has failed or sinned, and left the thing imperfect" (EIVPref). It is legitimate to speak of 'ends' in human affairs, which are conceived primarily through the imagination, but it is a profound error to read such an idea back into nature, which is governed by eternal and necessary laws conceived by reason alone. Teleological explanation has an inevitable role in the explanation of human affairs but must be eschewed in the explanation of nature itself.[36] Yet some people want to claim that their exemplar of human nature, which they set before men as an end that ought to govern action, is itself an end of nature, thus confusing the realm of the imagination, which for the most part determines human values, with that of reason, which legitimately discerns the truths of nature.[37]

We see the problem most acutely when we consider the uses of Moses' prophetic pronouncement that the ancient Hebrews were chosen by God. The prophets used this idea to bridge the gap between personal interest in the state of nature and common interest in a civil society. The strategy worked because it appealed directly to the Hebrews while locating them within a story of universal significance; it explained what had happened and what they ought to do in the future. Although this narrative was teleological—that is, it established an end (a model of conduct) that the Hebrews were obliged to realize (or imitate) in their actions—it did not necessarily violate the epistemological limits of prophetic language. Moses himself, as Spinoza emphasizes,[38] knew that the Hebrews were "chosen" to be distinct from other nations, not for their wisdom or blessedness, but for their success in temporal matters. Moses spoke "according to the Hebrews' power of understanding" in order "to warn [them] in this way . . . so that he might bind them more to the worship of God" (iii, 5, G III 44). In other words, Moses used prophetic language for its effect, which was to strengthen the very institutions for which the Hebrews had been chosen in the first place, not because it taught anything about the workings of nature. The notion of a calling allowed the Hebrews to preserve themselves, by placing the self-interested desires of each individual in the larger framework of a divine plan that involved choosing the Hebrew nation as the main protagonist. On this level the teleological explanation of their actions was perfectly legitimate; there was no attempt to claim that the Jews were chosen for anything other than a certain form of conduct.

Moses was able to translate the prophetic idea of a calling directly into concrete social practices that preserved the state and protected its ideological (i.e., prophetic) foundation. In other words, he established a religion whose purpose was to maintain the social compact (in the form of a theocracy, in which power and right were symbolically transferred from the masses to God) through the institution of law. But at no point did Moses confuse the laws of the Hebrew theocracy, which were created by man and particular to it, with the eternal laws of nature decreed by God. Certainly, piety was identified with obeying the civil law, and that law was not distinguished from religious ceremonies and rites: "So, in this state civil law and Religion (which as we have shown, consists only in obedience to God) were one and the same thing" (xvii, 31, G III 205). Yet there was no confusion of this religious law, which encompassed both ceremonial and civil law, with the "divine law," which teaches the eternal truths of nature through the "natural light" of reason innate in every man.[39] Moses himself claimed no true knowledge of God[40] but only exhorted the Hebrews to right conduct: "The tenets of the religion were not teachings, but laws and commands; piety was thought to be justice, and impiety a crime and an injustice" (xvii, 31, G III 205). For the individual, obeying the ceremonial laws of religion was identical not only with his moral duty[41] but also with his political life: for "[a]nyone who failed in his Religious duties ceased to be a citizen, and for this alone was considered an enemy; anyone who died for Religion was considered to have died for his Country, and absolutely no distinction was made between civil law and religion" (xvii, 31, G III 205). So, for the state, the practice of these ceremonial laws by its citizens meant its continued existence. In this light, it was no accident that most of the religious ceremonies of the Jews could not be performed by an individual alone but only by a group.[42] Moses identified civil law and religious law in order to inspire obedience to the state, not through fear of an earthly authority, but through devotion to a divine being who had ordered the life of His chosen people in this particular manner, that is, through the practice of these laws and rituals.

Moses also showed that he was aware of the epistemological and practical limits of the prophetic foundation of the Hebrew state in the way he organized its constitution. Most importantly, he separated the powers of the political authorities, whom he charged with administering and enforcing the law, from those of the priestly caste, charged with interpreting the law. In order to foster the belief that God was the actual monarch, Moses constructed (with common resources) a "palace of God" that would serve as a visible reminder of the presence of divine authority (xvii, 42, G III 208). He also appointed one of the tribes, the Levites, to be "the courtiers and administrators of this divine palace (xvii, 43, G III 208). The chief of the Levites, Moses' brother Aaron, was "the supreme interpreter of the divine laws, the one who gave the people the replies of the divine oracle, and finally, the one who petitioned God on behalf of the people" (xvii, 43, G III 208). But Moses made sure that although they had the power to interpret God's law the priests did not have the authority to command. This he left exclusively in his own control. The priests perpetuated the illusion that God had ordained the state by performing the religious rites that were commanded by God and interpreting the law, and in this way, the actual leaders of the state, beginning with Moses himself, enjoyed a venerated status as "the ministers of God's state and . . . God's agents" without giving up any of their political authority (xvii, 65, G III 212). This separation of powers set limits on the leaders' authority, since they had to act within the law; and it preserved the integrity of the priestly caste, since they could gain honor only by their interpretations (xvii, 63–64, G III 212). Moses used the priests to maintain the fiction that preserved his authority. But he also realized the dangers involved. When he kept for himself the exclusive right of enforcing the law, he tried to make sure that the priests would not overstep their bounds and think that their privileged status as the interpreters of God's law gave them the power to enforce it, and thus undermine his own authority.[43]

However, the very fiction that had founded the state could be easily subverted by the priests in the service of their own ends. Spinoza sees the prophetic foundation of the Hebrew state as its greatest strength but also its fatal weakness. Prophecy could serve as the basis of a religion uniquely suited to bind the Hebrews together into a cohesive political entity, but it could also be distorted into superstitious beliefs that might tear them apart. Spinoza argues that the Levites were the ruin of the state for at least two reasons. First, their privileged status led to grumbling and division among the tribes. Even before Moses' death there were signs of discontent among the elite. The very success of the state constituted at Sinai had given men the leisure to question the divine authority Moses had claimed and to doubt his motives in establishing the Levites (with his brother at their head) as a special caste.[44] Once the veil of appearances that was so crucial to the maintenance of the state had been pierced, rebellion became so widespread among the people that it was only ended through some·"great calamity or plague" (xvii, 103–04, G III 219). This was a sign of things to come.

Second, and more importantly, the special role reserved for the Levites led them to abuse their power, creating turmoil in the state. Especially after

Moses died and no one assumed his exalted role, there was little to prevent
the Levites from claiming not only the right to interpret laws but also the
right to enforce them (xvii, 100, G III 218). They found the justification for
their actions in a new interpretation of God's word, provided by the "many
relentless and foolish Theologians" among them (xvii, 99, G III 218). These
men were not mindful of the limits of prophetic knowledge and interpreted
the laws of right conduct as if they were the laws of nature itself. Although
useful in justifying the priests' claim to political authority, this move had
catastrophic consequences for the state. Religious authority, originally instituted by Moses to benefit all, became the means of a small group's domination of the rest.

Spinoza thinks that in order to gain power the priests claimed not only
the right to interpret the laws but also the right to enforce them. They used
prophecy not to exhort the masses to right conduct, as originally intended,
but to manipulate the masses to their own ends. The very ignorance and fear
which made prophecy effective at the outset, now enabled the theologians
to transform their religion into superstition.[45] Ignorant of the divine law of
nature, the masses were quick to take anything extraordinary as a sign of
God's will. The vivid nature of prophetic language seemed a higher form of
knowledge,[46] so they were easily misled. Moses and other prophets had used
"miracles" not to teach about the nature of God but to guide the people.[47]
The priests now used them much as soothsayers used such wonders as the
entrails of animals to predict the future.[48] What had been used to exhort the
masses to right conduct now became a tool to inspire fear in them. But the
hollowness of such interpretations of religious law had a unfortunate effect:
they served the immediate interests of the priests but not the long term interests of the masses.

Introducing elements of superstition into the religious structure of the
Hebrew state served the priests well, at first. They were not interested in
maintaining order through a stable practice of religious rites that inspired
devotion among the masses. Rather, they ruled by introducing into the state
practices that encouraged the very passions that abound in the state of
nature. For the power of superstition plays even more intensely on individual hopes and fears than does religion. But it does not resolve them as religion does. Superstition, Spinoza argues, does not have any interest in allay-
ing the fears of an individual; it does not seek to transform fear into
devotion but uses this fear to maintain control of the state. "Fear then, the
reason why superstition arises, is preserved and is encouraged" (Pref., 5, G
III 5). So, instead of maintaining stable laws, the Levites began to increase
them constantly, "determining everything by priestly authority and daily
issuing, concerning ceremonies, the faith, and everything else, new decrees,
which they wanted to be no less sacred and to have no less authority than

the laws of Moses" (xviii, 8, III/221). The paradoxical effect of these decrees and the attendant theological disputes was to undermine the faith of the masses in the religious order of the state. Since the epistemic ground of priestly authority was ambiguous, and the priests had strayed from its proper domain, it was easy for others to dispute that authority. The signs that once had meant one thing could easily be twisted to mean something different.[49] The doubt that few had displayed in the time of Moses grew unchecked under the rule of the Levites. In response, the priests only redoubled their attempt to manipulate the passions of the people, allowing "great license" and agreeing to whatever the common people desired when fear was not effective.[50] The vacillation between hope and fear that had been endemic in the state of nature was reintroduced into the state by the very agents who had been appointed to preserve its stability. Thus weakened, the Hebrew state readily succumbed to foreign invaders.

Once the means of inspiring devotion among the people had broken down or proved inefficacious, something else was needed to keep the people in check. If the state was to be reconstituted, the only possible solution was to introduce an earthly sovereign to rule the masses in tandem with the priests. And that, as Spinoza tells us, is what the Hebrews did.[51] This act finally broke the political effectiveness of the covenant with God that Moses had instituted. If Moses' technique had been to gain assent to his authority through the perpetuation of a fictive covenant with God, the technique of the kings was, of necessity, more direct. It was the threat of force. The old theocracy thus devolved into something resembling Hobbes' "Leviathan,"[52] although preserving some annoying and dangerous relics of the past. The elite of the old order had survived and were content with their lot, but their successors were not and were continually trying to usurp command. The institution of the priesthood persisted and continued to treat the rights of the ruling authorities with disdain, looking always to reestablish its own prophetic rule. Thus, the Hebrew kings "had a state within a state, and ruled precariously" (xvii, 108, G III 220). The constant strife between priests and kings could result only in tyranny. Once "religion declined into a pernicious superstition and . . . the true meaning and interpretation of the laws was corrupted," dissension reigned and only force could settle matters (xviii, 9, G III 222).[53] The eventual collapse of the Hebrew state was caused not from without but from within.[54]

Whether this story accurately depicts the events recounted in the Hebrew Bible is far less important for us than the use Spinoza makes of it. On one level it appears simply to relate the rise and fall of the ancient Hebrew state. On another, it points a moral: the institutionalization of the priesthood leads to the state's ruin. As Spinoza writes, "the more I consider this change the more it compels me to burst out in the words of Tacitus: at that time God's concern was not with their security, but with vengeance" (xvii, 97, G III 218).[55] Going one level further, I think that Spinoza's story is a political allegory that aims to translate the awful mystery of "God's vengeance" on the Hebrews into a meaningful point about politics: that the imaginative means called upon to produce political community can also bring about its downfall. All of these elements are buried in yet another level of significance. For Spinoza uses the story itself as an exemplar. He is not only asking his readers to understand the underlying significance of the narrative of the Hebrew state, but exhorting others to regard it as an example to imitate.

THE HEBREWS AND THE DUTCH

What the prophets were to the ancient Hebrews, Scripture was to the Dutch. It was for this cultural and historical reason that Spinoza chose the ancient Hebrews as his example and exemplar in the *TTP*. He followed his own advice:

> If someone wishes to teach some doctrine to a whole nation, not to mention the whole human race, and wishes it to be understood in every respect by everyone, he is bound to confirm his teaching solely by experience, and for the most part to accommodate his arguments and the definitions of things to be taught to the power of understanding of the common people, who form the greatest part of the human race. (v, 37, G III 77)

Just as an appeal to reason would not have been effective with the Hebrews, Spinoza thought that he had to appeal to the experience of the Dutch if was to persuade them of anything. But the experience of a people is a broad and complex notion. As Simon Schama has so admirably shown, the seventeenth-century Dutch saw themselves in the light of three important sets of historical narratives or myths: the story of their own heroic struggle against the Spanish, which retroactively assumed a strongly nationalist bent; the story of the Batavians depicted in the writings of Tacitus (and other Roman historians) and drawn upon by Grotius (amongst others) to explain the ancient origins of the nation; and the story of the ancient Israelites.[56] It is with this last founding myth that Spinoza is obviously concerned in the *TTP*.[57] His interpretation of the rise and fall of the Hebrew state was not just a randomly chosen illustration of his political philosophy but a model chosen for very concrete reasons. Spinoza hoped to use the Hebrews to show that tolerance of opinion and belief was necessary for the welfare of the state.

Although it would take us far beyond the scope of this paper to explicate the full range of meanings that the story of the ancient Hebrews had for the seventeenth-century Dutch, we can focus on the aspects most relevant to Spinoza by returning to the painting described in the introduction, Ferdinand Bol's "Moses Descends from Sinai with the Ten Commandments," hanging in the Magistrates's Chamber (*Schepenkamer*) of the Amsterdam Town Hall. As the art historian Albert Blankert has pointed out, there are undoubtedly two reasons why this somewhat unusual subject was selected for so prominent a place.[58] The first and more general is the Calvinist influence on the Dutch state. From their earliest days the Calvinists had identified themselves with the exodus of the ancient Hebrews.[59] The second, more specific reason has to do with the troubled relations between the Calvinist clergy and the Amsterdam government. Let us look first at the general reason why this painting was commissioned before we look at its specific place in the debates of the time.

Bol's use of this scene from Exodus was not a mere conceit or mannered allusion. By 1665, the Dutch had repeatedly used the Hebrew Bible to describe their own trials and tribulations, especially with the Spanish. To break the siege of Leiden by the Duke of Alva in 1574, William of Orange had taken the desperate measure of breaking the great dykes that protected the city and surrounding land from the ocean. The Spanish, panicked by the rising waters, fled. Local historians and the city fathers described this event in providential terms. The hand of God had intervened on the side of his chosen people against their oppressors, who were compared to the Midianites. The parallel with the trials of the ancient Israelites was not expressed in words alone: the chronicle of this event was recited thereafter in a commemorative meal with food (bread and herring) that was supposed to remind the celebrants of the Leiden citizens' heroic sacrifice and providential salvation.[60] This "commingling of scripture and historical chronicle" helped foster the emerging Dutch nation's sense of separateness, creating a vision of destiny that transformed profane events such as battles, trade transactions, and even household chores into the unfolding of a sacred plan.[61] The Calvinist preachers produced a theology in which the Dutch Republic was the "New Canaan," and they saw their own position "as equal to the prophets of ancient Israel."[62] On this basis, the "more demanding Calvinists . . . attempt[ed] to establish godly norms of social behavior that were laid down as fitting for the new Chosen People. Conformity to these norms guaranteed perpetuation of the covenant; deviation from them, the downfall of the commonwealth."[63] Both politicians and preachers constantly exhorted their people to right conduct in terms of this scriptural identification. Close to a century after the events at Leiden, when Bol was commissioned to paint

Moses for the town hall, and when Spinoza was composing the *TTP*, the identification with Israel was well rooted in the imaginative and moral landscape of the nation.

The scriptural narrative, then, was exemplary for the Dutch in both structure and function: in structure, because it could appeal to the imagination of the individual in the guise of an end that appeared to have divine, and therefore universal significance; and in function, because it served to exhort the people to act in relation to an objective set of values and in prescribed ways. Yet the precise sense in which it was exemplary was not always agreed. A figure, like Moses, could be assigned different messages, religious or political. Catholic tradition viewed Moses as a "prophetic harbinger of the messianic return." The Dutch identified him at various times with William of Orange, the noble liberator, and with Oldenbarneveld, the magistrate who was "the first great patriot of the law" and a proponent of religious toleration.[64] As we have seen, Spinoza traces such divergences in interpretation of an exemplar to its foundation in an inadequately conceived universal. What appears to be universal actually reflects some more particular interpretation of experience. The idea that scripture is "revealed" hides its human origins, the source of an exemplar's strength but also of its weakness. It can appeal to a large group of people of diverse interests and ideas. But it can also be placed in service of those divergent interests. The Dutch drew upon scriptural history to understand and shape their common experience. But the divergences of interpretation opened the way for conflict. The image of Moses holding the tablets of the law was indisputably an image of authority for the Dutch nation in the seventeenth century, but it "was when individual Dutch men and women tried to discern what exactly it was that those tablets commanded . . . that the scriptural analogy began to lose clarity and coherence."[65]

The dispute over who had the ultimate right to interpret scripture and who had the authority to enforce its commands was the specific impetus for the commission and conception of Ferdinand Bol's painting of Moses. In 1665, the clergy was officially under state authority. Nonetheless, "a bitter controversy arose on the issue of the primacy of the church or the state."[66] Since the revolt against the Spanish in the sixteenth-century the head of the House of Orange-Nassau had led the army and, for a good part of that time, the country, through the office of the Stadtholder.[67] But after the sudden death of William II in 1650, the States party, led by Jan de Witt, formed a republican government without a Stadtholder.[68] Most of the Calvinist clergy stridently opposed the government of the States party, not least because of the relative tolerance it showed to other religions.[69] They bowed (voluntarily or perforce) to the power of de Witt's government. But their sympathies were with the Orangists,[70] who sought to use the clergy's influence over the populace to reestablish themselves at the head of the government. It is not surprising, then, to find the Calvinist clergy using biblical analogies to argue for the reinstitution of the stadtholderate.[71]

Blankert argues that the Amsterdam burgomasters chose Bol's painting and specified the depiction of its subject-matter to counter the claims of the Calvinist clergy—and the Orangist party—and thereby reassert their own position and that of the States party in Amsterdam.[72] The painting shows Moses as Lawgiver with his brother Aaron, the high priest, subordinate to him and the Law. As if worried that the point of the painting would be missed, the burgomasters, as we have noted, also commissioned the marble frieze beneath it, detailing the frenzied scene around the Golden Calf. "The relief as a whole," Blankert comments, "served as a warning of the chaos that results when the leadership of the people falls into the hands of the clergy" (65). Just in case the audience did not immediately grasp the visual evidence, a poem by Joost van den Vondel was also commissioned, apparently some time before the painting itself was completed:

> The Hebrew Moses has received the Law from God, with which
> he returns from above to the people, who greet him reverently and
> welcome him eagerly. The free State begins to flourish when the
> people respect the laws.[73]

Using images drawn from the Old Testament, the city authorities hoped to make a statement to the clergy (in their own language) and to the populace about the proper place of leadership in the state.[74]

Spinoza, like Bol, emphasized the image of Moses as lawgiver, because he wanted to argue for the priority of the state in all matters, secular or religious. It was Moses, as the prophetic founder of the state, who could lead the people from the state of nature into civil society; and it was Moses, as lawgiver, who organized the state to endure. Yet the means by which Moses founded the state could easily be perverted by others for their own interests, as we have seen. This precisely is the point where Spinoza's analysis of the causes and effects of the corruption of religion in the Hebrew state is deeply linked to his argument for toleration in the United Provinces.

Spinoza bases his argument for toleration on the distinction between the proper and improper use of exemplary language in the state. In the preface to the *TTP* he tells the reader of his twofold purpose in writing the work. His overarching aim is to show "not only that . . . freedom [of opinion and worship] can be granted without harm to piety and the peace of the State, but also that it cannot be abolished unless piety and the Peace of the State are abolished with it" (Pref., 12, G III 7). In order to achieve this end Spinoza thinks that he must first "indicate the main prejudices regarding religion, i.e. the traces of our former bondage, and then also the prejudices regarding the right of the supreme powers" (Pref., 13, G III 7). For "Many, with the most impudent license, are eager to take away the greater part of that right, and to turn the heart of the masses (who are still liable to pagan superstition) away from the supreme powers, so that all may rush again into slavery" (Pref., 13, G III 7). Spinoza intends to expose these prejudices and their causes by a thorough critique of Scripture, undermining those who seek to exploit the masses through the manipulation of superstitious beliefs.

Given the political and social conditions of the United Provinces of his time, Spinoza did not think it possible to deny any and all role to religious belief and practice. As he writes,

> For everyone knows how highly the people value the right and authority regarding sacred matters, and how much everyone hangs on the utterances of the one who has it, so much so that we can rightly say that the person who has this authority has the most powerful control over their hearts. (xix, 40, G III 235)

Accordingly, Spinoza found it necessary to appeal to familiar religious beliefs and practices and reinterpret them. In this light, the ancient Hebrews became not just an analogy, or illustration of a theoretical point, but an exemplar to be imitated. Spinoza saw that the same dynamics underlying Moses' appeal to revelation were at play in the Dutch identification with Biblical Israel. If Moses called his people chosen, to exhort them to right conduct, that is, to conduct that would best maintain the state, the Dutch Calvinist belief that the Dutch nation had been chosen to endure and triumph could also be used to maintain a certain political order. But the priestly caste, the Calvinist preachers, must not be allowed to overstep the bounds of their proper role. Bol's painting compresses the exemplary meaning of the narrative of the founding of the Hebrew state, as Spinoza has reconstructed it, in one highly symbolic moment: the priests must bow to Moses, who embodies the proper relation of prophecy to the law. The right to interpret the law must be distinct from the right to enforce the law. Only under this constitutional arrangement could the state persist.

In the Netherlands of Spinoza's time, the priests threatened to cross this boundary, claiming that they had the right not only to interpret the law but also to enforce their interpretation.[75] They pursued this claim, just as the ancient Levites had, not directly but indirectly through the establishment of a king whom they believed they would control. As the period during which the struggle between church and state, republicans and Orangists, reached its most intense, "[t]he idea of the Dutch Israel was given its most elaborate treatment," by Calvinist ministers for whom the "State existed for the sake of the Church."[76] Indeed, the strategy of the Calvinists was that of the "relentless and foolish" theologians whom Spinoza had singled out among the Levites of the young Hebrew nation: They claimed that their interpretation of the laws was identical with philosophical truth.[77] Once in power, Spinoza believed, the theologians would seek to suppress all interpretations of the law different from their own. For to allow a diversity of beliefs would effectively undermine their claim to power as exclusive arbiters of truth. But any such attempt would be illegitimate, impractical, and ill-advised: illegitimate, because each person has the natural right to maintain whatever idea or passion he may hold;[78] impractical because it is impossible for any individual (or group) to control the minds of the multitude;[79] and ill-advised, because the imposition of prophetic (i.e., exemplary) language into the realm of either intellect or belief would not succeed but would only be labeled tyranny [*imperium violentum*] and met with resistance.[80] What the priests and preachers had forgotten or purposefully ignored was that their role is to perpetuate language (and institutions that maintain this language) whose goal is to inspire conduct commensurate with the aims of the state—peace and liberty. What Spinoza did in the *TTP*, just as Bol attempted to do in his painting, was to remind interested parties of this fact. The toleration of belief and ideas, if not of action, was central to the maintenance of the social contract.

Spinoza was reading contemporary Dutch concerns into the scriptures. He was not concerned with the historical truth of the scriptural narrative, even if it could be found,[81] but only with the use of its contents for his own purposes. Like others before him who employed the rhetoric of exemplarity, Spinoza felt free to pick and choose from the enormous stock of examples collected in the scriptures in order to make his own point.[82] But his strategy is entirely consistent with his aim in the *TTP*. If we are talking about politics, we appeal primarily not to reason but to experience, which is constituted through the imagination and memory. In other words, we must use exemplary language. Spinoza starts with an imaginative universal, grounded in the scriptures, that has an important political and cultural function in Dutch society, and gives his own interpretation of it, one which he believes is consistent with its function: the preservation of a stable state. Of course, Spinoza could hardly have foreseen the traumatic overthrow of the States party by the Orangists during the French invasion, two years after the *TTP* was published in 1670.[83] But while he was writing the *TTP*, there is no doubt that he believed it imperative to intervene and to try to persuade his readers of the dangers involved in the Calvinists' misuse of prophetic language, not only for philosophers but for all citizens of the republican state.

CONCLUSION: THE HEBREWS, SPINOZA, AND US

As prophecy was for the ancient Hebrews, or the scriptures for the Dutch, Spinoza's *Tractatus Theologico-Politicus* is to the contemporary political theorist: an exemplar. We have seen that, in his analysis of the Hebrew state, Spinoza argues that prophecy was the means by which Moses could persuade individuals led by their passions and perceived self-interest that they should join together into a state governed uniformly by a rule of law. We have also seen that Spinoza chose the example of the ancient Hebrews precisely because the seventeenth-century Dutch saw themselves as the new Israel. In both cases, the notion of "chosenness" played an important role in the construction of an exemplar. Both prophets and preachers used this idea because it effectively appealed to individuals to see themselves within a divine plan, whose realization depended upon their actions. Both prophecy and scripture, then, are exemplars in the sense that Spinoza defined it in the *Ethics*: imaginative universals that function to create a standard on the basis of which value can be defined and right conduct urged. What I hope to have shown in the preceding discussion is that exemplars play as important a role in politics as they do in ethics.

From the very first sentence of the *TTP*, Spinoza emphasizes that the power of reason over human affairs is limited. Again and again he argues that most people are ruled by their passions and best reached through the imagination. To convince another of something, one "should not connect his arguments or give definitions . . . Otherwise he will write only for the learned, i.e., he will be intelligible only to a few men compared with the others" (v, 37, G III 77). Rather, he must accommodate his arguments to the understanding and experience of the common people through the use of narratives that appeal to the imagination.[84] This does not mean, of course, that reason has no role in politics. Reason teaches that society is the best means to preserve individual existence, and it shows us ways to improve society for that end (iii, 14, G III 47). Moreover, it is an insight of reason, and amply demonstrated by experience, that people cannot escape being influenced by the passions and the imagination.[85] But although reason teaches important principles about politics, reason alone cannot solve the preeminent political problem: how to convince people led by their passions that their interests are best served in society.

In order to do that, the theorist as well as the politician must appeal to the imagination to address the very passions and interests that dominate most people's lives. The same principles that apply in the creation of political society through prophecy thus also apply to the interpretation of prophecy itself. It is necessary to use examples like that of the Hebrews not just to prove theoretical points but to exhort people to act in a certain way. In contemporary language, we could say that Spinoza profoundly understood the performative dimension of political discourse. He did not choose the Hebrews merely because they were an appropriate example for his theory but because they already functioned as an exemplar, as a model that ought to be imitated. In offering his own interpretation of this exemplar he is seeking to govern its meaning and use in political life.

Spinoza chose to focus on the Hebrews because of the cultural resonance of scripture in seventeenth-century Dutch society. We choose to analyze Spinoza's work because it has a resonance of its own in some small part of our own society, among academics and other "learned men." But if we wish seriously to address the problem Spinoza did, if we intend to use Spinoza's *TTP* in our time as he intended it to be used in his, not just as an example to be used in intellectual discussion, but as an exemplar to imitate in service of establishing a free and tolerant political order, then we must look to the Hebrews, and ask ourselves what imaginative notions lie at the foundations of our own society and how ought we to interpret them.

NOTES

An earlier version of this article was published in *History of Poltical Thought* 18 (1997): 207–41. For their comments on the draft of that version I would like to thank Ann Jensen Adams, Daniel Brudney, Edwin Curley, Daniel Garber, Joseph Stern, and Janelle Taylor. For their helpful editorial advice on this version I thank Lenn Goodman and Heidi Ravven.

1. For my discussion of this painting I draw upon two works of Albert Blankert, *Kunst als regerinzszaak in Amsterdam in de 17e eeuw: Rondom schilderijen van Ferdinand Bol* (with summary in English), (Lochem: Uitg. Mij. De Tijdstroom B.V., 1975), and *Ferdinand Bol* (Doornspijk: Davaco Publishers, 1982); and the doctoral dissertation by Barbara Joyce Buchbinder-Green, "The Painted Decorations of the Town Hall of Amsterdam" (Evanston, Illinois: Northwestern University, 1974). There is some uncertainty as to the actual date of this painting. It was probably commissioned in 1659, though it was not actually hung until 1664, at the earliest. Bol did not receive payment for it until 1666. See Blankert (1982), 109–10, and Buchbinder-Green, 152–53.

2. According to Buchbinder-Green (153–54), it was Jan van Eyk in 1758 who first suggested this interpretation of the painting in *Kunst en historiekundige beschryving en aanmerkingen over alle de schilderyen op het stadhuis te Amsterdam* (Amsterdam: Pieter Yver, 1758), 139. See also Blankert (1982), 110. On this point, both Buchbinder-Green and Blankert refer to an article by Christian Tümpel, "Studien zur Ikonographie der Historien Rembrandts," *Nederlands Kunsthistorisch Jaarboek*, XX (1969): 169–75, which compares Bol's Moses with that of Rembrandt.

3. See Katherine Fremantle, *The Baroque Town Hall of Amsterdam* (Utrecht: Haentjens Dekker & Gumbert, 1959), 77; and also Blankert (1975), 32–33, 65.

4. See letters 29 and 30 (IV/165–66), respectively from and to Oldenburg. For more on the structure and composition of the *TTP*, see Edwin Curley, "The *Theological-Political Treatise* as a Prolegomenon to the *Ethics*," in *Central Themes in Early Modern Philosophy*, ed. J.A. Clover and Mark Kulstad (Indianapolis, Ind.: Hackett, 1990). Since Bayle's *Dictionary* entry, most scholars agree that some of the *TTP* was drawn from an earlier (and now lost) defense Spinoza had written for himself and his principles at the time of his ban [*herem*] from the Amsterdam Jewish community in 1656 (see Henry E. Allison, *Benedict de Spinoza: An Introduction*, [New Haven: Yale University Press, 1987], 7).

5. Although Spinoza says in the Preface to the *TTP* that "I do not ask the common people to read these things" (34; G III 12), in a letter to Oldenburg he had said that one reason why he was undertaking the project that culminated in the *TTP* was to avert the accusation held by the "common people" [*vulgus*] that he was an atheist (Letter 30 to Oldenburg, September or October 1665, in Wolf, ed. *Correspondence of Spinoza*, 206, G V 166). Spinoza did not permit the translation of the *TTP* from Latin into Dutch, but this was perhaps due more to the unexpectedly strong reaction that the book had provoked rather than an original plan to limit its audience (Letter 44 to Jarig Jelles, 17 February 1671, Wolf, 260, G V 227). I will return to this issue again in the conclusion. All that we need assume at this point is that the audience is composed of persons other than those led exclusively by reason, which is most people.

6. André Tosel, "Y-a-t-il une philosophie du progrès historique chez Spinoza?" in *Spinoza: Issues and Directions* ed. P.-F. Moreau and Edwin Curley (Leiden: E. J. Brill, 1990), 306–26. A. Matheron also points to passages in which Spinoza emphasizes the primitive aspect of the Hebrews (see e.g., *Le Christ et le salut des ignorants chez Spinoza* [Aubier-Montaigne, 1971], 14), but he would not, I think, subscribe to all other aspects of Tosel's interpretation.

7. See Shlomo Pines, "Spinoza's *Tractatus Theologico-Politicus*, Maimonides and Kant," in *Scripta Hierosolymitana*, ed. Ora Siegel, vol. 1 (Jerusalem: Magnes Press, 1968), and more recently, Steven B. Smith, "Spinoza's Paradox: Judaism and the Construction of Liberal Identity in the *Theologico-Political Treatise*," *Journal of Jewish Thought and Philosophy*, 4 (1995), 203–25.

8. Lewis S. Feuer, *Spinoza and the Rise of Liberalism* (Boston: Beacon Press, 1958), 119.

9. Sylvain Zac, "Spinoza et l'état des Hébreux," in *Philosophie, théologie, politique dans l'oeuvre de Spinoza* (Paris: Vrin, 1979), 145–89. Etienne Balibar, in *Spinoza et la politique* (Paris: Presses Universitaire de France, 1986), also places the *TTP* within the political struggles of the time.

10. P.-F. Moreau, in "Les Principes de la lecture de l'Ecriture Sainte dans le T.T.P.," *Groupes des Recherches Spinozistes: Travaux et Documents*, no. 4 (Paris: 1992): 119–31, compares Spinoza's use of the Hebrews to that of his contemporaries (e.g., Koerbagh, Meyer) and concludes that "Il est donc possible de reprendre comme exemple [i.e., the Hebrew state] ce que l'on refuse comme modèle" (127). In the same volume are useful articles on other uses of the Hebrew state: F. LaPlanche, "L'érudition Chrétienne aux XVIe et XVIIe siècles et l'état des hébreux" (133–47), and C. R. Ligota, "Histoire à fondement théologique: la republique des hébreux" (149–67).

11. Norman O. Brown, in his article, "Philosophy and Prophecy: Spinoza's Hermeneutics," *Political Theory* 14, no. 2 (May 1986): 195–213, also considers the function of prophetic language in the political argument of the *TTP*, though he focuses on its transformative rather than its exemplary effect.

12. The general sense in which I use the term *exemplar* is indebted to two recent discussions of this rhetorical concept: Timothy Hampton, *Writing from History: The Rhetoric of Exemplarity in Renaissance Literature*, (Ithaca, N.Y.: Cornell University Press, 1990); and John D. Lyons, *Exemplum: The Rhetoric of Example in Early Modern France and Italy*, (Princeton, N.J.: Princeton University Press, 1989).

13. In the Preface to part IV, Curley renders the Latin 'exemplar' as 'model'. I prefer to use the cognate 'exemplar' in order to maintain the dual sense of 'example' and 'model' in the original.

14. I am indebted for this way of putting the problem of value in Part IV of the *Ethics* to an article by Edwin Curley, "Spinoza's Moral Philosophy" in *Spinoza*, ed. Marjorie Grene (Notre Dame: University of Notre Dame Press, 1979), 354–76.

15. *Ethics*, Part IV, Pref. (G II 206). I have retained the Latin 'exemplaria' here instead of Curley's uniform translation of it as 'models' because I want to argue that the word means both 'model' and 'example'. I think the first instance of the word in this passage could be translated as 'model' while the second could be translated as 'example'.

16. As Spinoza writes, "Those notions they call 'Universal,' like Man, Horse, Dog, etc., have arisen . . . because so many images (e.g., of men) are formed at one time in the human Body that they surpass the power of imagining—not entirely, of course, but still to the point where the Mind can imagine neither slight differences of the singular [men] (such as the color and size of each one, etc.) nor their determinate number, and imagines distinctly only what they agree in, insofar as they affect the body. For the body has been affected most [forcefully] by [what is common], since each singular has affected it [by this property]. And [the mind] expresses this by the word *man*, and predicates it of infinitely many singulars" (EIIP40S1).

17. Memory is nothing other than the association of two or more images following the order of a body's interactions with the external world. See EIIP18S.

18. Spinoza sums up the difference between adequate and inadequate ideas in EIIP29S, where he writes: "I say expressly that the Mind has, not an adequate, but only a confused [and mutilated] knowledge, of itself, of its own Body, and of external bodies, so long as it perceives things from the common order of nature, i.e., so long as it is determined externally, from fortuitous encounters with things, to regard this or that, and not so long as it is determined internally, from the fact that it regards a number of things at once, to understand their agreements, differences, and oppositions. For so often as it is disposed internally, in this or another way, then it regards things clearly and distinctly. . ."

19. ". . . to retain the customary words, the affections of the human Body, whose ideas present external bodies as present to us, we shall call images of things, even if they do not reproduce the [external] figures of things. And when the Mind regards bodies in this way, we shall say that it imagines" (EIIP17S).

20. See *Appendix Containing Metaphysical Thoughts*, Part 1, Chapter 1: "So when Plato said that man is a featherless biped, he erred no more than those who said that man is a rational animal. For Plato was no less aware than anyone else that man is a rational animal. But he referred man to a certain class so that, when he wished to think about man, he would immediately fall into the thought of man by recalling that class, which he could easily remember. Indeed Aristotle erred very seriously if he thought that he had adequately explained the human essence by that definition of his. Whether, indeed, Plato did well, one can only ask" (CW, 301; G I 235).

21. "We see, therefore, that all the notions by which ordinary people are accustomed to explain nature are only modes of imagining, and do not indicate the nature of anything, only the constitution of the imagination. And because they have names, as if they were [notions] of beings existing outside the imagination, I call them beings, not of reason, but of imagination." (EIApp.; G II 83/11–17). See also Martial Gueroult, *Spinoza* (Aubier-Montaigne, 1974) vol.2, 415.

22. Edwin Curley, in "Spinoza's Moral Philosophy," thinks that Spinoza "must be saying that we can form an idea of human nature, which is rightly used as a standard of judgment" (364). Curley holds that there are adequate ideas of human nature, which, because an individual will necessarily desire to realize them (as a function of his or her *conatus*), are objective. For other views on the relation of an adequate idea of human nature and the ideal of the "free man," see Dan Garber's recent paper delivered to the Jerusalem Spinoza conference, "Dr. Fischelson's Dilemma: Spinoza on Freedom and Sociability"

(forthcoming), and Lee Rice's "*Tanquam Naturae Humanae Exemplar*: Spinoza on Human Nature," in *Modern Schoolman* 68 (May 1991): 291–303.

25. Passages from the *TTP* are cited by chapter, paragraph number, and reference to Gebhardt's edition of Spinoza's *Opera*. All translations are taken from a typescript copy of the second volume of *The Collected Works of Spinoza*, translated and edited by Edwin Curley. I would like to thank Professor Curley for allowing me to use his work before it has been published.

24. "Moses was easily able to retain this dominion, because he excelled the others in divine power, persuaded the people that he had it, and showed this by many testimonies" (v, 28, G III 75).

25. "Moses, by the divine power and command, introduced religion into the Body politic, so that the people would do their duty not so much from fear as from devotion" (v, 29, G III 75).

26. In the *Discourses on Livy* , Machiavelli makes a similar argument. Numa was able to transform Rome from a city based on force to a city founded on principles of law and obedience, through the use of religion (Book 1, §11). On this parallel see also Norman O. Brown, "Philosophy and Prophecy, 208–09.

27. See also xvii, 26, G III 205.

28. See Matheron, *Le Christ et le salut des ignorants chez Spinoza*, 10. Douglas Den Uyl argues that the Hebrews were not in the "state of nature" because they already had the rudiments of social life (*Power, State, and Freedom: An Interpretation of Spinoza's Political Philosophy* [Assen: Van Gorcum, 1983), chapter 2.

29. See also xvii, 13–16, G III 203.

30. Spinoza gives the example of a person who disingenuously contracts with a robber to deliver goods to him at a later date. Spinoza thinks that when the person is later released he has no obligation whatever to make good on the promise; indeed he is fully rational to renege on it (xvi, 16–19, G III 192). As Curley notes, this contrasts starkly with Hobbes's view of the same example (see *De cive* ii, 16; *Leviathan*, xiv).

31. It is not a coincidence that the opening sentences of the *TTP* and the Preface to Part IV of the *Ethics* both begin with a reference to fortune—the power of external things over human affairs. While here I assume the theoretical construct of the state of nature, I think Spinoza does provide a deeper metaphysical reason for its actual existence, which he calls the power of "fortune." For the role of "fortune" in the *TTP*, see F. Mignini, "Theology as the Work and Instrument of Fortune," in *Spinoza's Political and Theological Thought*, ed. C. De Deugd (Amsterdam/New York: North Holland, 1984), 127–36.

32. Of course there still may be people who refuse to accept the prophet's teaching and continue to deceive others. But Spinoza's claim is that most

men will desire to accept it. From that point on, the few who do not could be compelled by force.

33. Machiavelli admires Moses—along with Romulus, Cyrus and others—for this same reason: "They owed nothing to fortune but the opportunity which gave them matter to be shaped into what form they thought fit; and without that opportunity their powers would have been wasted, and without their powers the opportunity would have come to nothing" (*The Prince*, chapter 6).

34. We see a parallel case in Machiavelli's *Discourses*, where, after having described the men who were persuaded by Numa's invocation of the gods as "rude" and "uncultivated," he ironically undercuts the distance between ancient Roman times and his own by pointing out that "[it] did not seem to the people of Florence that they were either ignorant or rude, yet they were persuaded by Friar Girolamo Savonarola that he had converse with God" (I,11).

35. One problem here is that Spinoza is not entirely consistent in the terms he uses for this distinction between the proper and improper use of prophecy. In the preface to the *TTP*, for instance, he refers to the difference between religion and superstition (3). But we must also keep in mind the difference between what Spinoza calls "true religion" (e.g., see xii, 22–23, G III 162–63) based on divine law, and ceremonial religion based on rituals, which is something like the distinction A. G. Wernham, in his introduction to *Spinoza: The Political Works* (Oxford, Clarendan Press, 1958), makes between "inward" and "outward" religion (34–35), though Wernham does not insist that inward religion must be true, only that it cannot be controlled by the sovereign. Curley also interprets Spinoza's reference to *superstitio animi* (Pref., 5, G III 6, literally, superstition of the mind) as "true superstition" in contrast to "false" superstition, which is "a manipulative use of seers which takes advantage of the people's belief in them" (see his footnote 2). I identify this "true" use of superstition with the proper function of "outward" religion. That is, it directs the populace to act in conformity with the precepts of inward religion (such as acts of charity, justice, and lovingkindness) even though they are not necessarily motivated in these acts by reason (see xii, 34–37, G III 165 for the foundations of Scriptural religion). In the "false" use of superstition, we find the confusion of speculative knowledge with the realm of the imagination, a confusion common (albeit in different ways) to both those theologians who would interpret Scripture on the basis of Platonic or Aristotelian categories and to soothsayers who would interpret events with the auguries of birds (Pref., 18, G III 9, and 5, G III 6). In both cases, the "seer" is using some notion of divine authority not to inspire "right conduct" but rather to "prop up his own inventions" and authority (xii, 40, G III 166). I would like to standardize these different terms in line

with my interpretation: that is, "religion" does not refer to the knowledge of the divine law (for that is "philosophy") but to the proper function of ceremonial law (i.e., to exhort to right conduct as true superstition does), while "superstition" refers to the perversion of the function of ceremonial law itself.

36. If man were able to live by reason alone, which would be to live and act in accordance with his determinate nature, then there would be no need for concepts of good and evil at all (EIVP67). For these concepts arise because man is dependent on external things in order to preserve his existence. Since an individual desires what he lacks, to the extent that external things prevent a person from living in full accordance with his nature, he will imagine and desire a more perfect nature, one that lacks nothing, as his "end."

37. For more on this point, see the appendix to Part I of the *Ethics*, especially from G II 81/25 through the end.

38. iii, 3, G III 44. Spinoza refers to Deuteronomy 9:6–7.

39. "By human law I understand a manner of living which serves only to protect life and the state; by a divine law, one which aims only at the greatest good, i.e., the true knowledge and love of God" (iv, 8, G III 59). Spinoza describes the universal character of divine law and the way in which the "natural light" (reason) discovers that it is common to all men in chapter i, 1–5, G III 16).

40. See iv, 29, G III 64.

41. Even general moral precepts were not taught to the Jews as true for all men but were accommodated to their particular understanding and practice (v, 7, G III 70).

42. See v, 2, G III 69. Conversely, the divine law does not require any ceremony at all (iv, 20, G III 62).

43. I neglect other features of the Hebrew state that Spinoza cites in chapter xvii as important reasons for its success: its citizen army (69); the fact that the leaders themselves were bound together through a common religion (70); the equal share in the ownership of all lands and fields (84); the feasts and rituals that inspired a joyful devotion (89–91); the reverence for the temple (92), etc.

44. Compare to Pref., 2, G III 5: "For no one has lived among men without seeing that, when they are prospering, even those who are quite inexperienced are generally so overflowing with wisdom that they believe themselves to be wronged if anyone wants to give them advice."

45. See Preface, 4, G III 5: "Because reason cannot show a certain way to the hollow things they desire, they call it blind and human wisdom hollow. The delusions of the imagination, on the other hand, and dreams and childish follies they believe to be divine answers."

46. "[T]he Prophets were said to have the Spirit of God because men were ignorant of the causes of Prophetic knowledge, wondered at it, and on that account, were accustomed to refer it to God—as they did all other abnormal phenomena—and to call it the knowledge of God" (i, 42, G III 27–28).

47. The true prophets did not think miracles were exceptions to the law of nature (vi, 6, G III 83), nor did they think they could be used to learn about the nature of God (vi, 30, G III 87). For a detailed analysis of Spinoza's discussion of miracles in the *TTP*, see the paper by Edwin Curley, "Spinoza on Miracles," in *Proceedings of the First Italian International Congress on Spinoza*, ed. Emilia Giancotti (Naples: Bibliopolis, 1985).

48. "Indeed, [men who immoderately desire uncertain things] believe God rejects the wise and writes his decrees not in the mind, but in the entrails of animals, or that fools, madmen and birds foretell his decrees by divine inspiration and prompting" (Pref., 4, G III 5). Hobbes also distinguishes between two senses of "prophecy": i) as God speaking to the people; and ii) as prediction of future events (see *Leviathan*, chap. 36, 456–58).

49. Compare to what Spinoza says about the conflicting interpretations of "universal ideas" in EIIP40S1 and *Metaphysical Thoughts*, part 1, chap. 1. These passages are quoted in notes 15 and 18 above.

50. See xvii, 106, G III 219, and xviii, 9, G III 222.

51. After the Hebrews had failed in their loyalty to divine worship, "there were great changes, and a great license to do anything, and extravagant living, and negligence, with everything going from bad to worse, until, after they had often been conquered, they completely broke away from the divine law, and wanted a mortal king, so that the royal house of the state would not be the Temple, but the court, and so that the tribes would all remain fellow citizens, not any longer in virtue of divine law and the priesthood, but in virtue of the Kings" (xvii, 106, G III 219).

52. See *Leviathan*, chap. 17.

53. See also xviii, 11, G III 223: ". . . we cannot have any doubt that the flattery of the Priests, and the corruption of religion and the laws, and the incredible increase in the number of the laws gave a very great and frequent opportunity for arguments and disputes, which could never be settled. For where men begin to argue with the fierce heat of superstition, and the magistrate aids one or the other side, they can never be calmed, but must be divided into sects."

54. Spinoza argues that "the necessity of solving this problem [i.e., of how to establish a regime in which people prefer public good to private advantage] has, indeed, compelled people to invent many solutions, still we have never reached the point where a state is not in more danger from its own citizens than from its enemies, and where those who have command do

not fear the former more than the latter" (xvii, 17, G III 203–04). He cites the example of Rome and refers to Tacitus (*Histories*, Bk. iv).

55. See also chap. xvii, 112, G III 220: "With this we see how Religion was introduced into the Hebrew state, and how its political authority could have been everlasting, if the just anger of the lawgiver had permitted it to stay the same. But because this could not happen, it had to perish in the end."

56. Simon Schama, *The Embarrassment of Riches*, part 1, chapter 2, *passim*. Grotius's account of the Batavian origins of the Dutch Republic, which includes a description of their manners and mores, is *Liber de Antiquitate Republicae Batavicorum* (1610). Schama's list of national origin myths (what I would call "exemplars") obviously should not be understood to exclude all other sources that may have contributed to the formation of Dutch character, political institutions, and intellectual life in the "Golden Age." In his book, *The Myth of Venice and Dutch Republican Thought in the Seventeenth-Century* (Assen: Van Gorcum, 1980), E. O. G. Haitsma-Mulier has stressed the importance of what he calls the "myth of Venice" in Dutch thought during this time and discusses its influence on Spinoza via the work of Pieter de la Court. Although the influence of this myth may well have been felt in higher intellectual and political circles, it does not seem to have had equal resonance in popular political culture. So while Venice may have served Spinoza in a variety of ways it was not useful to him as a common imaginative referent, an *exemplum*. That might explain why there are so few actual references to Venice in Spinoza's work, at least in the *TTP*.

57. In several places Spinoza directly compares the situation of the Hebrews to that of the Netherlands—see, for instance, xvii, 54, G III 210—but I am claiming a far more extensive parallel than these explicit comparisons alone would justify.

58. According to Blankert this was only the second treatment of this subject by a Dutch master (the other one was by Rembrandt) and the first to be hung in a courtroom anywhere in Europe. See the English summary of *Kunst als Regeringszaak in Amsterdam in de 17e eeuw*, 65. What follows is based on this source; on another monograph by Blankert, *Ferdinand Bol*, 50–51; and on Schama, 116–25.

59. G. Groenhuis, in his article "Calvinism and National Consciousness: The Dutch Republic as the New Israel" (in *Britain and the Netherlands*, ed. A.C. Duke and C.A. Tamse, vol. VII [The Hague: Nijhoff, 1981], 118–33) contests the view of some eminent Dutch historians (among them E. H. Kossman) who hold that while the Calvinists frequently made the analogy with ancient Israel they did not see themselves as the "inhabitants of a New Israel, as an elect nation." See also Dr. Groenhuis's work *De Predikanten* (with English summary), which Simon Schama draws upon.

60. Schama discusses this incident and its contemporary interpretation on pages 26–27. A fuller description of the military and political aspects of the siege can be found in Geoffrey Parker, *The Dutch Revolt* (Harmondsworth: Penguin, 1988). Groenhuis also notes many instances of the use of biblical imagery in the struggles of the early Dutch republic, as well as seventeenth-century uses, such as the poet Joost van den Vondel's comparison, in his play *Het Pascha* (The Passover), of the deliverance of the children of Israel with the liberation of the United Provinces (see "Calvinism and National Consciousness," 120–21 and passim).

61. Schama, 103. He also points to the curious way in which the Dutch penchant for cleanliness, frequently noted by foreigners, was a "militan[t] . . . affirmation of separateness": "What was cleansed was the dirt of the world that had obscured the special meaning of Dutch history and the providential selection of its people" (380).

62. Dr. G. Groenhuis, *De Predikanten*, 183.

63. Schama, 381.

64. Schama, 112–13.

65. Schama, 114.

66. Blankert, *Bol*, 65.

67. See H. H. Rowen, "Neither Fish nor Fowl: The Stadholderate in the Dutch Republic," in *Political Ideas and Institutions in the Dutch Republic* (Los Angeles: W. A. Clark Memorial Library, UCLA, 1985).

68. For a succinct discussion of Jan de Witt, see H. H. Rowen, *John De Witt: Statesman of the "True Freedom,"* (Cambridge: Cambridge University Press, 1986). For general background, see P. Geyl, *The Netherlands in the Seventeenth Century* (London: Ernst Benn, 1964), vol. 2.

69. See Groenhuis, "Calvinism and National Consciousness," 129, though P. Geyl, in *History of the Low Countries* (London: MacMillan, 1964), 165, notes that ". . . it would be wrong to conceive of Reformed and Statist as necessarily making a contrast. Most of the regents of the True Liberty brand were as good Reformed as any, and many Reformed ministers accepted them with befitting respect and submission as their lawful governors."

70. Groenhuis, "Calvinism and National Consciousness," 129–30.

71. Rowen, "Neither Fish nor Fowl," 19–20.

72. For a detailed discussion of the political debates among the Amsterdam regents and their role in the choice of subjects in the decoration of the Town Hall, see Margaret Deutsch Carroll, "Civic Ideology and Its Subversion in Rembrandt's *Oath of Claudius Civilis*," in *Art History* 9 (1986), 12–35.

73. Quoted in Katherine Fremantle, *The Baroque Town Hall of Amsterdam* (Utrecht: Haentjens Dekker Gumbert, 1959), 77. It derives from a poem by Vondel published in 1659. Vondel himself had been a target of the

Calvinist clergy in 1654 when his play *Lucifer* was banned (Schama, 119–21). While Fremantle thinks that the poem was actually inscribed beneath the painting, both Buchbinder-Green (153) and Blankert (*Bol*, 52) disagree. However, other expository poems by Vondel *were* inscribed under other paintings in Town Hall; for example, under Van Helt Stocade's *Joseph Distributing the Grain in Egypt*, which was in the Treasury Room [*Schoorsteenstuk*] (Buchbinder-Green, 110).

74. It is worth noting that a few years before the Magistrates commissioned Bol's painting to assert their own authority over and against the Calvinist ministers, they had also commissioned for another part of the town hall a large painting of the Batavians, depicting Claudius Civilis, who had led the Batavians in a revolt against the Romans. Claudius was readily identified with the first William of Orange who had led the Dutch in their revolt against the Spanish in the sixteenth century. The commission was a sign of respect made as a result of the reemergence of the Orangist faction, who claimed the stadtholderate for the young William of Orange, later to be William III. For a detailed discussion of this episode, see the article by Carroll, "Civic Ideology and Its Subversion," passim, and Blankert, 64. This example shows how different exemplars can be used in different (complementary and conflicting) ways at the same time.

75. Spinoza is not opposed to the various interpretations of scripture but only to the attempt by one sect to prohibit the interpretation of another (see xiv, 3, G III 173). For earlier disputes, see D. Nobbs, *Theocracy and Toleration: A Study of the Disputes in Dutch Calvinism from 1600–1650* (Cambridge: Cambridge University Press, 1938).

76. Groenhuis, "Calvinism and National Consciousness," 22–23. The books Groenhuis discusses are: Abraham van de Velde, *De Wonderen des Allerhoogsten* (The Miracles of the Almighty), published in 1668, and Herman Witsius, *De Twist des Heeren met syn Wyngaert* (The Quarrel of the Lord with his Vineyard), published in 1669.

77. We see Spinoza's opposition to this attitude reflected in his correspondence with Willem van Blijenbergh, who although himself not a Calvinist priest, believed that when the truths of reason and revelation were in conflict, the truth of revelation superseded that of reason. See letter 20, in *The Collected Works of Spinoza*, esp. 361–62 (GIV 97–98), and Spinoza's reply, letter 21, 375ff (IV/126f).

78. ". . . it cannot happen that a mind should be absolutely subject to the control of someone else. Indeed, no one can transfer to another person his natural right, *or* faculty of reasoning freely, and of judging concerning anything whatsoever, nor can he be compelled to do so" (xx, 2, G III 239).

79. ". . .however much the supreme powers are believed to have a right over all things, and to be the interpreters of right and religious duty, they will still never be able to bring it about that men do not make their

own judgment about everything, according to their own mentality, and that they are not, to that extent, affected with this or that affect" (xx, 6, G III 240).

80. "That is why rule over minds is considered violent, and why the supreme authority seems to wrong its subjects and to usurp their rights whenever it wants to prescribe to each person what he must embrace as true and what reject as false, and further, by what opinions each person's mind ought to be moved in its devotion to God. For these things are subject to each person's control, which no one can surrender even if he wishes to" (xx, 3, G III 239).

81. This is still a vexed question in modern biblical scholarship. The narrative accounts of events were themselves probably reconstructed for a religious purpose. Thus we have an interpretation of an interpretation, ad infinitum. For more on this question, see the anthology edited by Ronald E. Clements, *The World of Ancient Israel: Sociological, Anthropological and Political Perspectives* (Cambridge: Cambridge University Press, 1991).

82. See v, 41–42, G III 78. On the necessity for selection in an exemplar, see Lyons, *Exemplum*, introduction. As Lyons points out, the etymology of both *exemplar* and *exemplum* is in the terms *excisio*, which means "to cut out."

83. For a vivid account of the political events leading up to debacle, in which the De Witt brothers, leaders of the States party, were brutally murdered by a mob, see H.H. Rowen, *John De Witt: Statesman of the "True Freedom"* (Cambridge: Cambridge University Press, 1986), chapters 11 and 12. This occasion also gave rise to the story, probably apocryphal, that Spinoza, so incensed at the death of the two politicians, attempted to confront the mob with a sign reading "Ultimi barbarorum" (you are the worst of barbarians) and had to be restrained by his landlord who prudently feared for the philosopher's life (see Rowen, 220).

84. v, 37, G III 77 (quoted above) and 38–39. For further discussion of *accommodation* as a hermeneutical principle, see Norman O. Brown, "Philosophy and Prophecy," 202–05.

85. In the *Ethics*, Spinoza argues that "man is necessarily always subject to the passions, that he follows and obeys the common order of Nature, and accommodates himself to it as much as the nature of things requires" (EIVP4C).

PART IV

The Historical Setting

CHAPTER 10

Spinoza's Excommunication

RICHARD H. POPKIN

The excommunication of Baruch de Spinoza from the Portuguese Synagogue of Amsterdam on July 27, 1656 used to be portrayed as one of
the crucial events in the warfare between religion and science, the struggles
for human freedom against the closed mindedness of rigid orthodoxy. Brave
young Spinoza, then twenty-three years old, was portrayed as facing the
rage and intolerance of the bigots of Jewish orthodoxy. The excommunication also used to be seen as a tragic reversal. The Spanish and Portuguese
Jews of Amsterdam, who fled to the Netherlands in order to breathe the free
air and to practice their religion according to their own beliefs, had been the
victims of the Spanish and Portuguese Inquisitions. Yet, the old story goes,
within a generation or two they were expelling a free spirit from their midst,
the son of two Marranos who had been caught in the clutches of the Portuguese Inquisition and then fled to Amsterdam to live freely as Jews.

This version of the story, as the dramatic and tragic excommunication of
the enlightened Spinoza, appears in Will Durant's chapter on the philosopher
in his *Story of Philosophy*.[1] Durant includes the text of the condemnation of
the young Spinoza for all of the bad things he had done (never specified) with
all of the curses from the Bible, the admonition to the congregation to have
nothing more to do with the condemned one, to refuse him food, water,
shelter, comfort, and to refuse to read or listen to anything he wrote or said.
Spinoza was portrayed here as forever exiled from the Jewish world, living
out a lonely, isolated life. A dramatic, dismal ceremony is described as leading to this denouement. And poor Spinoza is depicted as having to go away
into the hostile Gentile world. This tale ranked the horrendous casting out
of Spinoza with the condemnation of Galileo in 1632 as one of the defining
events that led to modernity. The old guard of the Middle Ages was making

its last stand. Galileo in Italy and Spinoza in the Netherlands were to lead humanity into a new age, the age of Enlightenment, beyond superstition and irrationality.

We know from research in the last few decades into the background of Galileo's case that there is less there than meets the eye. Church politics, Galileo's way of stepping on the toes of the authorities, his loss of papal protection, all played roles in his condemnation and recantation.[2] And, as we know, the silenced Galileo died of old age under house arrest while works of his were being published in the Netherlands, by the Catholic priest, Marin Mersenne, and in translation in England by John Wilkins, future Bishop of Chester. His scientific ideas were accepted all over the Western world, providing the basis for modern science. While Galileo may have been forced to abjure publicly the Copernican hypothesis, many advanced thinkers accepted it. The actual condemnation may have been traumatic for Galileo, but it did not impede the making of the modern world. Even after the condemnation, Galileo received admirers like Thomas Hobbes at his home, and was able to play out his role as a founder of modern science. By the end of the seventeenth century, the Copernican theory and Galilean physics were taught in many of the leading universities in Europe.

In Spinoza's case, I think there is even more reason than in Galileo's for doubting the story of his martyrdom. Moreover, there is little reason to consider Spinoza's excommunication one of the monumental events of the seventeenth century.[3] We do not even know exactly why Spinoza was excommunicated. The actual ceremony seems to have been a minor scene carried out in the council chamber rather than in the synagogue proper and in Spinoza's absence. What we now know of the Jewish community in Amsterdam indicates that it was hardly a rigidly orthodox group unwilling to entertain new ideas. What we now know about Spinoza's life from mid-1656 until his death in 1677 (from consumption, not persecution) suggests that he was not isolated and was even in contact with some Dutch Jews. The excommunication seems hardly to have affected Spinoza personally. As far as we know, he never discussed the details with others, but said only that the Jews had excommunicated him.[4] In the first accounts of his life, the excommunication is in fact depicted as a minor event. But subsequent accounts of his life give it greater and greater emphasis, until Will Durant, 250 years later, portrayed the excommunication as a major tragedy and trauma of lasting historical import.

The entry in the Amsterdam synagogue's records of the excommunication occurred about six weeks after the event. Both the lateness of the entry and its exact wording have been analyzed carefully by Asa Kasher and Shlomo Biderman.[5] Research by I. S. Revah, Henri Mechoulan, Yosef Kaplan and others has revealed that excommunication (*herem*) was not uncommon in Amsterdam. There were over 280 excommunications during the seventeenth century for all sorts of offenses. It was by the *herem* that the synagogue authorities kept order and discipline.[6] People could be excommunicated for nonpayment of dues, for refusal to honor marriage contracts, for insulting one of the directors, etc. Only the Board of Directors, the *parnassim*, who were elected lay members, could decree an excommunication, with the advice of the rabbis.[7] In almost all known cases, the excommunicated person apologized, accepted a fine or punishment, and then was accepted again as a member in good standing of the synagogue. Only a handful of individuals were excommunicated for ideological reasons. Perhaps the best-known case now (but unknown in Spinoza's time) was that of Uriel da Costa, who was excommunicated in the 1630s for challenging rabbinic Judaism and denying the immortality of the soul. After being excluded from the Jewish world for a few years, Da Costa did apologize. He was apparently severely chastised, and then readmitted to the community. When he again asserted his 'heresies' he was excommunicated for a second time, and he then committed suicide.[8]

I. S. Revah discovered that Spinoza was part of a three-person rebellion. Spinoza, Juan (Daniel) de Prado, and Daniel Ribera were all accused of teaching bad views to the young; among other things, questioning the historical accuracy of the Bible.[9] Revah's findings and others by Yosef Kaplan,[10] show that Prado was the most important of the three. He had been a physician in Spain and had studied theology there. His classmate, Orobio de Castro, reported that Prado had already begun to cast doubt on all religions while still in Spain and had become a deist, whatever that may have meant in Spain at the time. Dr. Prado left Spain when the Inquisition questioned some of his relatives. He left in high style, travelling with his family to Rome in the entourage of a Spanish bishop who was to be elevated to cardinal by the Pope. After the ceremony, Prado and his family went north to Hamburg, where he joined the Jewish community. Next he moved to Amsterdam and earned part of his living teaching young Jewish students. He was highly educated and twenty years older than Spinoza.

When the three rebels were accused, Ribera just disappeared, probably returning to the Spanish Catholic world. The information we have shows that there was much pressure to get Dr. Prado to apologize and recant. The leaders of the Jewish community even offered him and his family, if he would not recant, an opportunity to resettle in some other Jewish community, far away, at the synagogue's expense.[11] Finally, according to the records, just before Spinoza's case was finalized, we are told that Dr. Prado stood up in the synagogue and apologized and recanted, said he would not spread such dangerous ideas, and so on. Charges against him were dropped. But the following year, he apparently again offered his critical ideas about the Bible and religion. He was then excommunicated, and he and his family disappeared into the New Christian world in Belgium.[12] However, he and Spinoza appear to have stayed close at least until 1659 when they are reported to have belonged to an informal discussion group at the home of a Spanish doctor in Amsterdam, along with Spanish Catholics and members of the Spanish Jewish community in Amsterdam. There are two reports about Spinoza and Prado that were given to the Inquisition in Madrid by a Spanish monk and a Spanish sea captain. We are told that the two rebels identified themselves as ex-Jews, having been excommunicated from the synagogue for their views "because they had become atheists." Specifically, they held that God existed, but only philosophically, that the soul dies with the body, and that Judaism was a fabrication not a true religion. Regarding their excommunications, Prado regretted that he no longer received charitable assistance from the synagogue, and they both regretted no longer having social relations with the Jewish community. But they were glad that they had stuck by their views.[13] This is the only information we have about how Spinoza felt about his excommunication. We do not know if he discussed his case in the lost *Apologie* that he apparently wrote shortly after the event to justify his position. In the *Tractatus theologico-politicus* of 1670, which is supposed to be a later revision of the *Apologie*, nothing is mentioned about how Spinoza and Prado were treated.

One more factor that has to be taken into account in evaluating Spinoza's excommunication is something I noticed in studying the relevant pages of the synagogue record book. The entries before and after that pertaining to Spinoza deal with the handling of a critical development in the community, the presence of thousands of Jewish refugees, some from Brazil and some from Poland, flooding into Amsterdam. The community's tacit agreement with the city included the commitment that the community and not the city would take care of the Jewish poor. Thousands of Sephardic Jews who had settled in Dutch-controlled Brazil fled in 1654-1655 when the Portuguese regained control of the territory. Many of them, including their rabbi, Isaac Aboab de Fonesca, were from the Netherlands originally or were related to Dutch Jews. The Amsterdam community felt obliged to find new homes for their brethren arriving in the Netherlands. Another wave of refugees from the east was more difficult to deal with. These were thousands of Polish Ashkenazi Jews driven from their homes when Swedish troops entered Lithuania, captured Vilna, and then struck deep into Poland itself. The entries in the synagogue records reflect the enormous efforts to hire ships to resettle the eastern Jews in Germany and elsewhere. In the meantime they were housed and fed in Amsterdam. This was the immediate, overriding problem for the Amsterdam Jewish community in the summer of 1656.[14]

In the midst of all of this relief effort, the problem of Spinoza and his two errant friends surfaced. Dr. Prado was taken to be the chief culprit and by extensive negotiations was brought temporarily back into the fold. Ribera just disappeared. But young Spinoza, himself the son of a *parnas*, refused any enticements. The statement of his case indicates that efforts were made to reach an agreement with the young rebel in which he would keep his opinions to himself and give nominal evidence of his membership in the community by appearing in the synagogue on the High Holidays. Beyond this, the community offered him a deal like the one offered to Dr. Prado, namely, that they would resettle him somewhere else where he could let his heresies loose on another group.[15]

The bitterness of the statement of Spinoza's excommunication apparently results from the failure of the community leadership to find a modus vivendi with the young Spinoza. The long list of curses taken from the Bible was merely a formula for getting rid of nudniks. The Venetian rabbis had given it to the Amsterdam community in the early seventeenth century.[16] The general public did not know this horrendous text until the nineteenth century. [17] It is only the preamble that is specific to the Spinoza case. It announces that the governing *parnassim* and the secretary treasurer,

> having long known of the evil opinions and acts of Baruch de Spinoza, have endeavored by various means and promises, to turn him from his evil ways. But having failed to make him mend his wicked ways, and on the contrary, daily receiving more and more serious information about the abominable heresies which he practiced and taught and about his deeds, and having numerous trustworthy witnesses who have deposed and borne witness to this in the presence of said Espinoza, they have become convinced of the truth of the matter, and after an investigation in the presence of the honorable *hakhamim* [the rabbis of the community], they have decided, with their consent, that the said Espinoza should be excommunicated and expelled from the people of Israel.[18]

No one signed the excommunication statement. Its operative phrase, "the abominable heresies that he practiced and taught and his monstrous deeds," comes with no specification or examples. So scholars have been speculating for centuries about what the young Spinoza might have taught and what he might have done to so offend the directors and the rabbis of the Amsterdam Jewish community.[19] The directors were leading businessmen of the community, most of whom had been Christians for some part of their lives. The secretary treasurer who entered the excommunication decree in the record book, one Isaac Lopes Suasso, had only recently metamorphosed from a Christian businessman in Antwerp to a major Jewish businessman in Amsterdam. He was now married to the daughter of one of the richest members of the Jewish community. There was no indication that

Lopes Suasso had been a Marrano in Antwerp. His brother was an important professor of Catholic theology in Bordeaux. Lopes Suasso apparently decided for business reasons to move his base of operations from Antwerp to Amsterdam and to quit the Catholic Church and join the Amsterdam synagogue. Contrary to the rules and regulations of the synagogue, which required three years of membership before one could become an officer, he was made secretary-treasurer soon after affiliating. He played no role in the intellectual and cultural life of the community and walked out of it when there was a major fundraising program to build the grand synagogue building that now stands at Meier Visserplein. So, it is hard to believe that he could have been overly shocked by whatever Spinoza was saying or doing.[20]

Kasher and Biderman explore all sorts of intellectual, philosophical, or theological possibilities as to what might have outraged the *parnassim* and the rabbis: Had the young Spinoza become a Cartesian? a follower of the Quakers? Had he become involved with the heretical views of Isaac La Peyrère, author of the *Prae-Adamites*, a book that challenged the accuracy of the Bible and the Mosaic authorship of the first five books—and on and on. They argue that there really is no basis for deciding, because the excommunication statement is deliberately vague.[21] But no matter what the abominable heresies or monstrous deeds were, the statement indicates that the congregation authorities would gladly have made a deal with Spinoza, if he had been willing to stop being such a nuisance.

That said, the excommunication could not have been traumatic to the congregation, nor to its authorities. They never, as far as we know, discussed the matter again. And the community grew and prospered without the young rebel. As we shall see, in spite of the admonition to the congregation not to have any commerce with Spinoza nor to read or discuss his views and his books, some did in fact do so, up to the end of his life.

Unlike the Galileo episode, Spinoza's excommunication was not a public event. It apparently took place in private in the council chambers, a small building next to the synagogue. All the fanfare that some commentators supposed from reading in the Mishna what an excommunication was supposed to be like does not seem to have taken place. Spinoza was not present, having already decided to leave the community. We are told that somebody had to be sent to find him and give him a copy of the excommunication document. It is obvious that the excommunication did not stop Spinoza from developing his "heretical ideas" and making them known to those interested at the time. He had no difficulty publishing his critique of the Bible and of organized religion. He had no trouble finding friends who were interested in his ideas. The excommunication seems to have had so little effect on Spinoza that he never discussed it in any of the materials that have come down to us. According to Colerus, he told people that he had been excommunicated by the Amsterdam Jews but gave no details. Apparently, this was just to explain why he was living by himself outside the Jewish community. He gave as his reason for leaving Amsterdam in 1661 that someone had tried to kill him with a knife. For years, he showed people the coat with the knife hole that he had been wearing at the time. But he did not show them the excommunication order or refer to it. In fact, Jarig Jelles, Spinoza's longtime friend, who knew him even before he was excommunicated, did not mention Spinoza's excommunication or his Jewish origin in his introduction to Spinoza's *Opera posthuma*, which was published just after Spinoza's death in 1677. Jelles tells us only that in his youth Spinoza studied theology and then went on in philosophy and that he left Amsterdam in order to pursue his intellectual interests and devote himself full time to the search for truth.

Perhaps more interesting is that in the first published account of Spinoza's life, Pierre Bayle, in his *Historical and Critical Dictionary* (1697–1702), gave a different version of Spinoza's early life than is found in other sources. Bayle said that he got his information from a "memoir sent to a bookseller."[22] No further identification is offered. This seems to be a text different from either Lucas's oldest biography or that of Colerus. Bayle said that as the young Spinoza developed a mathematical outlook, he found that he could not accept rabbinic doctrines. Spinoza voiced his negative opinions and freely set forth his doubts and beliefs. "It is said that the Jews offered to tolerate him provided that he would conform outwardly to their ceremonial practices."[23] They even promised him an annual pension. Spinoza would not submit to such hypocrisy. Little by little, he separated himself from the synagogue, and he might have kept up some connection with the Jewish community had he not been "treacherously attacked by a Jew who struck with a knife as he was leaving the theater. After this event he broke off from the Jewish community, and this was the cause of this excommunication." Bayle said that he tried to find out more particulars about the excommunication but was unable to do so.[24] It is important to take notice that Bayle, who was a great historical sleuth and who had many contacts in the Netherlands, did not learn anything more than this in the period up to 1697 when the article on Spinoza was published. Bayle cared very much about Spinoza. He gave him by far the longest article in the *Dictionary*, and the article was translated into Dutch and printed as a large book by itself. In the second edition, of 1702, Bayle reports that he sought out a disciple of Spinoza's with whom he went over the text of the *Ethics* line by line.[25] If Bayle was unable to ferret out the gossip circulating about Spinoza, I think we must conclude that it was extremely difficult to find out much about the life of Spinoza even twenty years after his death.

Bayle's good friend, Jacques Basnage, wrote the first history of the Jews[26] since that of Josephus about 1500 years earlier. It was published in 1705, translated into English in 1706, and an enlarged edition in fifteen volumes was published in 1716.[27] Basnage, like Bayle, had fled to the Netherlands in the 1680s.[28] He did a lot of research for his history of the Jews, including interviewing members of the Jewish community. Basnage's discussion of Spinoza's philosophy is in his volume on the Kabbalah.[29] He said that he asked the rabbi who had read out the excommunication order against Spinoza— he left the rabbi unnamed, although it may have been Aboab de Fonesca— about the heretic's philosophy. Basnage was told that Spinoza had merely plagiarized from the Kabbalists and put his theory in Cartesian terms to make it seem original.[30] The biographical materials about Spinoza, whom he characterized as one *"qui s'est rendu si fameux par un Atheisme nouveau,"*[31] appear in the last volume in the section on important Dutch Jews of the seventeenth century. Basnage claimed that Spinoza's study of Cartesian philosophy led him away from the principles of the rabbis, which did not meet Descartes' criterion of truth. [32] When it was noticed that Spinoza did not keep the Sabbath or attend the synagogue, the rabbis tried to keep him in the community by offering him a pension of 1000 Livres.[33] Spinoza's refusal led to hatred of him and the attempt to slay him with a knife as he left the synagogue. After the attack, Basnage suggested, Spinoza left Amsterdam because he did not feel safe there.[34] Basnage went on to tell of Spinoza's excommunication and his protest against the sentence that was given in his absence. Basnage offered no details whatsoever of the contents of the order of excommunication or of the sentence. Instead, we are told that Spinoza protested against the excommunication in a Spanish document addressed to the rabbis.[35] Basnage then moved on to discuss Spinoza's published writings and his life after leaving Amsterdam.[36] Basnage, like Bayle, portrayed the excommunication as formally marking the end of Spinoza's relations with the Jewish community. It took place *after* Spinoza had broken with the community and was no longer taking part in its activities. According to Basnage's account, the excommunication neither impeded Spinoza's development as a radical philosopher nor interfered with his relations with many important personages.

The most detailed account of Spinoza's life published in the early eighteenth century was that of Johan Colerus, a Lutheran minister in the Hague. Colerus had by chance rented a room that Spinoza had lived in and got interested in finding out what he could about the man. Colerus cultivated Spinoza's last landlord, Hendrik van der Spijk, and reported much information from him and his wife about Spinoza's last six years, and also about his earlier life from what Spinoza had told them. Colerus's short account appeared in Dutch, German, French and English in 1705–1706. He began by saying, "Spinoza, that philosopher whose name makes a great noise in the world, was originally a *Jew*."[37] He then gave some details about the family, refuting the view that Spinoza came from a poor family, a claim that was made in the contemporaneous *Vie de M. Spinosa* attributed to Jean-Maximillien Lucas. Colerus wrote that because Spinoza was so bright and interested in many things, the family hired a Latin tutor, Francis Van den Enden, and it was he who sowed the seeds of atheism among his students. Colerus said that he could substantiate this "by the testimony of several honest Gentlemen who are still living, some of whom have been elders of the Lutheran church at Amsterdam."[38]

Knowing Latin, Spinoza found Descartes' philosophy. He was, according to Colerus, "charmed" by Descartes' criterion of truth, and saw "that the ridiculous Doctrine and Principles of the Rabbins could not be admitted by a Man of Sense; because they are entirely built upon the Authority of the *Rabbins* themselves" and do not come from God.[39] Spinoza avoided the rabbis and kept away from the synagogue as much as he could. The rabbis were afraid that he would leave the Jewish community and become a Christian. Colerus incorporated the story from the Dutch translation of Bayle's article on Spinoza about the offer of a large pension to stay within the community and appear now and then at the synagogue. Colerus maintained that Spinoza affirmed the truth of the offer several times to the van der Spijks and to others, but said that had they offered him ten times as much he still would not have remained, because he was not a hypocrite and sought only the truth.[40] Colerus also repeated Bayle's story about the attack upon Spinoza as he left the theater but suggested that the story must be corrected, insofar as Spinoza had told the van der Spijks that the episode took place as he was leaving the synagogue.[41]

We are further told that no sooner had Spinoza left the Jewish community than he was prosecuted juridically and excommunicated. Spinoza broke off all friendships and correspondence with members of the community. Colerus then reported that some Jews of Amsterdam who knew Spinoza well confirmed this account of the excommunication and added that the sentence of excommunication was publicly pronounced by "the Old Man Hakham Aboab, a Rabbin of great reputation about 'em."[42] Colerus tried in vain to find out what sentence had been pronounced. He asked the rabbi's sons, and they said that they could not find it among their father's papers. Colerus had doubts about their claim but he was unable to find anyone who could tell him what had been said and done.[43]

At this point, Colerus sought help elsewhere—namely, from experts on Jewish law, to determine what a Jewish excommunication would be like. A learned Jew in the Hague referred him to a passage in Maimonides. Then he found Selden's account of three different kinds of Jewish excommunication. Colerus looked up other authorities and found Lightfoot's account of banishment from the synagogue accompanied by many curses. Finally, Surrhensius, Professor of Hebrew in Amsterdam, gave him the text of a traditional excommunication.[44] Colerus reconstructed from these sources a sober picture of the terrifying ceremony, a picture that then became generally incorporated into accounts of Spinoza's fate. None of this, however, dealt with Spinoza's case. All was drawn from texts about Jewish ceremonies. Only after spending pages reporting his researches into the matter and entertaining various possible scenarios, did Colerus mention that Spinoza was not in attendance and had to be sent a copy of the pronouncement, to which he forthwith responded in a protest written in Spanish. It is worth underlining that Colerus could not find out what had actually happened, nor could he find anyone who had been present. His long conjectural description of Spinoza's excommunication, however, was accepted as fact in the popular literature. But in his reprint of Colerus's text, Pollack omitted the excommunication scene entirely. He presents the excommunication as the end of the affair, having taken place when Spinoza had already removed himself from the Jewish community and was on the verge of leaving Amsterdam for good. In continuing his account of Spinoza's life, Colerus maintained that Spinoza flourished outside of the world of the synagogue and was sought after by leading intellectuals and personalities.

The last of the early accounts is the so called "oldest biography" attributed to one Jean-Maximillien Lucas, *La Vie de feu de Monsieur de Spinosa*. After some prior circulation, the manuscript was printed in 1719 along with *L'Esprit de M. Spinosa, or the Three Imposters, Moses, Jesus and Mohammed*. It was banned but reprinted later on in the eighteenth century.[45] The purported author, Lucas, who died in 1697, was a Huguenot journalist and a member of a group of freethinkers in the Netherlands.[46]

The text portrays the struggle of a poor young Spinoza against Chief Rabbi Saul Levi Morteira. It is the only old source that portrays the young Spinoza first as the finest disciple of Morteira, then as a rebel who drew down the wrath of his mentor and the horrendous excommunication, which was followed by the rabbis' trying to get the civil authorities of Amsterdam to help them exile the forlorn Spinoza. There is much pathos about Spinoza losing his friends and having to slink away from Amsterdam to a lonely, miserable life. The text gives much more detail than any other source about Spinoza's early Bible studies, his language abilities, his Talmudic studies, and his budding objections to the rabbinic point of view. But it gives no indication of how the information was obtained or from whom. Since it purports to be the work of a friend and disciple of Spinoza's, it has been given much credence as an important source of information about Spinoza's early life. Some scholars, however, have utterly rejected it.[47]

I am sceptical about the Lucas text, since in some matters we know it is in error, for example, its contention that Spinoza came from a poor family. Nothing that we now know about Morteira would indicate that he was a rigidly orthodox rabbi who could not abide dissent. Morteira was a cosmopolitan figure. Born and raised in Venice, he went to the French court at the Louvre with Elijah Montalto, physician to Queen Marie de Medici. He stayed there for seven years and left only after Montalto died. He carried the body of Montalto to Amsterdam for burial and then remained there. He led the Sephardic community until his death in 1660, and he introduced famous dignitaries, such as Queen Henrietta Marie, the wife of Charles I, to the synagogue. His major work, although unpublished at the time of the excommunication, was an important attack on Christianity. He was not a significant Talmudist. Hundreds of his sermons have been found and in none of them is Spinoza or his excommunication mentioned. He hardly seems to have been the terrible figure portrayed by the "Lucas" text.

Who actually wrote the Lucas biography of Spinoza remains a mystery, as does the nature of the relationship between the author and Spinoza. The question of who wrote the companion piece, *L'Esprit de M. Spinosa*, seems to have been settled by Silvia Berti.[48] Her candidate for authorship, Jan Vroesen, was not, as far as we know, directly connected with Spinoza. The Lucas text may be a compilation of diverse memories and rumors. For the purposes of this paper, it is important to underline only that the information in the Lucas text about Spinoza's vehement quarrel with Chief Rabbi Morteira and about Morteira's attempt to get the civil authorities to exile Spinoza from Amsterdam appear nowhere else; nor are they substantiated by any independent sources.[49] Since only the *parnassim*, the Board of Directors, could excommunicate anyone, Morteira, no matter how angry he became, would have had to turn the case over to these lay authorities.

Furthermore, the Lucas text was unknown in the seventeenth century; it was known slightly in the eighteenth century and received serious attention only in the nineteenth, with the first scholarly biographies of Spinoza. So, the account of the excommunication with all its terror and gloom, the black candles, upside down and dripping like blood on the floor, the pronouncement of the terrible curses and the wail of the shofar, was not reported by anyone who might have been in attendance. In fact, when I was working on the manuscripts of Ets Haim in the summer of 1961, I was given a place to sit and study in the council chamber, located next to the synagogue from which Spinoza was excommunicated. Dr. Israel Fuks, who was then cataloguing the manuscripts, told me that I was sitting in Morteira's chair and that it was in this very room that the excommunication had taken place. If so, then it was not part of a general service and could only have been witnessed by the council members, namely, the *parnassim*, the secretary-treasurer, and the rabbis.

To come to a conclusion, I think that what was known about Spinoza's excommunication from its official occurrence on July 27, 1656 until about fifty years later, was only that some such event took place, putting an end to Spinoza's relationship with the synagogue, that Spinoza was not in attendance, that he wrote a response, the *Apologie*, in Spanish, which was still extant when he died but has been lost and which may have been the ur-text for the *TTP*. What took place at the excommunication was not known at all to the general public. It was not a grand event like Galileo's condemnation. It took Colerus a good deal of effort to find out what a Jewish excommunication might have been like. He could not learn anything about Spinoza's actual excommunication from anyone who had witnessed it. Nor did he obtain any information about it from the son of Rabbi Aboab, who was supposed to have read out the excommunication decree. So Colerus offered his readers a range of possibilities garnered from sources about Jewish law. But he did not offer any information about the event itself. Spinoza himself never seems to have told anybody more than the fact of his excommunication. People who dealt with him thereafter did not seem to care about the details. Spinoza moved into the Christian world and found housing and friendship with the Collegiants and others. He probably was already participating in some Collegiant activities while still a member of the Portuguese Jewish community. In fact, many Christian Millenarians, including Collegiants and Quakers, came to the services at the Amsterdam synagogue and conferred with its members afterwards.[50] So Spinoza was not adrift. He quickly found a place in his new world. The story about him and Prado meeting frequently with other Spaniards, both Catholic and Jewish, in 1659, suggests that neither was cut off from the Jewish community completely.

By 1660–1661 Spinoza was gaining a reputation among Cartesians and dissident Christians. Henry Oldenburg, Secretary of the Royal Society of England, in 1661 sought him out and began a fifteen-year, three-way correspondence with Spinoza and Robert Boyle. People came to consult with Spinoza. He had special students, mostly from the upper class of Dutch society, working with him. He published the *Principles of Descartes' Philosophy* and the *Tractatus Theologico-Politicus*, which brought him renown. Far from being persecuted, Spinoza was lionized by Dutch liberals, by French aristocrats, and by Heidelberg University's offer of a chair (1673), which he declined.

Had he not been excommunicated, he would have had to submit his writings to the *parnassim* prior to publication, and they would probably not have granted him permission to publish them. We are told by Sebastian Kortholdt that, in his last six years, all sorts of eminent people came to see Spinoza in his spare quarters in van der Spijk's house. There were at least two hundred charcoal drawings by Spinoza of his visitors, one of whom was Leibniz. As for the claim that the excommunication cut him off from all contact with the Jewish community, Kortholdt testifies that van der Spijk told him that Spinoza did not always exclude Jews from visiting him—Spinoza's reverse *herem*![51] A recently discovered document from 1672 reveals that Spinoza was a co-witness along with the son-in-law of Benjamin Musafia, the rabbi of Copenhagen, to the good character of a Dutch Jewish army officer.[52] Around the same time, Spinoza was friendly with a Dr. Henri Morelli, an Egyptian Jew, who became the physician to St. Evremond and the Countess of Huntington. According to Morelli, they spent much time discussing whether Spinoza should accept the invitation of the Prince of Condé to come and make his acquaintance while the Prince was stationed in Utrecht following the French invasion of the Netherlands in 1672.[53]

It is surprising how little of Spinoza's life and hard times have been documented. Perhaps further research into the circles in which Spinoza moved before, during, and after his excommunication, will throw more light on his life and contacts. From what we know now, I think it safe to say that his excommunication was not one of the traumatic events of the seventeenth century or a decisive turning point in the struggle between orthodoxy and modernity. It seems to have been a minor local event in the Amsterdam community, one that was never discussed later on. It was an event of some significance for Spinoza, but it clearly did not deflect his career. In fact it gave him the opportunity to devote himself to his research and writing and relieved him of immediate concerns with censorship. He was able to work out his revolutionary rejection of Judeo-Christian supernaturalism and to provide a metaphysics for the naturalistic, scientific world of the Enlightenment without any direct interference from civil or religious authorities. Whatever happened in 1656, for whatever reasons, certainly did not stunt Spinoza's intellectual growth, inhibit his development, or hinder others from discussing his views with him.

I suspect that the story of Spinoza's fierce mistreatment arose in part from a new anti-Semitism no longer based exclusively or even largely on theological beliefs: It was an attempt to blacken the name of the Amsterdam Jewish community and of the Jewish world at large. The Da Costa story, first published only in 1687 as an Appendix to a dispute between Philip van Limborch and Orobio de Castro, was broadcast by Bayle in his article "Acosta" in 1697. Over the next century Da Costa and Spinoza were depicted as martyrs who took a stand against Jewish orthodoxy. Their cases supposedly showed how backward orthodox Jews had been and still were. And they pointed toward a world beyond orthodoxy. The emancipation of the Jews at the end of the eighteenth century and at the beginning of the nineteenth seemed to have required a myth, in which the now familiar, lurid images of Spinoza's excommunication became a crucial part.

NOTES

1. Will Durant, *The Story of Philosophy. The Lives and Opinions of the Greater Philosophers* (New York: Simon and Schuster, 1953), chap. 8v, sec. 3, 117 n. 119.

2. See, for example, Mario Biagioli, *Galileo Courtier: The Practice of Science in the Culture of Absolutism* (Chicago: University of Chicago Press, 1993); Maurice Finocciaro, ed., *The Galileo Affair, A Documentary History*, (New York: Notable Trials Library, 1991) and Pietro Redondi, *Galileo Heretic-Galileo ereticom* (Princeton: Princeton University Press, 1989).

3. This picture of what Galileo's condemnation and Spinoza's excommunication signified appears in Andrew D. White, *The History of the Warfare Between Science and Theology* (New York, Appleton, 1896).

4. See Johan Colerus, *The Life of Benedict de Spinosa* (London: D. L., 1706). Most of the text is reproduced in Frederick Pollock, *Spinoza. His Life and Philosophy* (London: Duckworth, 1899), Appendix, 391.

5. Asa Kasher and Shlomo Biderman, "Why Was Baruch de Spinoza Excommunicated?" in ed. *Sceptics, Millenarians and Jews* D. Katz et al. (Leiden, E. J. Brill): 98–141.

6. Cf. Yosef Kaplan, "The Social Functions of the *herem* in the Portuguese Jewish Community of Amsterdam in the Seventeenth Century," in *Dutch Jewish History* Assen/Maastricht: Van Gorcum (1984)1: 117–34. See also Kasher and Biderman, 100–01.

7. This was important during the seventeenth and eighteenth centuries.

8. On Da Costa's case and his views see the edition of his *Examination of the Pharisaic Traditions*, ed. H. P. Salomon and I. S. D. Sassoon (Leiden: E. J. Brill, 1993). The Introduction, 2–50, goes over most of what is presently known about Da Costa.

9. See I. S. Revah, *Spinoza et Juan de Prado* (The Hague: Mouton, 1959); and "Aux origines de la rupture spinozienne: Nouveaux documents sur l'incroyance dans la communauté Judéo-Portugaise d'Amsterdam a l'époque de l'excommunication de Spinoza," in *Revue des Etudes Juives*, cxxiii (1964): 359–431.

10. Yosef Kaplan, *From Christianity to Judaism: The Life of Orobio de Castro* (Oxford: Oxford University Press, 1989), 123–60.

11. Revah speculates that they were offering to send Prado and his family to New Amsterdam. See *Spinoza et Juan de Prado*, 29–30.

12. See Revah, *Spinoza et Juan de Prado*, 29–33.

13. The original Spanish text of the two depositions about Spinoza and Prado given to the Madrid Inquisition in 1659 appears in Israel S. Revah, *Spinoza et Juan de Prado*, 61–68. What is known about the meetings of Spinoza and Prado with other Spaniards, Jewish and Catholic, is reported

in Yosef Kaplan, *From Judaism to Christianity: The Life of Orobio de Castro*, 133–34.

14. On this, see R. H. Popkin, chap IX "The Marranos of Amsterdam," in *The Third Force in Seventeenth Century Thought* (Leiden: E. J. Brill, 1992), 161–65.

15. This is what can be inferred from the official statement entered in the synagogue record book and from what Spinoza told people later on.

16. See H. P. Salomon, "Le vrai excommunication de Spinoza," in *Forum: Litterarum*, ed. H. Bots and M. Kerkhof (Amsterdam/Maaren: 1984), 181–99.

17. It appears in volume 4 of Bruder's 1842 edition of Spinoza's works, taken from the municipal archives.

18. This is the translation of the Spanish text as given in Kasher and Biderman, 98.

19. Several of the possibilities are discussed in Kasher and Biderman.

20. I first became aware of the role played by Isaac Lopes Suasso when I saw the exhibit at the Jewish Museum in Amsterdam about the Jewish role in William of Orange's move from the Netherlands to the English throne. The catalogue of the exhibit, mostly written by Daniel Swetschinski, led me to investigate as much as I could about Lopes Suasso. It would be interesting to learn if his brother the Catholic theologian showed any interest or concern in his brother's conversion or reversion to Judaism.

21. See esp. their conclusion, 140–41.

22. Pierre Bayle, art. "Spinoza: in *Historical and Critical Dictionary: Selections*, trans. Richard H. Popkin (Indianapolis, Ind.: Hackett Publishing Co., 1991), 292 n. c. Bayle's sources are discussed in K. O. Meinsma, *Spinoza et son cercle* (Paris: J. Vrin, 1989), 2. This edition of Meinsma's major study contains much additional material from the editors, Henri Mechoulan and P. F. Moreau and others.

23. Bayle, art. "Spinoza," *Selections*, 292–93

24. Bayle, art. "Spinoza," *Selections*, 290–92

25. Bayle, art. "Spinoza," noRem. DD.

26. Jacques Basnage, *Histoire des Juifs, depuis Jesus-Christ jusqu'à présent: Pour servir de Continuation à l'histoire de Joseph.*

27. This last edition was published by Henri Scheuleer in the Hague.

28. On Basnage's life and career, see Gerald Cerny, *Theology, Politics and Letters at the Crossroads of European Civilization. Jacques Basnage and the Baylean Huguenot Refugees in the Dutch Republic* (The Hague: Martinus Nijhoff, 1987).

29. It occurs in Livre IV, chap. vii.

30. Cf. R. H. Popkin, "Spinoza, Neoplatonic Kabblist?" In *Neoplatonism and Jewish Thought*, ed. Lenn Goodman, Albany: State University

of New York Press, 1992), 343–62; and Basnage, *Histoire*, 1716 edition, Livre IV, chap. vii, 133.

31. Basnage, *Histoire* (Henri Scheuleer: 1716), vol. 15: 1032.

32. Basnage, *Histoire* (Henri Scheuleer: 1716), vol. 15: 1033.

33. Basnage, *Histoire* (Henri Scheuleer: 1716), vol. 15: 1033.

34. Basnage, *Histoire* (Henri Scheuleer: 1716), vol. 15: 1033.

35. Basnage, *Histoire* (Henri Scheuleer: 1716), vol. 15: 1033.

36. Basnage, *Histoire* (Henri Scheuleer: 1716), vol. 15: 1033–41. The only source mentioned by Basnage is Colerus's *Life of Spinoza*, which we will discuss next.

37. Colerus, *Life of B. Spinoza* in Pollock, 387.

38. Colerus, *Life of B. Spinoza* in Pollock, 388.

39. Colerus, *Life of B. Spinoza* in Pollock, 389.

40. Colerus, *Life of B. Spinoza* in Pollock, 390.

41. Colerus, *Life of B. Spinoza* in Pollock, 390.

42. Rabbi Isaac Aboab de Fonesca was actually in his fifties at the time of the excommunication. He had just returned with the refugees from Brazil and was given Menasseh ben Israel's post, since the latter was in England negotiating with Cromwell about the return of the Jews to England. In 1655, he published a Hebrew abridgment of the work of his teacher, the philosophical Kabbalist Abraham Cohen Herrera, a work Spinoza is said to have read.

43. As mentioned earlier, note that the actual text, now so notorious, was not known publicly until the nineteenth century.

44. Surrhensius was then working on a Latin translation of the Mishna and a commentary on it.

45. The text has been republished from a manuscript edited by Abraham Wolf as *The Oldest Biography of Spinoza* (London: Kennikat Press, 1927). Wolf gives both the original French text and English translation. The manuscript Wolf used is in the Spinoza collection of Wolf now located in the Special Collections at UCLA.

46. For what is known about Lucas, see Meinsma, 6–11 and 17–19.

47. On the question of the reliability of the Lucas text, see editorial Note 16 by Pierre Francois Moreau in Meinsma, 17–19. Meinsma could find no evidence that the civil authorities were ever approached by the rabbis about punishing Spinoza.

48. See Silvia Berti, "L'Esprit de M. Spinosa: ses origines et sa première édition dans leur contexte spinozien," in *Heterodoxy, Spinozism and Free Thought in Early Eighteenth Century Europe: Studies on the "Traité des trois imposteurs,"* ed. S. Berti, F. Charles-Daubert, and R. H. Popkin (Dordrecht: Kluwer Academic Publishers, 1996), 3–53. For other possible sources of the text, see the articles by Francois Charles-Daubert, Miguel Benitez, and A. Fairbairn and Bertram Schwarzbach in the same volume.

49. Meinsma looked for any evidence of a civil procedure against Spinoza in the Amsterdam records and found nothing.

50. Menasseh ben Israel said in 1656 that more than half of the people who came to synagogue services were Christians.

51. Sebastian Kortholdt, "prefatio" to his father's *Tribus impostoribus*, 2nd ed. (Hamburg: J. Reimann, 1700). In Meinsma (15, n. 4), Moreau says that Kortholdt has turned out to be correct on many points on which he differs with other sources.

52. Michael Petry and Guido Suchtelen, "Spinoza and the Military: A Newly Discovered Document," *Studia Spinozana* I (1985): 359–69. The person in question was Gabriel Milan, a merchant and diplomat (for Denmark) who became Governor of St. Thomas in the Virgin Islands.

53. See R. H. Popkin, "Serendipity at the Clark: Spinoza and the Prince of Condé," *Clark Newsletter*, no. 19 (spring 1986): 4–7.

About the Contributors

Edwin M. Curley is a James B. and Grace J. Nelson Professor of Philosophy at the University of Michigan, where he has taught since 1993. He received his Ph.D. from Duke University in 1963, and subsequently held positions at San Jose State University, the Australian National University, Northwestern University, and the University of Illinois at Chicago. His research on Spinoza includes his translation of the *Collected Works* (vol. I, Princeton, 1985; vol. II forthcoming); *Spinoza's Metaphysics* (Harvard, 1969), *Behind The Geometrical Method* (Princeton, 1988) and numerous articles. He has also worked extensively on Descartes (*Descartes Against The Skeptics*, Harvard, 1978) and Hobbes (edition of *Leviathan*, Hackett, 1994). He is involved in producing an electronic edition of Spinoza's Latin works, soon to appear from the InteLex Corporation.

Lenn E. Goodman is a Professor of Philosophy at Vanderbilt University. His books include *On Truth: A Pluralistic Approach, Jewish And Islamic Philosophy: Crosspollinations In The Classical Age, Judaism, Human Rights And Human Values, God Of Abraham, Avicenna,* and *On Justice: An Essay In Jewish Philosophy*. A winner of the Baumgardt Prize of the American Philosophical Association and the Gratz Centennial Prize, Goodman translated and commented on the philosophical writings of Moses Maimonides in his *Rambam* and on Saadiah Gaon's Commentary On The Book of Job in *The Book Of Theodicy*. He also translated and commented on such Islamic classics as Ibn Tufayl's philosophical tale *Hayy Ibn Yaqzan*, and the 10th century ecological fable *The Case Of The Animals vs Man*, By The Sincere Brethren Of Basra. Goodman is a graduate of Harvard University and received his doctorate at Oxford University, where he was a Marshall Scholar. He is married and is the father of the novelist Allegra Goodman, and of Paula Goodman Fraenkel, a physician and medical researcher.

281

Warren Zev Harvey is Professor of Jewish Thought at the Hebrew University of Jerusalem. He is author of studies on medieval and modern Jewish philosophy, including *Physics and Metaphysics in Hasdai Crescas* (Amsterdam 1998). He studied at Columbia University (Ph.D., 1973), and taught at McGill University (1972–1977), before moving to Jerusalem in 1977.

Warren Montag is Professor of English (Eighteenth century British and European Literature, European critical theory) at Occidental College in Los Angeles. He is the author of *The Unthinkable Swift and Bodies, Masses Power: Spinoza and his Contemporaries* and editor (with Ted Stolze) of *The New Spinoza*.

Richard H. Popkin is Professor Emeritus from Washington University, St. Louis and Adjunct Professor of History and Philosophy at UCLA. He has written extensively on modern philosophy from the Renaissance to the Enlightenment and has written many articles on Spinoza.

Heidi M. Ravven is Professor of Religious Studies (Jewish Philosophy and Philosophy of Religion) at Hamilton College, Clinton NY. Since 1987 she has devoted herself to Spinoza's philosophy. She has published articles on Spinoza, Maimonides, Hegel, and Jewish feminist philosophy. Ravven is currently editing a volume of *Philosophy and Theology* (with Lee C. Rice) on Spinoza and Biblical Interpretation, and completing a study of Spinoza's moral and social psychology.

Lee C. Rice is Associate Professor of Philosophy at Marquette University. He has published numerous articles, book chapters, edited volumes, and reviews on Spinoza. Rice also has expertise in cognitive science and artificial intelligence.

Michael A. Rosenthal is Assistant Professor of Philosophy at Grinnell College in Iowa. His Ph.D. is from the University of Chicago and he has published articles on Spinoza's political philosophy. His interests range from early modern, medieval and Renaissance philosophy to contemporary political philosophy and Jewish philosophy.

Kenneth Seeskin is Professor of Philosophy at Northwestern University, where he has taught since 1972. He has published widely in Jewish philosophy. His books include: *Autonomy in Jewish Philosophy* (2001), *Searching for a Distant God: The Legacy of Maimonides* (2000), *No Other Gods* (1995), *Maimonides: A Guide for Today's Perplexed* (1991), and *Jewish Philosophy in a Secular Age* (1990).

Index

We wish to express our gratitude to Sushrut Acharya, Hamilton College '05, for his indispensable assistance in developing this index.